‘From cod liver oil to cultured meat, food marketing addresses anxieties about health and morality. This engaging volume explores the nexus of scientific/medical discourse, marketing enabled by mass communication, and the industrialized foodscape, offering cogent and compelling analyses of visual and material culture.’

Kathleen LeBesco, *Professor of Communication and Media Arts, Marymount Manhattan College*

‘Everywhere we now look food is being marketed as in some way healthy. Making an important and timely contribution to the field of food studies, the contributors of this book show how this is of concern across major food categories. Taking a historical approach, the oddity and cynicism of food marketing is drawn out by showing that it is nothing new.’

David Machin, *Professor of Linguistics, Shanghai International Studies University*

‘How is science employed in food communication, and why? This book presents an original and thorough investigation into the appropriation and reuse of scientific knowledge by food brands. Through qualitative research spanning both contemporary and historical contexts, this collective work unveils insights crucial for understanding food communication across the world.’

Simona De Iulio, *Professor of Information and Communication Sciences, University of Lille*

Food Marketing and Selling Healthy Lifestyles with Science

This book sets out to historicise our understanding of contemporary trends by studying the long relationship between science, food and drink marketing and the promotion of healthy lifestyles. It aims to bring together contemporary and historical research from a multimodal perspective, considering how scientific discourse and ideas about health and nutrition are channelled through visual and material culture.

Using examples of advertisements, commercials and posters, the 16 chapters in this book will foster a cross-disciplinary and cross-temporal dialogue, uncovering links between past and present ways that manufacturers have capitalised upon scientific innovations to create new products or rebrand existing products and employed science to make claims about health and nutrition. They will, thus, demonstrate the continuity of science in food and drink marketing—even if fundamental ideas of nutrition have evolved over time. The book provides crucial new insights into the significance of the late nineteenth and early twentieth centuries as a period of innovation in food and drink marketing and showcasing how many of the marketing strategies employed today, in fact, have a far broader historical trajectory.

It will be of great interest to students and scholars of Critical Food Studies, Media and Communication Studies, History of Science and Medicine and Cultural Studies, as well as nutritionists, dieticians, sportspeople, in addition to policymakers and practitioners working in the area of food and drink marketing.

Lauren Alex O'Hagan is a research fellow in the School of Languages and Applied Linguistics at the Open University (UK) and an affiliate researcher in the Department of Media and Communication Studies at Örebro University (Sweden). She specialises in performances of social class and power mediation in the late nineteenth and early twentieth century through visual and material artefacts, using a methodology that blends social semiotic analysis with archival research. She has published extensively on the sociocultural forms and functions of book inscriptions, food advertisements, postcards and writing implements.

Göran Eriksson started working on this book during his time as a professor of Media and Communication Studies at Örebro University (Sweden). Currently, he is a professor at the Institute of Corpus Studies and Applications at Shanghai International Studies University (China). He works in the field of discourse analysis and his current research is linked to the sociology of health and is concerned with multimodal representations of healthy food and healthy eating in different settings. Ongoing studies look at marketing and are especially interested in how science and scientific expertise is communicated. He publishes extensively in international peer-reviewed journals. Göran is associate editor of the SSCI-indexed journal Discourse, Context and Media.

Critical Food Studies

Series editors: Michael K. Goodman
University of Reading, UK

Colin Sage
Independent Scholar

The study of food has seldom been more pressing or prescient. From the intensifying globalisation of food, a worldwide food crisis and the continuing inequalities of its production and consumption, to food's exploding media presence, and its growing re-connections to places and people through 'alternative food movements', this series promotes critical explorations of contemporary food cultures and politics. Building on previous but disparate scholarship, its overall aims are to develop innovative and theoretical lenses and empirical material in order to contribute to—but also begin to more fully delineate—the confines and confluences of an agenda of critical food research and writing.

Of particular concern are original theoretical and empirical treatments of the materialisations of food politics, meanings and representations, the shifting political economies and ecologies of food production and consumption and the growing transgressions between alternative and corporatist food networks.

Hunger and Postcolonial Writing
Muzna Rahman

Food Sovereignty and Urban Agriculture
Concepts, Politics, and Practice in South Africa
Anne Siebert

The Rhetorical Construction of Vegetarianism
Edited by Cristina Hanganu-Bresch

Artists and the Practice of Agriculture
Politics and Aesthetics of Food Sovereignty in Art since 1960
Silvia Bottinelli

Food Marketing and Selling Healthy Lifestyles with Science
Transhistorical Perspectives
Edited by Lauren Alex O'Hagan and Göran Eriksson

For more information about this series, please visit: www.routledge.com/Critical-Food-Studies/book-series/CFS

Food Marketing and Selling Healthy Lifestyles with Science

Transhistorical Perspectives

Edited by Lauren Alex O'Hagan and Göran Eriksson

Routledge
Taylor & Francis Group
LONDON AND NEW YORK

First published 2025
by Routledge
4 Park Square, Milton Park, Abingdon, Oxon OX14 4RN

and by Routledge
605 Third Avenue, New York, NY 10017

Routledge is an imprint of the Taylor & Francis Group, an informa business

British Library Cataloguing-in-Publication Data
A catalogue record for this book is available from the British Library

ISBN: 978-1-032-58073-9 (hbk)
ISBN: 978-1-032-58481-2 (pbk)
ISBN: 978-1-003-45027-6 (ebk)

DOI: 10.4324/9781003450276

The Open Access version of Introduction and From Foods to Nutrients was funded by Orebro University.

Contents

Figures

Tables

Acknowledgements

The idea for this edited volume arose after several years of working in the field of food and communication studies, and especially so the work we both conducted within the project *Communication of "Good" Food and Healthy Lifestyles* at Örebro University (ORU). This included several studies using a historical multimodal approach to food marketing in the UK and Sweden, from which the idea of this book progressed. There are many people to thank for the completion of this book. Our heartfelt thanks to the 14 contributors; it has been a pleasure to work with you all and we have learnt so much about food marketing along the way. Our sincere thanks to the British Newspaper Archive, Prachi Priyanka and Faye Leerink at Routledge, and series editors Colin Sage and Mike Goodman for dealing with our many questions over the past two years. We also want to acknowledge the FoodKom network and all its members. Through your insightful and constructive comments, you have all contributed to the making of this book.

Lauren: I must confess that I stumbled into this area of research by chance back in 2018 during my time as a visiting researcher at ORU. So, it is only fair that I start my acknowledgements by thanking David Machin and my co-author Göran Eriksson for piquing my curiosity in food marketing and setting me on this research pathway. I must also thank many of my other colleagues at ORU with whom I've had so many interesting discussions since I started working on this book, particularly Lame Maatla Kenalemang-Palm, Helen Andersson, Peter Berglez and Gustav Westberg. My thanks also to all those I spoke with at the 2023 Food and Communication conference at ORU. My conversations with Simona de Iulio, Emma Robertson, Michal Salamonik and Cornelia Gerhardt were particularly insightful. I would also like to thank my current institution, The Open University, for enabling me to return to ORU as a visiting researcher in 2023. A particular shout-out to Regine Hampel, Caroline Tagg and Jane Seale for making this possible. As always, a huge thank you to my partner Diego who can never have a peaceful trip to the supermarket because I'm always taking photographs of food packaging and advertisements! And last but not least, to Rory, Phil and Tom—my musical safe haven whenever I'm feeling overwhelmed with work.

Göran: First, my thanks to Lauren, my co-author and the co-editor of this book. It is always a pleasure working with you and the work with this book is no exception. In addition to your wide-ranging academic expertise, I must say that the level of your efficiency and your organisational skills is remarkable. I would also like to thank Helen Andersson, Tanja Kamin, Gwynne Mapes, Ana Tominc and Andreja Vezovnik, all members of the FoodKom network. It is always great to meet you and continue our discussions about food and communication. Thanks to my friend David Machin for support and inspiration.

Contributors

Iben Bredahl Jessen is an associate professor of Media and Communication in the Department of Communication and Psychology, Aalborg University, Denmark. Her research focuses on multimodal representations and media aesthetics in market communication and advertising both from a contemporary and a historical perspective. Recent publications include articles on multimodality and authenticity in the branding of food (gourmet cheese) and beverages (coffee and beer).

Daniel Ewers is a WRoCAH-funded PhD candidate based in the School of Philosophy, Religion and History of Science at the University of Leeds working collaboratively with the History of Advertising Trust. His research examines the history of vitamin health claims in British advertisements for foodstuffs between 1930 and 1980 and how appeals to popular understandings of health, scientific authority and nutrition intersect within these sources.

Conor Heffernan is a lecturer in the Sociology of Sport at Ulster University. Conor has published numerous articles on the physical culture movement in Ireland, England, the United States and India. His work has appeared in the *Social History of Medicine, History, Gender & History, Rethinking History* and *Women's History Review*, among other journals. He is currently working on a transnational history of exercise practices in the nineteenth century. In 2021, Conor published the *History of Physical Culture in Ireland.* Conor also runs the history of fitness website, *Physical Culture Study*, is a regular contributor to popular fitness websites and has appeared in Rogue Fitness' documentary on the physical culturist Arthur Saxon.

Amber Hinde recently submitted her PhD in English Language and Linguistics at the University of Glasgow, and her research was funded by the Carnegie Trust for the Universities of Scotland. Her thesis is titled *The Rhetoric of Food Reform in Late Nineteenth and Early Twentieth Century Britain*, in which she focuses on two prominent food reformers: Thomas Allinson and Eustace Miles. Amber uses critical discourse analysis to explore the construction of identities, questioning how Allinson and Miles used textual strategies to create a persuasive ethos and convince the public to make lifestyle changes. Her research interests lie at the intersection of health communication, rhetoric and the history of science and medicine. Amber uses rich collections of historical texts to ask important questions surrounding the use of rhetorical strategies in health texts.

Jessica Loyer lectures in Australia's first Bachelor of Food Studies at William Angliss Institute. Her research investigates historical and contemporary nutrition and diet culture, including the roles of scientific practice and translation, media discourses and production-consumption values in shaping our nutrient-reductionist, market-oriented, morality-infused and individually focused food-health landscapes. Current projects focus on the cultural politics of superfoods and bush foods, and the translation of emerging science in nutritional discourses and marketplaces.

Veronica Sau-Wa Mak is an associate professor in the Department of Sociology at the Hong Kong Shue Yan University. Her research interests focus on food, technology, media and heritage politics in China, Hong Kong, Japan and Southeast Asia. She is the author of *Milk Craze in China: Body, Science and Hope* (2021). Veronica has also published professional papers in academic journals, such as *Food, Culture and Society, Ecology of Food and Nutrition, Food and Foodways, Health, Risk and Society, Global Food History* and *International Journal of Heritage Studies*. She also contributed chapters to *Digitised Health, Medicine and Risk*, edited by Deborah Lupton (Routledge 2018), *Globalised Eating Cultures, Mediatization and Mediation*, edited by Jörg Dürrschmidt and York Kautt (2019) and *Chinese Food and Foodways in Southeast Asia and Beyond*, edited by Tan Chee-Beng (2011).

Saurabh Mishra is a senior lecturer in Modern Asian History at University of Sheffield. He has published two monographs: *Pilgrimage, Politics and Pestilence: The Haj from the Indian Subcontinent* (2011) and *Beastly Encounters of the Raj: Livelihoods, Livestock and Veterinary Health in Colonial North India* (Studies in Imperialism Series, 2015). He is currently working on a monograph on amateur science in India, which will be published by the end of 2024.

Leif Runefelt is a professor of the History of Ideas at Södertörn University. He holds a PhD in Economic History from Stockholm University and has written extensively on consumption, consumer culture and advertising in Sweden from the seventeenth to the twentieth century. Recently, he has written about images of women in early illustrated advertisements in the Swedish press, 1870–1914, and analysed the Swedish market for itinerant entertainment in the late eighteenth and nineteenth centuries. He has also studied costume, fashion and gender from a number of different angles and phenomena, such as tableaux vivants, the hair care market in Stockholm, corset advertising and the view of the female foot in the Swedish press, mostly for the nineteenth century.

Lucy Jane Santos is a freelance historian examining the crossroads of health, leisure and beauty with science and technology. She has appeared as a contributor on TV and radio, and her historical research has been featured in *History Today*, *BBC History Revealed*, *Jezebel*, *LitHub*, *New York Post*, *Vogue*, and on the BBC2 documentary, *Makeup: A Glamorous History*. Lucy's debut book was *Half Lives: The Unlikely History of Radium* (2020, 2021). In 2021, *Half Lives* was shortlisted for the BSHS Hughes Prize, for books that bring scholarship to new readers by capturing the public imagination while conforming to the rigorous standards of academic research. Her next book *Chain Reactions: The Hopeful History of Uranium* will be published in 2024.

Lo Shuk Ying is a research associate at the Hong Kong Institute of Asia-Pacific Studies, the Chinese University of Hong Kong. Her research interests are social and cultural history in modern China, with special focuses on gender and children's issues. She is currently participating in research projects about the history of fishing communities in South China and families and ethnicities in Hong Kong.

Angela Smith is a professor of Language and Culture at the University of Sunderland, UK. She has published extensively in the areas of gender, media discourses and political discourse. With Dr Michael Higgins (University of Strathclyde), she has published the second edition of *The Language of Journalism* (Routledge, 2020) and with Drew Dalton (University of Sunderland), she has edited *Gender, Sexuality and the UN's SDGs* (2023). She runs the University of Sunderland's Gender Studies Interdisciplinary Research Network and, with Sunderland Council, manages the Rebel Women of Sunderland project, which seeks to raise awareness of remarkable women connected with the city. With Professor Clair Nally (Northumbria University), Angela co-edits the Bloomsbury Library of Gender in Popular Culture.

Caroline Tagg is a senior lecturer in Applied Linguistics at The Open University, UK. Her research into language and digital technologies rests on the understanding that digital communication practices are deeply embedded into individuals' wider lives. She is author of *Taking Offence on Social Media* (with Philip Seargeant and Amy Aisha Brown, 2017), *Message and Medium* (with Mel Evans, 2020) and *Mobile Messaging and Resourcefulness: a post-digital ethnography* (with Agnieszka Lyons, 2022). She is co-editor of the Routledge Focus series *Language and Social Media* (with Sirpa Leppänen) and editor-in-chief of the international journal *Discourse, Context & Media* (2021–2024).

Andreja Vezovnik is an associate professor of Media Studies and Senior Researcher at the Centre for Social Psychology, University of Ljubljana, Slovenia. Her background is in sociology, but her research is interdisciplinary. She focuses mainly on the study of food discourses, food consumption and the food industry. She is a member of the programme committee of the Food and Communication Conference and a founding member of the FoodKom network. Her current interests include exploring different types of discourses about protein alternatives (cultured meat, plant-based meat, fermentation, insects, etc.) and their impact on our culture, society and consumption patterns.

Pilar Zazueta is a historian and an associate professor of Instruction at the University of Texas at Austin. Currently, she serves as an associate director of Undergraduate Studies at the Teresa Lozano Long Institute of Latin American Studies and Nettie Lee Benson Latin American Collection (LLILAS-Benson). Her research focuses on the history of the processed food industry and how nutrition became a public policy issue in Mexico during the twentieth century. She has worked at the Earth Institute at Columbia University, as well as the University of Victoria, managing two grants for the Canadian Institutes of Health. Pilar studied International Relations at El Colegio de México and has a PhD from Columbia University.

Introduction

Food Marketing and Selling Healthy Lifestyles with Science

Göran Eriksson and Lauren Alex O'Hagan

Introduction

For food and drink manufacturers today, marketing products with health and well-being associations are of vital importance. For such marketing, references to science and technological development—whether through choices of language, image, colour or typography—play a crucial role in making food appear as healthy and providing well-being for consumers. But how novel are these practices? Perhaps not as novel as we might think.

The practice of selling food with scientific rationality, in fact, has a long history dating back to the mid-nineteenth century. This was a time when food production became industrialised, the field of modern nutrition science was established and scientific discoveries and inventions were occurring at a rapid rate (Scrinis, 2013). It was also a period marked by the expansion of mass-mediated communication, which facilitated more systematic and targeted marketing (Cross and Proctor, 2014). Together, these factors transformed the food advertising industry, inaugurating a new way of seeing things and fashioning a mythology of consumerism that set a precedent for the consumer economy in which we now live (O'Hagan, 2021a).

The introduction of scientific discourse into food marketing was innovative and created an artificial demand for products on the basis that trusting consumers thought that they would improve their lives (Loeb, 1994). By drawing upon scientific, medical and nutritional knowledge, manufacturers constructed authority and credibility, while also tapping into middle-class anxieties around health, morality and fitness, convincing consumers that certain products—and later, nutrients—were essential to the modern, "healthy" way of living. Technical descriptions, scientific buzzwords and testimonials from doctors and scientists were replete in food advertisements, along with infographics, diagrams, geometric shapes and photographs—all of which functioned to convey the "health-giving" properties of food products. Brands also continuously reshaped and remarketed their products in response to emerging and changing understandings of science, medicine and nutrition so as to remain popular and

DOI: 10.4324/9781003450276-1

relevant to consumers. However, at the same time, these products were shrouded with an air of mystique as their complexities were not readily understood by consumers, thus turning them into both mirrors and instruments of social ideas (O'Hagan, 2020).

While nutritional advice has evolved over the past 150 years, science still remains a central aspect of food and drink marketing. Moreover, despite stringent regulations now in place to combat false advertising, there are still loopholes that can be exploited, particularly when it comes to semiotics (e.g. the use of colour, typography, framing and composition). This can create "spaces of confusion" (Sprackley, 2020:57) for consumers upon which marketers capitalise, generating panic around what to consume and even creating new needs as consumers get caught on a "nutrient treadmill" (Scrinis, 2013:43) and believe that certain products will change their lives. To better understand the ideological patterns and discourses that govern contemporary food marketing, it is instructive to examine the historical circumstances in which the intersection of scientific, nutritional, medical, commercial and social interests first emerged.

With this in mind, *Food Marketing and Selling Healthy Lifestyles with Science: Transhistorical Perspectives* sets out to historicise our understanding of contemporary trends by studying the long relationship between science, food and drink marketing and the promotion of healthy lifestyles. Specifically, it aims to bring together qualitatively oriented contemporary and historical research, considering how scientific discourse and ideas about health and nutrition are channelled through visual and material culture (i.e. advertisements, food packaging and social media). In doing so, it seeks to foster a cross-disciplinary and cross-temporal dialogue, uncovering links between past and present ways that manufacturers have capitalised upon scientific innovations to create new products or rebrand existing products and employ science to make claims about health and nutrition. Its objective is to demonstrate the continuity of science in food and drink marketing—even if fundamental ideas about nutrition have evolved over time—showcasing how many of the marketing strategies employed today can, in fact, be traced to the late nineteenth and early twentieth centuries. Given this ambition to historicise the understanding of contemporary food marketing trends, we approach the topic from a *transhistorical* perspective.

Transhistoricising Food Marketing

Our drive to put together this edited volume goes hand in hand with the growing turn in Media and Communication Studies towards transhistorical research and the realisation that it could make a much-needed contribution to Critical Food Studies, specifically in the context of food marketing. The concept of "transhistorical" was popularised by the groundbreaking book *Message and Medium* (2020) by Tagg and Evans, which outlined exactly what transhistorical research entails and its importance for exploring communication.[1] Tagg and

Evans (2020:3) argue that looking at texts *transhistorically* rather than just *historically* enables communicative practices to be explored not only as:

> lived experiences grounded in historical contexts, but also to identify and explain those elements of human behaviour that transcend historical boundaries and, therefore, to look beyond particular developments in communication technologies to understand the enduring motivations, stances, relationships and identity performances that drive human communication

Message and Medium boldly attempted to bring together scholars from a range of disciplines (i.e. Media and Communication Studies, Sociolinguistics, Sociology, Cultural Studies and Social History), yet united in their belief that studies of communicative practices and technologies must provide "an interrogation of earlier practices and phenomena against which claims about novelty can be made" (2020:3).

Fundamentally, transhistorical research seeks to identify antecedents in the communicative histories of individuals and communities that shape a text's creation (Tagg and Evans, 2020). By "unpick[ing] the complex and multiple relationships between message and medium" (Tagg and Evans, 2020:1), it aims to place seemingly novel contemporary communicative practices in a wider history of technologically mediated change. In doing so, it reveals similarities in the forms and functions of texts, while also demonstrating that their creation is guided by different social, cultural, historical and ideological values and bounded by the potentials, norms and traditions of the period in which they were created. It, thus, demonstrates how the fundamentals of human communication endure across time and space, despite the evolution of technologies that shape their message.

Essential to transhistorical research are considerations of *affordance*, *provenance* and *power* (van Leeuwen, 2005). In this context, affordance can be understood as the qualities or properties of a text that define its possible use, provenance describes a text's materiality and what it has been repeatedly used to mean and do and power entails how the meaning potentials of a text can be framed by hierarchical relations and serve ideological interests. Delving further into these three concepts, Adami (2020) outlines three questions that transhistorical research broadly asks when approaching a text. These are questions directing the analyses conducted in the contributions to this volume and can be summarised as follows:

1 Affordance: How did materiality, social availability and individual creativity afford (or constrain) the text?
2 Provenance: What meaning potentials did the text have and how have these meanings changed (or stayed the same) across space and time?
3 Power: Who produced and engaged with this text, how is this similar (or different) to now and how do these changes affect present understanding of the past?

Another key part of transhistorical research is "remediation" (Bolter and Grusin, 2000), understood as the way that texts can repurpose and translate existing technologies in an *incremental* instead of a *transformational* way, which is deeply embedded in changing historical and cultural contexts. Remediation, therefore, allows communication to be understood as part of a "wider integrated communicative environment" (Tagg and Evans, 2020:6) that responds to changing communicative practices and technologies. A recognition of comparison and continuity is also essential in transhistorical research. In other words, transhistorical research is not simply about reading backwards to a finite point; rather, it concerns how a text builds upon historical communicative practices, as well as how these historical communicative practices may have grounded themselves in earlier historical conventions of meaning making.

Given its interdisciplinarity, there is no one set way to approach transhistorical research. As Tagg and Evans' book shows, it can draw upon a variety of methodological and theoretical perspectives, from pragmatics, rhetoric and social semiotics to paratext theory, corpus analysis and sociocultural theory. Equally, it can be conducted directly through comparative or contrastive analysis by contrasting the past with the present or indirectly by applying a concept from one time period to another. In all cases, however, transhistorical studies share a deep awareness of the wider historical trajectory in which texts occur and the importance of assessing (dis)continuities between contemporary and historical modes of communication. In line with this mindset, the current edited volume brings together contributors from a variety of disciplines, such as Media and Communication Studies, Critical Food Studies, Linguistics, History and Sociology. Likewise, the contributors draw upon direct and indirect forms of analysis, tracing the roots of "contemporary" food trends and buzzwords (e.g. Chapter 7 on coffee substitutes; Chapter 9 on ghee and Chapters 10 and 11 on "pure") and exploring the evolution of the same product over time (e.g. Chapter 2 on dairy products and plant-based alternatives; Chapter 4 on muesli and Chapter 6 on Ribena).

To date, most transhistorical research has been concerned with contemporary social media practices and their resemblance to earlier forms of communication (e.g. Golden, 2010; O'Hagan and Spilioti, 2021; Gillen, 2023) or the development and affordances of communication technologies (e.g. Fischer, 1994; Herring, 2013; O'Hagan and Serafinelli, 2022). Our volume, thus, develops this line of research by applying it to a new field of study—food marketing—thereby encouraging the identification of the (dis)similarities in past and present articulations of health and science and how "new" media always builds upon pre-existing media ecologies.

There have been innumerable studies centred on the use of science in historical (e.g. Qvarsell and Torell, 2005; Smith, 2008; Lonier, 2010; Scheire, 2015; Emery, 2017; Steinitz, 2017; Pohl-Valero, 2020; Nelson et al., 2020; Cesiri, 2022) or contemporary food advertisements (e.g. Koteyko, 2009; Prell et al., 2011; Frye and Bruner, 2012; Jovanovic, 2013; Andersson, 2019; Chen and Eriksson, 2019a, 2019b, 2022; Ledin and Machin, 2020a; MacGregor et al.,

2021). However, there have been relatively few studies that focus on the *trans*historical, using history as a lens through which to understand contemporary food marketing and centred particularly on the use of linguistic and other semiotic choices (e.g. image, colour, typography, layout, composition).

Our work as part of the FoodKom Research Network—established in 2015 at Örebro University (Sweden)—has been chiefly concerned with this emerging area of study. Such research has explored the historical origins of many contemporary food trends, including protein (O'Hagan, 2021b), functional drinks (O'Hagan, 2023a) and cannabidiol food products (Runefelt and O'Hagan, forthcoming). It has also outlined the ongoing transformation of late-nineteenth-century buzzwords, such as "pure" (e.g. O'Hagan, 2020) and uncovered forgotten fads, such as radium-infused products (e.g. Eriksson and O'Hagan, 2021).

Independently, similar transhistorical work has also been carried out at the University of Lille (France), led by Simona De Iulio. Focusing on food advertisements, De Iulio has explored the discursive strategies used to construct fun (2010), represent risk (2013) and signal trustworthiness (2019). More recently, De Iulio and Kovacs (2022) have investigated "eating knowledge" from a transhistorical perspective in a comprehensive edited volume that explores "the strategies and logics underlying food knowledge circulation and mediatisation" (2). Other scholars with a growing interest in transhistorical approaches to the study of food marketing include Ruth Gamble and Emma Robertson (2023), Michal Salamonik (2023) and Beth M. Forrest (2023), who presented early research findings on the evolution of rice, cannabis food products and Spanish cuisine, respectively, at the Third Conference on Food and Communication held at Örebro University in September 2023.

Food Marketing and Selling Healthy Lifestyles with Science takes further the arguments of Tagg and Evans (2020) and builds upon the growing body of work that explores food marketing transhistorically, offering the first concentrated volume on the topic. Bringing together cutting-edge research by emerging and established scholars in the field, it specifically seeks to answer the following overarching questions:

- How do food and drink manufacturers capitalise upon scientific innovations to create new products or rebrand existing products?
- How is science employed to make claims about health and well-being and how are these claims manifested linguistically and semiotically?
- How are products made to appear as good and healthy choices?
- How have these marketing strategies changed or stayed the same across time?

By emphasising the multimodality of texts in particular (i.e. the use of more than one mode of communication in a text to create meaning), its chapters will provide crucial new insights into the significance of the late nineteenth and early twentieth centuries as a period of innovation in food and drink marketing and the long history of how it has shifted in response to developments in scientific, medical and nutritional knowledge. They will also have practical implications for both consumers and policymakers, helping them to maintain a critical distance from their current experiences of marketing in order to reflect on the veracity of the scientific claims that they encounter in their everyday lives and the effectiveness of regulations in offering protection from false marketing.

Marketing, Multimodality and Health

A significant question to pose at this point is why conduct research on marketing? With its obvious goal of selling a product, marketing might come across as a trivial phenomenon to study from a communicative perspective. However, even though its goal is evident in the way that messages are conveyed, marketing offers a good entry point to explore culture and everyday lives, both contemporary and historical. Marketing reflects contemporary ideas, norms and values, with marketers sensitive to ongoing trends and to what can make consumer products desirable (Clampin, 2014). Marketers are also attentive to people's everyday lives and, through idealised, recontextualised social practices, they can relate to consumers' aspirations and expectations, but also their fears and worries (Schudson, 2000).

While marketing can be artistic, creative, emotional and funny, as Jaworska (2020) warns, it can also be manipulative. It is this manipulative function that requires marketing to be critically investigated (cf. Saren et al., 2007; Tadajewski and Brownlie, 2008; Tadajewski et al., 2018). Manipulation is a form of asymmetrical interaction in which the advertiser attempts to alter the (potential) consumer's attitude or behaviour by convincing them to purchase a particular product. However, while the advertiser is likely to benefit from this purchase, it is not always certain that the consumer will reap such benefits. For this reason, Cook (1992) argues that advertisements are a "parasitic" form of discourse, a type of exploitation and deception that taps into consumer anxieties and convinces them to spend money on products that they do not necessarily need.

These concerns are particularly relevant to food marketing because it:

> creates the conditions for nutrition confusion, a dependence on nutrition experts, a susceptibility to food marketing claims, and a general sense of anxiety about what to eat. It contributes to the creation of new needs and to the idea that people are "in need" – in need of nutrition information, dietary advice, and nutritionally engineered foods.
>
> (Scrinis, 2013:43)

While some consumers may feel empowered or critically informed by such information, others suffer from an information overload, which can disturb them and force them to buy products that they do not really understand or need. Writing in 1899 about food, Stead (1899) claimed that no other form of marketing had such opportunities of "penetrating into the very sanctum sanctorum of the consumer." Over 120 years on, it is clear that food marketing is fully immersed in the homes of today's consumers and is the primary means through which they access nutritional information (Scrinis, 2013). The danger of this is that consumers experience products as "wholes" in terms of "materiality, a physical presence and a design" (Ledin and Machin, 2018:3), which can make it challenging to separate out fact from fiction, product truths from advertising claims. Foods are increasingly performative devices used by companies to signal certain ideologies. Thus, it is evident that they can never be understood solely in terms of nutritional value and instead must be viewed within the notions of power, control and the reproduction of domination (Fairclough, 1995).

For these reasons, it is important to understand communication from a multimodal perspective (cf. Kress and van Leeuwen, 1996, 2001; Kress, 2010), which is often neglected in historical food marketing research. Although the multimodal analyses that make up the chapters in this volume vary in detail, they all stress the importance of understanding the visual design of marketing. The multimodal perspective on communication is informed by the communications theory of social semiotics (cf. Kress and van Leeuwen, 1996, 2001; Kress, 2010; Ledin and Machin, 2018, 2020b), which focuses on how communicative artefacts create meaning through the way they are designed. Design is, as Kress (2010:23) puts it, "prospective," that is, it is "a means of projecting an individual's interest into their world with the intent of effect in the future." This perspective, thus, emphasises the urge to consider the visual design of marketing and, in our case, to explore how the visual design works to relate to and associate products with science. It implies that we consider food and drink marketing as a result of a set of choices conducted to predict how potential consumers can connect to and come to think about certain products.

It is also relevant to ask why we have chosen to focus specifically on how science is used in food marketing to promote the health-bringing effects of food. We live in an era when governments and global health organisations are putting public health at the top of the agenda and are highly active in advancing food policies for healthier dietary habits (Slavin, 2015). Conscious of this push, food manufacturers are consequently increasingly marketing their products with a wide variety of health claims and well-being associations (Eriksson and Machin, 2020).

At the same time—and as pointed out by previous research in different areas—the notion of what healthy means in the context of food and drink consumption is far from unitary (de Ridder et al., 2017). Scholars within nutritional research can agree upon what *not* to consume too much of, such as sugar-sweetened drinks, trans-fat-based foods and salt, and most official dietary guidelines suggest a varied and balanced diet with a considerable amount of fruits and vegetables (de Ridder et al., 2017). Such advice, however, is provided in a context where the information regarding healthy diets is ubiquitous. Consumers access advice on healthy eating in newspaper articles reporting on research findings, in glossy magazines, in television shows and not least on social media by (often) self-appointed experts. On top of this, there is the extensive marketing that people meet in various media, online, in public places and in supermarkets. This massive amount of information is often contradictory, full of commercial buzzwords and creates confusion regarding what is healthy or should not be consumed. This confusion, paired with the pressure on people to maintain a healthy lifestyle, is what the food industry can make use of and benefit from (Eriksson and Machin, 2020).

Food Marketing and Selling Healthy Lifestyles with Science will show that these issues are nothing new. For over 150 years, health has been a selling point for food and drinks, and science has been used to promote products as healthy and significant for a healthy lifestyle (O'Hagan, 2021a). Furthermore, the way that products are marketed can transform our "beliefs, values and practices around health, food traditions and culinary practices" (De Iulio and Kovacs, 2022:2), while knowledge circulation strategies and notions of health can shift over time according to sociocultural context and the circumstances of the era (Scrinis, 2013), as well as changing consumer understandings and the emergence of new needs.

Cod Liver Oil: An Illustrative Example

To better illustrate these fundamental points that run throughout the edited volume, let us now briefly consider the history of cod liver oil. For centuries, cod liver oil was seen as an ill-tasting, unpleasant-looking and hard-to-sell product. However, the discovery of vitamin A (in 1913) and vitamin D (in 1922) suddenly offered scientific proof of its medicinal worth (Apple, 1996). The invention of new production techniques making the oil transparent and less smelly also improved the product's image, leading to a "cod liver oil boom" (O'Hagan and Eriksson, 2022) across many Western countries. Throughout the 1920s, newspaper articles emphasised the health benefits of cod liver oil and how it could support the maintenance of a healthy lifestyle, while extensive marketing took place across local and national newspapers, which was influential in constructing discourses of truth around the oil as a scientifically formulated healthy choice. Thus, cod liver oil producers, who had previously struggled to sell their product, were now able to trade with ease by stressing its proven health effects (O'Hagan and Eriksson, 2022). The market also saw a range of new cod liver oil products emerge, including chocolate, biscuits and cereal, all of which exploited the benefits of vitamins in their promotion (Apple, 1996). Across the board, advertisements claimed that cod liver oil did not just support general well-being, but also offered a cure for rickets, anaemia and bronchitis.

These cod liver oil advertisements often targeted women as those in charge of caring for the family and responsible for household purchases, using the strategy of "scientific motherhood" (cf. Apple, 1995), which positioned women as in need of expert intervention in order to look after their husbands and children properly. Marketing particularly tapped into women's fears about their children's health, with scaremongering headlines such as "Do you want your children to be well?" or "Protect your children immediately!" The underlying message was that if women did not follow this marketed advice, they were irresponsible and risked placing their children in danger (O'Hagan and Eriksson, 2022).

However, this expertise was not just conveyed through language; advertisements also frequently used eye-catching images and illustrations, which subtly advised mothers on how to act to ensure the future health of the population (cf. Loeb, 1994:55). We see this in a 1925 advertisement for Möllers Cod Liver Oil (Figure 00.1), which carries the headline "The child's growth is a key issue for all mothers." Despite its monochrome graphics, the advertisement has a rather advanced visual construction, organised in a way that highlights certain aspects. The heading—"The child's growth"—is in italics and bold, thus stressing the urge to care for the children, while the brand name—Peter Möllers Fiskleverolja—is placed in the centre of the text, its larger bold font giving it a very salient position. It, thus, appears to have a logical connection to the heading, linking the child's well-being to the product. Below the brand name, the text continues, with an indented, italicised line stating that "High vitamin content is guaranteed" and this is why cod liver oil brings "health and strength."

On the left is an illustration reflecting a "slice-of-life" (Nelson et al., 2020) scene of a mother measuring her child against a wall. The smiling child holds a little glass in their hand, connoting the intake of cod liver oil and its effect on

Figure 00.1 1925 Advertisement for Möllers Cod Liver Oil

Credit: *Svenska Dagbladet*, 25 January 1925, p. 1

their growth. The illustration signals happiness and health through the child's willingness to consume the cod liver oil without any effort from the mother. Furthermore, the mother's stylish outfit associates the product with what at the time appeared as a modern and middle-class lifestyle (O'Hagan and Eriksson, 2022). The illustration also taps into the connection in the public consciousness between health and morality, suggesting that protecting children's health is a moral duty, and to neglect this disharmonises with notions of what constitutes a good mother. Such links between health and morality—in line with the neoliberal self-care agenda—are still prominent in today's food and drink marketing (Andersson, 2019; Chen and Eriksson, 2022).

The discovery of vitamins was a breakthrough in nutritional research and the marketing of products, such as cod liver oil, transformed the way that we now conceive of food and nutrition. It, therefore, stands as a clear example of how the food industry has long exploited nutritional science discoveries for its own commercial gain. Even in today's highly regulated environment, similar strategies still occur and rules can even be circumvented in canny ways, as we shall see below.

Towards a Semiotic Approach to Food Marketing Regulation

Many of the advertisements under investigation in this edited volume were produced at a time when food marketing was still largely unregulated or regulations were still in their infancy. Although the United Kingdom was pioneering in passing a general food safety law in 1860, it was not until 1944 that the Labelling of Food Order was enacted, followed by the 1968 Trade Descriptions Act. Equally, in the United States, the Pure Food and Drug Act of 1906 sought to clamp down on adulteration, while the Federal Trade Commission Act of 1914 outlawed unfair acts or practices that affect commerce. However, the first proper regulation on food packaging did not come until 1966 with the Fair Packaging and Labeling Act. In other European countries, such as Sweden, it took until 1971 for a similar act to be passed. Throughout the nineteenth and much of the twentieth century, advertisements could, thus, make sweeping claims regarding a product's health effects and packaging was not required to feature a nutrition information panel.

Today's food marketing is widely regulated in order to help consumers make healthy dietary choices. Within the context of the European Union (EU), for instance, *Regulation (EC) No 1924/2006* seeks "to ensure a high level of protection for consumers and to facilitate their choice" and stipulates the nutritional claims that can be used for marketing purposes. Furthermore, *Regulation (EU) No 1169/2011* regulates the information that food producers provide on food packaging, ensuring that there is no "misleading labelling" and that claims like "natural," "traditional" and "fresh" are clarified. From a health perspective, a key element of this EU regulation is the mandatory nutrition information panel, which must contain evidence-based nutritional information. *Commission*

Regulation (EU) No 432/2012 provides a list of permitted health claims that can be made on foods, related to specific nutrients. In other countries relevant to the edited volume, similar regulations are in place, albeit to varying degrees (e.g. Food Safety and Standards Act 2006 in India; Food Safety Law in China; General Health Law on Advertising in Mexico; Public Health and Municipal Services Ordinance/Trade Descriptions Ordinance in Hong Kong).

Nonetheless, a major weakness in these regulations is their overwhelming focus on the use of written language and the need for evidence-based factual claims in food marketing, thereby paying considerably less attention to how visual design can be used to imply what cannot be overtly claimed in the text. Layout and composition, for example, can subtly convey healthiness through such techniques as salience, framing and visual hierarchies, while specific colour choices and shapes can also make products appear scientifically approved (Chen and Eriksson, 2019b). Although the EU decided in late 2022 to resolve some of the issues in its regulations, the proposed changes are linked to the setting of "nutrient profiles" to restrict health claims around foods high in saturated fat, sugar or salt, as well as health claims around "botanicals," particularly in reference to food supplements (Collins, 2022). This continues to leave the door open for consumers to be misled by visuals and potentially face similar misleading health claims to advertisements from more than 100 years ago. This surprising link between past and present marketing strategies—despite regulation now in place to protect consumers—makes this topic one of major importance. Engaging more with historical *and* multimodal insights could help policymakers cast a more critical eye over the way that semiotic resources continue to be exploited by food marketers and, therefore, develop more robust regulations that truly safeguard consumers from deceptive marketing and unfair practices.

Themes

The chapters in this volume were chosen to illustrate the wide range of work that is being carried out by scholars across the world and across different disciplines. Although they represent such fields as Media and Communication Studies, Critical Food Studies, Linguistics, History and Sociology, there are overlaps in their theoretical orientation and the ways they approach how science is used to promote food and drinks as healthy. The 13 contributions demonstrate how products were sold as scientific innovations, often with references to their nutritional content and by stressing their superiority over other traditional products. They also show that marketing strategies employed today, in fact, have their roots in the late nineteenth and early twentieth centuries. These strategies seem to be independent of national borders and continental belongings and are not restricted to specific groups of products. Many, thus, come across as general, globally present and recurrent throughout various historical eras.

One such strategy found across many chapters in the book is "scientific motherhood" (Apple, 1996), which implies that advertisements largely address women as the primary household shoppers and in charge of caring for the family. Through this strategy, food producers position women as incapable of looking after their children without expert advice and advise them to purchase certain products in order to maintain their health (O'Hagan, 2021a). Scientific motherhood remains an effective marketing technique today, using scientific rationale to tap into women's fears of being "good" mothers and convincing them to listen to experts so as to avoid putting their children in danger (cf. Foss, 2010; Orland, 2023; Davis et al., 2019; Merrigan, 2022). In the current book, we see examples of this strategy in Saurabh Mishra's analysis of how hydrogenated oil was marketed in the context of late- and post-colonial India (Chapter 9). It is also present in the marketing of Ribena blackcurrant in post-war Britain, as Daniel Ewers shows (Chapter 6), and in the marketing of powdered milk in 1920s China, as demonstrated by Lo Shuk Ying (Chapter 5). There are also some links to this strategy in advertisements for coffee substitutes in late nineteenth-/early twentieth-century Sweden, as Leif Runefelt indicates (Chapter 7).

Another key strategy identified throughout this book is the paradoxical blend of science with tradition and/or nature (O'Hagan, 2022). This strategy serves to demystify modern science and cutting-edge technology by associating it with nature and (sometimes ancient) traditions. It dates back to the early 1900s and was, for instance, prominent in the marketing of radium products, where it aimed to link the "mysterious" and "natural" powers of radium to modernity and a modern lifestyle (Santos, 2020; Eriksson and O'Hagan, 2021). In the context of food marketing, this strategy promotes products as both natural and as a result of part of technologically advanced processes, as both ancient and modern (Hobart and Maroney, 2019). In doing so, it lends a mythical aura to the product in question, tapping into the quasi-nostalgic discourse of nutritional primitivism, while also obscuring the advanced processing of ingredients (Loyer and Knight, 2018; Andersson, 2019; Andersson and Smith, 2021). We find this strategy in Jessica Loyer's analysis (Chapter 11) of the marketing of chia seed products in contemporary Australia, Amber Hinde's study (Chapter 10) of Allinson's bread in early twentieth-century Britain, Andreja Veznovik's exploration of the growing cultured meat industry (Chapter 13) and Iben Bredahl Jessen's (Chapter 2) examination of the marketing of dairy products and plant-based alternatives in Denmark over the past 90 years. It is also apparent in the aforementioned chapter by Ying on the promotion of milk powder in China.

A third theme that runs across many chapters in this book is hygiene and cleanliness, particularly in relation to food safety and health values. These concerns date back to the late nineteenth century and are linked to the industrialisation of food production and the need for authorities to clamp down on the sale of illegally adulterated foods. In the United Kingdom, following the passing of the 1875 Sale of Food and Drugs Act, the term "pure" became particularly drawn upon by marketers to showcase their products as safe and, therefore, healthy options (O'Hagan, 2020). In a bid to show transparency, companies offered consumers "behind-the-scenes" views into their factories, with images of workers in white lab coats to signal safety and transparency (McClintock, 1995; Santos, 2020; O'Hagan, 2023b). Companies also employed representatives to travel around the country and demonstrate products in stores, such as Heinz's "girl in the white cap" (Domosh, 2003). Today, with more stringent regulations in place on food safety, the need to promote hygiene and cleanliness has become closely tied up with environmental and ethical concerns instead and the need to reduce one's carbon footprint and protect natural landscapes (Smith-Howard, 2017; Collinson, 2023). In the current volume, Lucy Jane Santos' study of the development of "electric restaurants" in early twentieth-century London addresses this theme (Chapter 12), as do the previously mentioned chapters by Vezovnik on cultured meat, Bredahl Jessen on dairy products and plant-based alternatives, Hinde on Allinson's bread and Runefelt on coffee substitutes.

The final recurring theme is that of healthism and the medicalisation of everyday life (Crawford, 1980, 2006). Healthism is an ideology that situates health problems as an individual responsibility, viewing health as something that one achieves through a self-care regime (Eriksson, 2022). In doing so, it turns health into a type of "aesthetic labour" (Elias et al., 2017), concerned with working on and perfecting bodily appearance. Food marketing plays a crucial role in reproducing healthism and has done so since the late nineteenth century and the growth of the Physical Culture Movement (O'Hagan, 2021b). Increased focus on bodily appearance as a sign of "good" health has also led to what Eriksson (2022) terms "fitnessism," whereby consumers are encouraged to exercise self-discipline and work on their bodies through the consumption of particular foods and commercialised fitness programmes to achieve a fit body—an outward sign of good and responsible citizenship (Bordo, 1993; Dworkin and Wachs, 2009; Monson et al., 2016). While fitnessism is particularly apparent today in modern makeover television shows and the social media accounts of influencers, like healthism, it has its roots in the late nineteenth century and the Physical Culture Movement. We see this particularly in Chapter 1 by Conor Heffernan who examines the medicalisation of food and how the language of science was used to promote new nutritional substances, extracts and diets in early twentieth-century Britain and Ireland. This theme is also present in Veronica Mak's (Chapter 8) study of adult formula milk products in contemporary China, and how the "vulnerable" bodies of elderly people are at the centre of marketing campaigns aimed at both staying and looking healthy. It is also a key aspect of Pilar Zazueta's (Chapter 3) exploration of ultra-processed food marketing in Mexico, and how different actors have adapted and recontextualised ideas about nutritional science and healthy eating to legitimise their interests in the public sphere and try to shape consumption. Chapter 4 by Angela Smith, which offers a comparison of the branding of muesli in the United Kingdom through a case study of Alpen and Troo

Granola+, also demonstrates how consumers are made individually responsible for the health of their bodies, as does the aforementioned chapter by Hinde on Allinson's bread.

In the volume's afterword by Caroline Tagg, a critical discussion of the above themes is brought together and responses are given to some of the key arguments and issues raised by contributors. Tagg focuses also on the importance of transhistorical approaches to the study of food marketing, particularly incorporating multimodality, and the novel insights that this can lead to.

Overall, it is hoped that this volume will offer innovative ideas and approaches to the study of the long relationship between science, food and drink marketing and the promotion of healthy lifestyles, thus fostering new dialogue on this underexplored yet important area of research and acting as a springboard for further—and much needed—studies from a transhistorical and multimodal perspective.

Note

1 The publication of *Message and Medium* and its warm response by scholars led to the founding of the Digital Correspondence Community Interest Group in 2023, which explores the linguistic and material facets of correspondence across the centuries and how they create meaning. For more information, see https://digitalhumanities-uk-ie.org/community-interest-groups/digital-correspondence/

References

Adami, E. 2020. "Transhistoricizing Multimodality: Reflections on the How-To" in *Message and Medium: English Language Practices Across Old and New Media*, edited by C. Tagg and M. Evans (Berlin: de Gruyter), pp. 359–363.

Andersson, H. 2019. Recontextualizing Swedish Nationalism for Commercial Purposes: A Multimodal Analysis of a Milk Marketing Event. *Critical Discourse Studies* 16(5):582–603.

Andersson, H. and Smith, A. 2021. Flags and Fields: A Comparative Analysis of National Identify in Butter Packaging in Sweden and the UK. *Social Semiotics* 33(4):861–882.

Apple, R. 1995. Constructing Mothers: Scientific Motherhood in the Nineteenth and Twentieth Centuries. *Social History of Medicine* 8(2):161–178.

Apple, R. 1996. *Vitamania: Vitamins in American Culture*. New Brunswick: Rutgers University Press.

Bolter J.D. and Grusin, R. 2000. *Remediation: Understanding New Media*. Cambridge: MIT Press.

Bordo, S. 1993. *The Male Body: A New Look at Men in Public and in Private*. New York: Farrar, Straus and Giroux.

Cesiri, D. 2022. The Representation of Baby Food Advertisements in the UK and the US from the Late 1880s to the 1940s. *Childhood in the Past* 15(2):96–104.

Chen, A. and Eriksson, G. 2019a. The Mythologization of Protein: A Multimodal Critical Discourse Analysis of Snacks Packaging. *Food, Culture and Society* 22(4):423–445

Chen, A. and Eriksson, G. 2019b. The Making of Healthy and Moral Snacks: A Multimodal Critical Discourse Analysis of Corporate Storytelling. *Discourse, Context & Media* 32, https://doi.org/10.1016/j.dcm.2019.100347

Chen, A. and Eriksson, G. 2022. Connoting a Neoliberal and Entrepreneurial Discourse of Science Through Infographics and Integrated Design: The Case of "Functional" Healthy Drinks. *Critical Discourse Studies* 19(3):290–308.
Clampin, D. 2014. *Advertising and Propaganda in World War II. Cultural Identity and the Blitz Spirit*. London: I.B. Tauris.
Collins, N. 2022. Nutrition and Health Claims in the European Union in 2022. *Regulatory Focus*. Available at https://www.raps.org/news-and-articles/news-articles/2022/9/nutrition-and-health-claims-in-the-european-union (Accessed: 18 January 2024).
Collinson, P. 2023. "Pure Food, Food Tourism and the Mythologising of Western Ireland" in *Pure Food: Theoretical and Cross-Cultural Perspectives*, edited by P. Collinson and H. Macbeth (New York: Berghahn Books), pp. 149–164.
Cook, G. 1992. *The Discourse of Advertising*. London: Routledge.
Crawford, R. 1980. Healthism and the Medicalization of Everyday Life. *International Journal of Health Services* 10(3):365–388.
Crawford, R. 2006. Health as a Meaningful Social Practice. *Health* 10(4):401–420.
Cross, G.S. and Proctor, R.N. 2014. *Packaged Pleasures: How Technology and Marketing Revolutionized Desire*. Chicago: University of Chicago Press.
Davis, T., Hogg, M.K., Marshall, D., Petersen, A. and Schneider, T. 2019. The Knowing Mother: Maternal Knowledge and the Reinforcement of the Feminine Consuming Subject in Magazine Advertisements. *Journal of Consumer Culture* 22(1), https://doi.org/10.1177/1469540519889990
De Iulio, S. 2010. The Construction of Fun in Food Advertisements Targeting Children. *Young Consumers* 11(2):96–107.
De Iulio, S. 2013. From Too Little to Too Much: A Short History of the Representations of the Risks Associated with Children's Food in Advertising. *Advertising & Society Review* 14(3), https://doi.org/10.1353/asr.2013.0017
De Iulio, S. 2019. Food Marketers at School: The Challenge of Trustworthiness in France (1900–2013). *Food and Foodways* 27(1–2):98–122.
De Iulio, S. and Kovacs, S. 2022. eds. *Food Information, Communication and Education: Eating Knowledge*. London: Bloomsbury.
De Ridder, D., Kroese, F., Evers, C., Adriaanse, M. and Gillebaart, M. 2017. Healthy Diet: Health Impact, Prevalence, Correlates, and Interventions. *Psychology & Health* 32(8):907–941.
Domosh, M. 2003. Pickles and Purity: Discourses of Food, Empire and Work in Turn-of-the-Century USA. *Social and Cultural Geography* 4(1):7–26.
Dworkin, S. and Wachs, F.L. 2009. *Body Panic: Gender, Health, and the Selling of Fitness*. New York: New York University Press.
Elias, A.S., Gill, R. and Scharff, C. 2017. *Aesthetic Labour: Rethinking Beauty Politics in Neoliberalism*. London: Palgrave Macmillan.
Emery, E. 2017. Viral Marketing: Mariani Wine Testimonials in Early French and American Newspaper Advertising. *Nineteenth-Century Contexts* 39(2):117–129.
Eriksson, G. 2022. Promoting Extreme Fitness Regimes Through the Communicative Affordances of Reality Makeover Television: A Multimodal Critical Discourse Analysis. *Critical Studies in Media Communication* 39(5):408–426.
Eriksson, G. and Machin, D. 2020. Discourses of "Good Food": The Commercialization of Healthy and Ethical Eating. *Discourse, Context & Media* 33, https://doi.org/10.1016/j.dcm.2019.100365
Eriksson, G. and O'Hagan, L.A. 2021. Selling "Healthy" Radium Products with Science: A Multimodal Analysis of Marketing in Sweden, 1910–1940. *Science Communication* 43(6):740–767.
Fairclough, N. 1995. *Critical Discourse Analysis: The Critical Study of Language*. London: Routledge.
Fischer, C. 1994. *America Calling: A Social History of the Telephone to 1940*. Berkeley: University of California Press.

Forrest, Beth M. 2023. Gastrónoma: Representations of Spanish Cuisine in Gourmet Magazine, 1941–2009. Presented at *Third Conference on Food and Communication*, Örebro University, Sweden, 13–15 September.

Foss, K.A. 2010. Perpetuating "Scientific Motherhood": Infant Feeding Discourse in Parents Magazine, 1930–2007. *Women & Health* 50(3):297–311.

Frye, J. and Bruner, M. eds. 2012. *The Rhetoric of Food: Discourse, Materiality, and Power*. London: Routledge.

Gamble, R. and Robertson, E. 2023. "Always packed fresh and clean": The Construction of Australian Rice for Local and Global Markets, c.1945 to the present. Presented at *Third Conference on Food and Communication*, Örebro University, Sweden, 13–15 September.

Gillen, J. 2023. *The Edwardian Picture Postcard as a Communications Revolution: A Literacy Studies Perspective*. New York: Routledge.

Golden, C. 2010. *Posting It: The Victorian Revolution in Letter Writing*. Gainesville: University Press of Florida.

Herring, S. 2013. "Discourse in Web 2.0: Familiar, Reconfigured, Emergent" in *Discourse 2.0: Language and New Media*, edited by D. Tannen and A.M. Trester (Washington, DC: Georgetown University Press), pp. 1–25.

Hobart, H.J. and Maroney, S. 2019. On Racial Constitutions and Digestive Therapeutics. *Food, Culture & Society* 22(5):576–594.

Jaworska, S. 2020. "Corpora and the Discourse of Advertising" in *The Routledge Handbook of Corpus Approaches to Discourse Analysis*, edited by E. Friginal and J.A. Hardy (London: Routledge), pp. 428–444.

Jovanovic, M. 2013. Selling Fear and Empowerment in Food Advertising. *Food, Culture & Society* 17(4):641–663.

Koteyko, N. 2009. "I am a very happy, lucky lady, and I am full of vitality!" Analysis of Promotional Strategies on the Websites of Probiotic Yoghurt Producers. *Critical Discourse Studies* 6(2):111–125.

Kress, G. 2010. *Multimodality: A Social Semiotic Approach to Contemporary Communication*. London: Routledge.

Kress, G. and van Leeuwen, T. 1996. *Reading Images: The Grammar of Visual Design*. London: Routledge.

Kress, G. and van Leeuwen, T. 2001. *Multimodal Discourse: The Modes and Media of Contemporary Communication*. London: Arnold Publishers.

Ledin, P. and Machin, D. 2018. *Doing Visual Analysis*. London: SAGE.

Ledin, P. and Machin, D. 2020a. *Introduction to Multimodal Analysis*. London: Bloomsbury.

Ledin, P. and Machin, D. 2020b. Replacing Actual Political Activism with Ethical Shopping: The Case of Oatly. *Discourse, Context & Media* 34, https://doi.org/10.1016/j.dcm.2019.100344

Loeb, L.A. 1994. *Consuming Angels: Advertising and Victorian Women*. Oxford: Oxford University Press.

Lonier, T. 2010. Alchemy in Eden: Entrepreneurialism, Branding, and Food Marketing in the United States, 1880–1920. *Enterprise & Society* 11(4):695–708.

Loyer, J. and Knight, C. 2018. Selling the "Inca Superfood": Nutritional Primitivism in Superfoods Books and Maca Marketing. *Food, Culture & Society* 21(4):449–467.

MacGregor, C., Petersen, A. and Parker, C. 2021. Promoting a Healthier, Younger You: The Media Marketing of Anti-Ageing Superfoods. *Journal of Consumer Culture* 21(2), https://doi.org/10.1177/1469540518773825

McClintock, A. 1995. *Imperial Leather: Race, Gender, and Sexuality in the Colonial Contest*. London: Routledge.

Merrigan, E. 2022. "Material Motherhood: The Disconnect of Science and Consumerism from Nostalgia in Baby Books" in *The Material Culture of Writing*, edited by C. Alexis and H.J. Rule (Denver: University Press of Colorado), pp. 89–114.

Monson, O., Donaghue, N. and Gill, R. 2016. Working Hard on the Outside: A Multimodal Critical Discourse Analysis of The Biggest Loser Australia. *Social Semiotics* 26(5):524–540.
"Möllers Cod Liver Oil Advertisement." 1925. *Svenska Dagbladet* (25 January), 1.
Nelson, M.R., Das, S. and Ahn, R.J. 2020. A Prescription for Health: (Pseudo)scientific Advertising of Fruits and Vegetables in the Early 20th Century. *Advertising & Society Quarterly* 21(1), https://doi.org/10.1353/asr.2020.0007
O'Hagan, L.A. 2020. Pure in Body, Pure in Mind? A Sociohistorical Perspective on the Marketisation of Pure Foods in Great Britain. *Discourse, Context & Media* 34, https://doi.org/10.1016/j.dcm.2019.100325
O'Hagan, L.A. 2021a. Blinded by Science? Constructing Truth and Authority in Early 20th-Century Virol Advertisements. *History of Retailing and Consumption* 7(2):162–192.
O'Hagan, L.A. 2021b. Flesh-Formers or Fads? Historicizing the Contemporary Protein-Enhanced Food Trend. *Food, Culture & Society* 25(5):875–898.
O'Hagan, L.A. 2022. All That Glistens Is Not (Green) Gold: Historicising the Contemporary Chlorophyll Fad Through a Multimodal Analysis of Swedish Marketing, 1950–1953. *Journal of Historical Research in Marketing* 14(3):374–398.
O'Hagan, L.A. 2023a. From Fatigue Fighter to Heartburn Healer: The Evolution of "Health Drink" Marketing in Early Twentieth-Century Sweden. *Journal of Food Products Marketing* 29(1):19–40.
O'Hagan, L.A. 2023b. "Welcome to Pure Food City": Tracing Discourses of Health in the Promotional Publications of the Postum Cereal Company, 1920–1925. *Journal of Historical Research in Marketing* 15(3):171–200.
O'Hagan, L.A. and Eriksson, G. 2022. Modern Science, Moral Mothers, and Mythical Nature: A Multimodal Analysis of Cod Liver Oil Marketing in Sweden, 1920–1930. *Food and Foodways* 30(4):231–260.
O'Hagan, L.A. and Serafinelli, E. 2022. Transhistoricizing the Drone: A Comparative Visual Social Semiotic Analysis of Pigeon and Domestic Drone Photography. *Photography and Culture* 15(4):327–351.
O'Hagan, L.A. and Spilioti, T. 2021. The Edwardian Selfies: A Transhistorical Approach to Celebrity Culture and Pictorial Bookplates. *Discourse, Context and Media* 43, https://doi.org/10.1016/j.dcm.2021.100522
Orland, B. 2023. "Motherhood and Scientific Innovation: The Story of Natural Versus Artificial Baby Food in the 19th Century" in *Gender in Science and Technology*, edited by W. Ernst and I. Horwath (Berlin: De Gruyter), pp. 129–146.
Pohl-Valero, S. 2020. The Scientific Lives of Chicha: The Production of a Fermented Beverage and the Making of Expert Knowledge in Bogotá, 1889–1939. *Osiris* 35:204–227.
Prell, H., Palmblad, E., Lissner, L. and Berg, C.M. 2011. Health Discourse in Swedish Television Food Advertising During Children's Peak Viewing Times. *Appetite* 56(3):607–616.
Qvarsell, R. and Torell, U. 2005. *Reklam och hälsa: Levnadsideal, skönhet och hälsa i den svenska reklamens historia*. Stockholm: Carlsson.
Runefelt, L. and O'Hagan, L.A. forthcoming. Hemp for Health: The Marketing of Cannabis-Infused Foods in Late Nineteenth-Century Sweden. *Journal of Historical Research in Marketing*.
Salamonik, M. 2023. The Power of Advertising: Products with Cannabis in Late Nineteenth-Century Sweden. Presented at *Third Conference on Food and Communication*, Örebro University, Sweden, 13–15 September.
Santos, L.J. 2020. *Half Lives: The Unlikely History of Radium*. London: Icon Books.
Saren, M., Goulding, C., Caterall, M., Maclaran, P. and Elliott, R. 2007. *Critical Marketing: Defining the Field*. London: Routledge.

Scheire, W. 2015. "Bring Joy to Your Home with the Real Frigidaire": Advertising the Refrigerator to Belgian Female Consumers, 1955–1965. *Food and Foodways* 23(1–2):57–79.

Schudson, M. 2000. Advertising as Capitalist Realism. *Advertising & Society Review* 1(1), https://doi.org/10.1353/asr.2000.0023

Scrinis, G. 2013. *Nutritionism: The Science and Politics of Dietary Advice*. New York: Columbia University Press.

Slavin, J.L. 2015. The Challenges of Nutrition Policymaking. *Nutrition Journal*, https://doi.org/10.1186/s12937-015-0001-8

Smith, D. 2008. Hail Mariani: The Transformation of Vin Mariani from Medicine to Food in American Culture, 1886–1910. *The Social History of Alcohol and Drugs* 23(1), https://www.journals.uchicago.edu/doi/abs/10.1086/SHAD23010042

Smith-Howard, K. 2017. *Pure and Modern Milk: An Environmental History Since 1900*. Oxford: Oxford University Press.

Sprackley, C. 2020. "Extractionist Logics: The Missing Link Between Functional Foods and Superfoods" in *Critical Approaches to Superfoods*, edited by E. McDonell & R. Wilk (London: Bloomsbury), pp. 57–76.

Stead, W. 1899. *The Art of Advertising*. London: T.B. Browne.

Steinitz, L. 2017. "The Language of Advertising: Fashioning Health Food Consumers at the Fin de Siècle" in *Food, Drink and the Written World in Britain, 1820–1945*, edited by M. Addyman, L. Wood and C. Yiannitsaros (London: Routledge), https://www.taylorfrancis.com/chapters/edit/10.4324/9781315183091-7/language-advertising-lesley-steinitz

Tadajewski, M. and Brownlie, D. 2008. *Critical Marketing: Issues in Contemporary Marketing*. Hoboken: Wiley.

Tadajewski, M., Higgins, M., Denegri-Knott, J. and Varman, R. 2018. *The Routledge Companion to Critical Marketing*. London: Routledge.

Tagg, C. and Evans, M. eds. 2020. *Message and Medium: English Language Practices Across Old and New Media*. Berlin: de Gruyter.

van Leeuwen, T. 2005. *Introducing Social Semiotics*. London: Routledge.

From Foods to Nutrients

150 Years of Modern Nutrition Science

Lauren Alex O'Hagan and Göran Eriksson

Introduction

In this chapter, we present a brief overview of major developments in the field of nutrition science over the past 150 years as a means of contextualising the 13 core chapters that make up *Food Marketing and Selling Healthy Lifestyles with Science*. Demonstrating how understandings around what we eat and how it affects our bodies have evolved from the late nineteenth century to modern day provides a framework for much of the discussion that follows in terms of how scientific claims are used in food marketing. Across the volume, we see how food advertisements are reflective not only of the social and cultural zeitgeist but are also strongly linked to nutritional and dietetic understanding. We begin this chapter by briefly exploring the concept of nutrition in the Ancient World and throughout the centuries that followed until the Chemical Revolution of the late 1700s when the foundations were laid for modern nutrition science. Our focus then shifts to key nutritional research conducted throughout the nineteenth and early twentieth centuries, which ultimately led to the identification of individual micronutrients. Finally, we outline how the now well-established field of nutrition science has continued to develop and the state of the research area today.[1]

Nutrition Science in the Ancient World

Theories on how food is used in our bodies date back to the Ancient World and classical antiquity, where both physicians and philosophers studied human diets and generally agreed that certain foods and drinks were important for preventing illness and restoring health. The first known teachings on nutrition are attributed to Imhotep of Ancient Egypt (4000 BCE), Emperor Huang Ti of China (2500 BCE) and the Indian Ayurvedic tradition (200 BCE), all of which stressed the link between a balanced diet and good health (Cannon, 2007). However, it is the work of Ancient Greeks, such as Pythagoras, Anaxagoras, Hippocrates and Galen, that is said to have provided the basis for Western nutrition and whose ideas remained in place up until the Age of Enlightenment (1685–1815).

DOI: 10.4324/9781003450276-2

Both Hippocrates and Galen promoted the concept of humourism, which dominated medical practice in Europe and the Middle East for centuries. According to humourism, the body consists of four fluids—black bile, yellow bile, blood and phlegm—that determine a person's temperament, and a correct diet is needed to balance them and stave off sickness (Conrad, 2011). Writing in 1621 in his *Anatomy of Melancholy*, Robert Burton blamed beef, venison, rabbit, milk, fish, pulses, fruit and vegetables for poor mental health, while in his *A Treatise of the Hypochondriack and Hysterick Passions* (1711), Bernard Mandeville claimed that mental illness was a result of overindulgence in rich food, strong liquor and self-drugging. George Cheyne's *The English Malady* (1733) also stated that lunacy, madness and a disordered brain could be "accounted for from no other natural Cause, but a Malregimen of Diet." It was not until the advent of germ theory in the 1850s that humourism began to fall out of favour as external causes for pathological changes in cells, tissues and organs were identified (Lagay, 2002).

Nutrition Science in the Chemical Revolution and Beyond

The Chemical Revolution in France, which took place at the end of the eighteenth century, is generally accepted as the first time that the relationship between food and our bodies was tested in a quantitative, scientific way through chemical analysis (Trüeb, 2020). A major figure in these early days of nutrition science was the French chemist Antoine Lavoisier who had a particular interest in metabolism. With his assistant Armand Seguin, Lavoisier measured human respiratory output of carbon dioxide (which he then called carbonic acid) both at rest and when lifting weights. They found that carbon dioxide increased with activity, which disproved previous theories that the sole purpose of respiration was to cool down the heart and that the weight of ingested material not recovered in stools or urine was lost through "insensible perspiration" (Carpenter, 2003a).

Lavoisier theorised that food was fuel and that the body, therefore, expelled carbon dioxide as a product of combustion (Stafford, 2010). In order to test this theory, together with mathematician Pierre-Simon Laplace, he designed an ice calorimeter and placed a guinea pig inside. They compared the heat produced by the animal with its production of carbon dioxide and then compared these results with the heat produced by a lit candle or burning charcoal. Their findings led them to conclude that respiratory gas exchange is a combustion, and this is what enabled the guinea pig to maintain its body temperature above that of its surroundings (Buchholz and Schoeller, 2004). Lavoisier's discovery was a major breakthrough at the time in terms of establishing that the body needed energy to function and that one major role of food was to supply it. This research formed the basis for determining what a person needs to survive and what causes weight gain or weight loss, as well as the relationship between food and physical labour (Stafford, 2010).

At the same time, many scientists were also investigating nitrogen and whether animals could use atmospheric nitrogen to "animalise" ingested foods of low nitrogen content. One of the pioneers in this area was French chemist Jean-Baptiste Boussingault who developed the first balance trial (i.e. an assessment of food input and waste output) in the 1830s. Boussingault compared the nitrogen content of hay, oats and potatoes fed to cows and horses to keep them at a constant weight with their excrement (and milk, in the case of cows). He discovered that animal feed contained sufficient nitrogen to meet bodily requirements, which ended the speculation that additional nitrogen was obtained from the atmosphere (Carpenter, 2003a).

Nutrition Science in the Mid-Nineteenth Century

Nutrition science experienced a huge growth in the mid-nineteenth century as a result of the emerging modern nation-state and governmentality (Cannon, 2007). In the 1840s, states became concerned about political turbulence across Europe, which had led to food supply shortages, and feared an outbreak of food riots. To govern the situation, they began to invest in nutrition research to find cheaper and easier methods to feed populations (Stafford, 2010). Concurrently, as industrialisation began and urban populations grew, retailers struggled to keep up with large-scale demand, which led them to resort to unscrupulous practices, adulterating their foods as a way of increasing profits and gaining a competitive advantage (Collins, 1993). Over the course of the 1800s, the dangers of food adulteration and impure foodstuffs were slowly exposed by chemists who found that it was a major contributor to the poor quality of life in industrial towns and cities, particularly for the working classes (O'Hagan, 2020). Following this exposure, states began to increasingly intervene in people's diets amid growing concerns about workers' efficiency and health, pumping vast sums of money into research institutes and university research centres (Kamminga and Cunningham, 1995). At the heart of this initiative were the beliefs that citizens had a duty to be fit in order to work, while the state was obliged to provide such conditions to do so (Kamminga and Cunningham, 1995). The food adulteration scandals also paved the way for stricter laws on food regulation across the Western world, led by the United Kingdom with its Adulteration of Food and Drugs Act 1860.

A notable figure in mid-nineteenth-century nutritional research was German chemist Justus von Liebig. By this time, the four elements of food had been identified (carbon, nitrogen, hydrogen and oxygen), as well as the three food constituents (carbohydrates, fats and protein). However, there was no knowledge of their chemical make-up. From his work in the area of plant nutrition, Liebig began to wonder whether physiological chemistry could be used to understand nature and, consequently, to engineer the food systems of industrialising countries (Cannon, 2007). With this in mind, he invented the *kaliapparat* to analyse carbon in organic compounds, publishing his chemical theory of metabolism in the treatise *Animal Chemistry* in 1842. Here, he argued that muscular labour by horses or humans required mainly protein, not carbohydrates and fats—something contradictory to what we know now. The isolation and identification of protein as a master nutrient was revolutionary and led to growing food experiments that sought to develop cheap protein-based foods to build up workers' resilience and create a national advantage (Cannon, 2007). Naturally, Liebig was at the forefront of these experiments.

Building on his claim that eating both meat juices and muscle fibre was important, Liebig established a formula to produce beef extract. In 1862, Belgian entrepreneur George Christian Giebert became interested in commercialising Liebig's formula and, three years later, they founded the Liebig's Extract of Meat Company together in London (Finlay, 1995). Through heavy marketing campaigns, they promoted their meat tea as curative and a highly nutritious alternative to real meat. They later shifted their focus towards convenience and flavour when questions were raised about its actual health benefits (Finlay, 1995). Liebig collaborated with popular cookery writers, such as Henriette Davidis and Katharina Prato, to popularise his meat tea. He also advertised the product with calendars, trading cards, games, posters and toys.

While Liebig was a pioneer in food engineering and marketing through science, he was not operating alone. Another major impetus was the Great Exhibition of 1851. Although it is oversimplistic to say that the Great Exhibition revolutionised food marketing, it certainly had an impact on the use of scientific discourse to sell products through its promotion of the latest technological advancements (Richards, 1990:39). Moreover, it showed producers the importance of knowing customers' desires to compete successfully and survive in an ever more competitive market (O'Hagan, 2019a).

Although there was a long history of (pseudo)science in advertisements for patent medicines (cf. Porter, 2000; Barker, 2009), this was not the case for food. Thus, the introduction of science into food marketing was both novel and powerful, shaping consumption patterns and consumer behaviour, particularly around the need to choose foods that promoted a healthy diet. From the 1850s onwards, advertisements for old products started to emphasise their improved scientific processes, while advertisements for new products began to foreground their scientific origins (Loeb, 1994:10). Emphasising a single health quality of a product created a "health halo" effect (Fernan et al., 2018), whereby consumers acquired positive impressions of other non-claimed health qualities, thereby increasing the perceived healthiness of the food or drink in question.

This practice increased throughout the nineteenth century as goods became branded and food manufacturers recognised their privileged position as knowledge shapers (Church, 2000:632). Narratives of health and wellbeing, therefore, became key in differentiating products from competitors and building consumer trust. Capitalising upon the public's growing knowledge of the latest medical and scientific advances, thanks to the popular press and increased literacy rates, manufacturers emphasised the importance of proper diet and good hygiene to prevent illness, as well as the strong link between health and morality (O'Hagan, 2020:57). Through this marketing, the public gained a new idea that certain food products could provide widespread benefits for them and their families and were encouraged to buy them, even if they did not fully understand the claims made and the information provided was not always strictly true (Hansen, 1999:632; Jones, 2012:387).

Here, then, we see the roots of the nutritionism ideology—what Scrinis (2013:2) describes as "a reductive *focus* on the nutrient composition of foods as the means for understanding their healthfulness, as well as a reductive *interpretation* of the role of these nutrients in bodily health." The major focus in this era on protein as essential to building strong bodies marked the start of "nutri-quantification" (Scrinis, 2013:42), with consumers repeatedly informed that an adequate quantity of a certain nutrient was necessary for good health. As Scholliers (2018) warns, this could, however, conceal the actual production and processing quality of foods and their ingredients, as well as fail to take into account broader contextual factors that may determine bodily health.

Nutrition Science in the Late Nineteenth and Early Twentieth Centuries

By the late nineteenth century, it was now widely accepted that there was a strong link between diet and physical vigour based on investigations of the physiology of nutrition in terms of quantitative chemistry (Kamminga and Cunningham, 1995). There was also a broad consensus that (1) health depends on the calorie content of diet; (2) the three major energy substrates (carbohydrates, fats and protein) can replace each other in proportion to their calorific content; and (3) different proteins have equivalent energy content (Kamminga and Cunningham, 1995).

The calorie offered a scientifically rational way to understand food and, according to Scrinis (2013:52), enabled the science of nutrition to be translated into everyday personal terms. It grew from an attempt to offer a nutritional version of Taylorism—a scientific measurement of the labour process and productivity, which conceived the body as "mechanomorphic" (Cullather, 2007:338). However, it took as given that all foods could be equally measured and compared in terms of the number of calories that they contained without considering how different food components and ingredients may have been transformed through processing techniques.

Throughout the early twentieth century, this gap was exploited by marketers who frequently used calories to present scientific comparisons between dissimilar foods. Their credibility was supported by the fact that many governments had adopted the calorie as a standard of food values. A 1919 British advertisement for Quaker Oats (Figure 0.1), for example, emphasises the government definition of a calorie and compares the calories in three different types of foods: eggs (624), fish (228) and Quaker Oats (1,810). Interestingly, no units are supplied alongside the numbers and the numbers indeed relate more to kilojoules than kcal, despite the claim of "calorie" in the government definition. Despite this ambiguity, the numbers work effectively in putting Quaker Oats forward as the best food for supplying workers with energy, its headline and accompanying photograph emphasising that one packet is equal to 40 eggs in food value.

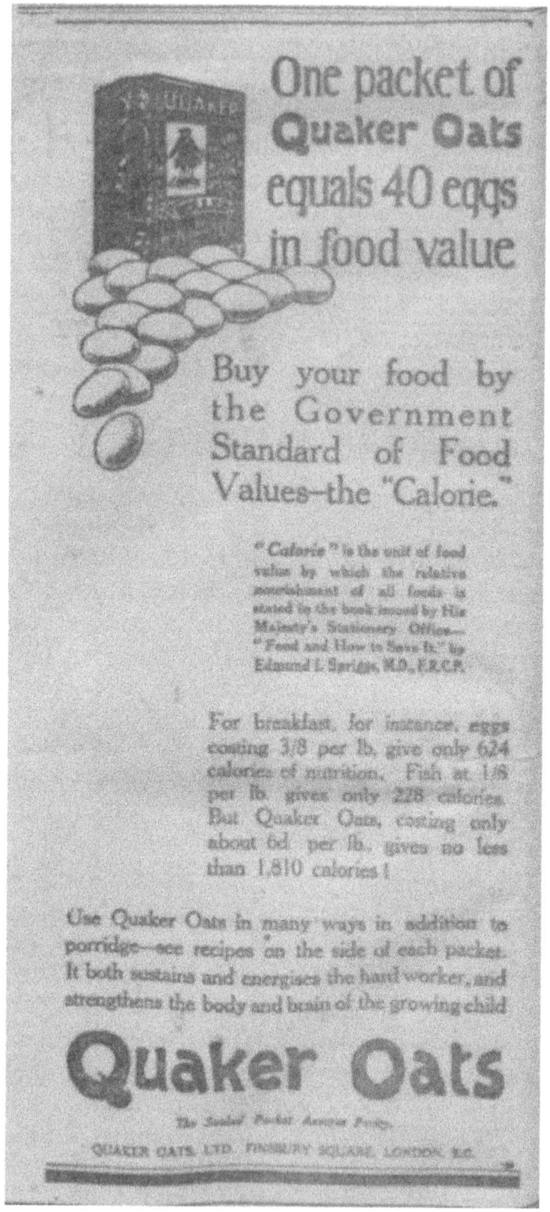

Figure 0.1 Calorie Comparisons in a Quaker Oats Advertisement (1919)

Credit: *Derby Daily Telegraph*, 20 January 1919, p. 4. With thanks to the British Newspaper Archive, on behalf of Reach, for permission to use.

Throughout the beginning of the twentieth century, nutrition research shifted from chemical physiology to biochemistry, with a move away from energy and macronutrients towards health and micronutrients. Marking a period concerned with *undernutrition*, scientists became particularly concerned with the links between nutritional deficiencies and certain diseases, such as rickets, scurvy and beriberi. It was Japanese physician Takaki Kanehiro who first demonstrated in the 1880s that beriberi (previously thought to be an infectious disease) actually came from nutrition, while Scottish physician James Lind first identified the link between a lack of citrus fruit and scurvy in the mid-1700s. However, at this time, the role of vitamins was not known. The big discovery came in 1912 when Polish biochemist Casimir Funk was studying beriberi and found that those who ate newly peeled rice rather than unpeeled rice felt weaker. This led him to investigate the rice husk, which he believed contained something essential for health that the human body could not produce, and he identified a nitrogenous compound (which today we know as thiamine B1). Funk named this mysterious substance "vitamine," implying that it was a "vital amine" (i.e. a nitrogenous organic compound essential to life).[2] Around the same time, American biochemists Elmer McCollum and Marguerite Davis were experimenting with rat diets. They discovered that rats stopped growing until they were fed certain egg or butter extracts, which brought about the conclusion that there were "certain accessory articles" in food essential for normal growth. They called this accessory article "factor A" (what we now know as vitamin A).[3]

Funk and McCollum's discoveries ushered in several decades of vitamin research with a clear focus on single-nutrient deficiency diseases (Trüeb, 2020). Between 1913 and 1948, all major vitamins were isolated and synthesised: vitamin E (1922), vitamin B1 thiamine (1926), vitamin C (1928), vitamin D (1932), vitamin B2 riboflavin (1934), vitamin B7 biotin (1936), vitamin B3 niacin (1937), vitamin B5 (1938), vitamin B6 pyridoxine (1938), vitamin K (1939), vitamin B9 folate (1941) and vitamin B12 (1948). These discoveries proved the nutritional basis of serious deficiency diseases, such as beriberi (B1), pellagra (B3), scurvy (C), pernicious anaemia (B12) and rickets (D), and led to dietary strategies to tackle them (Gibney et al., 2009). There was also a growing focus on mineral deficiencies, such as copper, zinc and magnesium, as well as increasing recognition of the link between iodine and thyroid problems and low fluoride and tooth decay (Carpenter, 2003c). Nutrition science was now well and truly consolidated as a discipline in its own right.

These discoveries accelerated interest in nutri-quantification, with the nutritionism paradigm increasingly infiltrating public understanding of food and dietary health. Specifically, food manufacturers began to focus on protective nutrients required for normal body functioning and to prevent nutrient deficiency diseases. Immediately, selected staple foods, such as bread, cereal, fat spreads, milk, juice and salt, became fortified with micronutrients and marketed as staving off single-nutrient deficiency diseases. These new marketing campaigns emphasised the vitamin or mineral content of products and their "protective" nature, thereby convincing consumers of their necessity. The discovery of vitamins also gave rise to an entire vitamin supplement industry (see Apple, 1996 for an excellent account of this within a US context). Although the industry and even health professionals have been criticised for working in a nutritionally reductive manner, offering people a "false sense of protection" (Guallar et al., 2013) and even increasing the risk of certain diseases, it remains a multi-billion-dollar industry today as people seek ways to keep healthy.

Women became particular targets of marketing campaigns, urged to buy such fortified foods for the sake of their children's health. This strategy—described by Apple (1995) as scientific motherhood—used scientific rationale to tap into women's fears about infant mortality, but also their concerns with respectability. From this point, we also witness the rise of the "nutricentric person" (Scrinis, 2013:32) who "accepts, embraces and internalises" the nutricentric understanding of foods and the body. However, this acceptance often comes from a place of anxiety and pressure to "keep up" to remain healthy. It, therefore, creates a false need for products as they question their own knowledge, develop a growing dependency on what experts say and become increasingly susceptible to marketing claims.[4]

Nutrition Science in the Mid-Twentieth Century

The interest in quantifying nutritionism continued up until the 1950s, gradually giving way to a new type of nutritionism focused on "good" and "bad" nutrients (Scrinis, 2013). This shift was motivated by growing concerns about the overconsumption of certain nutrients and foods and their link with chronic non-infectious diseases, such as heart attacks, strokes and cancer. In other words, quantifying nutritionism had successfully addressed nutritional deficiencies, yet the growth of processed foods and the consumption of too many "bad" nutrients had now brought about a new problem of *overnourishment.*

This finding emerged from epidemiological studies after World War Two, which revealed that the incidence of some chronic diseases was generally reduced as a result of rationing and food shortages. This led to the hypothesis that the dietary patterns of most affluent countries were conducive to chronic disease (Carpenter, 2003c). Such ideas were embraced by governments and public health institutions who produced the first recommendary dietary allowances (RDAs) and provided new guidelines for total calories and selected nutrients based on these "binary moral judgements" (Fischler, 1993). The new era of good and bad nutritionism, thus, became dominated by what Belasco (2007) calls "negative nutrition," with discourses emphasising the need to eat less "harmful" nutrients and using words like "avoid," "reduce," "limit" and "decrease."

Fears were particularly centred around "good" and "bad" fats and the link between high cholesterol and disease, as advocated by the diet–heart hypothesis. The diet–heart hypothesis was postulated by physiologist Ancel Keys who claimed that saturated fat caused cardiovascular disease by raising serum cholesterol. Keys based his hypothesis on animal data and feeding experiments conducted on humans, which suggested that high blood cholesterol caused fatty deposits that clogged arteries and caused heart attacks. He had also observed a lower rate of heart attacks in Mediterranean countries and linked this to their consumption of less saturated fat-rich foods (Teicholz, 2023).

The fears around "good" and "bad" fats played out particularly in the war between butter and margarine that took place during this period. While margarine had historically been seen as a "poor man's" food, lacking all the nutritional benefits of butter, it was now reframed as a medicinal product that had heart health benefits (O'Hagan, 2022). This was based purely on its unsaturated fatty acid profile, but also included partially hydrogenated oils—so-called trans fats—which were initially completely ignored (but later revealed to have similar associations with blood cholesterol concentrations as saturated fat). Margarine, thus, became what Scrinis (2013:30) calls a part of "everyday nutritionism," that is, an everyday nutritional expression, formulated within the logic of nutritionism, and that has been embraced and repeated by nutrition experts and the lay public alike. We see this in the 1977 Swedish advertisement for Flora in Figure 0.2 whose focus on nutrients undermines concerns of the quality of ingredients and processing techniques. The heading carries a big warning that children should be taught this in school, followed by the claim that saturated fat increases the risk of atherosclerosis but polyunsaturated fats decrease risk. A table is then presented with different cooking fats and types of fat, singling out Flora as best.

Mozaffarian et al. (2018) call out a major flaw with this type of nutritionism: it relied on the nutritional model developed to address deficiencies, which entailed identifying and isolating a single relevant nutrient, assessing its isolated physiological effect and quantifying its optimal intake level to prevent disease. This reductionist method translated poorly to non-communicable diseases and suggested a black-and-white one-dimensional understanding of the role of nutrients and biomarkers on bodily health, which blurred distinctions between whole foods and ingredients. This meant a "decontextualisation, simplification and exaggeration of the role of nutrients in determining bodily health" (Scrinis, 2013:5). Nonetheless, its ideas were still heavily taken up by the food industry and used in marketing.

At the same time as the "good" and "bad" fats debate, there was also a parallel discussion taking place, advocated by Dr Robert Atkins. In his 1972 book *Diet Revolution*, he promoted a low-carb, high-fat diet, arguing that carbohydrates, rather than fats, were the principal elements in foods that fatten people. This idea did not take off properly until the late 1990s. There were also other claims by John Yudkin about excess sugar and its link with coronary thrombosis. Yudkin published his ideas for a lay audience in the 1972 book *Pure, White and Deadly*, arguing that sugar was more harmful than refined grains. However, as has come to light since, the sugar industry paid scientists to play down the link and promote saturated fat instead as the culprit (O'Connor, 2016). The discrediting was largely successful. Instead, the decade was one of "at risk"

Figure 0.2 Everyday Nutritionism in a Flora Advertisement (1977)

Credit: *Svenska Dagbladet*, 24 March 1977, p. 17. With thanks to Upfield for permission to use.

bodies, with the vilification of saturated fat, the stigmatisation of cholesterol and a shift from "eat less" to "eat more" (Scrinis, 2013:79–80).

The 1970s were also marked by the rise of healthism, described by Crawford (1980:368) as a "heightened awareness and interest in health." Healthism is concerned with an elevated pursuit of personal health as a supreme goal, but this goes beyond illness and is concerned with responsibility for one's own health. These arguments bear some resemblance with the earlier Physical Culture Movement, which drew on Victorian self-help ideology and advocated regular exercise alongside broader health reforms, including vegetarianism, temperance, fresh air and frequent bathing, to avoid the physical degeneration of the human race and limit the burden that one might place upon society (O'Hagan, 2021).

By the 1980s, "good" and "bad" fats, coupled with healthism, were dominant strategies that guided marketing practices. This obsession also provided a lucrative opportunity for the food industry to introduce low-fat alternatives to the market. As Scrinis (2013:8) notes, such alternatives constructed a "nutritional façade" around the food that distracted attention from its other ingredients, additives and processing techniques. Geyskens et al. (2007), in fact, note that low-fat foods can encourage overconsumption because health claims on packaging exaggerate the role of a single nutrient and associate low fat with good health. As a result, people feel less guilty and tend to consume more, which has worsened rather than alleviated obesity problems.

Nutrition Science in the Late Twentieth Century Onwards

Moving into the late twentieth century, it became clear that the food industry had succeeded in exploiting the nutritionism paradigm and colonising the nutriscape. It was now the primary disseminator of simplified and reductive understandings of food and nutrients and was just as likely to shape and inform dietary advice and public understanding of food as scientists, nutritionists, governments and public health institutions (Nestle, 2018). As the number of nutricentric consumers grew, they looked increasingly to food marketing and packaging for advice, embracing and internalising the scientific and health discourses on display.

The 1990s began with a shift away from the "good" and "bad" fats paradigm. This was influenced by emerging research which showed that the decade of low-fat food marketing had actually coincided with a steady growth in obesity and diabetes levels. Furthermore, it found that the consumption of low-fat products did not translate into reductions in total fat consumption (La Berge, 2008). Additionally, new research revealed that trans fats were more harmful than previously thought. As a result, whole categories of foods suddenly became stigmatised based on their presumed trans fats content rather than distinguishing between good- and poor-quality versions (Scrinis, 2013:145). This is best exemplified through the case of margarine which, previously favoured as a healthy alternative to butter, was now seen as "a disastrous mistake" and its hydrogenation process as "the biggest food processing disaster in US history"

(Lawrence, 2010). In response, there was a general move towards alternative weight loss approaches instead of focusing around macronutrients and understanding food in terms of its macronutrient profiles. Scrinis (2013) has outlined three main trends in this respect: a return to nineteenth-century understandings of calorie reduction, low-carb diets (harking back to Dr Atkins' 1972 book) and low GI eating plans based on how foods affect blood sugar levels.

For the last three decades, we have been in a new period of functional nutritionism, which offers a "more positive and targeted view of nutrients and food as 'functional' in relation to bodily health" (Scrinis, 2013:12). Now, it is no longer enough to be healthy; there is an expectation that people should constantly look to enhance and optimise their bodies and that only certain nutrients can provide this enhancement and optimisation (Eriksson, 2022). In other words, we see a move towards a "biomedicalised food culture" (Durocher, 2020), which participates in defining how "healthy" food is understood and "healthy" eating is practised and creates new relationships between bodies and food. The emergence and popularity of functional foods—or superfoods—exemplify this point.

Functional foods are claimed to offer health benefits beyond their nutritional value, which can optimise the body's functioning and reduce disease risk. However, there is no common definition of a functional food, meaning that brands can use the term to construct a health halo around their products and create an "aura of precision" when it comes to the scientific knowledge underpinning the health claims that they put forward (Scrinis, 2013:197). This is apparent in food trends over the past decade, including quinoa, kale, turmeric, kefir and chia seeds (see Loyer's discussion in Chapter 11), as well as the rise of functional beverages, or nootropic drinks, marketed as actively improving one's health (Chen and Eriksson, 2022). While the term "functional food" is new, similar strategies have been used by marketers for the past 150 years, with the buzzwords "health drinks," "protein foods" and "nerve foods" just a few examples that presage today's obsession (cf. O'Hagan, 2019b, 2021, 2023). Sprackley (2020:76) notes how functional foods exist somewhere between food and medicine, and it is this liminality upon which marketers capitalise.

Numerous nutrients have been (re)positioned as *the* ultimate nutrient to consume in order to enhance a particular bodily function, whether that be brain health, digestion or sports performance. Recent years have seen emphasis placed on omega-3, vitamin D and biotin, as well as a growing interest in phytochemicals, antioxidants, plant sterols and probiotics, which are all seen as having medicinal or therapeutic qualities. This has created a sense that these functional nutrients cannot be obtained sufficiently from ordinary food, thus driving the market of dietary supplements and intensifying a perception of "nutrition scarcity" (Scrinis, 2013:259) that echoes the era of quantifying nutritionism. As Scrinis (2013) notes, the message has now changed to "eat smarter," with consumers informed that eating a balanced diet is no longer enough and that they must focus on particular bodily functions by optimising quantities and ratios of consumption.

Coupled with this interest in functional nutritionism has been the promotion of certain types of diets, such as palaeolithic or ancestral diets (consisting of foods thought to mirror those eaten by humans during the Palaeolithic era), the DASH diet (designed to reduce blood pressure and the risk of cardiovascular disease), the Mediterranean diet (inspired by the eating habits of Portugal, Spain, Italy and Greece) and the prudent diet (high intake of vegetables, fruit, legumes, whole grains and fish and other seafood). There has also been an accelerated growth in vegetarian and—more recently—vegan diets, with growing numbers of people turning to plant-based diets for health and environmental reasons. Gheihman (2021) argues that veganism has become an "emerging lifestyle movement" that, thanks to famous figures—or cultural entrepreneurs—has brought about a cultural shift into the mainstream, moving it away from traditional associations with animal rights activists.

Nutrition Science Now and in the Future

Mozaffarian et al. (2018) point out that, after decades of focusing on simple, reductionist metrics, the emerging true complexities of different foods and diet patterns are creating genuine challenges for understanding influences on health and wellbeing. In recent years, concerns about over-supplementation of vitamins have arisen (Forgie et al., 2023), for example, as well as the risk of "double burden"—that is, the combination of conventional malnutrition (insufficient calories and micronutrients) causing poor health and at the same time modern malnutrition (poor diet) increasing risk of obesity, cancer and heart disease (Kosaka and Umezaki, 2017). According to Mozaffarian et al. (2018), these issues have not been helped by nutrition policies, which continue to have a single nutrient or caloric focus. Although some nutrition policies do consider non-communicable diseases, they tend to overfocus on obesity, which fails to identify the root problem of unhealthy diets, as well as the various risk pathways and conditions affected by nutrition.

There are some promising advancements in the field of nutrition science that may help address such concerns, but they do not come without risks. Nutrigenomics, for example, studies the relationship between the human genome, human nutrition and health. It seeks to understand how people's responses to nutrients are influenced by their gene expression, with the ultimate aim of tailoring diets to people's genetic profiles to combat obesity and other health issues, such as diabetes and metabolic syndrome (Sales et al., 2014). Scrinis (2013:189) is sceptical of nutrigenomics, arguing that its promises are yet another claim by scientists that they have discovered the "truth" about food and health, but this time at a deeper molecular and genetic level. He argues that it is the paradigms within which this research and knowledge are interpreted and applied that will shape whether or not they perpetuate many of the issues with current nutrition science research and dietary advice.

Mainly in line with Scrinis's (2013) argument that food processing should be taken into consideration when considering the health value of foods, there has been increased support for the NOVA Food Classification system among scholars in the field of nutrition science (Montiero, 2018; Juul et al., 2021). Based on the level of processing that the products have undergone, this system differentiates between four categories: (1) minimally processed foods (e.g. fresh, dry or frozen fruits or vegetables); (2) processed culinary ingredients (e.g. olive oil, butter); (3) processed foods (e.g. canned fruits and vegetables); and (4) ultra-processed products (e.g. soft drinks, cereals, fast food and salty snacks). The latter category consists of foods that have gone through several stages of processing and contain additives, as well as often an assembly of unmodified and/or modified food substances. Montiero (2018:730) describes ultra-processed foods as "typically branded, distributed internationally and globally, heavily advertised and marketed, and very profitable." Generally, these foods are depicted as "junk food" (see Zazueta's discussion in Chapter 3). Summarising the existing evidence about the presumed associations between consumption of ultra-processed foods and the risk of cardiovascular diseases, Juul et al. (2021) put forward the argument that nutrition counselling as the cornerstone of preventive cardiology should address the problems of intake of such foods. If the aim is to help people follow healthier diets and maintain a healthy lifestyle, the best advice is to minimise the intake of ultra-processed foods and drinks (Montiero, 2018; Montiero et al., 2019).

Given growing environmental concerns, the decades ahead are also likely to see an extended interest in sustainable nutrition, particularly in terms of plant-based foods and upcycling (McClements and Grossman, 2021; Idrishi et al., 2022). The Nordic Nutrition Recommendations 2023 (Nordic Council of Ministers, 2023) take into consideration the impact of food consumption on the environment and the climate, with the ambition of "present[ing] the best available data for how to eat for the health of our bodies and for our planet" (6). In this context, the recent development in the field of nutrition science of "cultured meat" appears as a possible solution (see Vezovnik, Chapter 13 of this volume). Using tissue engineering techniques pioneered in regenerative medicine, animal cells are cultured *in vitro* to produce a lab-based meat, which may help address many of the ethical, environmental and public health issues associated with conventional meat production (Bryant, 2020). However, there are concerns that cultured meat may create more problems than it solves, as it lacks many of the vitamins and minerals present in "normal" meat (e.g. vitamin B1277, creatin, vitamin D3, iron) and may contain endocrine-disrupting chemicals that affect anabolic sex hormones (Treich, 2021). A 2023 report from the Food Standard Agency warns of the "promissory narrative" of cultured meat that purports it is healthier by design. They argue that controlling the amount of polyunsaturated fatty acids in cultured meat does not necessarily mean that the final product is healthier than "normal" meat. Moreover, this belief that it is healthier could even lead to overconsumption, as previously identified by Geyskens et al. (2007) and Scrinis (2013) with the low-fat trend of the 1980s.

Looking towards the future then, we can expect that other new products will continue to emerge, targeting ever increasingly more specific bodily functions. The importance of consuming prebiotics and postbiotics, in addition to the more established probiotics, will also continue to flourish. While research suggests that they can alleviate symptoms of digestive disorders and help increase body immunity, scientists warn of holding them up as a wonder cure, citing their adverse effects on immunocompromised individuals (Vallianou et al., 2020). While legislation is in place to protect consumers from harmful food labelling and marketing, new buzzwords keep surfacing and saturating products, from "flavonoid foods" to "bioactive foods." "The public is understandably bewildered by these evolving dietary messages," caution Mozaffarian et al. (2018). As Cannon (2007) emphasises, problematic food marketing messages are further compounded by the fact that much nutrition advice is distorted by trade groups or nutrition foundations who lobby legislators to protect their own personal interests.

Mozaffarian et al. (2018) believe that nutrition policies must move from simplistic reductionist strategies to multifaceted approaches that bring together modern scientific advances with trusted communication to the public and modern evidence on effective systems level behaviour change. Additionally, attention must shift from the global medicalisation of health to interconnected personal, community, sociocultural, national and global determinants of food environments and choices. Studies must also be carried out on the long-term health consequences of modern shifts in agricultural practices, livestock feeding, crop breeding and food processing methods, which remain poorly understood. Scrinis (2013) proposes a new food quality paradigm with a stronger contextualisation of foods and dietary patterns in order to reduce nutricentric analyses and ensure that research findings do not result in oversimplified or misleading interpretations. Arguably, it is only through knowledge of history that we can learn from past mistakes and apply these lessons to the future of nutrition science and food marketing, ensuring that it is less reductionist, fairer and has the public's best interests at heart. These arguments, grounded in a transhistorical approach, lie at the centre of *Food Marketing and Selling Healthy Lifestyles with Science*.

Acknowledgements

Our thanks to Marleen Lentjes for her excellent feedback, which helped improve the original draft of this chapter.

Notes

1 For a full account of the history of nutrition science, see the excellent articles of Carpenter (2003a, 2003b, 2003c, 2003d).

2 The name was subsequently changed to "vitamin" in 1920 to fit with the standard nomenclature of the Chemical Society and to reflect the fact that not all the substances were amines (Banoub, 2018:3). An alphabetical designation system was also developed, with substances labelled Vitamin A, B, C, etc.

3 It is also important to mention two early landmark studies in the discovery of vitamins. In 1881, Russian surgeon Nikolai Lunin demonstrated that mice could not survive on purified diets consisting only of carbohydrates, fats and protein, yet they developed normally when milk was added. This suggested that there was an unknown substance in milk that was an essential component of nutrition (Semba, 2012). Twenty years later, the English biochemist Frederick Gowland Hopkins challenged the view that all proteins are nutritionally equivalent when he discovered the amino acid tryptophan and showed that it (and other amino acids) could not be synthesised by the body and needed to be supplied in diet (Carpenter, 2003b).
4 It should be pointed out that not all fortification were superfluous or a "trend." Calcium fortification in flour in England, for example, as recommended by Elsie Widdowson, helped prevent point malnutrition in the 1940s (Burki, 2018).

References

Apple, R. 1995. Constructing Mothers: Scientific Motherhood in the Nineteenth and Twentieth Centuries. *Social History of Medicine* 8(2):161–178.
Apple, R. 1996. *Vitamania: Vitamins in American Culture*. New Brunswick: Rutgers University Press.
Banoub, D. 2018. Buying Vitamins: Newfoundland Cod Live Oil and the Real Subsumption of Nature, 1919–1939. *Geoforum* 92:1–8.
Barker, H. 2009. Medical Advertising and Trust in Late-Georgian England. *Urban History* 35(3):379–398.
Belasco, W.J. 2007. *Appetite for Change: How the Counterculture Took on the Food Industry*. Ithaca: Cornell University Press.
Bryant, C.J. 2020. Culture, Meat and Cultured Meat. *Journal of Animal Science* 98(8), https://doi.org/10.1093/jas/skaa172
Buchholz, A. and Schoeller, D. 2004. Is a Calorie a Calorie? *American Journal of Clinical Nutrition* 79(5):899–906.
Burki, T.K. 2018. Elsie Widdowson: Food for Thought. *The Lancet* 3(12), https://doi.org/10.1016/S2468-1253(18)30350-9
Burton, R. 1621 [2001]. *Anatomy of Melancholy*. New York: NYRB Classics.
Cannon, G. 2007. The Rise and Fall of Dietetics and of Nutrition Science, 4000 BCE–2000 CE. *Public Health Nutrition* 8(6A):701–705.
Carpenter, K.J. 2003a. A Short History of Nutritional Science: Part 1 (1785–1885). *History of Nutrition* 133:638–645.
Carpenter, K.J. 2003b. A Short History of Nutritional Science: Part 1 (1885–1912). *History of Nutrition* 133:975–984.
Carpenter, K.J. 2003c. A Short History of Nutritional Science: Part 1 (1912–1944). *History of Nutrition* 133:3023–3032.
Carpenter, K.J. 2003d. A Short History of Nutritional Science: Part 1 (1945–1985). *History of Nutrition* 133:3331–3342.
Chen, A. and Eriksson, G. 2022. Connoting a Neoliberal and Entrepreneurial Discourse of Science Through Infographics and Integrated Design: The Case of "Functional" Healthy Drinks. *Critical Discourse Studies* 19(3):290–308.
Cheyne, G. 1733 [2018]. *The English Malady*. London: Gale ECCO.
Church. R. 2000. Advertising Consumer Goods in Nineteenth-Century Britain: Reinterpretations. *The Economic History Review* 53(4):621–645.
Collins, E.J.T. 1993. Food Adulteration and Food Safety in Britain in the 19th and Early 20th Centuries. *Food Policy* 18(2):95–109.
Conrad, L.I. 2011. *The Western Medical Tradition, 800 BC to AD 1800*. Cambridge: Cambridge University Press.

Crawford, R. 1980. Healthism and the Medicalization of Everyday Life. *International Journal of Health Services* 10(3):347–511.
Cullather, N. 2007. The Foreign Policy of the Calorie. *American Historical Review* 112(2):337–364.
Durocher, M. 2020. Biomedicalized Food Culture: A Critical Analysis at the Intersection of "Healthy" Food, Bodies and Health. *Journal of Critical Dietetics* 5(1), https://doi.org/10.32920/cd.v5i1.1335
Eriksson, G. 2022. Promoting Extreme Fitness Regimes Through the Communicative Affordances of Reality Makeover Television: A Multimodal Critical Discourse Analysis. *Critical Studies in Media Communication* 39(5):408–426.
Fernan, C., Schuldt, J.P. and Niederdeppe, J. 2018. Health Halo Effects from Product Titles and Nutrient Content Claims in the Context of "Protein" Bars. *Health Communication* 33(12):1425–1433.
Finlay, M.R. 1995. "Early Marketing of the Theory of Nutrition: The Science and Culture of Liebig's Extract of Meat" in *The Science and Culture of Nutrition, 1840–1940*, edited by H. Kamminga and A. Cunningham (Amsterdam: Rodopi), pp. 48–75.
Fischler, C. 1993. "A Nutritional Cacophony, or the Crisis of Food Selection in Affluent Societies" in *For a Better Nutrition in the 21st Century*, edited by P. Leathwood, M. Horisberger and W. James (New York: Raven Press), pp. 57–65.
"Flora Advertisement." 1977. *Svenska Dagbladet* (24 March), 17.
Food Standards Agency. 2023. Identification of Hazards in Meat Products Manufactured from Cultured Animal Cells. Available at https://www.food.gov.uk/research/identification-of-hazards-in-meat-products-manufactured-from-cultured-animal-cells-hazards (Accessed: 18 January 2024).
Forgie, A.J., Pepin, D.M., Tingting, J., Tollenaar, S., Sergi, C.M., Gruenheid, S. and Willing, B.P. 2023. Over Supplementation with Vitamin B12 Alters Microbe-Host Interactions in the Gut Leading to Accelerated *Citrobacter rodentium* Colonization and Pathogenesis in Mice. *Microbiome* 11(1), https://doi.org/10.1186/s40168-023-01461-w
Geyskens, K., Pandelaere, M., Dewitte, S. and Warlop, L. 2007. The Backdoor to Overconsumption: The Effect of Associating "Low-Fat" Food with Health References. *Journal of Public Policy and Marketing* 26(1), https://doi.org/10.1509/jppm.26.1.118
Gheihman, N. 2021. Veganism as a Lifestyle Movement *Sociology Compass* 15(5), https://doi.org/10.1111/soc4.12877
Gibney, M.J., Lanham-New, S.A., Cassidy, A. and Vorster, H.H. 2009. *Introduction to Human Nutrition*. London: Wiley-Blackwell.
Guallar, E., Stranges, S., Mulrow, C., Appel, L.J. and Miller, E.R. 2013. Enough Is Enough: Stop Wasting Money on Vitamin and Mineral Supplements. *Annals of Internal Medicine* 159(12):850–851.
Hansen, B. 1999. New Images of a New Medicine: Visual Evidence for the Widespread Popularity of Therapeutic Discoveries in America after 1885. *Bulletin of the History of Medicine* 73(4):629–678.
Idrishi, R., Aggarwal, D. and Sharma, V. 2022. "Upcycling Technologies in the Food Industry" in *Smart and Sustainable Food Technologies*, edited by S. Shegal, B. Singh and V. Sharma (New York: Springer), pp. 367–392.
Jones, C.L. 2012. Re-Reading Medical Trade Catalogs: The Uses of Professional Advertising in British Medical Practice, 1870–1914. *Bulletin of the History of Medicine* 86(3):361–393.
Juul, F., Vaidean, G. and Parekh, N. 2021. Ultra-Processed Foods and Cardiovascular Diseases: Potential Mechanisms of Action. *Advances in Nutrition* 12(5):1673–1680.
Kamminga, H. and Cunningham, A. 1995. "Introduction: The Science and Culture of Nutrition, 1840–1940" in *The Science and Culture of Nutrition, 1840–1940*, edited by H. Kamminga and A. Cunningham (Amsterdam: Rodopi), pp. 1–15.

Kosaka, S. and Umezaki, M. 2017. A Systematic Review of the Prevalence and Predictors of the Double Burden of Malnutrition Within Households. *British Journal of Nutrition* 117(8):1118–1127.

La Berge, A.F. 2008. How the Ideology of Low Fat Conquered America. *Journal of the History of Medicine and Allied Sciences* 63(2):139–177.

Lagay, F. 2002. The Legacy of Humoral Medicine. *AMA Journal of Ethics* 4(7):206–208.

Lawrence, F. 2010. I can't believe it's not … healthy! *The Guardian* (23 January). Available at https://www.theguardian.com/environment/2010/jan/23/margarine-butter-health-wars (Accessed: 18 January 2024).

Loeb, L.A. 1994. *Consuming Angels: Advertising and Victorian Women*. Oxford: Oxford University Press.

Mandeville, B. 1711 [1976]. *Treatise of the Hypochondriack and Hysterick Passions*. New York: Arno Press.

McClements, D.J. and Grossman, L. 2021. A Brief Review of the Science Behind the Design of Healthy and Sustainable Plant-Based Foods. *npj Science of Food* 5, https://www.nature.com/articles/s41538-021-00099-y

Montiero, C.A. 2018. Nutrition and Health. The Issue Is Not Food, Nor Nutrients, So Much as Processing. *Public Health Nutrition* 12(5):729–731.

Montiero, C.A., Cannon, G., Lawrence, M., Costa Louzada, M.L. and Pereira Machado, P. 2019. *Ultra-Processed Foods, Diet Quality, and Health Using the NOVA Classification System*. Rome: FAO.

Mozaffarian, D., Rosenberg, I. and Uauy, R. 2018. History of Modern Nutrition Science—Implications for Current Research, Dietary Guidelines, and Food Policy. *British Medical Journal*, https://doi.org/10.1136/bmj.k2392

Nestle, M. 2018. *Unsavory Truth: How Food Companies Skew the Science of What We Eat*. New York: Basic Books.

Nordic Council of Ministers. 2023. Nordic Nutrition Recommendations 2023. Available at https://www.norden.org/en/publication/nordic-nutrition-recommendations-2023 (Accessed: 18 January 2024).

O'Connor, A. 2016. How the Sugar Industry Shifted Blame to Fat. *New York Times* (13 September). Available at https://www.nytimes.com/2016/09/13/well/eat/how-the-sugar-industry-shifted-blame-to-fat.html (Accessed: 18 January 2024).

O'Hagan, L.A. 2019a. The Advertising and Marketing of the Edwardian Prize Book: Gender for Sale. *English Literature in Transition, 1880–1920* 62(1):72–94.

O'Hagan, L.A. 2019b. Packaging Inner Peace: A Sociohistorical Exploration of Nerve Food in Great Britain. *Food and History* 17(2):183–222.

O'Hagan, L.A. 2020. Pure in Body, Pure in Mind? A Sociohistorical Perspective on the Marketisation of Pure Foods in Great Britain. *Discourse, Context and Media* 34, https://doi.org/10.1016/j.dcm.2019.100325

O'Hagan, L.A. 2021. Flesh-Formers or Fads? Historicizing the Contemporary Protein-Enhanced Food Trend. *Food, Culture and Society* 25(5):875–898.

O'Hagan, L.A. 2022. "Classifying" Margarine: The Early Class-Based Marketing of a Butter Substitute in Sweden (1923–1933). *Global Food History* 9(1):20–46.

O'Hagan, L.A. 2023. From Fatigue Fighter to Heartburn Healer: The Evolving Marketing of a Functional Beverage in Sweden. *Journal of Food Products Marketing* 29(1):19–40.

Porter, R. 2000. *Fakers and Charlatans in English Medicine*. Reading: Tempus.

"Quaker Oats Advertisement." 1919. *Derby Daily Telegraph* (20 January), 4.

Richards, T. 1990. *The Commodity Culture of Victorian England*. Stanford: Stanford University Press.

Sales, N.M.R., Pelegrini, P.B. and Goersch, M.C. 2014. Nutrigenomics: Definitions and Advances of This New Science. *Journal of Nutrition and Metabolism*, https://doi.org/10.1155/2014/202759
Scholliers, P. 2018. "The Popularization of a New Nutritional Concept: The Calorie in Belgium, 1914–1918" in *Proteins, Pathologies and Politics: Dietary Innovation and Disease from the Nineteenth Century*, edited by David Gentilcore and Matthew Smith (London: Bloomsbury), pp. 111–125.
Scrinis, G. 2013. *Nutritionism: The Science and Politics of Dietary Advice*. New York: Columbia University Press.
Semba, R.D. 2012. The Discovery of the Vitamins. *International Journal for Vitamin and Nutrition Research* 82:310–315.
Sprackley, C. 2020. "Extractionist Logics: The Missing Link Between Functional Foods and Superfoods" in *Critical Approaches to Superfoods*, edited by E. McDonell and R. Wilk (London: Bloomsbury), pp. 57–76.
Stafford, N. 2010. History: The Changing Notion of Food. *Nature* 468:16–17.
Teicholz, N. 2023. A Short History of Saturated Fat: The Making and Unmaking of a Scientific Consensus. *Current Opinion in Endocrinology, Diabetes and Obesity* 30(1):65–71.
Treich, N. 2021. Cultured Meat: Promises and Challenges. *Environmental and Resource Economics* 79(1):33–61.
Trüeb, R.M. 2020. *Nutrition for Healthy Hair*. New York: Springer.
Vallianou, N., Stratigou, T., Christodoulatos, G.S., Tsigalou, C. and Dalamaga, M. 2020. Probiotics, Prebiotics, Synbiotics, Postbiotics, and Obesity: Current Evidence, Controversies, and Perspectives. *Current Obesity Reports* 9:179–192.

Part 1

Food, Healthy Bodies and Nutritional Advice

1 Vim, Vigour and Vitality

Physical Culture Marketing and the Promise of a Better Life

Conor Heffernan

I love it! I love it! Let those who please
Enjoy a diet of nuts and peas;
Let Shaw compose his dramatic scenes
On cabbage, tomatoes and kidney beans
Let Eustace Miles find muscular force
In carrot cutlets with Plasmon sauce,
Or other equally messy slop –
But give me my old-fashioned mutton chop

(Heffernan, 2020:245)

This humorous rhyme, which appeared in a 1907 edition of *Truth Magazine*, mocked physical culturist and vegetarian athlete Eustace Miles. Whether *Truth* liked it or not, more and more British men and women were turning to strange—at times unpalatable—supplements and food substitutes in search of better health, energy and, in some cases, sexual prowess. This was part of a broader and powerful trend in British social life: the rise of the physical culture movement (PCM). Broadly defined, the PCM was a late nineteenth- and early twentieth-century phenomenon concerned with the "ideological and commercial cultivation of the body" (Budd, 1997:152). Put differently, the PCM can be understood as a time when the modern interest in gyms and fitness culture first crystallised on a serious and large scale.

While previous fitness iterations in England focused more on the group—or the collective—the PCM was decidedly individual. Seeking to improve their health, strength and vitality, British men, women and children began lifting weights, engaging in callisthenics and monitoring their bodies in previously untold numbers. They read physical culture magazines imported from the United States and mainland Europe, while England's own physical culture magazines were exported across the British Empire. Those promoting physical culture—be they physicians, politicians, coaches or entrepreneurs—often stressed the need to monitor one's diet in conjunction with their exercise. In the present age, neoliberal ideas about self-sufficiency, the importance of

DOI: 10.4324/9781003450276-4

keeping fit and the desirability of muscular bodies dominate the fitness industry (Brighton et al., 2020). As this chapter makes clear, direct parallels existed a century earlier, and turn-of-the-century strongman, Eugen Sandow, was the face of this movement.

Although histories of physical culture have often focused primarily on exercise and sporadically on nutrition, a growing body of work exists on physical culture foods, diets and supplements (Steinitz, 2021; Heffernan, 2022a; O'Hagan, 2022). Building on this work, this chapter examines the medicalisation of food within physical culture texts. Popular realms of physical culture—as opposed to medical or martial worlds—were inhabited by strongmen and women, gymnastic instructors and athletes rather than trained scientists or physicians. They represented a generation of "organic intellectuals" who, by dint of their physical qualifications, rose to prominence in British society (Strine, 1991). Co-opting the language of science, they employed scientific terms and methods to enhance their reputations and upsell their products. Studying this phenomenon, the chapter is divided into three distinct, but interconnected, sections. First, it discusses the PCM, the growing medicalisation of British health and the process of examining physical culture materials. Next, it explores implicit or "soft" uses of medical language to market physical culture goods and diets. The final section discusses Eugen Sandow's attempt to create a medical institute in 1907 and its successes. Overall, the chapter argues that the use of scientific language by physical culturists was often successful, adding gravitas to their marketing messages.

Methodological Note

The findings shared below are the result of extensive trips to archives in London (England), Austin, TX (USA) and Dublin (Ireland) over a period of several years. In London, the researcher visited the British Library and Wellcome Trust Library, where they consulted physical culture magazines and monographs from the 1890s to 1914. In Austin, the researcher visited the H.J. Lutcher Stark Center for Physical Culture and Sports, where they consulted physical culture monographs and magazines from the same period. Finally, in Dublin, the researcher utilised the National Library's collection of monographs and magazines related to sport and physical culture. Archival work was complemented by online searches of the *British Newspaper Archive*. In analysing the data, the researcher contextualised the sources with reference to secondary research and prior primary research in similar fields. As a methodological approach, the researcher was driven by the postmodern school, which seeks to deconstruct societal discourses and identities in the hope of uncovering broader, and often hidden, histories related to power. As will be explored, the asymmetry of knowledge between physical culturists and the public—wherein physical culturists typically knew a great deal more—resulted in questionable messages and practices being marketed in pursuit of profit. Employing a language of scientific progress and objectivity was central to this process.

Managing Physical Culture in Britain

Writing on sport and health culture in nineteenth-century America, Jan Todd (1998:11–16) coined the phrase "purposive exercise" to distinguish these worlds. While sport, even play, tends to be focused on the scoring of goals or the winning of games/prizes, purposive exercise is concerned with more immediate, corporeal goals. In other words, purposive exercise can be understood as the undertaking of exercise not for sporting reasons, but rather for health motives, ranging from the desire to look better aesthetically to rehabilitating injuries and/or strengthening specific muscles.

Purposive exercise is often associated with non-competitive gymnasium and callisthenic cultures rather than sports. This distinction is important because the intensification of modern sports in England during the nineteenth century has been well documented by scholars (Holt, 1990). Additionally, many individuals mistakenly take purposive exercise to be a modern phenomenon. While a great deal of attention has fixated on the "modernisation" (by which it meant the rigid organisation) of sport by British administrators and on the cultural export of said sport throughout the British Empire (Holt, 2014), important work has also been conducted on the rise of purposive exercise within Britain (Budd, 1997). From the early nineteenth century, educators, philosophers, politicians and, importantly, military thinkers began to promote the value of purposive exercise for men and, to a lesser extent, women.

Gymnasiums first emerged in Britain in the 1820s and 1830s and were formalised in 1860 when the British military created its own physical training programme and built its first military gymnasium in Aldershot (Bredin, 1960:568–573). Soon after, a decree went forth that gymnasiums were to be built in garrisons around the Empire. When discussing the rise of the PCM in the late nineteenth century, it is, thus, important to note that it did not emerge from a vacuum, but was instead the latest development in an ongoing interest in purposive exercise (Todd, 1995:7–11). What then was physical culture and what distinguished it from this previous gymnastic interest? The simplest answer is depth. The PCM surpassed the previous gymnastic movement due to its popularity in recreational and institutional cultures. While no scholar has yet been able to pinpoint a specific moment when the PCM began, the late 1880s is typically used as a starting point (Heffernan, 2022a). This was a time when recreational exercisers began to be exposed to a far greater variety of health and wellness products and the music hall welcomed strongmen and women performers, many of whom were able to secure outside opportunities. There was, in effect, a democratisation of fitness, which impacted both the professional athlete and the lay exerciser.

One of the most famous individuals was Eugen Sandow. Born Friedrich Wilhelm Mueller in Prussia in 1867, Sandow travelled to England in the 1880s where, after a weightlifting contest with fellow strongman "Samson," he became a sporting celebrity (Chapman, 1994). Throughout the 1890s and up to the Great War (1914–1918), Sandow's physical culture empire encompassed fitness books and magazines, nutritional supplements, exercise equipment, cooking ingredients, cigars, clothes and children's toys, among other products (Morais, 2013). Sandow was the most prolific entrepreneur, but he was not alone. Many of his contemporaries sold exercise courses, manuals, nutritional supplements and athletic aids. This commercialisation of health, in previously unrecognisable ways, defined the PCM in Britain. Equally important, however, was how respectable and mainstream it was.

At a time when the study of food and physiology was beginning to become more scientific, physical culturists latched onto growing anxieties about health and the healthy body to improve their standing (Holt, 2006). In Britain during this period, a considerable number of moral panics coalesced into cliched and repetitive worries that the population was becoming unhealthy. The most notable concern came in 1899 and the outbreak of the Second South African ("Boer") War. From 1899 to 1901, the British Empire appeared to struggle to overcome a much smaller South African military comprised of the Boer Republics. Embarrassing on a geopolitical level, the conflict was accompanied in Britain by concerns about the racial livestock of British men. Such concerns were fuelled by stories that scores of men were rejected for service due to ill health. Vanessa Heggie's (2008) research has made clear that these concerns were often embellished. Nonetheless, they struck a chord politically and led to an interdepartmental government enquiry into physical degeneration in the populace.

The language of this report was often shrouded in medical terminology and rhetoric around work output, health, digestion and nutrition. In a fascinating study on the history of calories, James Hargrove (2006) made clear that the terminology around food shifted during the nineteenth century to discussions of proteid, nitrogen and, in time, calories. A great deal of calorie talk in popular discourses stemmed from the United States. However, in England, these popular discourses around food became medicalised. This phenomenon was certainly seen in physical culture circles with regard to the products being sold and advocated by physical culturists. Lesley Steinitz's (2014) work on Plasmon, a milk-based protein powder promoted in early twentieth-century Britain, made clear that Plasmon's appeal came in part from the ability of advertisers to market it as scientific. The phrases used to promote Plasmon, and many other physical culture foods, stemmed around their proteid content, their blood-enhancing properties, nitrogen content and presence of fortifying substances. What is telling about this is how seemingly banal foods in the late nineteenth and early twentieth century suddenly became marketed as rudimentary superfoods. It was no longer Hovis Bread, but the strengthening aid, Hovis Bread, endorsed by weightlifters and strength athletes (Heffernan, 2019).

Pulling from more modern research, Macgregor et al. (2021) found that, in contemporary health circles, the term "superfood" is allowed to thrive in popular discourse because it is vague and ill-defined. The label takes advantage of the "halo effect" whereby foods and supplements are deemed inherently healthier based upon their supposed additional benefits (i.e. being gluten-free, organic, free range, etc.) (Fernan et al., 2018). Behavioural economists interested in food behaviours have scrutinised the power of the "halo effect" by showing that consumers often deem "organic" cookies to be healthier than "non-organic cookies," despite their nutritional profiles being indistinguishable (Drescher et al., 2014). Those marketing health foods and supplements in the early twentieth century were aware of this phenomenon and used it to sell products. Their messages combined the new language around food with older patent medicine style claims which spoke vaguely about improving vim, vigour, vitality and energy. While many physical culturists were sponsored athletes for products, some—such as Sandow—were actively involved in the marketing of their own products, akin to the modern fitness influencer who uses their profile to sell products (Morais et al., 2022). Regardless of a physical culturist's agency in marketing a product, physical culture goods were advertised within the language of science. The next section will discuss this in greater detail.

It is worth noting the use of anatomy and physiology in physical culture magazines and books to stress that the language of science was not just used to sell physical culture foods or supplements. In his 1908 monograph on physical culture, Alfred Wallace-Jones (1908:6) claimed that the exercises contained within his book could regulate the circulation of blood, thereby curing a litany of illnesses. They would also help to replace muscular wastage in the blood and ensure a vibrant rejuvenation of the body's tissues and cells. J.P. Müller (1911:34), whose physical culture system encompassed callisthenics and massage, quoted a Dr Wilhelm Schulthess (a Swiss orthopaedist) in passages discussing the ability of exercise and massage to rejuvenate muscle atrophy better than bandages. Eustace Miles (1907) quoted from agricultural and veterinary science works on the feet of animals to discuss the need for humans to maintain their gait and posture. Some, in contrast, did not bother at all to reference research, such as Sanford Bennett (1907:1–2) whose *Exercising in Bed* was a critical success and claimed to be guided by "the science of health, strength, elasticity of body and longevity." While it is tempting to see these efforts as cynical marketing ploys on the part of writers, it is worth noting the zeal with which physical culture was treated by some during this period and the reliance of British physicians on outside authorities when it came to physical activity. Heggie (2018) and Neil Carter (2012) have both traced the evolution of exercise and sports science from the mid-nineteenth century in Britain. What is important to stress about this development is that, although scientific research was being conducted on exercise, its influence had not fully penetrated more general medical discussions.

Thus, before and after this period, many physicians relied upon gymnastic or physical culture instructors for insights on training. This was the case for Donald Walker, an amateur writer, whose Indian club swinging exercises were prescribed by physicians in the 1830s and 1840s (Heffernan, 2019), and for

Sandow, whose dumbbell workouts were prescribed in the 1900s (Morais, 2013). It is not inconceivable to think that many physical culturists presumed themselves to be spearheading a new kind of "health science." Certainly, Müller (1911) did so and even included quotes from physicians praising him for being "decades in advance of medical science" when it came to both physical culture and general hygiene. This co-opting of science, or veneer towards a quasi-medical approach, was found in the anatomical charts which often accompanied physical culture books. Such charts were included to help readers distinguish between different muscle groups while simultaneously stressing the physical development of physical culturists themselves.

Figure 1.1—a 1903 advertisement for Plasmon protein powder—does a good job illustrating the importance of comparison in fitness ephemera during this period. The left side of the image depicts the "Plasmon household," wherein the svelte woman of the clean and sterile house embodies modernity and scientific living. The contrast is, of course, depicted on the right as "The Past." Here, a dark and squalid room is shown with a woman wearing ragged clothes as the focus. The woman, notably shorter and heavier than the figure on the left, is seen to embody the "problems" of previous generations—their ill health and dirt. The message is clear: science and scientific living improved both body and mind. Consuming Plasmon, thus, brought one towards clean, beautiful (albeit sterile) health.

Figure 1.1 1903 Plasmon Advertisement

Credit: Author's own image

The Process of Science and Selling: Physical Culture Commerce

Attention will now be drawn to three distinct physical culture products and their advertising rhetoric, which marked a clear effort to situate them as scientific products or, at the very least, as supported by scientific research. They are Plasmon, a dried milk powder sold as a physical culture supplement; muscle embrocation creams, sold to relieve muscle aches; and spring-grip dumbbells, which promised increased strength and musculature. These products differed in their promises and co-option of science but spoke to a trend within the late nineteenth- and early twentieth-century physical culture of marketing products through the language of science. Diet and fitness were essential to the PCM. Nutritional supplements were not at the margins, but central.

Plasmon

Plasmon, whose history has been further covered elsewhere (Heffernan, 2020; O'Hagan, 2022), was unique in physical culture circles in that it began as a medical substance and was subsequently converted into a physical culture food. Plasmon was a dried milk powder first used as a restorative drink given to convalescing patients in German hospitals. In the late nineteenth century, the patent for Plasmon was sold to a consortium interested in transforming its usage. Thus, when Plasmon emerged in the early 1900s in Britain, its target audience were no longer patients, but rather British men and women interested in increasing the "proteid" content of their food (Heffernan, 2020). Due to its high concentration of milk protein, Plasmon was marketed as an easy way of increasing the nutritional value of one's food. This was seen, most plainly, in a Plasmon cookbook published in 1904. Promising to marry "the science of dietetics [...] with the art of cookery," the recipes contained therein were "flesh forming" meals enjoyed by the whole family (1–4). Through the "art of science," it was promised that just a single teaspoon of Plasmon contained the "same proteid and nutrients as ¼ pound of prime fillet of beef" (1). While the cookbook only alluded to science and scientific studies, previous Plasmon advertising specifically named individuals. Much was made of a report conducted by a legitimate physician, Dr C.R. Virchow, on Plasmon, which included the following evaluation:

> There is no food-preparation known to us equal to Plasmon, either as regards constancy of composition as guaranteed by its source or in respect to the proportion, solubility, and digestibility of the nutritive constituents.
>
> (Plasmon, 1906:1–2)

Plasmon sold itself as a scientific breakthrough which promised to revolutionise cooking through its concentrated formulas. Images of Plasmon (such as Figure 1.1), thus, played with its scientific associations. Plasmon was a deeply intriguing product for many, despite its relatively short shelf-life in Britain (it disappeared almost entirely prior to the Great War). What is missing from this story thus far, of course, is the association with physical culture.

Aside from its more generalised marketing campaign, Plasmon created relationships with three high-profile physical culturists: C.B. Fry, Eustace Miles and the previously mentioned Sandow (Heffernan, 2020). Fry was a Victorian gentleman and amateur athlete who excelled in cricket, athletics and football, while Miles was a vegetarian tennis player and progressive social figure who sought to combine health with equitable policies concerning class and gender. Sandow, on the other hand, was a Prussian strongman who was, at that time, attempting to pivot away from weightlifting competitions and music hall feats of strength towards becoming a more general, and respectable, expert on health and fitness.

Of the three, Sandow was the most attractive for Plasmon's agents. Often advertised as the world's most perfectly developed specimen (Chapman, 1994:5–6), Sandow was a prototype bodybuilder whose aesthetic build had long been the talk of British society. In the *Plasmon Cookery Book* (1904), several pages are dedicated to Sandow's use of the product. Likewise, Sandow spent a considerable amount of time speaking positively of Plasmon in newspapers. His testimonies proved revealing, most notably the claim that he survived for several days consuming nothing but Plasmon. Not only did his strength and musculature maintain, but he also got stronger (Plasmon, 1904:6–8). Prior to selling his own supplements, which came later in the decade, Sandow claimed that Plasmon was the most efficient and nutritious food that a physical culturist could consume. Eustace Miles made similar claims, but Sandow carried a much higher social prestige (Heffernan, 2020). The basis of these claims—that Plasmon could sustain a physical culturist's lifestyle—relied on Plasmon's proteid content, its scientific method and its position as a nutritional powerhouse. Just as today, celebrities were used to promote these products with outlandish claims (Pilgrim and Bohnet-Joschko, 2019).

Sandow's Embrocation

It was not just foods, or food supplements, that were promoted in the pursuit of a healthy lifestyle. Equally important were nostrums, presented as legitimate medicines. Muscle embrocation (typically a cream or liquid) was one such example. Beginning in the 1880s and running until the interwar period in Britain, muscle embrocation creams and liquids were advertised in newspapers and physical culture magazines as a "cure all" for muscle pain and stiffness. One of the first high-profile physical culturists to endorse some form of muscle embrocation was Victorina, an 1880s strongwoman who briefly toured Great Britain (Heffernan, 2021:360–363). Sandow was one of the first physical culturalists to promote his own products rather than acting as a sponsored athlete, launching "Sandow's Muscle Embrocation" from the mid-1900s (*The Scotsman*, 21 February 1906). While his product was unremarkable in its advertising, it was the most ubiquitous in newspapers. Promoted as "concentrated," which was a loosely veiled effort to co-opt the language of science, advertisements promised the embrocation would treat muscle pain and discomfort, but also rheumatism, lumbago and neuralgia (*Daily News*, 1 October 1907). Additionally, the advertising copy situated Sandow as the "greatest living authority on muscular and nervous disease."

What was in the embrocation? After all, physical culturists were told the primary ingredients in Plasmon. Sandow proved far coyer on this point. Claiming to have worked with "some of the finest scientists" in some sources and claiming that he came across a powerful "compound" through trial and error in other sources, Sandow presented his embrocation as a strong, even medicinal, product. Eriksson and O'Hagan's previous work (2021) on nutritional supplements has cited the ability of supplement entrepreneurs to blend scientific language with a sense of mysticism. Sandow did just that. One important outlet for this, where he was subject to much less scrutiny, was his own magazine. Founded in 1899, *Sandow's Magazine of Physical Culture* (as it was initially titled) included an "Ask the Editor" section in which readers could submit nutritional, exercise or medicinal questions to Eugen Sandow. In his responses, Sandow (although it is impossible to know whether it was him or a ghostwriter) diagnosed medical and training issues and advised "massage with Sandow's Embrocation." Sandow's Embrocation promised to "hasten recovery of muscular tone" thanks to its patented compound (Sandow, 2014:45). For those who took Sandow's advice and purchased the embrocation, they were given a 32-page illustrated book, "showing the correct method of application for each of its many purposes" (Sandow, 2014:145). Previous work on magnetics and magnetic belts in Victorian and Edwardian England (Rains, 2014) has discussed the importance of mimicking medical and scientific procedures. In this instance, advertisements and writings on the correct application of the product, its need for a detailed application and its ability to cure or solve injuries or illnesses mimicked legitimate medicines.

Spring-Grip Dumbbells

The final physical culture product to consider is spring-grip dumbbells, which were popularised especially in the *fin de siècle* period. Spring-grip dumbbells represented an attempt on the part of physical culturists to popularise weight training for the public as safely and as accessibly as possible. Weighing at most five pounds, spring-grip dumbbells promised miraculous body transformations of strength and muscularity through the use of springs. They were presented as safer than traditional heavy weights, which famous physical culturists had used to build their bodies. Terry Todd (1985) previously commented on the ingenuity, if not cynicism, of physical culture entrepreneurs in marketing spring-grip dumbbells. At the beginning of the twentieth century, the medical consensus around weight training was predominately centred on the idea that it was injurious to the heart, made one inflexible and could cause a variety of injuries (Park, 1987). Light-weight training, on the other hand, was deemed safe and advantageous to those desirable of a healthy life. How then did they work? Put crudely, the spring-grip dumbbells were based on a sandwich design. In between two steel handles was a series of springs. The goal for exercisers was to compress the steel springs and, in doing so, join the handles together. Underlying this practice was the idea that concentrating one's energy forcefully into the dumbbells would create an efficient means of training. In this regard, the dumbbells, and their advertisements, played on scientific ideas of invention, innovation and efficiency.

Once more, it is useful to examine Eugen Sandow as his spring-grip dumbbells were among the most popular of the age. Part of this stemmed from Sandow's own rigid enforcement of intellectual property. An example of this came in 1903 when Sandow's company brought legal proceedings against a fellow physical culturist, Professor Josef Szalay, whose own spring-grip dumbbells were deemed to be *ersatz* imitations of Sandow's (*Westminster Gazette*, 8 December 1903). Sandow's "invention," according to his own advertising copy, was:

> The greatest invention for giving perfect physical development and fitness [...] It is so arranged that the sturdiest athlete or the weakest child may use it with equal success [...] The whole series of exercises are carefully planned to give the greatest benefit in the shortest amount of time.
>
> (*Modern Man*, 28 August 1909)

Much like the previously mentioned magnetic belts, Sandow's advertisements played on three key themes in an age when scientific advancement was in itself deemed to be socially desirous. The first was transferability—the product was so "scientifically" developed by Sandow that it could be used by anyone. The next was the idea of ultimate progress which, in this case, referred to the idea of perfect physical development. On this point, Sandow's advertisements and training manuals (Sandow, 2014:60–62) stressed the importance of concentration and force (as applied to gripping the dumbbell), which they dressed in a vaguely understood language of physics. Finally, and perhaps most importantly, the quoted advertisement stressed the concept of efficiency. As Dorothy Porter (1991) made clear, popular understandings of the scientific method in England during this period often centred on efficiencies. This was particularly attractive, given that a common concern publicly and personally for many was the idea that life had reached a near-chaotic level of busyness and that free time was at a minimum. Sandow's dumbbells provided the "best" method in the shortest period. While the advertisements and training instructions often focused more so on physics and concentration, the advertised benefits were decidedly in keeping with public appropriations of science's presumed benefits. Some, as the next section discusses, took this appropriation to an astonishing level.

The Sandow Curative Institute of Physical Culture

When discussing physical culture products, it is inevitable, albeit at times repetitive, to focus on Eugen Sandow. At the time of writing, he is the only physical culturist to enjoy two academic biographies and scores of articles. However, other physical culturists existed and were also entrepreneurial. In 1860s America, George Barker Windship used his medical credentials as a physician to promote his own exercise equipment known as the "health lift" (Todd, 1993). The previously mentioned Josef Szalay created his own spring-grip dumbbell, while Edward Aston promoted an "anti-barbell," which was effectively a bar with weights on one side only (the theory being that the gravitational forces would produce greater musculature) (Aston, 1911). Bernarr Macfadden hosted physique competitions and ran his own magazines, while world tours were part of the trade for multiple strongmen and women (Todd, 1987).

The reason why Eugen Sandow has often been the lightning rod for historians' interest, and at times ire, was not because he did any of these individual things, but rather because he was one of the few—if not only—physical culturists to combine these various revenue streams and, in the case of his Curative Institute, create something entirely new. Sandow's Curative Institute was, as the name suggests, an establishment created to treat a variety of illnesses (Heffernan, 2022b). What is most fascinating about Sandow's Institute for the purposes of this chapter was his desire to straddle the line between medical and folk medicine, or between the scientific and unscientific. His institute promised to cure illness and ailment without the "use of harmful purgatives or drugs," while simultaneously using medical doctors and an advertised "scientific" method of diagnosis (Sandow, 1907:12–15). Significantly, Sandow presented his system as an evolution of the current medical model.

What did this system entail? In simple terms, very little that had been offered elsewhere. Regardless of their ailments, patients were issued with dietary advice and an exercise programme centred around both Sandow's exercises and his exercise equipment (be it the spring-grip dumbbell or his "Sandow Developer"). The idea of exercise as medicine was obviously not born with Sandow's Institute, but what did make it unique was Sandow's use of medical doctors. Sandow's Institute, which was established in London in 1907, used a two-tier system for patients. Upon entering the Institute, patients were examined by a medical doctor who determined the nature of their illness. Suitably diagnosed, the patients were then referred to Sandow for treatment with the understanding that the doctors themselves were only there to diagnose and were not officially stating that Sandow could cure an individual's ailment or illness (Sandow, 1914). The physicians employed by Sandow were later disbarred from practicing by the General Medical Council (GMC) in Britain after it was deemed that they had openly endorsed Sandow's Institute.[1]

It is telling that, during the physicians' legal case with the GMC, instances were brought up, whereby former clients of Sandow's Institute had injured themselves or, in one case, died from a serious illness following treatment

(General Medical Council, GD5/1/48, n.d.). While it was stated that the physicians had the power to turn away clients if they felt their diagnosis too serious to be treated by Sandow's dietary and exercise advice alone, there is little indication of how common an occurrence this was. Nor do we have a sense of how many clients Sandow treated in his physical location in London or in the mail-order treatments he also advertised, due to the loss of Sandow's personal and professional papers. In 1922, Sandow published a book entirely composed of his clients' testimonials (all anonymous), which featured hundreds of names. We do know, however, that the Institute lasted several years, and even survived the GMC case involving its physicians. We also know a great deal about how Sandow sought to advertise his clinic. Focus will be given in this final section to the Institute's advertising of "objective" facts and its scientific method.

Advertisements for Sandow's Institute mixed fact and fiction in some truly fascinating ways. In 1907, *Truth*—a magazine known for its searing exposés—published what appeared to be an in-depth examination of Sandow's clinic. In it, an unnamed reporter detailed their experiences interviewing Sandow, uncovering his method and, most importantly, his clinic's success rates. While the interview and reporting worked as a thinly veiled advertisement, the success figure given by *Truth* was 99% of all cases (Sandow, 1922:7). Treating illnesses ranging from cancer to obesity, only 1% of individuals who attended Sandow's clinic did not improve in some way. Later advertisements latched onto this figure of 99% success, despite never given an indication as to how this figure was reached or, equally importantly, what success entailed. Given that Sandow's clinic advertised that "willpower increased; the various organs brought to and maintained in a health condition and the individual made physically perfect," it seemed a high threshold. Sandow later clarified this figure as follows:

> Any Medical Man or bona fide sufferer can see in strict confidence the originals of the above reports and tens of thousands of others, which verify "Truth's" famous Report that the Sandow Treatment gave great relief in 99 cases out of every 100 and effected complete cure in 94.
>
> (Sandow, 1922:34–35)

Perhaps a less incredulous number, designed to show the Institute's success in a clinical and objective manner, was the use of weight and waist measurements. Despite the fact that many of the illnesses Sandow claimed to treat were internal issues, many of his testimonials centred on changes in a client's weight, waist size and muscle gain. As has been well studied elsewhere, weight measurements became increasingly important at the end of the nineteenth century as a means of quantifying one's health (Zweiniger-Bargielowska, 2005). This is not to say that weight and body size had not previously been a component of Western medicine, but rather that broader efforts were made at this point to standardise weight targets across populations. The United States was a particularly fertile ground in this regard, especially given the publication of weight measurements from US insurance companies as a means of creating "healthy" weight targets for the general public (Gilman, 2008:4). The nineteenth century and the rise of the PCM also brought with it a greater focus on individual bodily measurements, with an intensity similar to that found in modern fitness cultures (Brighton et al., 2020). In the United States, the phrenology movement quite literally linked the size of one's physique, and indeed body parts, to personality and behavioural traits. Therefore, when some phrenologists promoted physical activity in the mid-nineteenth century, they did so with the claim that larger muscles would correspond to desirable traits like intelligence (Mrozek, 1987:77–80).

Sandow's Institute benefitted from a conflux of phrenology, eugenics and weight concerns. When Sandow toured the United States in the mid-1890s, he was subject to measurements by Dudley Allen Sargent, the gymnasium instructor for Harvard University. Over the course of several decades, Sargent measured scores of men and women, seeking to determine the most perfectly developed body. Based upon this experience, he deemed Sandow to be the most perfectly developed man he had ever measured (De la Peña, 2003:7–11). Sandow spent a great deal during the 1890s and 1900s using this claim to market his shows and products. In Britain, he linked the ability to increase or decrease one's physique measurements to Britain's eugenics movement and the quest to birth healthier generations. Advertisements and published testimonials for Sandow's Curative Institute, therefore, focused on "objective" physique measurements which sought to use weight loss, reductions in waist size or increases in muscle size as a proxy for good health or effective treatment. What is telling in this regard is how spurious the connections were regarding individual treatments. Thus, one individual noted that their condition (unspecified) had improved. Evidence of this was the two-inch increase in their chest size and their 14 lbs weight gain (Sandow, 1922:14). Case No. 19,256, who suffered from "General Debility," happily reported a 5 lbs increase in weight (Sandow, 1922:26). Those suffering from a "weak chest," like Case No. D 22,613, cited their weight gain as evidence that Sandow's method worked, while Mr. W. of Wakefield believed that his continual weight gain proved his neurasthenia was in remission (Sandow, 1922:34). Similar instances could be found among the testimonials given by those suffering from liver or kidney disorders (Sandow, 1922:54).

As part of his Curative Institute, Sandow also ran a mail-order health service, where individuals could write in and, for a small fee, receive both a diagnosis and treatment by post (Sandow, 1914). In their postal consultation form, men and women were instructed to take strict measurements of their body, regardless of their medical complaints. In time, they were encouraged to measure themselves again and compare their new measurements to the initial numbers sent to Sandow. The logic of this was that increases in muscular size, especially around the upper body, were indicative of better health outcomes. The same was true for weight and/or waist measurements. Figure 1.2 shows how measurements, illustrations and text came together in the consultation form to create a seemingly scientific and respectable examination.

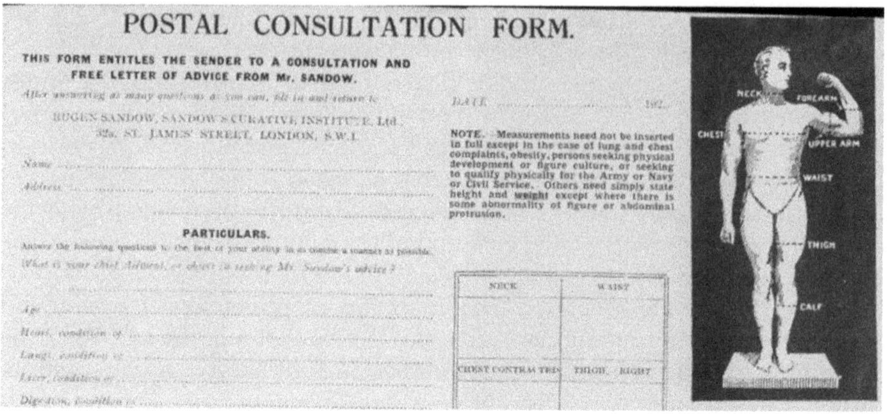

POSTAL CONSULTATION FORM.

THIS FORM ENTITLES THE SENDER TO A CONSULTATION AND FREE LETTER OF ADVICE FROM Mr. SANDOW.

After answering as many questions as you can, fill in and return to

EUGEN SANDOW, SANDOW'S CURATIVE INSTITUTE, Ltd.,
32a, ST. JAMES' STREET, LONDON, S.W.1.

DATE .... 192..

Name ....

Address ....

NOTE.—Measurements need not be inserted in full except in the case of lung and chest complaints, obesity, persons seeking physical development or figure culture, or seeking to qualify physically for the Army or Navy or Civil Service. Others need simply state height and weight except where there is some abnormality of figure or abdominal protrusion.

PARTICULARS.

Answer the following questions to the best of your ability in as concise a manner as possible.

What is your chief Ailment, or object in seeking Mr. Sandow's advice?

Age ....

Heart, condition of ....

Lungs, condition of ....

Liver, condition of ....

Digestion, condition of ....

NECK	WAIST
CHEST CONTRA[illegible]	THIGH, RIGHT

Figure 1.2 Sandow's Postal Consultation Form

Credit: Sandow (1914), *How I Conduct Curative Physical Culture by Correspondence*, p. 27.

The form shows a beautiful blending of classical antiquity with modern desires to measure the body. Here Sandow, and his agents, co-opted a very distinct idea of the past (and the social capital that Greco-Roman cultures had in England in the twentieth century) with a new scientific measurement. This was, of course, standard practice for Sandow whose own strongman performances often opened with poses mimicking Greco-Roman statues, before embarking on a "scientific" discussion of physical culture. Much like the Greco-Roman statue, whose remains were often partial (missing a limb or even head), the illustration shows a body divided into separate sections. Health was now measured in broad terms, but also in the minutiae of one's measurements. Good health required attention to detail and, more importantly, "scientific" measurements were not a luxury, but a requirement.

While it was alluring and simple to quantify health in this way, this had little basis in patients' treatments. In fact, the General Medical Council later complained that Sandow's Institute focused far too much on meaningless measurements to the detriment of patient health in a parallel later studied in Scrinis' (2013) work on *Nutritionism* and the rise of quantitative nutrition. This pattern remains within popular discussions of health and fitness, whereby the "quantified self"—the self understood through numbers and metrics—is taken as a proxy for overall health and well-being (Lupton, 2016). While Sandow also promoted this type of approach in his more popular fitness tracts, it was far more problematic when attached to his Curative Institute of Physical Culture and the illnesses which his Institute purported to cure.

As a final point in this regard, it is important to stress just how popular Sandow's Institute was. In 1910, the Institute was embroiled in a legal battle with the GMC which alleged that the Institute's physicians had grossly overstepped their profession's ethics by appearing in advertisements. The trial, which was reported widely throughout Britain, uncovered stories about malpractice, inefficient treatments and Sandow's own lack of medical knowledge (Heffernan, 2022b). At the conclusion of the trial, the Institute's physicians were removed from the medical bar, although they continued to work at Sandow's Institute (and continued to appear in its advertising). What should have been a massive image problem for the Institute—it presented itself as a hybrid between orthodox and complementary medicines, but having the support of orthodox medicine—did little to temper its popularity (Sandow, 1922). Despite its failings in the eyes of traditional physicians, the Institute held a strong grip on the public's imagination thanks to its combination of showmanship and questionable science. While the outbreak of the Great War did more to impact its popularity, the Institute continued until Sandow's death in 1925. Likewise, Sandow's 1922 book of testimonials from his Institute's clients included scores of individuals who continued to attend or seek treatment after 1910.

Conclusion

In 1967, American physician and crusader against questionable medical claims, Ronald Deutsch, published a book on medical "quacks" labelled *The Nuts Among the Berries* (1967). Focused on the American context, and deliberately written with an inflammatory title, it told stories of questionable healers and, at times, dangerous cures. What was striking about the book was how many of Deutsch's targets were attached to physical culture in some way, shape or form. In a similar vein, Graeme Kent's (2012) work *The Strongest Men in the World* sardonically commented on the world of British physical culture and its flair for the ridiculous in the early 1900s. Physical culture operated as a subcultural movement, critiquing traditional medical norms and institutions, while simultaneously appropriating many of their traits and behaviours. This is still occurring among influencers who critique conventional medicine, while adopting its scientific language. In the late nineteenth and early twentieth century, physical culture was often presented by physical culturists as new, modern and entirely unlike anything which had come before it. The movement was concerned with individual health, not in the medical sense of freedom from illness or disease but rather in a holistic sense, which centred on living life vibrantly and with "vim" or "vigour," to use the parlance of the time.

Physical culture was about health, but it was also about commerce. At the height of the pre-war PCM, enterprising health entrepreneurs capitalised on individual and state-wide fears that Britain's population was becoming physically degenerate and that individual action was necessary to stem the tide. The answer, unsurprisingly, often came in the form of esoteric equipment, gymnasium memberships and nutritional supplements, accompanied by outlandish claims about their efficacy. Central to these marketing campaigns was the ability of the individual entrepreneur to explain their product, at least partially, through the language of science. The PCM was not a scientific movement, despite what individuals like Eugen Sandow may have advertised. It did, however, capitalise on ideas of modernity, the clinical efficiency of the laboratory and the objectivity of "facts" to sell to a willing public. Early physical culturists of the time created a ploy so effective and popular that many of these traits and behaviours have been found repeatedly over the past century in wellness cultures. The formula remains the same: advertise a desirable physique, adapt its appearance to a specialised system of product and reap the rewards.

Note

1 At that time, physicians were not allowed to openly advertise goods or services as part of the orthodox medical community's desire to distinguish themselves from alternative practices.

References

Aston, E. 1911. *The Superman Course*. London: Edward Aston Courses.

Bennett, S. 1907. *Exercising in Bed: The Simplest and Most Effective System of Exercise Ever Devised*. San Francisco: E. Hilton Company.

Bredin, A.E.C. 1960. The Army Physical Training Corps Centenary: 1860–1960. *Royal United Services Institution Journal* 105(620):568–570.

Brighton, J., Wellard, I. and Clark, A. 2020. *Gym Bodies: Exploring Fitness Cultures*. Abingdon: Routledge.

Budd, M.A. 1997. *The Sculpture Machine: Physical Culture and Body Politics in the Age of Empire*. New York: New York University Press.

Carter, N. 2012. *Medicine, Sport and the Body: A Historical Perspective*. London: A&C Black.

Chapman, D. 1994. *Sandow the Magnificent: Eugen Sandow and the Beginnings of Bodybuilding*. Chicago: University of Illinois Press.

De la Peña, C. 2003. Dudley Allen Sargent: Health Machines and the Energized Male Body. *Iron Game History* 8(2):3–19.

Deutsch, R.M. 1967. *The Nuts Among the Berries*. New York: Ballantine Books.

Drescher, L.S., Roosen, J. and Marette, S. 2014. The Effects of Traffic Light Labels and Involvement on Consumer Choices for Food and Financial Products. *International Journal of Consumer Studies* 38(3):217–227.

Eriksson, G. and O'Hagan, L.A. 2021. Selling "Healthy" Radium Products with Science: A Multimodal Analysis of Marketing in Sweden, 1910–1940. *Science Communication* 43(6):740–767.

Fernan, C., Schuldt, J.P. and Niederdeppe, J. 2018. Health Halo Effects from Product Titles and Nutrient Content Claims in the Context of "Protein" Bars. *Health Communication* 33(12):1425–1433.

"Free Trial of Sandow's Spring Grip Dumbbells." 1909. *Modern Man* (28 August), 23.

General Medical Council. *Minutes of Meeting*, 702(62), Lothian Health Services Archive, Edinburgh, GD5/1/48.

Gilman, S.L. 2008. *Fat: A Cultural History of Obesity*. Cambridge: Polity.

Hargrove, J.L. 2006. History of the Calorie in Nutrition. *The Journal of Nutrition* 136(12):2957–2961.

Heffernan, C. 2019. "Born Swinging": Tom Burrows and the Forgotten Art of Endurance Club Swinging. *Sport in History* 39(1):45–73.

Heffernan, C. 2020. Superfood or Superficial? Plasmon and the Birth of the Supplement Industry. *Journal of Sport History* 47(3):243–262.

Heffernan, C. 2021. "A Strong Woman's Troubles": Victorina and the Strong Woman in Victorian Britain. *Women's History Review* 30(3):354–374.

Heffernan, C. 2022a. State of the Field: Physical Culture. *History* 107(374):143–162.

Heffernan, C. 2022b. Desirable Bodies and Eugen Sandow's Curative Institute in Edwardian England. *Social History of Medicine* 35(1):195–216.
Heggie, V. 2008. Lies, Damn Lies, and Manchester's Recruiting Statistics: Degeneration as an "Urban Legend" in Victorian and Edwardian Britain. *Journal of the History of Medicine and Allied Sciences* 43:178–216.
Heggie, V. 2018. *A History of British Sports Medicine*. Manchester: Manchester University Press.
Holt, R. 1990. *Sport and the British: A Modern History*. Oxford: Oxford University Press.
Holt, R. 2006. The Amateur Body and the Middle-Class Man: Work, Health and Style in Victorian Britain. *Sport in History* 26(6):352–369.
Holt, R. 2014. Historians and the History of Sport. *Sport in History* 34(1):1–33.
Kent, G. 2012. *The Strongest Men on Earth: When the Muscle Men Ruled Show Business*. London: Biteback Publishing.
Lupton, D. 2016. *The Quantified Self*. New York: John Wiley & Sons.
MacGregor, C., Petersen, A. and Parker, C. 2021. Promoting a Healthier, Younger You: The Media Marketing of Anti-Ageing Superfoods. *Journal of Consumer Culture* 21(2):164–179.
Miles, E. 1907. *The Eustace Miles System of Physical Culture. With Hints as to Diet: Fully Illustrated and Containing Two Charts of Exercises for the Cultivation of a Healthy and Well-proportioned Physique for Men and Women*. London: Health & Strength.
Morais. D. 2013. Branding Iron: Eugen Sandow's "Modern" Marketing Strategies, 1887–1925. *Journal of Sport History* 40(5):193–214.
Morais, D., Hemme, F. and Reyes, C. 2022. Tap 'Follow'# FitFam: A Process of Social Media Microcelebrity. *Qualitative Research in Sport, Exercise and Health* 14(2):289–305.
Mrozek, D.J. 1987. The Scientific Quest for Physical Culture and the Persistent Appeal of Quackery. *Journal of Sport History* 14(1):76–86.
Müller, J.P. 1911. *My System for Ladies*. London: Ewart, Seymour & Co.
O'Hagan, L.A. 2022. Flesh-Formers or Fads? Historicizing the Contemporary Protein-Enhanced Food Trend. *Food, Culture & Society* 25(5):875–898.
Park, R.J. 1987. Physiologists, Physicians, and Physical Educators: Nineteenth Century Biology and Exercise, "Hygienic" and "Educative". *Journal of Sport History* 14(1):28–60.
Pilgrim, K. and Bohnet-Joschko, S. 2019. Selling Health and Happiness: How Influencers Communicate on Instagram About Dieting and Exercise: Mixed Methods Research. *BMC Public Health* 19:1–9.
Plasmon, 1904. *Plasmon Cookery Book: Dainty, Nutritious and Economical Dishes for Every Household*. London: International Plasmon Ltd.
Plasmon, 1906. *Plasmon: The Mainstay of Life—What is It?* London: International Plasmon Ltd.
Porter, D. 1991. "Enemies of the Race": Biologism, Environmentalism, and Public Health in Edwardian England. *Victorian Studies* 34(2):159–178.
Rains, S. 2014. "Do You Ring? Or Are You Rung For?": Mass Media, Class, and Social Aspiration in Edwardian Ireland. *New Hibernia Review/Iris Éireannach Nua* 18(4):17–35.
Sandow, E. 1907. *The Construction and Reconstruction of the Human Body: A Manual of the Therapeutics of Exercise*. London: Sandow's Curative Institute.
Sandow, E. 1910. *Sandow Chest Expander Accessory—Booklet with Fold-Out Charts*. London: Sandow's Curative Institute.
Sandow, E. 1914. *How I Conduct Curative Physical Culture by Correspondence*. London: Sandow's Curative Institute.
Sandow, E. 1922. *Reports of a Few of the Thousands of Cases Successfully Treated by the Sandow Method of Curing Illness by Natural Means*. London: Sandow's Curative Institute.

Sandow, E. 2014. *Sandow's Magazine of Physical Culture, January to June 1900*. New York: Literary Licensing.
"Sandow's Dumbbell Action." 1903. *Westminster Gazette* (8 December), 17.
"Sandow's Embrocation." 1906. *The Scotsman* (21 February), 15.
"Sandow's Marvellous Success." 1907. *Daily News* (1 October), 2.
Scrinis, G. 2013. *Nutritionism: The Science and Politics of Dietary Advice*. New York: Columbia University Press.
Steinitz, L. 2014. "Making Muscular Machines with Nitrogenous Nutrition: Bovril, Plasmon and Cadbury's Cocoa" in *Food & Material Culture: Proceedings of the Oxford Symposium on Food and Cookery 2013* (Oxford: Oxford Symposium), pp. 289–303.
Steinitz, L. 2021. Transforming Pig's Wash into Health Food: The Construction of Skimmed Milk Protein Powders. *Global Food History* 9(3):290–323.
Strine, M.S. 1991. Critical Theory and "Organic" Intellectuals: Reframing the Work of Cultural Critique. *Communications Monographs* 58(2):195–201.
Todd, J. 1987. Bernarr Macfadden: Reformer of Feminine Form. *Journal of Sport History* 14(1):61–75.
Todd, J. 1993. Strength Is Health: George Barker Windship and the First American Weight-Training Boom. *Iron Game History* 3(1):5–6.
Todd, J. 1995. From Milo to Milo: A History of Barbells, Dumbbells, and Indian Clubs. *Iron Game History* 3(6):4–16.
Todd, J. 1998. *Physical Culture and the Body Beautiful: Purposive Exercise in the Lives of American Women, 1800–1870*. Macon: Mercer University Press.
Todd, T. 1985. Historical Perspective: The Myth of the Muscle-Bound Lifter. *Strength & Conditioning Journal* 7(3):37–41.
Wallace-Jones, A. 1908. *Fifty Exercises for Health and Strength*. London: Health & Strength.
Zweiniger-Bargielowska, I. 2005. The Culture of the Abdomen: Obesity and Reducing in Britain, Circa 1900–1939. *Journal of British Studies* 44(2):239–273.

2 Multimodal Representations of Health and Science in Danish Advertisements for Dairy Products and Plant-Based Alternatives

A Diachronic Study

Iben Bredahl Jessen

Introduction

Messages about what to eat and drink to live a healthy life are abundant in the media. Public authorities, experts and, not least, marketers communicate about nutrition and health, aiming to guide or convince consumers about the ingredients of a healthy lifestyle. Throughout the history of mass media, advertisements have promoted viewpoints of relations between humans, products and well-being (cf. Leiss et al., 2018), and some types of food and drink advertising have emphasised the dietary benefits of products or the more general impact on aspects of health (Zwier, 2009; Prell et al., 2011; Gunter, 2016).

This chapter focuses on references to "science" in communication about health and healthy lifestyles in Danish advertisements for dairy products and plant-based alternatives. These product categories are at the centre of discussions on nutrition and health (Jallinoja et al., 2016; Thorning et al., 2016) due to evolving dietary advice from public authorities and guidelines from other expert systems circulating in the media. Until 2011, for example, the food pyramid from Coop Denmark (first published in 1976)—which reflects official dietary advice from the Danish authorities—placed dairy products in a higher position than vegetables in terms of what to consume most. While the rationale for this change was linked to new understandings of nutrition and health, products like milk have a long history of different meanings, traditions and consumption patterns across cultures (Wilken and Knudsen, 2008; Valenze, 2011), as well as conflicting viewpoints about their benefits. Today, there is also a growing consideration of climate when it comes to dietary advice (Coop, 2022; Nordic Council of Ministers, 2023), as well as a surge in "healthy" plant-based alternatives.

Against the backdrop of changing dietary advice and divergent understandings of healthy lifestyles, this chapter presents a diachronic study of the multimodal strategies involved in promoting dairy products and plant-based alternatives by means of verbal, visual and auditory semiotic resources. The study is text-oriented and inspired by social semiotics and theories of multimodal meaning-making and legitimation. Based on a sample of Danish print

DOI: 10.4324/9781003450276-5

and audiovisual advertisements from 1930 to 2019, the chapter traces historical shifts and continuities in representations of healthy lifestyles and ways of referring to science in order to legitimate claims of product benefits. The selected product categories for the study include milk and plant-based drinks, butter and margarine (including mixed products and pure vegetable variants). By including different types of products, the purpose is to explore how meaning patterns connected to health and science relate and fluctuate within and between product types over time.

Dairy Products and Plant-Based Alternatives: Historical Perspectives

The promotion of dairy products and plant-based alternatives with arguments related to health has a long history. In a historical study of Swedish dairy marketing in the 1920s and 1930s—which mentions similar promotional initiatives during this period in several other European countries, Canada and the US—Martiin (2010) identified a combined focus on public health, product quality and hygiene in advertisements, along with socioeconomic considerations in terms of incentives to support farmers and the countryside in a period with limited exports. The promotion of dairy products connected national health and wealth, and it was presented as a Swedish "duty to produce and consume as much dairy produce as possible" (Martiin 2010:229). Equivalently, a report on Danish dairy history points to the agricultural crisis in the 1930s as the reason behind the Danish Dairy Board's decision to initiate campaigns to increase the consumption of milk, butter and cheese, using posters with such slogans as "milk is health" (Rasmussen, 1982:208). Historically, milk has been associated with health-giving qualities (Jönsson, 2005), and school milk programmes have been introduced accordingly, which educate children to become milk consumers (Atkins, 2005). Butter and margarine, on the other hand, have had more challenging histories, with evolving—and even conflicting—views throughout the twentieth century on their potential benefits (Pantzar, 1995; Levene, 2014; O'Hagan, 2023).

Despite historical and contextual differences, health in advertisements for dairy products and plant-based alternatives has been connected to the strengthening of bodily health by proper nutrition. In dairy advertisements, this implies an idea of health as something that is derived from product qualities, that is, if the product is "natural" or "pure," it is good (for your body). To support this understanding, references to scientific knowledge within nutrition and vitamin research are included (Smith-Howard, 2013). Moreover, health in advertisements for dairy products and plant-based alternatives appear to be intertwined with other discourses prevailing in the social world at a given time, such as expressions of nationality and "food citizenship" (Lieffers, 2015:340), class (Levene, 2014; O'Hagan, 2023) and gender/family (Hand, 2017). This is also the case in Fuentes and Fuentes' (2017) study of contemporary marketing materials promoting vegan alternatives to milk, whereby health is implied in discourses of sustainability and ethical consumption. Not unlike the reciprocal orientation in advertisements for butter and margarine (margarine imitating butter and vice versa) demonstrated in the diachronic study by Pantzar (1995), Fuentes and Fuentes (2017) show how vegan milk substitutes are marketed in relation to their dairy "counterparts" by offering healthy alternatives, while at the same time suggesting similarity. This chapter will take these investigations further through a textual and multimodal analysis of representations of health and science from a diachronic perspective.

Research Methodology

The present study explores the multiple meanings surrounding representations of health and science in advertisements for dairy products and plant-based alternatives, using a broad perspective on health inspired by Prell et al.'s (2011) analysis of food advertising in which health messages are identified as references to the body, emotions and social relations (e.g. care of children and family).[1] Likewise, references to science will be approached broadly as the use of scientific or technical vocabulary (e.g. terms and values for nutritional content) and visualisations (e.g. concepts, graphs and charts), quotes from scientists or scientific institutions and any references to "science," "research," "laboratories," "reports," "studies" and "analyses" (cf. Pitrelli et al., 2006). Multimodal strategies in advertisements will be explored in terms of written and spoken words, music, still and moving images, graphics and colours. The concern is how messages about health and science are *constructed* and *represented* in marketing materials over time, not whether actual scientific evidence exists.

The analysis is inspired by social semiotic theories of multimodal meaning-making and exemplifies an "archaeological" approach described by Höllerer et al. (2019:52) as an approach in which texts "serve as a cultural memory – as the 'storage' or 'crystallization' of social knowledge." Formats of advertising and marketing texts are considered as cultural constructions of the social world (cf. Hall, 1980; Wharton, 2013), signifying viewpoints of health and healthy lifestyles. The analysis examines multimodal structures of representational meaning related to the advertised products and how health claims are legitimated by references to science. Representational meaning is analysed with a focus on dairy products and plant-based alternatives as represented "participants" (cf. Kress and van Leeuwen, 2021:45) that enter into relationships with other participants (e.g. humans, objects, phenomena) and settings by means of verbal, visual and auditory semiotic resources (e.g. combinations of written words and images).

In this way, the analysis addresses understandings of what humans "do" to products and what products "do" to humans in terms of health benefits and the semiotic resources chosen to express such relationships. The semiotic resources are analysed with a focus on meaning potentials (van Leeuwen, 2005:4), hereby including the multimodal connotations and symbolic meanings ascribing health-related values to the advertised products. On this basis, legitimation by references to science is analysed, considering multimodal legitimation as all forms of expressions that "seek to give meaning to social practices" (van Leeuwen, 2017:219). Inspired by van Leeuwen (2017), representations of health and science are considered and discussed in relation to different types of legitimation: (1) legitimation by reference to authority (e.g. "expert authority" or "authority of tradition"); (2) legitimation by rationalisation, including "instrumental rationalisation" (i.e. legitimation by emphasis on "goals, uses and effects") or "theoretical rationalisation" "by reference to a theory of 'how things are'" (van Leeuwen, 2017:229); and (3) legitimation based on moral- or value-based evaluations by reference to value systems (e.g. that something is "healthy" or "good").

The analysis is based on a sample of Danish print and audiovisual advertisements for milk, butter, margarine and plant-based drinks from 1930 to 2019. The year 1930 has been selected as a starting point due to the availability of relevant materials in the applied archives. The collected material consists of:

1 Print advertisements in the consumer magazine *Samvirke* from 1930 to 2019. *Samvirke* has been published by the consumer cooperative Coop Denmark since 1928 (until 1945 published under the name *Brugsforenings-Bladet*) as a service to its members. Today, *Samvirke* is the most-read magazine in Denmark, with more than one million readers per year (Kulturministeriet, 2021). The magazine covers a broad range of consumer topics, among these health and food. All issues of *Samvirke* are accessible digitally in the public e-archive *Samvirke Classic*. Advertisements of relevance for this study have been identified by using a keyword search.
2 Audiovisual advertisements from 1930 to 2019, available in the media archives of the Royal Danish Library. Collections of material from these archives are challenged by archival differences as regards to what and how materials are available across time. A combined collection procedure involving two archives (the advertising and the television archive) was, therefore, applied. In the advertising archive, Danish cinema advertisements from 1907 to 1995 are available, as well as commercials from the Danish channel TV 2 from 1988 to 2005. From this archive, relevant advertisements were identified by product category and keyword searches. In the television archive, a sample of television commercials from 2006 to 2019 are available from TV 2. From this archive, commercial breaks before the news at 19:00 pm were screened for relevant commercials.

This process resulted in the collection of 233 advertisements. Only advertisements addressing aspects of health were included in the sample, and identical advertisements were only registered once. Table 2.1 presents an overview of the collected print and audiovisual advertisements distributed into product categories.

As only advertisements including signifiers of health were collected, the sample is not representative of the frequency of advertisements within product categories as such. For example, numerous butter and margarine advertisements during the 1960s have been left out as they merely focus on taste,

Table 2.1 Overview of the 233 Advertisements in the Sample Distributed by Product Categories

		Number of collected advertisements with references to health (Advertisements with references to health and science)									
		1930–1939	*1940–1949*	*1950–1959*	*1960–1969*	*1970–1979*	*1980–1989*	*1990–1999*	*2000–2009*	*2010–2019*	*Total*
Print	Milk	-	-	-	-	-	1	3 (1)	3 (1)	3 (2)	10 (4)
	Butter	-	-	-	-	2 (2)	2 (2)	-	-	-	4 (4)
	Margarine	4 (1)	6 (6)	12 (6)	8 (1)	24 (20)	26 (23)	12 (10)	3 (3)	-	95 (70)
	Plant drink	-	-	-	-	-	-	5 (5)	10 (9)	1 (1)	16 (15)
Print in total		**4 (1)**	**6 (6)**	**12 (6)**	**8 (1)**	**26 (22)**	**29 (25)**	**20 (16)**	**16 (13)**	**4 (3)**	**125 (93)**
AV	Milk	-	1	-	8	11 (2)	11 (5)	7 (4)	16 (4)	3 (1)	57 (16)
	Butter	-	-	-	2	-	1	1	-	-	4
	Margarine	1	-	-	4 (2)	4	2 (2)	22 (7)	11 (8)	3 (1)	47 (20)
	Plant drink	-	-	-	-	-	-	-	-	-	-
AV in total		**1**	**1**	**0**	**14 (2)**	**15 (2)**	**14 (7)**	**30 (11)**	**27 (12)**	**6 (2)**	**108 (36)**
Print and AV in total		**5 (1)**	**7 (6)**	**12 (6)**	**22 (3)**	**41 (24)**	**43 (32)**	**50 (27)**	**43 (25)**	**10 (5)**	**233 (129)**

Credit: Author's own image

cooking capacities and presentations of recipes. Variations in the number of collected advertisements over the years can be explained by the archival and sampling differences described above, as well as a range of other circumstances possibly influencing the occurrence of advertisements, such as structural developments within the dairy industry (e.g. dairy products becoming branded goods available in retail shops and not delivered by the local dairy), economic and cultural developments in consumer society (e.g. increased purchasing power, greater availability of goods and brands, changing ways of eating), an evolving media landscape and shifting preferences towards advertising media (e.g. in recent years, a possible shift towards online and social media).

The collected advertisements were transcribed and subjected to a detailed thematic analysis in order to identify common traits and variations related to representations of health and science from a diachronic perspective. Based on iterative readings of the transcriptions, six coding categories summing up the health-related signifiers in the material were identified: (1) hygiene and control; (2) nature; (3) nutritional content; (4) general well-being and care; (5) diet and keep fit; and (6) environment and climate (see Table 2.2).

Table 2.2 Coding Categories and Examples of Signifiers of Health

Coding categories	*Examples of signifiers*
	Production environment
Hygiene and control	Informative labelling
	Laboratory analyses
	Plants
Nature	Fields
	Landscapes
	Animals
	Types of fat
	Proteins
Nutritional content	Vitamins
	Minerals
	Additives
	Strength
	Growth
General well-being and care	Feelings of energy
	Mental well-being
	Nutritional care of children and family
	Low fat
	Low calories
Diet and keep fit	Low sugar
	Prevention of disease and discomfort
	Slim waistline
	Low carbon footprint
Environment and climate	No pesticides
	Reduced use of resources

Credit: Author's own image

A second coding process then took place to identify references to science across the health-related themes. As can be seen in Table 2.1, a total of 129 out of the 233 advertisements in the sample included references to science (55%). However, references to science were more prevalent in print advertisements (74%) than in the audiovisual advertisements (33%).

Multimodal Representations of Health and Science

The subsequent analysis identifies the semiotic meaning potentials connected to the aforementioned themes and examines how they are represented. The analysis is based on excerpts and illustrative examples from selected advertisements in search of common traits and variations.[2] In this way, the analysis will not provide exhaustive analyses of singular texts. The analysis is organised chronologically in periods of three decades (1930–1959, 1960–1989, 1990–2019) in order to show how the themes interact. Apart from dividing the material into periods of equal length (albeit with varying amounts of collected material), the division marks significant developments within nutrition science. For example, the 1960s saw growing attention towards fat types and health effects, while the early 1990s was a time when the first publications on unhealthy trans-fatty acids appeared (Scrinis, 2013).

1930–1959: Hygiene and Vitamins

The first three decades in the sample show less material than the two periods that follow (cf. Table 2.1), perhaps due to other more prevalent advertising media at that time not included in the collection of materials, such as newspapers, posters, collectors' stamps and illuminated advertising (Strandskov et al., 1998:291ff.). The collected material with references to science only includes print advertisements, and they all promote margarine from the Danish Co-operative Wholesale Society's (F.D.B.) own factory, which gained a market share of 25% in the 1930s (Strandskov et al., 1998:408). Although Denmark had a large butter production at the time, this was mostly for export (Rasmussen, 1982:196). The cheaper substitute, margarine, was the most consumed fat product in the country throughout the 1930s, the late 1940s and the 1950s. In fact, pre-war statistics show the Danes as the most margarine-consuming population in the world (see Berg, 2013:97). However, during the Second World War, as margarine production ceased due to lack of raw materials and margarine and butter became rationed, this consumption pattern turned upside down, with butter taking the lead (Jensen, 2012). These conditions are reflected in a post-war advertisement announcing that low-cost margarine is back and that socially responsible consumers should "not forget that the return of margarine means larger export of agricultural produce" (46 Margarine, August 1946a).

Health-related themes in connection with references to science are dominated by articulations of nutritional content and hygiene and control. This focus on nutritional content reflects the Danish legalisation of margarine fortified with vitamins A and D in 1937, which "had for some time been a desire of the margarine industry as it wanted its products to mimic the nutritional composition of butter" (Jensen, 2012:39). However, hygiene and control were by far the most dominating theme, as well as concerns about the purity of margarine. As explained by the head of F.D.B.'s central laboratory in articles in *Brugsforenings-Bladet* in the first part of the 1930s, scientific results and methods from bacteriology played an important role in margarine production and guided the measures taken to keep out damaging microorganisms, such as putrefactive bacteria and mould which made margarine inedible (Ring, 1932, 1935).

The importance of hygiene and control manifests in a PAN/Trekroner margarine advertisement from September 1931 in which a drawing of wrapped rolls of margarine is accompanied by a copy, stating that the margarine "aided by science and hygiene has come as close to the ideal as ever possible in our time." In this advertisement, "science" comes into play as an abstract authoritative expertise juxtaposed to (and, thus, connected with) "hygiene" as a warrant of food safety and health, in this way combining legitimation by expert authority and theoretical rationalisation (van Leeuwen, 2017). The meaning potential of "the ideal" here implies reference to the (previous) state of affairs in which hygiene and quality supposedly were not always the best and a reassurance that it is safe to consume the product.

Likewise, in the collected advertisements from the 1940s and 1950s, references to science manifest in the copy as arguments of product quality and safety, while the illustrations mostly consist of drawings of the product (either packaged or loose), sometimes situated in a kitchen setting with a woman cooking. Several advertisements, especially in the mid-1940s, stress nutritional content by declaring margarine as vitaminised. Visually, a connection between the vitaminised product and nature is alluded to in the logo on the illustrated margarine packaging with graphic lines forming the shape of a sun and the sun's rays (see 46 Margarine, September 1946b in Figure 2.1). Legitimation by moral evaluation here shows as "analogy" (van Leeuwen, 2017:227) to common understandings of the sun as life- and health-giving (cf. O'Hagan, 2022).

In the verbal descriptions, references to science in relation to hygiene and control are emphasised in connection with modern production facilities, laboratory control and skilled specialists. In margarine advertisements from 1946, it is accentuated that no human hands have touched the product, as in this example:

> [...] and skilled specialists in connection with thorough laboratory control and completely modern production equipment guarantee that you from F.D.B always get a consistent first-class product, which – untouched by human hands on its way to the consumers – is also second to none as regards hygiene.
>
> (46 Margarine, August 1946)

Figure 2.1 1946 Advertisement from F.D.B. "46 Margarine"

Credit: Published in *Samvirke*, September 1946, p. 12. Reproduced with permission.

Compared with the abstract articulation of science as a discipline in the margarine advertisement from 1931, human agents are here mentioned as “skilled specialists”—an expert authority ensuring “clean” products. Humans control, but do not touch.

Other advertisements further explain that, during production, margarine is “protected against harmful microorganisms” (Trekroner, July 1949a) and examined in “reassuring hygienic control” (Trekroner, September 1949b). In this way, possible concerns of the housewife regarding safety and nutritional quality are addressed; the product is not contaminated and is a source of vitamins for the family. This is expressed explicitly in an advertisement with a yellow background (connoting sun and health) and drawings of girls eating slices of bread, as well as the concluding statement: “Therefore, it is safe to give the children Trekroner margarine” (Trekroner, September 1949). Here, the enlightened and responsible housewife is addressed, perhaps educated through the many cookbooks and nutrition guides available at that time about the scientific advances within bacteriology and nutrition science of relevance for daily cooking practices (Nyvang, 2022).

1960–1989: Fat Types and Diet

The collected material from the 1960s, 1970s and 1980s shows more advertisements with references to science than in the previous three decades, but these are unevenly distributed (cf. Table 2.1). Only three advertisements with references to science date from the 1960s, while 24 and 32 advertisements are recorded in the 1970s and 1980s, respectively. The health-related themes connected to science are more varied than in the previous three decades. Nature, nutritional content and general well-being and care appear as more dominant themes in relation to science, while the theme “diet and keep fit” appears with more and more weight, hence reflecting a new nutritional era from the beginning of the 1960s characterised by “good-and-bad nutritionism” (Scrinis, 2013:73) and a focus on fat types and the link between saturated fats and risk of heart disease. Compared with the previous three decades, hygiene and control feature remarkably less.

In the sample as a whole, print advertisements from the 1960s comprise several margarine advertisements simply pointing at vegetable margarine as a healthy (and cheap) product well suited for lunchboxes at school or work. Science is only alluded to in one advertisement in which it is assured (in a footnote) that “declaration of content” and “quality control” are in order (Trekroner, December 1969). Likewise, among the collected audiovisual advertisements (recorded during the 1960s from the Danish Dairies), several milk advertisements point to health as general well-being and care by describing milk as “great” and by showing both famous and ordinary people drinking milk while performing their job. The slogan “Milk must be drunk ‘the right way’ – often and cold” is hardly to be considered as dietary advice, if so, vague.

More explicit references to science manifest in two margarine advertisements in which health is connected to nutritional content, as well as general well-being and care. In a 1965 Bellis cinema commercial, the voiceover states that "vegetable margarine contains nutrients that children need, and adults should not do without." Although it is not clear who the authority behind this statement is and which nutrients are referred to, the message involves an idea of fact or knowledge about what "children need." The suggestion of an expert authority, thus, goes hand in hand with legitimation by moral evaluation, implying what is good and healthy. Moreover, a connection to nature is established in the visuals by scenes of a family in a summer cottage by the seaside having lunch outside and by the voiceover's figurative description of margarine that "tastes like sun and summer" (1965 Bellis cinema commercial). In this way, nature and sun are represented as inherent qualities of the product and as the abstract provenance of the nutrients.

Likewise, in another Bellis margarine commercial (this time from 1968), the voiceover mentions "places where the sun shines all year round" as the place where "the light nutrient-rich vegetable fats" come from. Accordingly, nutritional care of children is metaphorically stated as advice to "give your children a mouthful of sunshine" (1968 Bellis margarine commercial) (similar references to the sun are identified in O'Hagan, 2022; O'Hagan and Eriksson, 2022). Health is expressed as "eating nature" and nature is presupposed as "good" (cf. Jönsson, 2005). For the first time in the sample, this commercial also articulates vegetable fats as "light." However, it is not further explained what "light" means or what the benefits of "light" are. The theme "diet and keep fit" is, thus, suggested, but in this commercial, "light" seems more connected to general well-being and nutritional care of the family.

During the 1970s, more examples of the theme "diet and keep fit" were identified, especially in print advertisements. Several margarine advertisements from F.D.B. promote so-called "diet margarine" with more polyunsaturated fat and, in Danish, "minarine" ("low-fat spread") with less fat and more polyunsaturated fat. These advertisements are often accompanied by an extensive copy with declarations of nutritional contents and types of fats, thus at the same time connoting a system of expertise and theoretical rationalisation. As emphasised in an F.D.B. Plantemargarine advertisement from September 1972, the promoted margarine is provided with a declaration of contents showing "which nutrients you bring home to your family." Perhaps because many of the print advertisements are promoting the cooperative's own products (and in line with the editorial profile of the magazine), some advertisements bear resemblance to consumer information, for example, by listing the nutritional content of different margarine types for the consumer to compare and choose.

In an F.D.B. advertisement from May 1973b with an image of an open box of low-fat spread surrounded by mushrooms, a tomato and parsley as "symbolic attributes" (Kress and van Leeuwen, 2021:102), characteristics of consumer information manifest in the headline: "What do you need to know when choosing? 2 things are of vital importance: the content of fat and the content of linoleic acid (polyunsaturated fat)." Here the consumer is "educated" in nutrition to be able to make qualified decisions for the household. Statements linked to the theme "diet and keep fit" also show a focus on reducing calorie intake to maintain slimness. Slimness, thus, becomes a symbol of a light and healthy lifestyle and a way of translating the paradigm of "good-and-bad nutritionism" (Scrinis, 2013) into a marketing context.

In another version of the aforementioned F.D.B. low-fat spread advertisement, published in April 1973a, references to science appear in combining vocabulary of nutritional values with diet, hence suggesting legitimation by authority, moral evaluation and rationalisation at the same time: "Slim down with a healthy novelty [...] 'Minarine' is low in calories [...] 'Minarine' contains only 40% fat. Hereof 40% linoleic acid (polyunsaturated fat). And 'minarine' is enriched with vitamin A, D and E."

A somewhat different approach to health and nutrition is expressed in Lurpak/Danish Dairies print advertisements from 1970a featuring two well-known television chefs as endorsers of butter. The "role model authority" (van Leeuwen, 2017:224) of the endorsers is represented in the copy, signalling a down-to-earth attitude towards the focus on nutrition: "We will not tire you with listing the nutritional content of butter [...] we know that butter is a pure natural product that does not contain other fats than those in the cow's milk" (Lurpak/Danish Dairies, March 1970b). Here, butter is articulated as healthy because it is made from cow's milk, thereby pointing at nature as the source of healthy dairy products (cf. Pantzar, 1995). Moreover, expertise is assigned to the dairies where the products are "controlled and tested in every way so the splendid quality is maintained" (Lurpak/Danish Dairies, March 1970), and, in another advertisement, it is further explained that the dairies know how to preserve "the vital nutrients" in milk (Lurpak/Danish Dairies, February 1970). In this way, butter is characterised as a natural and pure (not mixed) product which, as expressed by the implicit comparison in the slogan, "taste twice as good."

The description of milk as "great"—which characterised the milk advertisements of the 1960s—is reframed in the milk advertisements from the Danish Dairies in the 1970s by a description of milk as "new energy." Here, milk is represented in relation to general well-being and care by connections of milk and physical activity (mostly sport) and by emphasising milk as a source of calcium. Likewise, the milk commercials from the Danish Dairies in the audiovisual material from the 1980s continuously represent milk as "new energy," and the benefits of milk are described as "strengthening the bones" and "strengthening the teeth" (Danish Dairies, 1988a, 1988b). The emphasis on physical activity also shows in a 1984 Danish Dairies cinema commercial in which a group of comedians sing about milk and people exercising: "One wants to run, one wants to swim [...] / [...] vitamins are medicine for your condition/small minerals and protein/all of it gives energy."

Physical activity is also prevalent in relation to the theme "diet and keep fit" and shown in a 1988 television commercial for the low-fat spread Lätta (the Swedish brand name referring to "light"), which emphasises the well-trained body with the slogan "Have you chosen never to be fat?" Fitness culture linked to arguments of a nutritionally balanced or "correct" diet manifests in the print material from the 1980s as well. In a January 1984 advertisement for Brugsen Minarine low-fat spread, information on nutritional content is presented with a picture of a woman's lower leg in gym leggings and legwarmers, a dog and a ghetto blaster and the headline "minarine/music/gymnastics." According to the copy, "gymnastics and fewer calories can quickly make you lose weight" (Brugsen Minarine January 1984 ad). Similarly, in a September 1985 advertisement for Brugsen Minarine low-fat spread, a picture of a woman lying in workout clothes while holding leashes connected to two boxes of low-fat spread is metaphorically explained as "keep the calories on a leash." Through a narrative structure (cf. Kress and van Leeuwen, 2021) in which the woman is represented as an actor with power and control, the individual is represented as capable of being in control of calorie intake and weight.

The focus on calories shows in "prior" references to official dietary advice as represented in the Cooperative's food pyramid by the slogan "Live better," which became part of the food pyramid in 1984 (Coop, 2022). In a Brugsen advertisement from March 1983a presenting low-fat spread together with other low-fat products, the consumer is encouraged to "Live light – and live better" and, in another Brugsen advertisement from August 1983b, "Live better – eat less fat. One of the five good pieces of dietary advice that also keeps you slim." However, to judge from a Danish Dairies butter advertisement from September 1983, the focus on calories and fat types has seemingly resulted in some confusion. Illustrated by an image of glistening vegetables and the headline "It tastes like butter… because it is butter," the advertisement points out that not all types of margarine can be used for "everything" as butter can, and, from a record comparing the content of fat in butter and different types of margarine, it follows that only low-fat spread ("minarine") contains less fat ("40%" compared to "80%"). Again, butter is emphasised as a natural and pure product by means of theoretical rationalisation, and possible doubts as to the content of fat are met with reference to regulations: "Butter is pure pleasure from nature – without artificial colour or other additives. There is the same amount of fat in butter and margarine (determined by law) and therefore the energy content is the same" (Danish Dairies Sept 1983 ad). Mentioning the "law" exemplifies legitimation by "impersonal authority" (van Leeuwen, 2017:222).

In this connection, a more general tendency in the print advertisements shows in statements about what is *not* in the products (e.g. "no colours added"). Sometimes this also includes milk. In a Brugsen Diætmargarine advertisement from September 1982, it is explained that the spread is "made for those who must – or want to – avoid milk ingredients." Similarly, in a May 1982 Natura advertisement promoting health food as a way to "a better life," vegetable margarine is described as "not added milk, salt or aromatics, but 55% polyunsaturated fat […] that is healthy for you." In a November 1987 advertisement for PAN vegetable margarine, the consumer is encouraged to "break with tradition and get something better"—here referring to margarine with animal fat as "old-fashioned" because the level of polyunsaturated fat is lower. In line with the paradigm of "good-and-bad nutritionism" (Scrinis, 2013), polyunsaturated fat is further linked to disease prevention in a Brugsen Diætmargarine advertisement (September 1984) suggesting that this type of fat "is believed to prevent cardiovascular disease" and further (tentatively): "Polyunsaturates are not a 'panacea', but they can help to lower the cholesterol level." Modern consumers are, thus, assumed to consider such health issues when buying food.

1990–2019: Green Alternatives

The three decades from 1990 to 2019 count about the same number of advertisements with references to science as in the previous three decades, but due to different procedures of collection in the audiovisual archives, there is a rather low number of advertisements from the 2010s (Table 2.1). The presence of themes in advertisements with references to science is still varied. Nutritional content is a continuously dominating theme and is now marked by an increased focus on the harmful trans-fatty acids resulting from the chemical processing (hardening) of vegetable oils (Scrinis, 2013). In Denmark, a threshold value for the level of industrially produced trans-fatty acids was determined by law in 2003 and later regulated by the EU rules (Fødevarestyrelsen, 2023). Hygiene and control are almost absent as themes, supposedly reflecting a greater level of regulation and the fact that food safety is now taken for granted. The environment and climate increasingly play a role.

In 1990, the first advertisement for plant-based drinks appeared. A print advertisement introduces a soy drink as a "pure natural product"—resonated in the brand name Naturli'—and as a "healthy alternative to milk" (Naturli', September 1990b). The resemblance to milk is emphasised by an image of a child with a milk "beard," and the natural is described as originating from "the protein-rich and natural soya bean, raw cane sugar and coarse sea salt – and no additives" (Naturli', September 1990b). Although promoted visually as a product for the whole family (e.g. by an image of a family in a kitchen), the drink is also accentuated as "without cholesterol" (Naturli', September 1990b) and "as lowering cholesterol because of the special combination of vegetable proteins" (Naturli', January/February 1990a). Furthermore, in an advertisement with a picture of a man holding a baby and the headline "A healthy 'Naturli' ["natural"] family," the product's health benefits are described as: "Low fat content and rich on polyunsaturated fats, lesser carbohydrates, without cholesterol and milk fat […] Now with extra calcium for everyone, not least children, breastfeeding or elderly, when bones and teeth should be strengthened" (Naturli', June/July 1991). In this way, a variety of nutritional needs is articulated. The product is legitimated by combining value-based evaluation and rationalisation (pointing at bodily benefits), supported by abstract references to systems of expertise by the use of technical concepts.

In June/July 1995, considerations of the environment are identified in a Naturli' advertisement showing a range of cartons of plant-based drinks. Under the subheading "Research and Development" and supported by bullet points listing the "healthy qualities" of the product, the copy stresses "ecology and health" and "considerations of the balance of nature and the use of the earth's resources" (Naturli', 1995). The qualities related to the word "balance" exemplify moral evaluation by abstraction, yet, once again, in combination with expertise-based rationality. A similar Naturli' advertisement with a focus on research, health and nutrition shows in September 1998, but supplemented with a focus on "lifestyle," "ecological balance and quality of life" and a reference to "people from the East" with a long tradition of profiting from the qualities of the soya bean. The pointing at cultures from the East—characteristic of the health food tradition (Jönsson, 2005:107)—illustrates how "mythopoesis," defined as "legitimation conveyed through narratives" (Höllerer et al., 2019:163), supplements the moral evaluation legitimating the product as "good."

The theme "diet and keep fit"—identified from the 1960s onwards—remains present in the advertisements from the 1990s, yet with new nuances. A September 1991 print advertisement for Lätta low-fat spread has the slogan "Have you chosen never to be fat?" and a picture of a woman in fitness wear, and connects slimness and health to looking good: "For you who live a healthy life and want to keep looking good." Low-calorie intake is furthermore linked to the clearing of one's conscience since the product also figuratively "leaves a good taste in the mouth" (Lätta, 1991). Slimness is also explicitly addressed in a 1991 MD Foods television commercial in which a young couple dancing to the rhythms of Latin music is shown together with numerical indications of the fat content in yoghurt and milk. In the lyrics, the low-fat product range "Cheasy" is cheered and phonetically "caressed" by the verse "Che, che, che, Cheasy, oooh Cheasy," yet the product's consumers, represented by the dancing couple, are also cheered in the lyrics by the repetition of "it is cool to be slim." The coolness or attractiveness of "slim" is emphasised visually by the man dancing (with his eyes closed) after his partner has left the dance floor, with his hands still "holding" the absent partner, thus forming the shape of a slim waist. The slim waistline is also suggested graphically by curved lines on the packaging. The attractiveness of the product is, thus, visually connected to the attractiveness of the slim figure as an ideal.

Considerations of fat types and a nutritionally balanced diet persist as a theme in the 1990s, now with statements indicating that the product is free from unhealthy trans-fatty acids (such messages are identified in the sample from 1995). Several margarine advertisements specify the type of plant oils, such as sunflower oil or rapeseed oil. In an Alfa advertisement from November 1995, the natural origin is illustrated by a picture of a rapeseed field in bloom and a blue sky with the headline: "Health from the yellow fields." The absence of animal fats is accentuated in an AMA margarine advertisement, also from November 1995, with a large bouquet of sunflowers and a copy assuring that the margarine "contains no animal fats, only pure oil from sunflower oil and other plants. For that reason, it is rich on the important poly- and monounsaturated fats, whereas it is totally free from trans fatty acids."

Children's nutrition is a recurrent theme in print advertisements from the 1990s, especially in relation to dairy products. In a Danish Dairies milk advertisement from December 1998, parents' responsibility for ensuring children's intake of calcium is addressed: "Milk is one of the best sources of calcium and with ½ litre every day you can be sure that your child will have sufficient calcium." This is repeated in television commercials from the 1990s and 2000s as general advice. For example, in a 2000 MD Foods television commercial, an adult character watching cartoons is interrupted by an off-screen voice teaching him "that you need calcium – also as an adult," but that low-fat milk is recommended.

However, references to science in the advertisements from the 2000s are dominated by messages regarding fat types and cholesterol. In a print advertisement for Benecol, published in November 2000, in which parts of the written text are censored, the reader is urged to "fill in the blanks" and guess what the plant-based spread "lowers." By referring to an impersonal authority in terms of regulations regarding health claims in marketing, the advertisement claims that the product is "healthier than allowed by the law." Furthermore, it indicates theoretical rationalisation by stating that "the effect is documented in more than 30 clinical studies" (Benecol, 2000). Other advertisements are more explicit. For example, in a Becel advertisement from November 2003a, it is argued that the promoted spread "contains plant sterols which are documented to be able to lower the level of cholesterol." Yet, it is also pointed out that the spread should be part of healthy dietary habits to show effect. While "documentation" in this advertisement is represented as an abstract idea, other advertisements "document" by means of testimonials and graphs on the screen. Moreover, in a 2003b Becel television commercial, the effect of plant sterols is emphasised both in written and spoken words as "scientifically proven," and the lowering of cholesterol is illustrated by a slice of bread with spread on which a downward-sloping curve is drawn with a knife as the curve turns red. The shift of the curve from "spread" to red indicates something worthy of attention. At the same time, everyday food intake is visually connected to "science" by imitating its techniques of representation.

Connections between dietary habits and cholesterol are also represented in narratives of a value-based cultural clash. In a 2001 Becel television commercial, "Danish people" are introduced by a voiceover as "having a relaxed relationship to health and things like that." The statement is illustrated by a Christmas lunch with people eating plates of fatty food, while exclaiming food-related clichés, such as "there is plenty more where that came from." As opposed to "the typical Danes," some "dissidents" among the Danes are introduced. The voiceover presents the "dissidents" as those who use the advertised low-fat spread "not to increase their cholesterol level" and claims that the "behaviour of the dissidents is very provocative." This is illustrated by a scene in a supermarket with a woman trying to hide the product she just took down from the shelf while being addressed by another customer as a "weak eater." The "dissidents" must, therefore, meet secretly to eat healthy. The use of humour by means of contrast and exaggeration also shows in a 2009 Milda television commercial with a more explicit focus on the content of fat types. The contrast is here established in a more positive way as the commercial portrays a family who use liquid margarine with "unsaturated fat and omega 3 and 6" as smarter than their neighbours who have bought enormous quantities of fish to obtain the same nutrients (thus seemingly also being aware of nutrition and fat types, unlike the "typical Danes" mentioned above).

Representations of plant-based drinks from Naturli' in the advertisements from the 2000s share features with the themes identified in the plant-based drink advertisements from the 1990s, and declarations such as "free from cholesterol" and "no trans-fatty acids" identified in other product categories also appear here. For example, it is claimed that "25g soya protein per day can lower your cholesterol – establish American and British health authorities" (Naturli', February 2005). However, a new attribute is the emphasis on plant-based drinks as "green." In advertisements from 2002, plant-based drinks are articulated as "green milk" and "nature's green alternative to cow's milk" (Naturli', February 2002a), and the consumer is encouraged to "choose green" (Naturli', September 2002b). The meaning of the "evaluative adjective" (van Leeuwen, 2017:227) "green" is both related to the provenance from plants and environmental considerations. In this regard, consuming plant-based products is a choice "for everyone who does not tolerate or does not want cow's milk and those who want to live a healthy life" (Naturli', February 2002a). Choosing "green" is furthermore connected to descriptions of the product as "more than a drink – it is a lifestyle" (Naturli', February 2002a). Besides health, this lifestyle is explained to involve care of nature's resources, as well as animal welfare. However, nature and environmental care are visually most prevalent, for example, in a March 2009 advertisement with images of green leaves with drops of water and the globe with a huge green sprout, and in a March 2010 advertisement entitled "You and the Earth" with an image of plant-based drink packaging imprinted with the globe and a sprout on the side (see Figure 2.2). In these advertisements, global responsibility is motivated by bullet points (connoting rationality) with "facts" regarding environmental benefits of the green lifestyle. The advertisement from 2010 asks consumers: "Did you know that production of vegetable protein means: 5 x less use of cultivated areas, 10 x less use of water, 4 x less CO_2 emission?" Although it is not explained what "less" is to be compared to, vegetable protein production is provided with an idea of "better." Healthy lifestyles are, in this way, not only a matter of bodily health but are closely related to an individual's responsibility for nature and climate. The choice of plant-based products is articulated as "your contribution to a sustainable world" (Naturli', 2009).

In the collected material from the 2010s, a certain fatigue or confusion towards the abundance of messages claiming health benefits is suggested. In a 2011 Becel television commercial promoting margarine with "a high natural

Figure 2.2 2010 Advertisement from Naturli'

Credit: Published in *Samvirke*, March 2010, p. 27. Reproduced with permission.

level of unsaturated fatty acids and omega 3," a humorous sketch with two comedians includes the question "is it also good for the ears?" Reference to the abundance of messages about health explicitly shows in a 2019 Arla television commercial pointing at "the many truths out there." The point is illustrated by a scene with schoolchildren having lunch as they comment on what they eat, for example, referring to a glass of milk, "Do you really want to drink that?" (Arla, 2019). The "many truths" here imply reference to a conflicting discursive field including scientific, pseudo-scientific and non-scientific claims about what is "good" to eat and drink.

Conclusion

As demonstrated in the analysis, ways of reasoning "good" dairy products and plant-based alternatives have changed over time. In the 1930s, 1940s and 1950s, references to science were linked to hygienic measures and bacteriology, with advertisements addressing the fear of contamination by unclean food. Nutritional arguments were also prevalent in references to scientific knowledge about vitamins and disease prevention established at the beginning of the twentieth century (Scrinis, 2013). From the 1960s onwards, the emphasis on hygiene as a marketing message gradually disappeared; instead, control became oriented towards declaration of content. In Denmark, a declaration board was established in 1957 (Nyvang, 2022) around the same time that fat types and health effects came into focus in nutrition science and turned up as marketing messages in favour of vegetable margarine. In response, butter advertisements pointed at value systems of "good taste" and "good food habits"—values that have a long history in the "class conflict" between margarine and butter (cf. O'Hagan, 2023). Likewise, milk was articulated as "simply good," but turned up in low-fat variants, hence meeting contemporary dietary advice on reducing the intake of fats. Slimness started to appear in advertisements as a dominant message from the early 1970s, thereby ascribing "good" products not only to nutritional values but also to meanings related to the "ideal" body. However, over time, slimness disappeared as a marketing message and ethical concerns related to the environment became more prevalent. In the 1990s, advertisements for organic dairy products and plant-based drinks represented a new kind of value-based consumption in which individual health and healthy lifestyles are linked to environmental responsibility, hereby involving references to systems of knowledge beyond nutrition. In the plant-based advertisements, climate considerations are also expressed, indicating an early example of an area of concern which has become a focus area across product categories and industries today.

By considering the rationale underlying the multimodal strategies involved in promoting "good" dairy products and plant-based alternatives from a historical perspective, it becomes possible to understand current meaning patterns related to food and drink marketing which otherwise may be considered as "new." Marketing messages such as "light," "plant-based" and "green" all have historical meaning potentials and should be considered as interacting with other prevailing value systems at given times.

Notes

1 This approach follows a definition of health as both "physical, mental and social well-being" (World Health Organization, 2020:1).
2 All translations have been carried out by the author.

References

"46 Margarine." 1946a. *Samvirke* (August, issue 3), 16.

"46 Margarine." 1946b. *Samvirke* (September, issue 2), 12.

"Alfa." 1995. *Samvirke* (November), 36.

"AMA." 1995. *Samvirke* (November), 64.

Arla. 2019. *Der er mange sandheder derude* (29 secs). [Television advertisement], Royal Danish Library's media collections.

Atkins, P.J. 2005. Fattening Children or Fattening Farmers? School Milk in Britain, 1921–1941. *Economic History Review* 58(1):57–78.

Becel. 2001. *Danskerne* (45 secs). [Television advertisement], Royal Danish Library's media collections.

"Becel." 2003a. *Samvirke* (November), 65.

Becel. 2003b. *Becel Pro Active* (30 secs). [Television advertisement], Royal Danish Library's media collections.

Becel. 2011. *Becel* (14 secs). [Television advertisement], Royal Danish Library's media collections.

Bellis. 1965. *Sæt det sunde i centrum* (29 secs). [Cinema advertisement], Royal Danish Library's media collections.
Bellis. 1968. *Gi' Deres børn en mundfuld sol, gi' dem Bellis plantemargarine* (26 secs). [Cinema advertisement], Royal Danish Library's media collections.
"Benecol." 2000. *Samvirke* (November), 51.
Berg, B.Å. 2013. "Margarine – A Scapegoat Milked by Many Maids. A Brief History of Margarine in Sweden with an International Background" in *From Local Champions to Global Players. Essays on the History of the Dairy Sector*, edited by P. Rytkönen, L.A.G. Hernandez and U. Jonsson (Stockholm: Stockholm Studies in Economic History 61), pp. 95–110.
"Brugsen." 1983a. *Samvirke* (March), 54.
"Brugsen." 1983b. *Samvirke* (August), 54.
"Brugsen Diætmargarine." 1982. *Samvirke* (September), 64.
"Brugsen Diætmargarine." 1984. *Samvirke* (September), 64.
"Brugsen Minarine." 1984. *Samvirke* (January), 56.
"Brugsen Minarine." 1985. *Samvirke* (September), 88.
Coop. 2022. Madpyramiden. Available at https://madpyramiden.dk/ (Accessed: 8 January 2024).
"Danish Dairies." 1983. *Samvirke* (September), 48–49.
Danish Dairies. 1984. *Karoline* (40 secs). [Cinema advertisement], Royal Danish Library's media collections.
Danish Dairies. 1988a. *Mælk* (15 secs). [Television advertisement], Royal Danish Library's media collections.
Danish Dairies. 1988b. *Mælk* (15 secs). [Television advertisement], Royal Danish Library's media collections.
"Danish Dairies." 1998. *Samvirke* (December), 50–51.
"F.D.B." 1973a. *Samvirke* (April), 40.
"F.D.B." 1973b. *Samvirke* (May), 40.
"F.D.B. Plantemargarine." 1972. *Samvirke* (September, issue 1), 32.
Fuentes, C. and Fuentes, M. 2017. Making a Market for Alternatives: Marketing Devices and the Qualification of a Vegan Milk Substitute. *Journal of Marketing Management* 33(7–8):529–555.
Fødevarestyrelsen. 2023. Transfedtsyrer. Available at https://www.foedevarestyrelsen.dk/ (Accessed: 8 January 2024).
Gunter, B. 2016. *Food Advertising: Nature, Impact and Regulation*. Cham: Springer International Publishing.
Hall, S. 1980. "Encoding/Decoding" in *Culture, Media, Language: Working Papers in Cultural Studies, 1972–79*, edited by S. Hall, D. Hobson, A. Lowe and P. Willis (London: Routledge), pp. 117–127.
Hand, J. 2017. Marketing Health Education: Advertising Margarine and Visualising Health in Britain from 1964–c.2000. *Contemporary British History* 31(4):477–500.
Höllerer, M. A., van Leeuwen, T., Jancsary, D., Meyer, R.E., Andersen, T. H. and Vaara, E. 2019. *Visual and Multimodal Research in Organization and Management Studies*. New York: Routledge.
Jallinoja, P., Jauho, M. and Mäkelä, J. 2016. Newspaper Debates on Milk Fats and Vegetable Oils in Finland, 1978–2013: An Analysis of Conflicts over Risks, Expertise, Evidence and Pleasure. *Appetite* 105:274–282.
Jensen, T. 2012. The Consumption of Fats in Denmark 1900–2000, *Anthropology of Food* S7, https://doi.org/10.4000/aof.7100
Jönsson, H. 2005. *Mjölk – en kulturanalys av mejeridiskens nya ekonomi*. Stockholm: Brutus Östlings Bokförlag Symposion.
Kress, G. and van Leeuwen, T. 2021. *Reading Images: The Grammar of Visual Design*. London: Routledge.

Kulturministeriet 2021. Mediernes udvikling i Danmark. Magasiner og ugeblade 2021. Available at https://mediernesudvikling.kum.dk/2021/ (Accessed: 8 January 2024).
Lätta. 1988. *Beach* (30 secs). [Television advertisement], Royal Danish Library's media collections.
"Lätta." 1991. *Samvirke* (September), 78.
Leiss, W., Kline, S., Jhally, S., Botterill, J. and Asquith, K. 2018. *Social Communication in Advertising*. New York: Routledge.
Levene, A. 2014. The Meanings of Margarine in England: Class, Consumption and Material Culture from 1918 to 1953. *Contemporary British History* 28(2):145–165.
Lieffers, C. 2015. "A Wholesome Article of Food": Rhetoric of Health and Nation in Canada's Oleomargarine Debates, 1917–1924. *Canadian Bulletin of Medical History* 32(2):337–362.
"Lurpak/Danish Dairies." 1970a. *Samvirke* (February, issue 2), 3.
"Lurpak/Danish Dairies." 1970b. *Samvirke* (March, issue 2), 3.
Martiin, C. 2010. Swedish Milk, a Swedish Duty: Dairy Marketing in the 1920s and 1930s. *Rural History* 21(2):213–232.
MD Foods. 1991. *Cheasy* (35 secs). [Television advertisement], Royal Danish Library's media collections.
MD Foods. 2000. *Husk mælken* (35 secs). [Television advertisement], Royal Danish Library's media collections.
Milda. 2009. *Milda margarine* (25 secs). [Television advertisement], Royal Danish Library's media collections.
"Natura." 1982. *Samvirke* (May), 26.
"Naturli'." 1990a. *Samvirke* (January/February), 27.
"Naturli'." 1990b. *Samvirke* (September), 55.
"Naturli'." 1991. *Samvirke* (June/July), 27.
"Naturli'." 1995. *Samvirke* (June/July), 15.
"Naturli'." 1998. *Samvirke* (September), 64.
"Naturli'." 2002a. *Samvirke* (February), 91.
"Naturli'." 2002b. *Samvirke* (September), 94.
"Naturli'." 2005. *Samvirke* (February), 51.
"Naturli'." 2009. *Samvirke* (March), 65.
"Naturli'." 2010. *Samvirke* (March), 27.
Nordic Council of Ministers. 2023. *Nordic Nutrition Recommendations 2023. Integrating Environmental Aspects*. Available at https://pub.norden.org/nord2023-003/ (Accessed: 8 January 2024).
Nyvang, C. 2022. *Stegt flæsk med persillesovs. 100 danmarkshistorier*. Aarhus: Aarhus Universitetsforlag.
O'Hagan, L.A. 2022. Selling Swedish Summer: The Marketing of Pommac, 1920–1960. *History of Retailing and Consumption* 8(2):171–199.
O'Hagan, L.A. 2023 "Classifying" Margarine: The Early Class-Based Marketing of a Butter Substitute in Sweden (1923–1933). *Global Food History* 9(1):20–46.
O'Hagan, L.A. and Eriksson, G. 2022. Modern Science, Moral Mothers, and Mythical Nature: A Multimodal Analysis of Cod Liver Oil Marketing in Sweden, 1920–1930. *Food and Foodways* 30(4):231–260.
"PAN." 1987. *Samvirke* (November), 70.
"PAN/Trekroner." 1931. *Brugsforenings-Bladet* (September, issue 2), 436.
Pantzar, M. 1995. Public Dialogue Between Butter and Margarine in Finland 1923–1992. *Journal of Consumer Studies and Home Economics* 19(1):11–24.
Pitrelli, N., Manzoli, F. and Montolli, B. 2006. Science in Advertising: Uses and Consumptions in the Italian Press. *Public Understanding of Science* 15(2):207–220.
Prell, H., Palmblad, E., Lissner, L. and Berg, C.M. 2011. Health Discourse in Swedish Television Food Advertising During Children's Peak Viewing Times. *Appetite* 56(3):607–616.

Rasmussen, J.D. 1982. "Dansk mejeribrug 1914–55" in *Dansk mejeribrug 1882–2000*, edited by C. Bjørn (Odense: De Danske Mejeriers Fællesorganisation), pp. 189–308.
Ring, V. 1932. Lidt om Margarine og Margarinefabrikation. *Brugsforenings-Bladet* 9(2):442–444.
Ring, V. 1935. Behandlingen af Bakterier og andre Mikroorganismer. Om Levnedsmidler – og specielt Margarines – bakteriologiske Forhold. *Brugsforenings-Bladet* 5(2):240–242.
Scrinis, G. 2013. *Nutritionism. The Science and Politics of Dietary Advice*. New York: Columbia University Press.
Smith-Howard, K. 2013. *Pure and Modern Milk: An Environmental History Since 1900*. New York: Oxford University Press.
Strandskov, J., Sørensen, P. and Pedersen, K. 1998. *Pioneren Otto Mønsted – Sig navnet…* Aarhus: Systime.
Thorning, T.K., Raben, A., Tholstrup, T., Soedamah-Muthu, S.S., Givens, I. and Astrup, A. 2016. Milk and Dairy Products: Good or Bad for Human Health? An Assessment of the Totality of Scientific Evidence, *Food & Nutrition Research* 60(1), https://doi.org/10.3402%2Ffnr.v60.32527
"Trekroner." 1949a. *Samvirke* (July, issue 1), 16.
"Trekroner." 1949b. *Samvirke* (September, issue 1), 16.
"Trekroner." 1969. *Samvirke* (December, issue 1), 40.
Valenze, D.M. 2011. *Milk: A Local and Global History*. New Haven: Yale University Press.
van Leeuwen, T. 2005. *Introducing Social Semiotics*. London: Routledge.
van Leeuwen, T. 2017. "Legitimation and Multimodality" in *The Routledge Handbook of Language and Politics*, edited by R. Wodak and B. Forchtner (New York: Routledge), pp. 218–232.
Wharton, C. 2013. "Spreads Like Butter – Culture and Advertising" in *Advertising as Culture*, edited by C. Wharton (Bristol: Intellect), pp. 53–79.
Wilken, L. and Knudsen, A.C.L. 2008. Milk, Myth and Magic: The Social Construction of Identities, Banalities and Trivialities in Everyday Europe. *Kontur* 17:33–41.
World Health Organization. 2020. *Basic Documents* (49th ed.). Geneva: World Health Organization.
Zwier, S. 2009. Medicalisation of Food Advertising. Nutrition and Health Claims in Magazine Food Advertisements 1990–2008. *Appetite* 53(1):109–113.

3 Consumer Activism, Ultra-Processed Food Marketing and the Meaning of Healthy Eating in Mexico

A Diachronic Study

Pilar Zazueta

Introduction

Since the mid-twentieth century, public debates in Mexico about ultra-processed foods (UPFs) have been characterised by suspicion and ambivalence, not only of the products and producers themselves but also of the claims and methods of marketing. Popularly known as "junk food," UPFs are industrialised formulations of whole foods or organic substances that tend to have high contents of salt, sugar and fats, and lack fibre, proteins and micronutrients.[1] The majority of UPF companies in the country are foreign or franchises, which has also contributed to the belief that their actions are not necessarily in the best interests of local consumers, but rather in the bottom-line of investors who live abroad. Companies and state actors have equated UPFs to "the progress of civilisation" and in opposition to peasant lifestyles.

Historian Julio Moreno (2003) has identified a key feature of popular and commercial visual culture in mid-century Mexico: an interplay and tension between "scientific knowledge," coded as foreign, modern and artificial, and "traditional knowledge," coded as natural, local and ancient. The advertising industry in Mexico has used these two ideas to promote different products since the start of the post-revolutionary period in the 1930s. The case of food marketing is particularly interesting because diets and food customs have been a central part of Mexican nationalist discourses since the twentieth century. It is through cuisine and food that the government, business interests, the media and the artistic community have "sold" Mexico as a tourist attraction with a unique cultural heritage (Pilcher, 2010). Moreover, the Mexican government has played a central role in the food system in general (intervening in the production, distribution, marketing and sales of staple foods) and has funded research in nutritional sciences in order to make claims and promote ideas about what a healthy diet and lifestyle means. Just like food companies and advertisers, the government and public health activists selectively utilised and emphasised the discourses of "scientific knowledge" and "traditional knowledge" to pursue different policy goals depending on political circumstances.

In this chapter, I will examine the interactions between government officials, health experts and transnational companies that have set the terms about what

DOI: 10.4324/9781003450276-6

constitutes "healthy eating" in Mexico and how these interactions have shaped messages in commercial advertisements, as well as public advocacy campaigns. The first section is about the influence of colonial social hierarchies and nineteenth-century modernisation discourses on ideas about food and nutrition in Mexico. In the second section, I explain the changes in the food industry and advertisements in the twentieth century. It was during this period of import substitution industrialisation (ISI) when companies such as Bimbo, which manufactured boxed bread and pastries, were founded, and the sugar industry and transnational soft drink companies began to expand their market. Then, I analyse state-sponsored public awareness campaigns designed to inform consumers about "junk food" advertisements during the late 1970s and late 1980s. Finally, in the last section, I trace the transformation of UPF marketing after the passage of the North American Trade Agreement (NAFTA) in 1994 and NGO-based activism to reform the advertising and sales of these products. Activists and public health authorities focused on using messages about healthy eating and nutritional sciences to counter the marketing strategies of companies such as Kellogg's (sugary breakfast cereals and other ultra-processed grain-based products). Kellogg's, in turn, tried to improve their public image by funding nutritional research and incorporating new ingredients, such as "ancient grains," into their formulations.

Contextualising Ideas about Food and Nutrition in Mexico

In Mexico, debates and tensions about what is a good and healthy diet have been present since the earliest stages of colonisation by Europeans (Earle, 2012). Since Europeans were at the top of social hierarchies for more than 300 years, their foods were coded in society as civilised and prestigious. After Latin American nations became independent in the 1820s, the existing class and racial hierarchies were disrupted, but not totally overturned. Nineteenth-century scientific discourses asserted that European staple foods were healthier than the staple foods from other parts of the world. Post-independence elites, mostly Mexican *criollos* (descendants of Europeans born in the Americas) or *mestizos* (descendants of Europeans and Indigenous people) aimed to "modernise" the lifestyles of the "poor" mostly rural populations through urbanisation, industrialisation or the expansion of new forms of wage labour (Pilcher, 1998).[2] During this century, the majority of the Mexican population was rural subsistence farmers who cultivated mostly corn, beans and complementary vegetables like squash and tomatoes. Mexican intellectuals, scientists and doctors disseminated the idea that a better diet would improve health, longevity and work performance. Experts considered animal proteins as "protective" and qualitatively better than the vegetarian rural diet (Aguilar-Rodríguez, 2007).

However, it was not until the twentieth century, in part as a consequence of the Mexican Revolution (1910s to the late 1940s), that the state was able to substantially intervene in the food market. As the country descended into civil war, food production and consumption became matters of military and political strategy, as different political factions created bureaucracies to maintain the supply of staple foods to the cities (Ochoa, 2000). The authoritarian single-party system that emerged after the Revolution did not dismantle these bureaucracies, but rather reformed them with different goals in mind: subsidising workers' salaries as part of an ISI strategy through the control of the prices of staple foods in urban centres.

Before the 1930s, public officials did not produce any systematic and rigorous assessments to prove their claims that traditional Mexican peasant diets were inferior. With the consolidation of the post-revolutionary state, government institutions started using clinical trials to study diets (Baz, 1942:270–271), but not to make new discoveries or challenge the status quo. For state officials, any publicly funded research had to be prescriptive; in other words, experts had to recommend changes to the diet, not determine whether these changes were necessary. The state founded a National Institute of Nutrition (NIN) in the 1940s[3] and, in that same decade, began to invest in healthcare and social security. Federico Gómez, a pioneer in the treatment and diagnostics of malnourished children, was a central figure in Mexico's new public hospital system. Gómez published one of the most influential studies in Latin American paediatrics in 1946 in which he defined malnutrition as the deficient assimilation of food by the organism, which led to a pathological state of different degrees of gravity and diverse clinical manifestations. Gómez's landmark contributions were the use of an anthropometric measure (weight-for-age) and the classification of patients into three groups according to severity (de Onis, 2000).

Policymakers in the food state bureaucracies and the healthcare system used the research of the NIN and the Gómez classification to argue for the need to continue intervening in the food market, particularly subsidising staple foods. One of the most important claims was that most low-income Mexicans, particularly children, suffered from second-degree malnutrition according to the Gómez classification. The general goals of the state agencies and nutritional research in Mexico were to support the work of food distribution agencies, which changed names over time but were consolidated in the 1960s as the National Company of Popular Subsistence (CONASUPO) (Ochoa, 2000). Through the media and official communications, the government insisted on the importance of eradicating child malnutrition and supplying the cities with enough food in order to support industrialisation and economic development (Zazueta, 2021).

The Post-Revolutionary State, Advertisements and Food Companies

The use of commercial advertisements to sell food products is a relatively recent development in Mexico. Given that before the 1910 Revolution most people were illiterate or semi-literate, product sales were carried out with eye-catching signs and street billboards. Elite newspapers and the penny press included almost no advertisements for food and drinks, other than imported alcohol (Bunker, 2012). The advertisement sector began to thrive after the 1930s, with the implementation of ISI.

While the state and local industrialists exalted nationalist sentiments in the economic sphere, they also cultivated a close relationship with their powerful neighbour, the United States. Julio Moreno (2003:12) explains how pioneering US advertising companies established themselves in Mexico during the 1930s and 1940s and radically changed the sector:

> advertising agents defined themselves as 'prophets of capitalism' who supported Mexico's prosperity by generating economic growth that would raise the standard of living for Mexicans [...] Yet advertising agents also endorsed the nationalist and social democratic ideals of the Mexican Revolution.

A good example of the interrelationship between government action and marketing strategies adopted from the United States is the case of the baked goods company Bimbo. In post-revolutionary Mexico, bread production monopolies—controlled by Spaniards and aided by state policies—consolidated in several cities. For example, from 1934 to 1940, the national government helped larger bakeries in Mexico City "to repress competition" (Weis, 2012:152), mainly by outlawing smaller bakeries whose workers could not join state-sponsored unions. The state also allowed large bakeries to divert the use of state-subsidised flour for the manufacture of cheap loaves of bread (*bolillos*) to other products such as pastries, which were not subject to price controls (Weis, 2012).

Bimbo's history begins when founding partner Lorenzo Servitje inherited the pastry shop *El Molino* (founded in 1928) from his father, a Catalan immigrant. The idea behind Bimbo was to recreate the way bread was sold in the United States by packaging it in a box or plastic bag and modifying the recipe to make it last longer. Bimbo's owners learnt about the new bread production techniques through specialised magazines and trips abroad (Cherem, 2016). In 1954, Bimbo created the Keik brand (renamed Marinela in 1957) to manufacture industrialised pastries, also in the American style, inspired by the famous "twinkies" (in Mexico called *gansitos*) (Andrade, 2017).

Bimbo's partners were the creative force behind its best spokesperson: the Bimbo bear—a white bear with a hat and baker's utensils. Several scholars in Europe and North America have studied how mascots can help create brand recognition and loyalty and quickly convey complex ideas and messages to the public. Brand mascots can even function as "agents of social empowerment" as they tend to symbolise the efficiency and democratising effect of mass production to fulfil consumer needs and desires (Hornsey, 2018). In the case of Bimbo, the bear tied the brand to concepts of whiteness and purity, associated with white bread since colonial times in Mexico. It was also a way of leaving behind the unwanted racial and class connotations of the other bread: that of the Spanish bakeries, which were demonised by the press and the public as late as the 1940s (Weis, 2012). The baker's bear, on the other hand, represented boxed bread—an accessible, hygienic and practical product for the urban middle and popular classes that aspired to be modern and consume American products. According to Servitje (cited in Cherem, 2016), the idea of the bear, but also the company's name Bimbo, was to be associated with the tenderness of childhood, as the products were going to be intentionally marketed to children. Later in the chapter, I explain how the government's consumer agency, as well as civil society organisations, took advantage of the identification between the brands and their mascots. Just as the brands could construct an image of mascots as friendly to children, the state and health activists could claim the opposite: mascots were "trojan horses" working purely on behalf of the companies' commercial interests.

Servitje emphasised the importance of advertising for the company's business plan. Before opening their first factory, the partners consulted a North American soft drink company's manual (Cherem, 2016:83). Servitje then transferred successful formulas from the soft drink industry to bread. In Servitje's own words (Cherem, 2016:88):

> In the bakery industry, advertising or promotional campaigns were hardly ever used. Our success was to have thought of them as a fundamental tool from the beginning [...] we flooded radio, cinema, and press [...] two full pages were paid for in *Excélsior* [wide circulation Mexican newspaper], in the cinema newscasts we featured inauguration [of the factory].

According to the Bimbo manual, salespeople had to emphasise the freshness of the product and the importance of boxed bread for nutrition to the owner or store manager and their staff (Cherem, 2016:407).

Sugar producers, and later soft drink companies, also made claims linking their products to modernity, hygiene and nutritional sciences. Since the end of the Revolution, the sugar industry was subsidised mostly due to political reasons. Sugar production tended to be localised in the areas where the most radical revolutionary peasants, the *Zapatistas*, were dominant. Large plantation owners lost their property through land reform, but some managed to retain their sugar mills (Singleman, 1993:68). In 1938, the mill owners organised under a collective name, National Union of Sugar Producers (UNPASA), and backed by state loans, would become the sole suppliers of sugar to the country. The cane producers became dependent on the mills "for credits for sowing and cultivation, and for fertilizers, irrigation, and transportation" (Kaufman Purcell, 1981:215). During the Second World War, when most staple foods were scarce, sugar retained its value and, in the following years, it remained a very important commodity, which Mexico used to maintain favourable terms of trade. In the war years, UNPASA publicised its role as a productive sector of the Mexican economy that maintained fair prices. The organisation started an advertising campaign promoting sugar as a healthy and nutritious food and celebrating its consumption.

An UNPASA advertisement published in 1940 in *Revista Hoy* made the following claims:

> The Mexican people have sensibly increased their sugar consumption since the year 1939. The most important factor is that a small volume of sugar provides energy and resistance. It also has a very agreeable flavour. It is also the cheapest food out there thanks to the efforts of UNPASA. Before, sugar was a luxury product, but now it is a product of common and current use.

Production of sugar increased in the 1950s and mill owners used advertisements to promote messages about the nutritional qualities of sugar to expand sales. During this decade, there was no generalised public discussion about the downsides of eating too many sweets. An article published in the Medicine section of the national newspaper *El Universal* on 13 June 1954 summarised some of the nutritional information circulating at the time:[4] "is refined sugar, which is the source of most of our [Mexico's] carbohydrate consumption, bad for your health? This is a very complex question. There is some evidence that yes, it could have noxious effects, but research is still needed." The article advocated avoiding excessive consumption to prevent tooth cavities and diabetes (in older age), but such recommendations for moderation were no match for the government's and the sugar producers' economic and political interests in maintaining high internal sugar consumption.

In the mid-1950s, UNPASA's advertisements depicted workers, athletes, Indigenous people and housewives eating or drinking foods or drinks prepared with sugar. For example, an advertisement, published in *Revista Hoy*, featured an industrial worker and claimed the following: "He needs sugar. Industrial labourers' work capacity results in increasing production. The tired worker produces less. The worker conquers his fatigue with sugar. That is why sweetened beverages should never be absent in the workshop or the factory." The same advertisement also claimed that sugar "did not make you fat" (UNPASA, 1955). A decade later in 1969, an UNPASA advertisement (Figure 3.1) in *Boletín Azucarero Mexicano* featured a black and white photograph of a young Mexican boy flexing his bicep muscle, which stated:

> He wants to grow up. He wants to be strong, have energy. And it is not difficult from him to achieve it. Sugar gives you '*fibra*'. It is tasty and cheap. In no other country is it as cheap as in Mexico. Give your son energy and happiness, give him sugar.

The word *fibra* in twentieth-century Mexican working-class slang means effort or physical strength, as it is a reference to muscle fibres, not dietary fibres. The advertisement uses this second meaning of the word and local observers are meant to understand this by the quotation marks around the word and by looking at the image of the boy flexing his arm.

Figure 3.1 The Best and Cheapest Sugar in the World (UNPASA)

Credit: Unión Nacional de Productores de Azúcar (Mexico), *Boletín azucarero mexicano*, August 1969, p. 47.

The soft drink industry benefitted second-hand from UNPASA's promotion of refined sugar and used marketing to insist on the safety of their products. In Mexico, like in the United States and Europe, food and beverage companies used "purity" as a rhetorical device. Purity means cleanliness, but also transparency, accountability, reliability and even spiritual probity (Petrick, 2011; O'Hagan, 2020). Soft drinks became an attractive investment in Mexico since large sectors of the public believed that these products were cleaner than tap water. Long articles with photographs of soft drink plants and how they operated appeared in national newspapers, with the purpose of showing that the water taken from the municipal system and used in the plants was filtered and disinfected (Ruiz Sandoval, 1959). The message was that soft drink companies, not the municipal water supply, were the ones that provided Mexicans with a reliably clean product. Famously, the slogan of one of the oldest soft drink companies in Mexico, Sidral-Mundet, was "pasteurized and healthy" (Mundet, 1974).

Many advertisements for UPFs (1950s–1970s) focused on children and parents. Given the government's own efforts to promote nutritional research in the service of improving the diets of children and eradicating malnutrition, processed food producers capitalised on these ideas to sell their own products. For example, a Bimbo print advertisement from 1973 featured a black and white photograph of a dark-haired schoolboy happily relaxing near a stream: "Bimbo will be next to the wonder of being a kid. Bimbo bread, enriched with milk, sugar, vitamins, minerals and proteins. The happy years are even happier, with good nourishing food like Bimbo Bread." Given public anxieties about malnutrition and hunger, Bimbo communicated a message of safety, even in the face of economic hardship. In a similar fashion to the UNPASA sugar advertisement from 1969, the Bimbo advertisement stated that boxed bread was part of a happy childhood experience. As Eileen Ford (2016) has argued, the Mexican print media (1940s–1960s) regularly featured photographs of children that portrayed "both extreme poverty and idealized middle-class childhood," contributing "to the ideological opening of modern childhood as an ideal for which Mexicans, both as parents and as citizens, should strive" (128). The black and white photographs of children in the UNPASA and Bimbo advertisements were part of these representations of an aspirational childhood. The texts that explained the nutritional benefits of eating sugar and bread were used to tell parents that they could access this middle-class life for their children.

Nutrition, Health and State-Led Consumer Activism (1976–1983)

In the late 1970s, the government started taking a more critical stance towards private UPF companies, the advertising industry and consumerism in general. The reason behind this new posture was that the economic model was failing to produce sustained GPD growth without inflation. Officials at the Ministry of the Treasury were worried that Mexico had been rapidly accumulating foreign debt and thought that, in order to maintain growth, they had to do something to control consumption, especially upper- and middle-class consumption patterns. Miguel de la Madrid, Under Secretary of the Treasury (who later became President in 1983), criticised "unnecessary consumption and lifestyles incongruent with reality" because, "given the need of the great majorities," this consumption not only provoked "social irritation but it also affected savings" (de Cervantes, 1976:5). Government officials thought that working-class consumption, especially food consumption, could be optimised and rationalised, making the working class better off. Additional political motivations behind implementing consumer protection policies were to curb the unrest provoked by growing inflation and to address union demands.

In 1976, the government created two new public agencies to protect consumers. The first was the National Consumer Institute (INCO)—a cabinet-level independent consumer protection agency with broad powers to intervene on consumers' behalf, conduct public information campaigns and enforce consumer regulation. The second was the Federal Consumer Protection Agency (PROFECO)—an organism that was to act as an arbiter in any dispute between individual consumers and individual producers or service providers. During the late 1970s and early 1980s, the INCO used radio, television and print media to promote the idea of responsible consumption among the Mexican public. For the government, a "good consumer" was "a person who thought about consumption according to a scale of needs," planned their expenses, spent less than they earned and had cash reserves (INCO, 1977:4).

The INCO positioned itself as a public advocate that would repeatedly uncover the artifice or manipulation of marketing and commercial advertising by providing reliable and expert information. INCO's communication materials often included quotes or interviews with experts, particularly scientists, nutritionists, doctors, economists and psychologists. The *Newspaper of the Consumer*, which was sold and distributed in government-run supermarkets and intended for low-income consumers, included numerous segments about healthy eating and wellness. The cover of the inaugural issue was an article about how soft drinks were "bad for your health and your wallet," featuring one of Mexico's most famous athletes: boxer Pipino Cuevas. Besides a statement from Cuevas saying that he ate healthy and never consumed soft drinks, the short article included quotes from a doctor and the head of the chemistry laboratory of a public university. The experts explained that Coca-Cola and other soft drinks were not healthy due to their high sugar content, as well as the presence of colourants and preservatives. Instead, the experts insisted that people should consume natural and homemade "*aguas frescas*" made with local fruits, which had the additional benefit of being cheaper than soft drinks (INCO, 1980c). These campaigns were an example of economic nationalism, but the INCO did not limit itself to criticising transnational and North American companies; they also critiqued local Mexican brands that produced UPFs and all types of consumer products.[5]

The INCO based their consumer education campaigns on the proposition that the cost per nutrient in industrialised foods tended to be higher. For example, a series of posters produced in a collaboration between the consumer agency, food distribution agency and the National Labor Congress (a confederation of workers' unions) incited consumers to "compare before buying" and repeated the message that natural products were better and cheaper than industrialised ones (Figure 3.2). The white bold print at the top of the poster draws the eye to the main message: that consumers had to consider their options. It compares two products: homemade juices made with fruit and industrialised soft drinks. On the "natural" side, the fruits are arranged neatly on a tray accompanied by a pitcher of *agua de Jamaica* (a drink made out of

Figure 3.2 Compare before Buying (INCO, Mexican Labor Congress, CONASUPO, 1980d)

Credit: National Library of Medicine

hibiscus flowers and sugar). On the industrialised side, the soft drinks are also neatly organised, but in a way that highlights the different kinds of packaging, not the content. The words, images and colours work together to make the advertisement communicate impartiality, only providing the "facts" and inviting consumers to decide for themselves which products represent the more "rational" choice. These types of campaigns reflected the idea that consumers could "live with less" and still improve their nutrition.

The INCO used various "selling" techniques to connect with the audience, such as incorporating working-class slang, catchy songs and jingles and visuals from comic books and tabloids into their campaigns. The goal was to appeal to nationalism and working-class pride and instigate some adversarial feelings towards big corporations, both foreign and Mexican. Using surveys and interviews with the public, the INCO wanted to counter what they saw as the negative values behind advertising campaigns: promotion of consumerism, admiration for US culture in detriment to Mexican traditions and unrealistic expectations, as well as alienation from family and community (INCO, 1981c).

The way food advertisers targeted children became a point of bitter contention between the state and companies. Improving child nutrition had been a central preoccupation of public health authorities since the 1940s, but in the late 1970s, it acquired a new urgency. Researchers from the NIN were featured regularly in the media explaining that Mexican children were malnourished, and this was a threat to the nation's prospects (Zazueta, 2021). Thus, consumer agencies tried to sell healthy choices to parents by criticising advertisements targeting children. The INCO encouraged parents to tell their children that advertisements were "fairytales" which used cartoon characters or television personalities to sell junk food (INCO, 1980b). The children's newsletter, *El Brinco*, which was included for free with the *Revista del Consumidor*, encouraged children to save money and not spend it on junk food. *El Brinco* also featured interviews with the "cousins" of junk food mascots like *Gansito* (Bimbo's Little Goose). The "cousins" were equally cute, but ate fresh food instead of sugary snacks and warned children that, in the long run, *Gansito* "would end up fat" (INCO, 1982a, 1982b). The *Revista del Consumidor* also warned parents that the very popular television character *Mimoso Ratón* (Adorable Mouse) would "die of malnutrition" because he ate "junk food" all day (INCO, 1982c).

The INCO also emphasised the individual responsibility of parents as consumers. For example, Fernando Cesarman, a prominent psychology professor at the National University (UNAM) was quoted saying that the consumption of junk food "had a filicidal intention on the part of the parents" and that instead Mexicans had to eat their "true traditional food" (INCO, 1981d:5). Another feature in the magazine, called "Tribulations of a Complacent Mother," shot in the style of Mexico's popular *fotonovelas* (photo based comics with soap opera storylines), questioned the parenting decisions of working-class mothers. The "complacent mother" is depicted having a discussion with her bratty daughter who demands all kinds of junk food, repeats verbatim the lines of television advertisements and throws a tantrum when she does not get her way (Isabel, 1982).

The government's message became a partial reversal of previous forms of framing healthy eating in Mexico: now, it was the traditional Mexican crops and foods that were desirable, not the industrialised UPFs. Officials and health experts spoke publicly of destigmatising foods that were associated with the working class and Indigenous people (Zubirán, 1974). Through the INCO, the government—in alliance with workers' organisations—promoted the image of nutritional science experts standing with the working class against the foul play of big companies. The project was to highlight "real" Mexican food products in all their media campaigns, providing information about nutritional content, prices and forms of preparation (Navarro de Macias, 1988). The government criticised the strategy of transnational companies selling foods "with names in English" to sound "sophisticated." Instead of getting "carried away" with the idea that, for example, "*Kellogs Corn Flaics*" (which government documents intentionally misspelt to mimic local pronunciation) were healthy (INCO, 1980a), consumers were encouraged to learn about the nutritional properties of traditional Mexican crops and to use science to combine all of these foods for a healthy diet (INCO, 1981b).

In December 1981, the private sector responded and launched a critical campaign against INCO and its messages. The head of the Joint Chambers of Industry and Commerce, Jorge Chapa Salazar, attacked the consumer protection agencies, claiming that they were giving the public false information about food prices and were undermining the Mexican economy. The largest private television network *Televisa* aired a programme that featured the interview and attacked INCO's public education campaigns. The representatives of the private sector were particularly irked by the very popular jingle and advertisements featuring the song "Abelardo, Take Care of Your Year-End Bonus" and the slogan "give affection, don't buy it" (*PROFECO Retro*, 2009). Abelardo was a mascot (a lion), which was also featured in print advertisements alongside "health buddies": fruits, vegetables and milk (INCO, 1981a). Numerous columnists and commentators supported the work of INCO in national newspapers, sometimes citing research by the consumer protection agencies and the NIN to document the "terrible" eating habits of Mexicans and blaming the private sector and television for promoting these habits (Colmenares Páramo, 1982).

Pressure from industry, but mostly the economic crisis, ended up changing the government's priorities and the INCO ceased abruptly with its public awareness campaigns against the marketing of "junk food." The collapse of oil prices and the subsequent financial crisis of the early 1980s slashed government budgets and initiated a period of government austerity, privatisation and divestment from public services that lasts to this day. The NAFTA, which liberalised the markets in many sectors, including food and agriculture, accelerated the changes in the diets of the Mexican population towards even more reliance on UPFs (Gálvez, 2018).

Current Disputes about UPF Marketing and Advertising in Mexico (1999–2022)

Since the late 1990s, public health officials in Mexico have become increasingly alarmed about the obesity epidemic in the country. The publicly funded National Institute of Public Health (NIPH) had found that "increasing obesity prevalence trends in 1999–2006 were among the highest documented in the world" (Barquera et al., 2013). Between 2006 and 2012, obesity increased again, but at a lower rate, particularly among children and people living in poverty. Experts have called this phenomenon "the nutrition transition," which consists of a "reduced intake of legumes, coarse grains, and other vegetables," with increased access in developing countries to cheaper, processed foods that are high in fat, added sugar and salt (Popkin et al., 2012).

Growing obesity rates have catalysed a new form of activism, led by an alliance of NGOs, in particular one called *El Poder del Consumidor* (EPC), as well as individual health researchers, all of them represented under an umbrella organisation called the Alliance for Food Health. The alliance has focused on lobbying for a front-of-package labelling system for UPFs, the regulation of marketing of foods and drinks to children and adolescents and soft drinks taxes. At the same time, UPF companies, and the trade organisations that represent them, have pushed back, presenting a series of initiatives and marketing campaigns to shift the blame of the obesity epidemic from increased consumption of UPFs to lack of exercise, genetics and the consumption of "unhygienic" street foods (Gálvez, 2018; Sarmiento, 2020).

Some of the first actions by the EPC were to file complaints against different companies before PROFECO and the Ministry of Health. In 2007, the NGO presented the research and surveys conducted by the NIPH to demand that Kellogg's cease advertising its sugary breakfast cereals to children. The advertisement that caused the complaint featured mascot Tony the Tiger claiming that Frosted Flakes gave children energy to be healthy—the same message UNPASA had used in the past (Medina, 2007).

UPF companies in Mexico began to sponsor advertising campaigns and initiatives to counter the narrative presented by the EPC and their allies in the health sector. Kellogg's is a relevant case study because of how the company introduces health and wellness narratives into its advertisements, as well as its continuing efforts to fund nutritional research to improve its image. This company has had a presence in Mexico since the 1950s (Kellogg's, 2022), but experienced an unprecedented period of growth with the passage of the NAFTA in 1994.

The Mexican press has regularly published Kellogg's press releases about the health benefits of their products as news articles. For example, in 1999 as part of the launch of *VitaHierro*, a new iron supplement, the President of the National Association of Paediatrics served as a spokesman for the company and insisted that it was important to add "fortifiers to cereals." The doctor claimed this supplementation was absorbed "three or more times more than iron in other foods" (Uribe, 1999:19). Company-affiliated scientists and executives also talked to the press to "raise awareness" of the symptoms of anaemia and prevention of malnutrition (Lara, 1999). This strategy of recruiting experts for advertising purposes culminated in 2005 when the brand founded the Kellogg's Institute of Nutrition and Health (INK). Immediately, articles started appearing about how Kellogg's supported "scientific research in nutrition so that Mexicans have the tools to make better decisions regarding their health" (*Reforma*, 4 October 2012). The institute was officially inaugurated during a visit by Vicente Fox—the President at the time (2000–2006) and former corporate executive of Coca-Cola—to a Kellogg's plant in the state of Queretaro (Jiménez, 2006). For more than a decade, INK has funded the research of numerous scientists who focus on population health, child nutrition, anaemia and obesity at public and private universities (*Reforma*, 5 January 2010; *Reforma*, 29 September 2013).

Kellogg's also started appealing to "naturalness" and social responsibility through the adoption of new ingredients like "ancient grains." The hype about "ancient grains" had swept the North American markets in the late 1990s and early 2000s, making once-unknown products like quinoa popular in restaurants and as added ingredients in ultra-processed energy bars (Seligmann, 2023:157). In Mexico, many public universities trained scientists to specialise in research about regional crops with the intention of finding new industrial and commercial uses. In a compilation summarising all of this research for the general public entitled *Magical Foods of Indigenous Mesoamerican Cultures* (2006), plant scientists affirmed that corn, beans, amaranth and cactus leaves (nopales) could be classified as "nutraceuticals" (a neologism that combines the term nutrition and pharmaceutical) used not only to "nourish the body but to cure illnesses" (Paredes-López et al., 2006:6). The national press covered this research, in many cases publicising the health benefits of these "forgotten" Indigenous crops and the new uses scientists found for them (Aguilar, 2003; Paredes López, 2003).

Kellogg's had already been sourcing quinoa from the Andes and, based on this experience, started releasing products with amaranth—a crop identified with Indigenous Mesoamerican culture—as an added ingredient. One of the publicised health benefits of amaranth was its high amino acid (lysine) content, compared with other grains which, according to the press release, could "combat obesity and malnutrition" (Godoy, 2010:1). Kellogg's started buying amaranth from local producers and adding it to their breakfast cereals and energy bars (Martínez, 2009). Partnering with the amaranth producers also provided Kellogg's the opportunity to tell a different story about themselves, in particular in light of the growing criticisms by NGOs and the controversy of rising obesity rates in children and adults. The characterisation of these crops as "natural and healthy" and the emphasis on their "indigeneity" is part of a long history of using resources, such as foodstuffs, of colonised peoples or economically marginalised communities to benefit colonial settlers or "cure" diseases of high-income populations (Hobart and Maroney, 2019).

In the Mexican case, Kellogg's and the press publicised a story about one of the groups from which they sourced amaranth, *San Miguel de Proyectos Agropecuarios* (SMPA), and used it to promote a narrative of corporate responsibility and commitment to healthy eating. SMPA secured positive coverage in the press and was credited with creating "jobs, wellbeing, community cohesion" in an impoverished rural town. In 1986, founder Dr Benito Manrique de Lara y Soria invested in machinery developed by a Mexican agricultural engineer to produce protein supplements which his company delivered to local children. By the mid-1990s, "Dr Amaranth" and his company had helped "reduce malnutrition from 65 percent to 25 percent" in the region (Simonnet, 2014). The director of Kellogg's Latin America at the time wrote:

> Kellogg's is proud of having bought amaranth from *SMPA* for more than 10 years. First with Nutri-Grain® bars, and most recently, with Special K® cereal and Kellogg's® Ancestral Grains cereal and bars sold in Latin America [...] The entire company is built on working with the community and building economic growth using local knowledge
>
> (Mejia, 2017)

Another partnership was with *Mexico Tierra de Amaranto*, an NGO that received funds from Kellogg's to train rural women facilitators to teach communities to grow and harvest amaranth. The facilitators also gave educational talks to communities about the importance of breakfast and nutrition (Kellogg's, 2014; Sánchez, 2017).

One of the Alliance for Food Health's most successful media stunts was the "Junk Food Cartel" (2016) in which they directly blamed Kellogg's, McDonald's and Coca-Cola for Mexico's child obesity epidemic. A parody of Mexico's brutal drug war, the media campaign was a fake television police sting where the captured capos were actually junk food mascots: Kellogg's Tony the Tiger and Melvin the Elephant accompanied by Coca-Cola's polar bear and Ronald McDonald. A popular soap opera actor played the main cop and accused the companies of "pushing" unhealthy food on children and not complying with their promise of retiring advertisements targeted to children younger than 12 (Villanueva, 2013; *El Cártel Chatarra*, 2016). The implication was that, just like a drug cartel, transnational UPF companies were a public health menace, violated the law and were incapable of self-regulating.

The Alliance for Food Health struggled against the UPF industry in a highly mediatic battle that resulted in accusations of conflicts of interest and collusion between government officials and the companies. The NIPH stood with the Alliance in advocating for public policies such as soft drink taxes, modified front-of-package information for UPFs and better advertising regulations (Perlroth, 2018). During the administration of President Enrique Peña Nieto (2012–2018), the NIPH and the Alliance were at times in direct confrontation with the heads of other state agencies (e.g. Mercedes Juan López, Minister of Health, 2012–2016), who were not supportive of the proposed policies. Industry lobbyists allied with the Ministry to create the Mexican Observatory of Non-Transmissible Diseases to try to debunk the links between increased UPF consumption, diabetes and obesity (Soto, 2020; *El Peor de los Mundos*, 2023). NIPH researcher Dr Simón Barquera has stated that the Observatory "brought experts who came to testify that the increase in obesity was due to a virus or to the fact that people had stopped smoking or had genetic predispositions" (El Peor de los Mundos, 2023) and denied any links to changes in diet.

After more than a decade of activism, Congress did approve most of the policies proposed by the Alliance, first the soft drink taxes in 2014 and then the front-of-label regulations in 2020. The representatives of UPF companies have resisted the passage and implementation of these regulations and continue to do so. Both the Alliance and the industry representatives employ strategic communication tactics that seek to debunk or question the scientific research and surveys that each side presents to back up their respective claims.

Conclusion

From the 1940s until the end of the twentieth century, Mexico transitioned from a context where anxieties about food scarcity and malnutrition dominated public discussions and policy priorities to one in which experts and civil society considered excessive consumption of UPFs as one of the main health challenges facing the country. UPF companies, both local and foreign, have been key players in this transition, consolidating their market share and promoting discourses of safety and modernity by making health- and nutrition-related claims. They have used "science" discursively, first in the 1940s to 1970s, to highlight the presence of certain ingredients in their products (sugar, vitamins and "enrichment") and promote the idea that these ingredients could provide "energy" and general well-being. The explosion in rates of obesity, diabetes and other diet-related health risks catalysed a new wave of consumer activism in the 1990s focused on regulating advertising and sales of UPFs. This led UPF companies to use "science" as a marketing device once again, both defensively, to counter claims by health activists, but also offensively, as a mechanism to rebuild public trust. Transnational cereal company Kellogg's is a case in point, funding local nutritional research and pursuing "socially responsible" partnerships to recontextualise discourses surrounding "traditional knowledge" and "natural foods."

A transhistorical perspective, which takes into account differences between regions and countries, helps better explain how and why sellers and advertisers select certain scientific and nutritional claims to promote their products, particularly in contexts of rapid social transformation. Nutritional sciences are notoriously "inexact" in the sense that specific causal mechanisms between diets and health effects continue to be poorly understood or at least a matter of heated debate. Due to the complexity of how human nutrition actually works, it is relatively easy to misinform; in other words, to give consumers information about food that, while not necessarily false, leads them to think that some food products are healthier or at least better choices than others. Food companies take advantage of these uncertainties and use seemingly scientific statements in order to be seen as entities acting not just on behalf of their own economic interests but also as social actors promoting values such as modernisation, knowledge and convenience. The complexity of nutrition affects governments, experts, civil society and the media who are forced to substantiate or contradict the claims of industry that a relationship exists, or does not exist, between specific foods and a positive or negative health outcome.

For the humanities and social sciences, a critical research agenda can centre not only on examining the cultural and political contexts in which health or scientific claims emerge but also on how these discourses are deployed rhetorically and visually by social actors in different times and regions. Since UPF companies have operated and continue to operate on a global scale, and their main communication tool is advertising, research also needs to be transnational. This will lead us to improve the way that national and international regulators provide resources for consumers in order to evaluate these health claims more effectively in the face of uncertainty. Current public discussions in Latin America—and elsewhere—have been focused on what regulators can do to monitor how corporations communicate with children and understand what role advertising plays in habit formation. Decisions about children's diets can generate anxiety, particularly when caregivers feel that they have limited options or control to provide "healthy food," either due to poverty and inequality or the structure of the food market. We need to continue to investigate how public disputes about UPFs and their effects on health have occurred to help us understand both the nature of scientific messages deployed on behalf of commercial interests and how these messages are embedded in particular visions about economic class, social mobility, nationalism and ethnicity.

Notes

1 Examples of UPFs include soft drinks, industrialised white bread, crisps and breakfast cereals. Most of the ingredients in UPFs are preservatives and other additives used to stabilise, emulsify, dissolve or modify the flavours and aesthetics of the food (Monteiro et al., 2018).

2 Like in other Latin American countries, Mexican experts involved in the fields of medicine and public health used scientific studies about human diets produced in Europe and North America to justify their policy proposals. By the mid-nineteenth century, many of them were also heavily influenced by French neo-Lamarckian eugenics (Stepan, 1996; Pilcher, 1998; Pohl-Valero, 2014).

3 The newer institute was founded by Dr Salvador Zubirán, former Dean of the National University and personal physician of several Mexican presidents. The institute now has his name.

4 Although Mexican scientists did publish research on specific fields of nutritional sciences, the majority of the information about nutrition came from the United States, Europe and international organisations. During World War Two, research conducted by the highly influential Nutrition Foundation and Harvard University generated knowledge about nutrition "at a time when health officials believed deficiency diseases posed a threat to economic productivity and military fitness" (Johns and Oppenheimer, 2018). Only in the 1950s, did these institutions start to study the links between particular foods, weight gain and health risks. There is ongoing scholarly debate on whether in the 1960s and afterwards the US sugar industry, for example, "downplayed or suppressed evidence linking sugar and heart disease" (Johns and Oppenheimer, 2018).

5 During the 1970s, the relationship between the Mexican government and national economic elites (organisations representing industrial, banking and commercial interests) was, at times, tense. Cooperation existed, but there were also significant disagreements, particularly about labour relations and macroeconomic policies (Whitehead, 1980; Bazdresch and Levy, 1991).

References

Aguilar, I. 2003. Amaranto: Un himno a la alegría. *Reforma* (6 June), 1.
Aguilar-Rodríguez, S. 2007. Cooking Modernity: Nutrition Policies, Class, and Gender in 1940s and 1950s Mexico City. *The Americas* 64(2):177–205.
Andrade, F. 2017. Forjó un imperio con sentido social. *Reforma* (4 February), 8.
Barquera, S., Campos, I. and Rivera, J.A. 2013. Mexico Attempts to Tackle Obesity: The Process, Results, Push Backs and Future Challenges. *Obesity Reviews* 14(S2):69–78.
Baz, G. 1942. *Informe de labores presentado al H. Ejecutivo de la Unión por el Dr. Gustavo Baz secretario del ramo 1941–1942*. Mexico City: Secretaría de la Asistencia Pública.
Bazdresch, C. and Levy, S. 1991. "Populism and Economic Policy in Mexico 1970–1982" in *The Macroeconomics of Populism in Latin America*, edited by R. Dornbusch and S. Edwards (Chicago: The University of Chicago Press), pp. 223–262.
Bunker, S.B. 2012. *Creating Mexican Consumer Culture in the Age of Porfirio Díaz*. Albuquerque: University of New Mexico Press.
"Celebran 5 años de apoyar la investigación en nutrición." 2013. *Reforma* (29 September), 1.
Cherem, S. 2016. *Al grano: vida y visión de los fundadores de Bimbo*. Mexico City: Editorial Planeta Mexicana.
Colmenares Páramo, D. 1982. Ofensiva Empresarial Contra el INCO. *El Periódico del Consumidor*, January edition.
de Cervantes, L. 1976. Fue censurado el consumo suntuario. *Excélsior* (1 April), 5.
de Onis, M. 2000. Measuring Nutritional Status in Relation to Mortality. *Bulletin of the World Health Organization* 78(10):1271–1274.
Earle, R. 2012. *The Body of the Conquistador: Food, Race, and the Colonial Experience in Spanish America, 1492–1700*. Cambridge: Cambridge University Press.
ElCártelChatarra.2016.Availableathttps://www.youtube.com/watch?v=vG7kkU8uvYQ (Accessed: 4 May 2023).
El Peor de los Mundos. 2023. Available at https://www.youtube.com/watch?v=KcY-hyFoQfM (Accessed: 3 May 2023).
Ford, E. 2016 Childhood and Modernity in Mexico City: Print Media and State Power during the "Mexican Miracle". *The Journal of the History of Childhood and Youth* 9(1):118–139.
Gálvez, A. 2018. *Eating NAFTA: Trade, Food Policies, and the Destruction of Mexico/ Alyshia Gálvez*. Berkeley: University of California Press.
Godoy, E. 2010. Amaranto combate la desnutricion y la obesidad en Mexico, *La Nación de Costa Rica* (25 May). Available at https://www.nacion.com/ciencia/amaranto-combate-la-desnutricion-y-la-obesidad-en-mexico/6YFHYAFW65H3NP3CRUIPMFEGMI/story/ (Accessed: 3 May 2023).
Gómez, F. 1946. Desnutrición, *Boletín Médico del Hospital Infantil* 3:541–543.
"Hasta dónde es buena la azúcar como alimento." 1954. *El Universal*, 13 June (unpaginated). From Archivos Económicos de la Biblioteca y Hemeroteca Lerdo de Tejada, Mexico City, Mexico.
Hobart, H.J. and Maroney, S. 2019. On Racial Constitutions and Digestive Therapeutics. *Food, Culture & Society* 22(5):576–594.
Hornsey, R. 2018. "The Penguins Are Coming": Brand Mascots and Utopian Mass Consumption in Interwar Britain. *Journal of British Studies* 57(4):812–839.
"Incentiva Kellogg Company investigaciones en nutrición." 2010. *Reforma* (5 January), 1.
INCO. 1977. El perfil del buen y el mal consumidor. *Revista del Consumidor* (March ed.), 4.
INCO. 1980a. Corn Flakes. Mucho Pochismo y Poca Alimentación. *El Periódico del Consumidor* (September ed.), 1.

INCO. 1980b. Cuénteles a sus hijos los cuentos de la publicidad. *Revista del Consumidor* (special no.), 32–33.
INCO. 1980c. El Refresco daña la salud y el bolsillo. *El Periódico del Consumidor* (July ed.), 1.
INCO. 1980d. Compare antes de comprar. Poster created for Mexican Labor Congress, CONASUPO, held in National Library of Medicine, Bethesda MD, United States.
INCO. 1981a. Abelardo te presenta a los cuates de tu salud. *Revista del Consumidor* (April ed.), poster insert.
INCO. 1981b. Aplíquele Ciencia a su Comida: en la Variedad está el Gusto. *El Periódico del Consumidor* (August ed.), 3.
INCO. 1981c. El SAM propone, La Publicidad Dispone. *Revista del Consumidor* (March 49), 32–35.
INCO. 1981d. Los niños son lo que comen. *Revista del Consumidor* (April 50), 1.
INCO. 1982a. Entrevista al primo del gansito. *El Brinco*, 1.
INCO. 1982b. Entrevista al vecino de Pancho Pantera. *El Brinco*, 10.
INCO. 1982c. No Tarda: Mimoso Ratón va a Morir de Desnutrición. *El Periódico del Consumidor*. 4.
"Incrementa INSK apoyo a investigación en salud." 2012. *Reforma* (4 October), 1.
Isabel, M. 1982. Tribulaciones de una mamá complaciente. *Revista del Consumidor* (August ed.), 46–47.
Jiménez, B. 2006. Celebra Fox avance en poder adquisitivo, *Reforma* (31 May), 6.
Johns, D.M. and Oppenheimer, G.M. 2018. Was there ever really a "sugar conspiracy"? *Science* 359(6377):747–750.
Kaufman Purcell, S. 1981. Business-Government Relations in Mexico: The Case of the Sugar Industry. *Comparative Politics* 13(2):211–233.
Kellogg's. 2014. Kellogg's Committed to Empowering Women and Smallholder Farmers, *Kellogg Company Newsroom*. Available at https://newsroom.kelloggcompany.com/2014-01-08-Kellogg-Committed-To-Empowering-Women-And-Smallholder-Farmers (Accessed: 9 May 2023).
Kellogg's. 2022. Empresa. Historia en Latinoamérica. Crecimiento global. *Kellogg's®*. Available at https://www.kelloggs.com.mx/es_MX/empresa/historia-latinoamerica.html (Accessed: 10 May 2023).
Lara, A. 1999. Harán cereales más nutritivos. *Reforma* (23 January), 5.
Martínez, V. 2009. Multiplican el uso de viejos cultivos. *Reforma* (30 November), 13.
Medina, L.A. 2007. Consumidores indefensos. *Reforma* (19 August), 8.
Mejia, M.F. 2017. Amaranth: A Case Study of Eradicating Malnutrition, *Kellogg Company Newsroom*. Available at https://newsroom.kelloggcompany.com/amaranthsanmiguel (Accessed: 28 April 2023).
Monteiro, C.A., Cannon, G., Moubarac, J.C., Bertazzi Levy, R., Louzada, M.L.C. and Jaime, P.C. 2018. The UN Decade of Nutrition, the NOVA Food Classification and the Trouble with Ultra-Processing. *Public Health Nutrition* 21(1):5–17.
Moreno, J. 2003. *Yankee Don't Go Home!: Mexican Nationalism, American Business Culture, and the Shaping of Modern Mexico, 1920–1950*. Chapel Hill: University of North Carolina Press.
Mundet. 1974. Sidral Mundet. *Revista Gente* (2 February), Back cover.
Navarro de Macias, M. 1988. *Development Policy and Nutrition: A Case Study of the Nutrition Education Campaign of the Sistema Alimentario Mexicano (SAM)*. Stanford: Stanford University.
Ochoa, E. 2000. *Feeding Mexico: The Political Uses of Food Since 1910*. Wilmington: Scholarly Resources.
O'Hagan, L.A. 2020. Pure in Body, Pure in Mind? A Sociohistorical Perspective on the Marketisation of Pure Foods in Great Britain. *Discourse, Context & Media* 34, https://doi.org/10.1016/j.dcm.2019.100325

Paredes López, O.P. 2003. Revolución del huarache. *Reforma* (6 June), 6.
Paredes-Lopez, O.P., Guevara Lara, F. and Bello Pérez, L.A. 2006. *Los alimentos mágicos de las culturas indígenas mesoamericanas*. Mexico City: Secretaría de Educación Pública.
Perlroth, N. 2018. Spyware's Odd Targets: Backers of Mexico's Soda Tax, *The New York Times* (20 January). Available at https://www.nytimes.com/2017/02/11/technology/hack-mexico-soda-tax-advocates.html (Accessed: 19 February 2019).
Petrick, G.M. 2011 "Purity as Life": H.J. Heinz, Religious Sentiment, and the Beginning of the Industrial Diet. *History and Technology* 27(1):37–64.
Pilcher, J. 1998. *¡Que vivan los tamales! Food and the Making of Mexican Identity*. Albuquerque: University of New Mexico Press.
Pilcher, J. 2010. "José Cuervo and the Gentrified Worm: Food, Drink, and the Touristic Consumption of Mexico" in *Holiday in Mexico: Critical Reflections on Tourism and Tourist Encounters*, edited by D. Berger and A.G. Wood, Durham: Duke University Press, https://doi.org/10.1515/9780822391265-010
Pohl-Valero, S. 2014 "La Raza Entra Por La Boca": Energy, Diet, and Eugenics in Colombia, 1890–1940. *Hispanic American Historical Review* 94(3):455–486.
Popkin, B.M., Adair, L.S. and Ng, S.W. 2012. Global Nutrition Transition and the Pandemic of Obesity in Developing Countries. *Nutrition Reviews* 70(1):3–21.
PROFECO Retro. 2009. Available at https://www.youtube.com/watch?v=JtyGD4obeG8 (Accessed: 10 May 2023).
Ruiz Sandoval, H. 1959. Lecciones industriales de Excélsior: la fabricación de refrescos. *Excélsior* (21 December), 1–2.
Sánchez, A. 2017. Siembran oportunidad. *Reforma* (23 October), 10.
Sarmiento, S. 2020. JAQUE MATE / Engañoso etiquetado. *Reforma* (3 March), 10.
Seligmann, L.J. 2023. *Quinoa: Food Politics and Agrarian Life in the Andean Highlands*. Urbana: University of Illinois Press.
Simonnet, C. 2014. Una utopía llamada amaranto. *Reforma* (26 January), 12.
Singleman, P. 1993. The Sugar Industry in Postrevolutionary Mexico: State Intervention and Private Capital. *Latin American Research Review* 28(1):61–88.
Soto, D. 2020. Cuestionan consejo "antiobesidad": Covid-19. *Reforma* (2 September), 13.
Stepan, N.L. 1996. *The Hour of Eugenics: Race, Gender, and Nation in Latin America*. Ithaca: Cornell University Press.
UNPASA. 1940. Consuma Usted más Azúcar. *Revista Hoy* (unpaginated).
UNPASA. 1955. Él necesita azúcar. *Revista Hoy* (1 October), 2.
UNPASA. 1969. La mejor y más barata azúcar del mundo. *Boletín azucarero mexicano* (August ed.), 47.
Uribe, E. 1999. Prevenga la anemia. *Reforma* (27 November), 19.
Villanueva, P. 2013. Urgen ONG a restringir publicidad de "chatarra". *Reforma* (30 April), 15.
Weis, R. 2012. *Bakers and Basques: A Social History of Bread in Mexico*. Albuquerque: University of New Mexico Press.
Whitehead, L. 1980. La política económica del sexenio de Echeverría: Qué salió mal y por qué? *Foro Internacional* 20(3):484–513.
Zazueta, M. del P. 2021. ""Hay desnutrición, no hambre": nutrición y políticas públicas en México, 1960–1997" in *El hambre de los otros: Ciencia y políticas alimentarias en Latinoamérica, siglo XX y XXI*, edited by S. Pohl-Valero and J. Vargas Domínquez (Bogota: Universidad del Rosario), pp. 341–366.
Zubirán, S. 1974. *La desnutrición del mexicano*. Mexico City: Fondo de Cultura Económica.

4 A Better Way to Start the Day

Pseudoscience, Health and Synthetic Personalisation in Breakfast Cereal Packaging

Angela Smith

Introduction

As the meal that breaks the overnight fast, breakfast is represented as providing sustenance and energy for the day ahead. For many, cereal is an important breakfast food and has been recognised for many years as essential to a balanced diet. Nonetheless, breakfast cereals are a relatively recent invention, having arrived on US breakfast tables in the late nineteenth century and UK breakfast tables some 20 years later. Muesli—a Swiss cereal made primarily from rolled oats—did not reach the US or UK until even later in the 1960s. Since then, it has grown to become a popular cereal choice, particularly for the health conscious.

This chapter will explore the evolution of the branding of muesli as a breakfast cereal in the UK, comparing early and contemporary examples of packaging. Specifically, it will look at Alpen, first introduced to the UK in 1971, and Troo Granola+, on the market since 2018. As Maffei and Schifferstein (2017:142) have observed, food packaging operates "like a foreword to a book, the functional and aesthetic elements of packing contextualise and introduce the food," and, thus, merits further study. This is particularly relevant for breakfast cereals as most breakfast options in the UK (e.g. toast, "full English" fry-up) do not require packaging.

Looking at the same product from two different brands over changing periods of time will demonstrate how cultural norms allied with developments in nutritional science have influenced their packaging, the health claims made and how the consumer is addressed. Additionally, it will show how scientific discourses come to be prioritised or backgrounded at various moments in time, although the concept of "purity" is a continuous discourse that runs throughout. The historical trajectory of food packaging has been explored elsewhere (i.e. by Spiekermann, 2011; Oswald, 2012; Haydu and Skotnicki, 2016; Barnes, 2017), all of whom demonstrate the development of brands from their novelty on introduction to the common sense of their consumption once established. As this chapter will show, this is also happening in the case of muesli.

DOI: 10.4324/9781003450276-7

The chapter will start with a brief overview of the development of packaged breakfast cereals, exploring how health and purity were embedded from the very beginning. It will then move on to explore how different emphases are placed on these elements from 1971 to modern day. It will conclude by summarising the similarities and differences between Alpen and Troo Granola+, thereby highlighting the importance of transhistorical approaches to food marketing.

Breakfasting Food and Health

Corresponding to broader developments in the government of population (Foucault, 1991), the twin influences of religion and medicine started to influence the representation of diet in the mid-nineteenth century. The rise of Christian fundamentalism, particularly in the United States, saw the re-emergence of diets that were "pure"—something that recurs in various forms of religion throughout history. In the nineteenth century, purity was linked to new developments in food and nutrition, with particular emphasis on digestion and the accompanying development of health hotels, or spas. As O'Hagan (2020) shows, the use of "pure" in food advertising was also linked with the panic over food adulteration in the mid-nineteenth century which, in Britain, resulted in many new laws and marketing materials prioritising a discourse of purity in food products. Just as the industrialised processes of the early twentieth century accelerated food production in novel directions (see Mozaffarian et al., 2018), it also established a dynamic tension, with the identification of vitamins providing nutritional solutions for the government on public health (particularly with some of the B vitamins and vitamin C). The Great Depression of the 1930s and then the Second World War saw governments fixate upon the diets of their populations, leading to the arrival of recommended daily allowances of selected nutrients and the start of calorie intake guidelines. In all of this, the first meal of the day—breakfast—came to be seen as the most important (Spence, 2017).

In the UK, breakfast cereals took off in the 1930s, with many brands, such as US-based Quaker and Kellogg's, starting to package their cereals in ways that are still recognisable today. The arrival of mass-produced breakfast cereals saw a move away from a time-consuming cooked breakfast, requiring less preparation and washing-up. The successful US brands were soon copied by well-established UK brands, such as biscuit manufacturers Huntley & Palmer and grocers J. Sainsbury, who produced their own in-house version of products, such as cornflakes.

One of the biggest selling points for such products was their combination of long shelf life and freshness. Kellogg's Corn Flakes at this time boasted that they were "oven fresh flavour perfect," while the packaging itself prioritised the established red "signature" of the Kellogg's brand, which still features on their products and provides a sense of continuity and trustworthiness. Other products prioritised the speed with which they could be prepared to serve.

J. Sainsbury's cereal, for example, highlighted that it was "ready to serve," whilst Scott's Porage Oats "cooks in five minutes" (the slogan appearing between two clock faces, the one to the left being five minutes earlier than the one to right).

There was also an emergence of consensus about the nutritional properties of cereal, with the Quaker in Quaker Corn Flakes' logo connected to a speech bubble declaring, "They're malted," and HO Mills boasting "whole wheat cooked with malt" for their corn flakes. This articulation between health and natural content can be linked with the scientific discoveries of the early part of the twentieth century, which had identified individual nutritional factors, as well as the links between diet and weight (e.g. sugar and fat with weight gain). Thus, breakfast cereals were well placed to provide a solution to "unhealthy" breakfast options that had been established over the previous century.

The promotion of a healthy lifestyle through nutritional information provided on food packaging has been a topic of a range of studies in recent years, many of which have looked at drinks. Ledin and Machin (2020), for example, have explored the brand Oatly, while Chen and Eriksson (2021) have investigated energy and health-promising drinks, following Burges Watson et al.'s (2009) discussion of probiotic drinks. Chen and Eriksson (2019) have also explored the application of scientific language to protein snacks. Conversely, research by Mapes (2020) has shown a shift in some branding to make food more artisanal and, therefore, appear less mass-produced. This chapter will add to this growing body of work by providing further insights on style and address in the context of scientific claims in the branding of breakfast cereals. To date, there has been some historical research carried out on the history of breakfast cereal, most notably in a US context (e.g. Gitlin and Ellis, 2012; Severson, 2016). However, to date, there have been limited studies on the history of breakfast cereal packaging, with most focusing on children's responses to increasingly sugar-laden (and, thus, "unhealthy") cereals aimed specifically at that consumer group (Reece et al., 1999; Hill and Tilley, 2002; Lodolce et al., 2013). This study will, thus, also add to this growing research area through an exploration of muesli packaging—a previously unexplored area.

Methodology

The data used in this chapter has been selected by type of product rather than specific brand in order to allow a more detailed analysis of how nutritional science has guided developments in how products are marketed to consumers, including products that are more recent innovations rather than re-packagings of established brands with existing reputations and corporate styles. Although muesli was first introduced to the UK in the 1960s in the form of Bio-Bircher Muesli, it was not until the arrival of Alpen in 1971 that the market took off. Alpen has led the muesli market ever since, hence the decision to include Alpen packaging as the first point of analysis in this chapter. Over the last few decades, numerous competitors to Alpen have appeared on the market, including Troo Granola+, which emerged in 2018. Troo Granola+ is also marketed as innovative and has, therefore, been chosen because it represents a rich source for multimodal analysis, providing what Pollan (2006) terms a "food story." The selection of these two products will clearly demonstrate the evolution of cereal packaging from its first introduction to current times.

The concept of "food stories" is rooted in the marketisation of social movements whose interest in food and food production created a need for context and discussion, and generated a new genre of lifestyle blogs, television and cookery books. Subsequently, food stories have been appropriated by food producers and marketers as a selling point (Pollan, 2006). In Pollan's version of "storied food," the narrative is invoked by a food producer or marketer and serves as "an imperfect substitute for direct observation of how a food is produced, a concession to the reality that most people in an industrial society haven't the time or the inclination to follow their food back to the farm" (Pollan, 2006:137). Images of raw ingredients set within a rural idyll are used to establish a set of positive connotations for foods that have long been separated from small-scale agricultural production. In this sense, "storied food" serves as a narrative, non-standardised form of eco-labelling organic, fair trade and grass-fed produce (Pollan, 2006).

In common with other marketing constructions, food stories contribute to and build on claims of difference and uniqueness, as a result of well-thought-out branding strategies. Chen and Eriksson (2019) show how companies construct their food production as morally righteous and remote from industrial food production in ways that reveal an affinity with both the consumer and the environment. Equally, Ledin and Machin's (2020) study of the ethically branded product Oatly shows how ethical issues are colonised and communicated to consumers in a playful and antagonistic style, inviting them to ally with the company's political struggle against corporate giants and an unsustainable dairy industry. Food stories replete with claims about locality, morality and sustainability are used in marketing to invest within consumers the power to "do good," both for the environment and for their own health (Chen and Eriksson, 2021). It is, thus, a way for food producers to add value to both production and consumption and, by extension, to be seen to empower purchasers.

In order to understand the multimodal construction of these food stories and their representation and reproduction of nutritional discourses, the data analysis used here draws on the principles of social semiotics and multimodal critical discourse analysis (MDCA) (Machin and Mayr, 2012; Ledin and Machin, 2018). Accordingly, strategies that are used in packaging design are considered ideological; they are used by designers and producers to shape the representations of events, actions, participants and settings for particular ends and with political and cultural implications. Beyond its instrumental obligation to protect and convey its content, packaging is used to communicate information about the food, through production and consumption, and to avail the customer of its qualities in a manner that they will find satisfying (Ledin and Machin 2018).

The analysis used here seeks to identify which semiotic choices have been used in the construction of these multimodal stories and how these choices are used to create meaning. Semiotic modes, such as iconography, form, layout, colour, text and typography, are regarded to communicate the interests, values, ideas and/or perspectives that the products convey within a social environment (Ledin and Machin, 2018). As this study is concerned with the use of "science" in these products, specific attention will also be paid to register, determined by three factors: *field*, which refers to the subject matter of the discourse; *tenor*, which refers to the role being played by the speaker/producer and the resulting level of formality in the situation; and *mode*, which usually refers to the medium of communication (Thomas et al., 2004:219).

This study will also draw upon the concept of "synthetic personalisation" (Fairclough, 2001), arguing that the linguistic features of informal, conversational language are deployed to create a sense of familiarity with consumers. In addition to representing social practices, packaging is often also used to explain, justify, legitimate and evaluate the product (Ledin and Machin, 2018), and synthetic personalisation is employed to engage consumers, addressing them in an appropriately biddable manner and convincing them of the good that will come from consuming this breakfast cereal.

MCDA will, therefore, allow an exploration of the commonalities of Alpen and Troo Granola+, while also highlighting the differences that mark these two products apart.

The Science in Food: The Development of Muesli, 1900–1971

Muesli was developed by Swiss physician Maximilian Bircher-Benner in 1900.[1] Consisting of oats, nuts and grated apple, it was served with cream to patients in Bircher-Benner's hospital as a form of appetiser, thereby associating the product with health from its very beginning. An earlier form of muesli—granula—was "invented" and trademarked by American Dr James Caleb Jackson in 1863. Made of baked oats sweetened with honey breakfast cereal, granula was served at sanatoriums throughout the United States. Around the same time, a similar product was also developed by John Harvey Kellogg; although originally also called granula, Kellogg decided to rebrand it "granola" to avoid legal problems with Jackson.

The first mass-produced muesli was launched onto the market in 1959 by Swiss company Somalon AG who used Dr Bircher-Benner's recipe to create Bio-Bircher Muesli. The product was subsequently exported to Germany, Austria, the Netherlands, the US and the UK.[2] However, it failed to take off. It was not until the launch of Alpen in 1971 by Weetabix that muesli grew to become a popular cereal in the UK. According to Alpen's website, muesli was "discovered" by a Weetabix executive on a skiing holiday in Switzerland in the late 1960s, where his personal chef had served it to him at breakfast. At that time, there was a rise of bohemian living, as evidenced in the hippy movement, which drew on nature, social liberalism and spirituality. For the Weetabix executive, muesli—with its established history as a health food and its rustic appeal—perhaps fits very well with this ethos. Thus, he was able to recognise an opportunity, drawing a link between his Swiss breakfast and an emerging hippy consumer market back home.

By 1971, Weetabix had developed a version of the dish including dried rather than fresh fruit, which had a much longer shelf life. They called it Alpen as a nod to its Swiss origins. In large part as a consequence of its development through the Alpen brand, the generic term "muesli" was the name to come to prominence in the UK. As we will see, packaging of breakfast cereals follows what Hine (1995) has observed of most supermarket food packaging, which seeks to move our gaze away from the "life and death matter of eating" as found in the traditional marketplace (i.e. unwashed vegetables and bloodied animal carcases) to something more sanitised. In the case of breakfast cereal, the products sought a closer link with a sanitised version of nature to enhance a sense of purity that fits with the hippy ethos.

The first boxes of Alpen helpfully gave the basic ingredients a key place on the front of the box (see Figure 4.1). This is found as a strapline to underscore the brand name ("Mixed cereal with raisins and nuts"), which is dominated by a photograph of a rustic table displaying the raw ingredients: grapes, shelled nuts, bunches of oats and rye, reading left to right, where an earthenware flagon of milk sits (described in the ingredients list as "a natural mixture"). The strapline at the bottom of the front of the box reads: "Made from good things from the good earth," linking the product to nature through the noun

Figure 4.1 Alpen packaging, 1971

Credit: Author's own image

phrase ("good earth") and drawing emphasis away from the manufacturing process (stressing instead the raw ingredients in the image). It is also worth noting the use of the second noun phrase's employment of the determiner "the." This creates a sense of common ground and fits with the wider discourse of wholesomeness and naturalness.

The back of the box shows the same unprocessed ingredients, but this time set on a table beneath a window. The window has homely, Swiss-style wooden shutters, with cut-out three-leaf clover patterns, ajar to disclose an Alpine scene with rocks and fir trees in the foreground and a snow-topped image of the Matterhorn behind. The product is at once simple in form and set amid the spectacle of Alpine nature.

The text, in white print over the dark brown area between the window and the raw food, uses block capitals to highlight the name of the product repeated as a three-part list:

> ALPEN is a natural breakfast food, pure and simple.
> It contains no preservatives—no additives—nothing artificial—just a crunchy mixture of natural foods.
> ALPEN is a delicious cereal derived from an old Swiss recipe.
> In Switzerland, it would be called Muesli where for many years it has been popular not only for breakfast but as a snack or even as a dessert.
> ALPEN is so satisfying you will find that a serving of one-half cup per person is sufficient. Just add milk. No need to add sugar.

Like with the nineteenth-century branding of processed foods that O'Hagan (2020) mentions, there is an emphasis on purity. This is seen in the images, through the connotations of rustic nature in the Swiss cabin with its view across to the Alps, and linguistically in the emphasis on "pure and simple." Here, though, this is combined with the myths around natural splendour and abundance, while claiming established legitimacy in according muesli the status of a proper noun through initial capitalisation. O'Hagan's (2020) argument about the use of "pure" is also relevant here, as Alpen sets itself up as a contrasting product to the more industrialised processed corn and rice that dominated the market at this time. This is something that O'Hagan and Eriksson (2022) have also commented on in respect of the marketing of cod liver oil.

Alpen also provides a helpful guide on how to eat the product, which is expanded on the side of the box. This widens the categorisation of the food beyond a breakfast dish to a broader claim of an all-day health food, consistent with its roots in therapy and convalescence described earlier:

> IMPORTANT
> SERVE SMALLER PORTIONS THAN FOR OTHER KINDS OF BREAKFAST CEREAL
> Average serving is just one-half cup
> AS A BREAKFAST CEREAL

Simply add milk, no need to add sugar. You'll also find Alpen with milk is even more delightful when fresh or canned fruits are added.
AS A DESSERT
Serve Alpen and fruit as above with some whipped cream topping or even over ice cream.
AS A LATE-NIGHT SNACK
Alpen is ideal. A crunchy mixture with nuts and raisins you can eat right from the box.

Interestingly, both the back and the side of the box emphasise portion size. While the rationale here is that a smaller portion is "satisfying," the use of block capitals and the headline "IMPORTANT" bear the connotations of an official warning, introducing a register in keeping with a more medical discourse and with the claims to legitimacy in capitalising the product's generic name. This is only partly ameliorated by the list of potential uses of Alpen, all of which relate to different meals in chronological order during the day. Again, there are connotations of easification (Fairclough, 2001) in "simply add milk" and "eat right from the box." The personalisation of the text, in particular using the second person pronoun "you" in the elliptical form "you'll" includes the implicature that the product is delightful, but will be even more delightful if fresh fruit is added. Thus, we see the combination of a product with weighty natural heritage and health benefits, expressed in a manner that emphasises accessibility and ease in its relationship with the consumer.

Muesli as a Cultural Symbol, 1970s–2000s

Alpen remained the market leader in the UK to the point of becoming a generic name for muesli by the end of the first decade of its presence. However, the purity and goodness of Alpen and muesli, in general, began to attract negative overtones, with the emphasis on wholesomeness coming to be associated with a specific type of self-denying, joyless diet, which was linked to the rise in "healthy eating" in the 1990s. This was not helped by the relative absence of colour in traditional muesli, leading it to be likened to the texture and perhaps taste of sawdust. Alpen's own packaging at this time had not changed from the muted browns of its early incarnation, seemingly priding itself on this "classic" look to the point that it offered tokens to collect for "free" gifts, such as branded aprons, tin boxes to store the muesli and logo-embellished cereal bowls, all carrying the Alpen packaging image. This was in the face of more colourful packaging in their rivals' products from the 1980s onwards, yet as the market leader, Alpen's increasingly drab and dated look informed general perceptions of muesli.

By the 1990s, a clear relationship between food and health had developed based on the notion of "healthy food" and "unhealthy food." Empirical studies by sociologists such as Blaxter and Paterson (1983) framed "healthy" food as being that which had minimal processing in its preparation and was deemed "natural" (as we see in the packaging of Alpen). This was contrasted with highly processed food containing excess sugar, fat and salt, which was termed "junk food" and was, therefore, "bad" for one's health. As Chen and Eriksson (2019, 2021) and Eriksson and Machin (2020) have argued, this emphasis on health has shifted more recently towards a neoliberal ideology of self-management that has passed into a level of common sense. Again, in keeping with Foucault's (1991) work on governmentality, state responsibility for the health of citizens has become articulated as a matter of self-care and mutual moral judgement and surveillance. This regime of common sense draws upon the assumption that as long as the "correct" diet is followed faithfully, then longevity and good health can be secured.

While there is a long history of breakfast cereals being associated with healthy living, this growing interest in the dichotomy between "healthy" and "unhealthy" food offered breakfast cereal producers a chance to foreground the supposed health-giving properties of their products. When scientific research into heart disease and diet appeared to show that the consumption of oats had a health benefit, Quaker Oats, for example, began to market their product with this claim. In 1997, they rebranded their Oats with the prominent band "Oatmeal helps reduce cholesterol," linking the message to approval by the Food and Drug Administration in the United States. It is interesting to note that there is no hedging in this assertion, but there is an amelioration: the oatmeal "helps" reduce cholesterol, which carries the implicature that there are other factors that will also play a role.

In her study *Food, the Body and the Self* (1996), Lupton interviewed people about their diets and in particular the ways in which these "healthy eating" messages were being received. In her interviews, she found the participants' descriptions of food described as "healthy" typically included vegetables and fruit (particularly if "fresh"), salads, whole grains, lean meat, chicken and fish (81). These findings are also found in earlier studies, such as Charles and Kerr (1988) and Chapman and Maclean (1993), and show that at least some "healthy eating" messages about specific foods were getting through.

Lupton's (1996) interviews and focus groups—all in a British context—also expressed views and attitudes towards these foods. In her data, there are attitudes towards breakfast cereals reflecting the complex claims of these products: the tension between health and pleasure. In other words, we eat things because we have been told they are good for us rather than for their flavour. She gives the example of Simon who said that he forced himself to eat foods that he disliked purely for their health-giving properties. He explicitly cites muesli in this category, perhaps influenced by the common perception of it as being akin to sawdust. In talking about the first time that he tried muesli, he says, "I almost puked [...] So I didn't like muesli, but I forced myself to like it [...] I guess, mainly, I force myself to eat foods for health reasons" (Lupton, 1996:82; see also DeVault, 1991). Muesli, in particular, has been successfully marketed as a health food since its arrival in 1971. It is often associated with the health-conscious, left-leaning consumer to such an extent that, in the UK, a common putdown of someone who is perceived to be too left-leaning or "woke" is that they are "*Guardian*-reading, lentil-loving, muesli-munching." Muesli has taken on a status that journalist Ian Jack (2016) wryly refers to as gastro-synecdoche.

This all links with moral meanings and judgements which are associated with definitions of "healthy" and "unhealthy" foods. There is a binary opposition set up between categories that are termed "good," "healthy" and "natural" and those which are "bad," "unhealthy" and "artificial." An individual's choice of food is, therefore, a potent sign of that person's degree of self-control, self-esteem, knowledge of nutrition, commitment to bodily health, awareness of the origin and constitution of food and level of spirituality (Lupton, 1996:93). As Chen and Eriksson (2019) show in the case of high-protein foods, food producers reinforce the myth of such consumption by linking it to neoliberal ideas about individual wellness and the accompanying demands to display an active lifestyle.

As mentioned earlier, Alpen changed its packaging very little between the 1970s and 1990s. By the late 1990s, the semiotic code of food packaging that tended to use blue to indicate lower fat or sugar, with red as the "original" version (see also Andersson and Smith, 2021 for this feature of butter packaging), was well established in cereals, and more companies were producing low-sugar muesli in an increasingly competitive market. In 1995, Alpen eventually switched from brown to this red colourway for the "original" version, with a blue version for "no added sugar." It is interesting to see that the higher sugar version is referred to as "original," glossing over the high sugar content in a context where this was seen to be unhealthy. The underlying assumption is that the "original" version has added sugar, and a careful look at the ingredients list on the original packaging shows mention of "golden brown sugar" in addition to the sugar that would be found in the dried fruit. Despite the positive adjectives used to premodify the sugar, by the late 1990s, the impact on health of sugary foods was starting to change food packaging (see also Hill and Tilley, 2002), and muesli was being marketed as a low-sugar health food once more.

Pseudoscience and Synthetic Personalisation: New Approaches to Muesli in the Twenty-First Century

As mentioned earlier, the scientific evidence to support the consumption of oats as part of a diet to help reduce cholesterol emerged in the 1990s. As more muesli brands appeared on the market, new brands were forced to create a space for themselves with a unique selling point beyond the now-established link between oats and health. Troo Granola+ was launched in the UK in 2018. This brand's food story credits its origins to a young couple who were seeking a low-sugar, gut-healthy granola for their two children. The brand initially started in 2017 as a make-your-own kit that prioritised environmental packaging issues. Consistent with a discursive style that will be explored in more detail later, the company website highlights the personal story of the product, with the two company founders—Mike and Helena—presented as well-meaning amateur nutritionists.[3] Claiming the authenticity of diligent practice, Mike "stumbles upon chicory root fibre (aka inulin)" while reading articles about low-sugar ingredients. The food story that this product is framed by is one in which named individuals are helping unknown consumers improve their health.

In terms of packaging, Troo uses valuable space to declare its environmental aims, explaining in detail how the packaging is 100% compostable. Emphasising that their virtue extends to the product inside, the brand foregrounds discourses of good health. The cartoon birds that appear on the website and also on other packaging show a ribbon banner declaring, "Helping people live longer, happier and healthier lives" above a handwritten style "through better" and then clean, white block capital sans serif text: "GUT HEALTH," claimed and lent individual agency as their "mission." Thus, we can see a company ethos of health, focusing on gut health coupled with environmentalism, expressed in a manner that emphasises the personalised agency of the producers. These priorities are expressed most vividly on the cereal box (see Figure 4.2).

The front of the box carries the slogan "GUT HEALTHY GOODNESS," but this time rendered in a playful typography with a curving line beneath the double "oo" in "goodness," imitating a smiling face. The same pattern is used in the upward tilting brand name "TROO," both of which are marked as corporate items by the trademark logo. The brand name Troo is itself a playful pun drawing on its homophone "true." This links the product with the honesty

Figure 4.2 Troo Granola+ packaging, 2019

Credit: Author's own image

and purity associated with muesli in particular as we saw with Alpen, but also with an underlying playfulness in the linguistic strategies in this branding that will be explored further.

The muesli box is a cheerful purple ground, hinting at luxury and lusciousness and linking with a key ingredient: blueberries. The animal symbol for this particular product is a blue and pink parrot, which is shown holding a fresh raspberry in its beak; the berry still has a green leaf attached. The largest image aside from these is an elliptical white bubble, pointing left to right. The text in this box highlights the sugar and fibre in the product: "low sugar" and "9g fibre per bowl." Along with the upbeat and positive messages elsewhere on the packaging, this invites our trust in the product and its benefits.

The text beneath the product name is in a handwritten style, encouraging ideas of reliability and authenticity: the immediacy and honesty of the author's own hand. Even while invoking the personalising discourse of a handwritten font, this text draws on buzzwords in food and nutrition: super berry. Super berries are part of a group of food types that can be referred to as "super foods," but which carry no official scientific sanction. A 2012 European Food Information Council (EUFIC, 2012) report into superfoods reported the widespread use of "super food" and "super berry," but warned that this could be misleading because what is really needed is a balanced diet that includes a greater quantity and variety of fruits and vegetables. In particular, blueberries have been identified as "super berries," and indeed this is what we find on the box illustration for Troo Granola+. A small, upward tilting "window" indicating the box content (the only photo of "real" food on the package) has a couple of plump raspberries and two burnished blueberries on the left, with two more blueberries (their freshness emphasised with the addition of a green leaf) towards the right where the window meets the parrot image. Thus, we can see a health message being drawn on without explicit reference to the benefits. As the 2012 EUFIC report highlighted, the term "super berries" was already commonly found; so by the time of Troo's launch in 2018, the concept existed at the level of common sense and required no further explanation.

The side of the box offers a "Gut health glossary," helpfully outlining the main scientific claims of the product in an attempt at demystification. This sort of easification is also aligned with the need to explain a new product to consumers, where there are elements involved that are beyond the well-known or common-sense features such as the super berries. It should be noted, however, that unlike in the case of Alpen, it is the science that is being made more accessible rather than the consumption of the product, as we saw earlier. The cheerful blue and pink parrot from the front of the package reappears with a speech bubble: "Gut health can be quite confusing and complicated – so we've created this glossary to demystify some of the jargon." In terms outlined by Fairclough's (2001) notion of synthetic personalisation, we can see that the talking parrot is part of the Troo team: it is "we," not "I." It also claims to empathise with consumer bewilderment at the demands and complexities of gut health, glossed here as "confusing and complicated."

Significantly, we can see synthetic personalisation in action throughout this area of the packaging. There is reference to "your gut" in several places, as well as an overwhelming positivity associated with these scientific terms—for example, "Prebiotic – a type of functional fibre that helps nourish your good gut bacteria" and "Polyphenols – Micro nutrients from plants that can enhance the growth of good gut bacteria." Again, and exploiting the conversational style, we can see the use of hedging in this latter statement: the micronutrients *can* be of benefit, not the more certain modality of *will* or *shall*. Importantly, there is a concentration of these scientific terms on the side of the box.

There is a much denser concentration of text on the back of the box. Below the upper slogan, synthetic personalisation is in action again, with a conversational invitation to consumers of this product:

> Feeling fruity? Then this is the one for you. Enjoy our fibre packed roasty toasty oats, nuts and seeds boosted with super berries and vitamin C which can help boost immunity.

There is titillating innuendo in the opening question where, in the British English context, "fruity" contains strains of sexual connotation. This is pitched as a suggestive question—"feeling fruity?"—and we can see that there is an implied "yes" from the consumer, before presenting Troo as the solution. The playful neologism of "roasty" mirrors the existing adjective "toasty." This, in turn, reassures us that the sexual connotations are lessened by an overall mood of informal fun.

The conventional muesli ingredients that were established by Alpen in 1971 are here supplemented by "super berries" and, rather more opaquely, "vitamin C," with the repeated offer of boosting immunity that was printed on the front of the box. As mentioned earlier, vitamin C was one of the earliest vitamins to be identified and, thus, is one that exists at the level of common sense in that we are all supposed to recognise its positive value to health. This might explain partly why the asterisks beside this on the front of the box do not link to any visible text, unlike the double and triple asterisks elsewhere on the box.

The parrot again returns as the bearer of the corporate message with a speech bubble. This time, the text is represented in a hand-written font, which breaks up the block of text:

> Join us in our mission to improve the nation's gut health through eating more fibre every day! You need to aim for 30 g of fibre per day, let us help you on your way...

The complex shift in address in this section warrants some discussion. There is the initial "us," which is the personalised company that addresses "you," the responsible consumer (urged to aim for 30 g daily fibre). The address also shifts to the collective "nation," but ends by emphasising the individual agency of the consumer. In keeping with the earlier references to governmentality, the product is, thus, situating itself in the context of wider debates about national health concerns. There is also an absent agent at work: who is urging us to consume 30 g of fibre a day? The force that is behind this is hidden but is being trusted by Troo on our behalf, the brand helping us fulfil this "need" to be healthier.

This easification of digestive health, glossed throughout this packaging as "gut health," sets the Troo company out on a nationwide mission which consumers can join by consuming their products. This fits with the neoliberal ethos that Chen and Eriksson (2021) argue is part of the move to self-help eating. The parrot's speech here adds drama and excitement to this mission, indicated through the use of the exclamation point. There is also a helpful reference to a recommended daily intake of fibre, stated here to be 30 g. From the front of the box, we know that a standard bowl of Troo Granola+ contains a positive amount of fibre, and the promise here is that Troo ("us") can "help you on your way" to achieve the 30 g goal.

The largest block of text on the back of the box also assumes the casual and personal style of a handwritten style font to help sustain the informal address through a list of scientific claims:

> Research from the World Health Organization suggests that eating at least 30g of fibre per day could really improve your health. All our yummy Troo products contain at least 25% of your daily fibre requirements in one portion! They have been especially developed to contain lots of functional fibre** that helps support gut health as well as excluding gut irritants. The perfect way to start the day or to nibble on as a health snack.

As we can see, there is an explicit reference (without actually saying precisely what this is) to an official health agency, the World Health Organization, to back up the claims about fibre and health that the packaging is making. There is no link made to a specific report, but instead, there is a pattern of science/quirky personalisation that is found across this packaging. The use of the adjective "yummy" in relation to Troo products is hyper-informal, more generally found in relation to young people and children's language. The link between this juvenile language and the product can perhaps be explained in that "gut health" is traditionally a taboo topic and, thus, it is being demystified and rendered accessible through a variety of strategies, of which this is one. It also fits with the register found elsewhere, such as the "roasty toasty" neologism mentioned earlier, where such playful language carries juvenile connotations.

However, the scientific claims persist across the packaging. We see again reference to "functional fibre" with two asterisks, traditionally used in print to refer to a footnote. This footnote appears on the back of the box:

> **Oat fibre is a functional fibre in relation to its contribution to an increase in faecal bulk. Each 45g portion of Troo Granola+ contains over 20g of oats and at least 9g of fibre.

There is a shift in linguistic strategy here to be more formal and less personal. The use of "faecal bulk" is interesting as it is a medical term which, in turn, links with the subsequent more detailed breakdown of ingredients into specific weights. It is notable that "functional fibre" is not one of the jargon terms found on the side of the box; rather, more Latinate terms are displayed to increase the scientific attitude that the brand adopts at certain times.

The final minor sentence in this section returns the engaged consumer to a note of positivity and joy, with the product being promoted as a "healthy snack" in the same way as we saw Alpen being marketed in 1971. That this snack is to be "nibbled" takes us back into the register of juvenile language that is found at various points in this branding.

The lower section of the three infographics continues with the positivity found elsewhere on the box:

> Boosted with Vitamin C
> Each bowl contains 6g prebiotic fibre***
> No fake news. Honest healthy goodness.

Again, a three-part list is provided. The two scientific claims are summarised and boosted by an informal claim in the third item of the list. The first two infographics are speckled with stars, highlighting the positivity of their messages. As mentioned earlier, the side of the box, with its promise to demystify jargon, does so apparently without much reference to the rest of the text. However, there is one item from that list that we do find here: prebiotic fibre. In addition to the rather confusing use of weights for fibre, there is a new one here: 6 g. The three asterisks refer the interested consumer down to the bottom of this side of the box where the smaller text of black on purple is difficult to read, but the main aspect of interest for the consumer is rendered more visible by it appearing in white text on the purple ground:

> *** Each 45g portion contains 6g of your 12g per day of chicory inulin which contributes to normal bowel function by increasing stool frequency – how Troo is your poo?!

This footnote shows what we can see is an established shift from a scientific register to a jocular, informal register. Visually, it is more accessible than the one discussed earlier in that the shift in font colour to highlight the section "6g of your 12g per day of chicory inulin" gives the answer to the curious consumer's question about just what "6g prebiotic fibre" is. Chicory inulin is what the founders of the brand discovered in their early experiments and is highlighted on the company's website. On the cereal box, it is further explained as being an active agent in "gut health," which is here clarified for the only time on the box as "increasing stool frequency." In keeping with the established patterns, the explicit nature of this is then rendered more jocular with the indulgence in scatological humour, punning the brand name: "how Troo is your poo?!" In using both a question mark and an exclamation point, this question is made more playful. "Poo" is also the more juvenile term for faeces, so can be linked to the use of such linguistic features elsewhere on this packaging. Perhaps, it is here acting as a way to lessen the potential offensiveness of this topic.

The final infographic on this line—"No fake news: honest healthy goodness"—has a link with the contemporary political public sphere, where the term "fake news" gained currency during the presidency of Donald Trump who used it to dismiss any assertion that challenged his version of the truth. In this case, the phrase is being used playfully to highlight the health message of the product.

Overall, although Troo Granola+ has many similarities with the original Alpen branding for muesli, there are also some significant differences. For example, while the "natural" and "homemade" elements of the product remain, in the case of Troo, these are now tied to scientific findings relating to diet and health. Moreover, while both products are promoted as at any time of the day, Troo links this to the World Health Organization's message about the importance of fibre in the diet rather than Alpen's timesaving strategy, as found in its earlier packaging. The most significant similarity between the two products relates to the way that sugar is used as a marketing tool, as mentioned in the case of Alpen earlier.

While in the case of the early packaging of Alpen, there was a backgrounding of science, what we see with Troo is the foregrounding of science through the use of scientific language used to market the product as healthy. This can be linked to more established brands where science has been used to promote cereal-based products since the late nineteenth century. Here, this extends to a lengthy attempt to demystify the jargon associated with such science—an attempt that is curiously lacking in usefulness in the rest of the packaging. Most importantly, there is an individual responsibility on the part of the consumer, linked with the neoliberal discourse that Chen and Eriksson (2021) have observed in other health foods, and the inclusion of "fake news" fits with contemporary discourses of political populism and entitlement.

Conclusion

As breakfasts have diversified and normalised the consumption of muesli in the last 50 years, the early branding of these products as being time-saving has faded into the background. This points to an underlying assumption that these products can be served instantly with very little preparation beyond opening the packet—a knowledge that has become embedded in cultural consciousness and, thus, operates at the level of common sense.

With muesli-type products, this is clearly linked to nature, with a continuation of the rustic appeal of the early Alpen branding being found in that of Troo. In looking at these two products at their point of introduction to the UK market, we can see just what has changed in the appeals made to consumers. In Troo's case, this is more clearly linked to health benefits that are specifically aimed at "gut health," with the unglamorous world of gastric health being given a jolly makeover with their bright packaging. Both packagings use easification, with the Alpen box introducing us to a product that requires minimal preparation, which was a major selling point at that time. In the case of Troo, this easification is used in an attempt to make science more accessible, again reflecting contemporary debates on breakfast foods. Troo also claims to be demystifying jargon, although on this particular product, this is largely jargon that exists beyond the specific product. The extensive use of synthetic personalisation to present a youthful, playful product in Troo can be seen as an attempt to shift the product from the gastro-synechdotal links with unglamorous, old-fashioned hippies to a more contemporary, youthful consumer. This is reinforced by the product name, Granola, rather than the more traditional "muesli" that was so negatively portrayed in Lupton's study.

What we can see is that, over the period of 50 years, breakfast muesli has developed in line with growing understandings of health and well-being. The rise of neoliberalism, as shown by Chen and Eriksson (2021), places responsibility on the consumer to invest in their own health, and these products add to this growing market. The cheerful makeover of muesli, as found in Troo, shows us that there is a concerted effort to make this product more attractive to a wider range of consumers. The use of MCDA can help us understand this more clearly than other methods, enabling the common themes of health and purity found in both Alpen's 1971 packaging and Troo's 2019 packaging to be unpicked and their similarities and differences to be uncovered.

Notes

1 See www.alpen.co.uk for the full story of the history of muesli.
2 See https://eatguud.com/blogs/blog/the-history-of-muesli for more details on early mass-produced muesli.
3 See www.eattroo.com for details.

References

Andersson, H. and Smith, A. 2021. Flags and Fields: A Comparative Analysis of National Identify in Butter Packaging in Sweden and the UK. *Social Semiotics* 33(4):861–882.

Barnes, A. 2017. Telling Stories: The Role of Graphic Design and Branding in the Creation of 'Authenticity' Within Food Packaging. *International Journal of Food Design* 2(2):183–202.

Blaxter, M. and Paterson, E. 1983. "The Goodness Is Taken Out of It: The Meaning of Food to Two Generations" in *The Sociology of Food and Eating*, edited by A. Murcott (Aldershot: Gower), pp. 95–105.

Burges Watson, D.L., Moreira, T. and Murtagh, M.J. 2009. Little Bottles of the Promise of Probiotics. *Health: An Interdisciplinary Journal for the Social Study of Health, Illness and Medicine* 12(2):219–234.

Chapman, G. and Maclean, H. 1993. "Junk Food" and "Healthy Food": Meanings of Food in Adolescent Women's Culture. *Journal of Nutrition Education*, 24:108–113.

Charles, M. and Kerr, M. 1988. *Women, Food and Families*. Manchester: Manchester University Press.

Chen, A. and Eriksson, G. 2019. The Mythologization of Protein: A Multimodal Critical Discourse Analysis of Snack Packaging. *Food, Culture & Society* 22(4):423–445.

Chen, A. and Eriksson, G. 2021. The Making of Healthy and Moral Snacks: A multimodal Critical Discourse Analysis of Corporate Storytelling. *Discourse, Context & Media* 32, https://doi.org/10.1016/j.dcm.2019.100347

DeVault, M. 1991. *Feeding the Family: The Social Organisation of Caring as Gendered Work*. Chicago: University of Chicago Press.

Eriksson, G. and Machin, D. 2020. Discourses of "Good Food": The Commercialisation of Healthy and Ethical Eating. *Discourse, Context and Media* 33, https://doi.org/10.1016/j.dcm.2019.100365

European Union Food Information Council. 2012. What Are Superfoods and Are They Really Super? Available at https://www.eufic.org/en/healthy-living/article/the-science-behind-superfoods-are-they-really-super (Accessed: 8 August 2022).

Fairclough, N. 2001. *Language and Power*. London: Longman.

Foucault, M. 1991. "Governmentality" in *The Foucault Effect: Studies in Governmentality*, edited by G. Burchill, C. Gordon and P. Miller (Chicago: Chicago University Press), pp. 87–105.

Gitlin, M. and Ellis T. 2012. *The Great American Cereal Book: How Breakfast Got Its Crunch*. New York: Abrams Image.

Haydu, J. and Skotnicki, T. 2016. Three Layers of History in Recurrent Social Movements: The Case of Food Reform. *Social Movement Studies* 15(4):345–360.

Hill, H. and Tilley, J. 2002. Packaging of Children's Breakfast Cereals: Manufacturers Versus Children. *British Food Journal* 104(9):766–777.

Hine, T. 1995. *The Total Package*. Boston: Little, Brown and Company.

Jack, I. 2016. Why Should Muesli Munching Be a Term of Abuse? It's the Fault of Orwell, *The Guardian* (9 January). Available at https://www.theguardian.com/commentisfree/2016/jan/09/why-should-muesli-munching-be-a-term-of-abuse-its-the-fault-of-orwell (Accessed: 4 August 2022).

Ledin, P. and Machin, D. 2018. *Doing Visual Analysis: From Theory to Practice*. London: SAGE.

Ledin, P. and Machin, D. 2020. Replacing Actual Political Activism with Ethical Shopping: The Case of Oatly. *Discourse, Context & Media* 34, https://doi.org/10.1016/j.dcm.2019.100344

Lodolce, M., Harris, J.L. and Schwartz, M.B. 2013. Sugar as Part of a Balanced Breakfast? What Cereal Advertisements Tell Children About Healthy Eating. *Journal of Health Communication* 18(11):1293–1309.

Lupton, D. 1996. *Food, the Body and the Self*. London: SAGE.

Machin, D. and Mayr. A. 2012. *How to Do Critical Discourse Analysis: A Multimodal Introduction*. London: SAGE.

Maffei, N. and Schifferstein, H. 2017. Perspectives on Food Packaging Design. *International Journal of Food Design* 2(2), https://doi.org/10.1386/ijfd.2.2.139_2

Mapes, G. 2020. Marketing Elite Authenticity: Tradition and Terror in Artisanal Food Discourse. *Discourse, Context & Media* 34, https://doi.org/10.1016/j.dcm.2019.100328

Mozaffarian, D., Rosenberg, I. and Uauy, R. 2018. History of Modern Nutrition Science – Implications for Current Research, Dietary Guidelines, and Food Policy. *The British Medical Journal* 361, https://doi.org/10.1386/ijfd.2.2.139_2

O'Hagan, L.A. 2020. Pure in Body, Pure in Mind? A Sociohistorical Perspective on the Marketisation of Pure Foods in Great Britain. *Discourse, Context & Media* 34, https://doi.org/10.1016/j.dcm.2019.100325

O'Hagan, L.A. and Eriksson, G. 2022. Modern Science, Moral Mothers, and Mythical Nature: A Multimodal Analysis of Cod Liver Oil Marketing in Sweden, 1920–1930. *Food and Foodways* 30(4):231–260.

Oswald, C. 2012. *Marketing Semiotics: Signs, Strategies, and Brand Value*. Oxford: Oxford University Press.
Pollan, M. 2006. *The Omnivore's Dilemma: A Natural History of Food in Four Meals*. New York: Penguin Books.
Reece, B.B., Rifon, N.J. and Rodriguez, K. 1999. "Selling Food to Children. Is Fun Part of a Balanced Breakfast?" in *Advertising to Children: Concepts and Controversies*, edited by L.C. Machlin and L. Carlson (Thousand Oaks: SAGE), pp. 189–208.
Severson, K. 2016. A Short History of Cereal, *New York Times* (22 February). Available at http://www.nytimes.com/interactive/2016/02/22/dining/history-of-cereal.html?_r=0 (Accessed: 19 May 2023).
Spence, C. 2017. Breakfast: The Most Important Meal of the Day? *International Journal of Gastronomy and Food Science* 8:1–6.
Spiekermann, U. 2011. Redefining Food: The Standardisation of Products and Production in Europe and the United States, 1880–1914. *History and Technology* 27(1):11–36.
Thomas, L., Waring, S., Singh, I. Stilwell Peccei, J., Thornborrow, J. and Jones, J. 2004. *Language, Society and Power: An Introduction*. London: Routledge.

Part 2

Drinks as Elixirs of Health

5 Best for Babies? Powdered Milk and Scientific Discourse in Early Twentieth-Century China

Lo Shuk Ying

Introduction

Over the last two decades, the study of dairy advertisements in modern China has become a popular research topic, with scholars paying increased attention to milk powder and milk varieties, such as fresh milk and condensed milk. Studies have concerned the relationship between milk and modernity (Li, 2010; Wang, 2011), the promotion of milk as an infant food (Chou, 2010) and how milk powder companies reshaped motherhood by encouraging artificial feeding (Lo, 2018). Research has also examined Liberty Farms (*Ziyou Nongchang*)—a fresh milk brand in Shanghai—demonstrating how the concept of *xiao jiating* (nuclear family) was marketed through its "smart" consumption by women (Glosser, 2003). This chapter contributes to this growing body of research by investigating how manufacturers interpreted scientific knowledge in the context of milk powder, marketing the product as the "best choice" for infants in early twentieth-century China.

Specifically, this chapter analyses milk powder advertisements in *Shenbao* [*Shanghai Post*]—a nationwide Chinese commercial newspaper founded in Shanghai in 1872.[1] The advertisements under exploration come from three milk powder companies: Lactogen, Momilk and Vitamilk. Lactogen was the flagship brand of the Nestlé Company, introduced to China around 1920. Nestlé had set up a sales office in Shanghai in 1908, making it one of the first foreign enterprises stationed in China (Nestlé's Management of Dairy Supply Chain in China, 2008). Its milk powder was released onto the market via local agents and trading companies (Zhang, 2020:110). Momilk—an American product manufactured by Brewer & Co. Inc[2]—was put on the Chinese market in 1924. Without an overseas office, Momilk employed local agents to deal with its business in China. Vitamilk (*Huimin Naifen*), on the other hand, was a domestic brand of the Wei Min Co. Ltd., established in 1927 by William Yinson Lee (1884–1965), a former agent of Brewer & Co. Inc.[3] Its products were given to distributors in various large Chinese cities, such as Hankou, Chongqing, Nanjing, Fuzhou, Ningbo, Wanzhou and Lanxi, for wholesale and retailing (*Shenbao*, 14 May 1930).

DOI: 10.4324/9781003450276-9

The chapter adopts a content analysis approach to the milk powder advertisements, focusing on both the written text and visual presentations.[4] Images disseminate messages to consumers in a direct and simple way, meaning that even those with limited literacy can interpret them. Images also express "symbolic, metaphorical and allegorical interpretation of collective ideas" (Reichardt, 1989:224–225), as well as experiences of people which might otherwise be hidden in written texts. The findings demonstrate that all three companies adopted similar commercial strategies and promotional techniques to sell their products, misinterpreting scientific ideas or blending such knowledge with traditional Chinese medical concepts. Companies also made use of medical authorities to build their reputations, reinforcing the safe and healthful images of the products. These advertisements, thus, illustrate not only the application of scientific discourse in commercial activities but also what type of scientific knowledge common people acquired in early twentieth-century China.

The chapter is divided into two parts. The first part provides an overview of the use of cow's milk and infant feeding practices in pre-twentieth-century China, while the second part examines how scientific discourses were manipulated to promote powdered milk in the 1920s.

Cow's Milk and Traditional Chinese Infant Feeding Practices

Cow's milk was not a customary constituent of the Chinese diet nor was it a typical infant food. Chinese infants were only fed animal milk when there was a lack of breast milk from either their mothers or wet nurses. Chinese medical practitioners recommended feeding infants with pig's milk, for example, because it could alleviate illness caused by umbilical tetanus (Li, 1987 [c. 16th century], *juan* 50, Part I). Cow's milk, in contrast, had no such medical function and was even known to cause digestion problems (Li, 1987 [c. 16th century], *juan* 50, Part II).

Economic reasons also contributed to cow's milk not being fed to infants in Imperial China. Cattle were important working farm animals and, thus, it was illegal and immoral to eat beef (Goossaert, 2005). Milking was also considered to affect agricultural output. From a species perspective, most cattle in China were buffalo and yellow cattle, both of which have poor lactation rates. An inadequate supply would, therefore, have prevented cow's milk from becoming a common substitute for breast milk (Lo, 2018:18–20).

Western merchants introduced the milk-drinking habit to Chinese people in the early nineteenth century. As fresh milk was not easily found in Chinese markets at the time, foreign merchants brought dairy cattle with them. William C. Hunter of Russell & Co., for example, mentioned that his company fleet—which included three boats—was full of factory coolies, cows and provisions when it departed from Macau for Canton on 4 October 1831 (Hunter, 1882:83). This suggests that fresh milk was in short supply even in Canton—the only designated port open to foreign trade under the Canton System[5] before the outbreak of the First Opium War in 1839.

Gradually, the dairy industry developed to cater for Westerners who were permitted to stay in treaty ports after the First Opium War. In 1855, for example, there were eight milk stores and 24 cowsheds located at Kwun Tai Loo in Victoria City, Hong Kong (Wong, 2020:80–81), while European-owned cowsheds were founded in the International Settlement of Shanghai in 1870. By 1898, there was a total of 53 dairy farms in the Settlement, six of which were run by foreigners. The remaining were Chinese owned, of which only 17 were officially registered (*MCSR*, 1874:59; *MCSR*, 1899:121). It was during this period that condensed milk also became widely available. Imports of condensed milk were recorded in Shanghai, Ningbo, Fuzhou, Dalian, Xiamen, Shantou, Canton, Kowloon and Mengzi (*RTTR*, 1895:289, 295, 341, 366, 388, 408, 436, 460, 490, 565, 606).

By the late nineteenth century, some Chinese people who lived in coastal cities and constantly interacted with foreigners and Western cultures began to drink milk; Sheng Xuanhuai—an entrepreneur and politician in the late Qing Dynasty—is one such example (Huang, 2020). In Chinese fiction, milk started to be portrayed as a component of breakfast among well-off people in Shanghai (Wu, 1977 [1933]:chap. 52). Even prostitutes became aware of milk's "magic" power in maintaining life (Ceng, 1991 [1904]:chap. 28). These examples show that, at this time, Chinese adults were more likely to consume milk than infants. However, milk was not yet a popular beverage, even among the wealthy, because fresh milk and condensed milk were expensive commodities.

Artificial feeding was introduced to China in the early twentieth century. In response to the tensions of internal rebellions and foreign invasions, the Late Qing Reforms (1901–1911) were launched, which included the provision of female education with home economics. The Chinese literati—both conservatives and radicals—believed that home economics was an excellent discipline to train female students to be "good wives and wise mothers" (*xianqi liangmu*) in order to achieve the ultimate goal of "strong nation and strengthening race" (*qiangguo qiangzhong*). Home economics covered several areas, including childcare. Breastfeeding, as home economists stressed, was the ideal infant feeding method since breast milk contained all the nutrients infants required. The moral responsibility of mothers to breastfeed was emphasised. Some even argued that breastfeeding was a "natural duty" (*tianzhi*) of women (Shimoda, 1902:12–13; Adachi, 1908:13; Hattori, 1908:28, 30). If mothers were short of breast milk and a wet nurse was not available, they could switch to artificial feeding. Home economists discussed the benefits and uses of various types of milk. In general, fresh milk was considered the best option in terms of nutrition, but condensed milk was deemed to be the most hygienic dairy product. Similar ideas and advocacies have also been emphasised in the United States since the late nineteenth century. Such beliefs—described as "scientific motherhood" by Apple (2006)—stressed that mothers needed scientific and medical guidance to raise children in a proper way.

These modern scientific ideas—often translated and disseminated through printed media, such as newspapers—were novel to Chinese people. Although

China had a low literacy rate in the late Qing Dynasty,[6] newspaper readership was relatively high. One copy of a newspaper was typically shared between ten and 20 readers, while outdated newspapers were distributed to inner and rural regions of China for further circulation. Furthermore, newspapers were often posted on walls or boards for passers-by to read. They could also be read aloud in public spheres, such as teahouses and schools, thereby increasing access for illiterate people (Lee and Nathan, 1985:372).

At this time, milk powder was not studied in home economics books or mentioned in newspapers because it had not yet been invented. The so-called "milk powder" (*niunai fen*) of the time was not pure solid dried milk, but a mixture of wheat flour, malt flour and cow's milk, such as Horlicks or Mellin's Food. When milk powder—as we understand it today—became available in the 1920s, however, companies quickly ensured that they emphasised how the product "overcame" the shortcomings of the cow's milk varieties available for infant feeding. As we will see below, they did so through the use of scientific discourse.

Vitamins and Cow's Milk

As previously indicated, home economists first recommended giving infants cow's milk in the late Qing era. Their analysis on the chemical differences between human milk and cow's milk (mostly fresh and canned milk) demonstrated that both included varying proportions of the same chemicals, such as fat, protein, water and minerals. The health-giving benefits of milk became further promoted following the discovery of vitamins by Western scientists in the 1910s, which led to a subsequent emphasis on nutrition as a means of preventing illnesses and diseases.

Elmer McCollum—an American biochemist credited with discovering vitamins A, B, D and E—advocated the use of vitamins as an indicator of food value and stated that milk was a good source of the nutrients that the human body needed. He argued that the diets of people in North America and Europe typically included milk and its byproducts; thus, they attained greater size and greater longevity, and were much more successful in the rearing of their young. They were also more aggressive than non-dairy users and obtained much greater advancements in literature, science and art (McCollum, 1918:150–151). Consequently, cow's milk became celebrated as a "protective food" that contributed to national strength and civilisational progress (Valenze, 2011:12). McCollum's findings, as well as the discoveries of other "new" nutritionists in the United States, were quick to be manipulated by the food industries for promotion (Levenstein, 1988:150–156).

McCollum's ideas on milk were introduced to China in the early 1920s through the article "Milk as a Factor in Race Development." This was a period of change in the country, sparked by the May Fourth Movement in 1919, which saw the faculty and students of Peking University call for "Mr Democracy" (*de xiansheng*) and "Mr Science" (*sai xiansheng*) to change the nation and its people. As a result, Western science soon became a guideline for Chinese diets. Chinese milk advertisements from the period show the clear influence of McCollum's ideas. A 1920 advertisement for Gail and Bordon Condensed Milk in *Shenbao*, for example, argues that dairy products make up 15% to 25% of the diets of Europeans and North Americans. Therefore, they grow stronger, live longer, have a lower mortality rate and achieve better in literature, science and art (*Shenbao*, 23 May 1920). Liberty Milk (*Ziyou Nongchang*) was another brand that appropriated McCollum's ideas to market the benefits of giving fresh milk to infants. Nevertheless, there were no milk powder companies in China interested in McCollum's theory in the early 1920s.

Although vitamin knowledge was almost simultaneously transmitted to China, it was not until the late 1920s that the benefits of vitamins became widely known. Wu Xian—a professor in biochemistry at Peking Union Medical College—was one of the first scientists to introduce the concept of vitamins (including vitamins A, B, C, D and E) to China. Wu emphasised that specific vitamin deficiencies played a significant role in the development of illnesses, including rickets, beriberi, septicaemia and xerophthalmia. To prevent these diseases, Chinese people were advised to consume a wide variety of nutrient-dense foods or adjust their eating habits. They were particularly told to drink milk because of their unbalanced diet and lack of "good" protein from animal sources. Nevertheless, cow's milk, as Wu stressed, had an excessive amount of protein and was deficient in carbohydrates, which meant that it was not ideal for infant feeding (Wu, 1977 [1933]:8).

Despite the many benefits of cow's milk, greater access to scientific information also made Chinese people more aware of its limitations for artificial feeding. It was claimed, for example, that dairy products could become contaminated and transmit tuberculosis and other diseases to infants if milk was not pasteurised or processed properly (Chen 1926:1–3; Yu 1935:22–24). Scientific discourse, thus, did not overwhelmingly support the use of cow's milk, particularly for infant feeding. As we will see below, when milk powder arrived on the market, manufacturers selectively picked and chose arguments from the debate to create favourable perceptions of their goods.

The Introduction of Milk Powder

Milk powder first became available on Chinese markets in the 1920s, but almost all products were imported. The earliest product was Lactogen, manufactured in 1920 by the Nestlé Company, and the first commercial commodity to be showcased in a window display in China (Xu, 1995:4). In the first quarter of 1924, the sales volumes of Lactogen surpassed those of Horlicks (*Shanghai Huojia Jikan*, 2005 [1924]:3).

From 1923 to 1937, over half of China's net imports of milk powder came from Australia and New Zealand, followed by the United States. It was not until 1927 that the first domestic brand of milk powder—Vitamilk—was put on the Chinese market. Keen competition pushed companies—both global and local—to adopt innovative promotion strategies. Advertisements, presented as written texts and sometimes supplemented by visual images, were the primary way for companies to approach consumers.

With well-designed branding and marketing plans, foreign milk powder enterprises still needed to refresh their promotional strategies when they entered the Chinese market. These companies could not simply copy and translate the advertisements they had previously used because the Chinese were neither traditional dairy consumers nor used to bottle-feeding babies with cow's milk. Advertisements, thus, had to be adapted in terms of content, style and presentation in order to meet the needs of Chinese consumers. The English version of Lactogen advertisements in China, for instance, typically used several short sentences or slogans to highlight the essential features of the product, along with the image of a chubby baby popping out of the tin. Such a presentation embedded the product and the infant together, illustrating that Lactogen was able to nurture healthy and fat babies. Its Chinese advertisements, in contrast, contained heavy doses of written material and often highlighted the following characteristics: (1) being equivalent to breast milk; (2) suitable for newborns; (3) ability to be stored for a long period, even in the hot summer and (4) ease of preparation by diluting with hot water. It then guided customers to obtain a trial sample and a child-rearing handbook published by Lactogen (Figure 5.1).

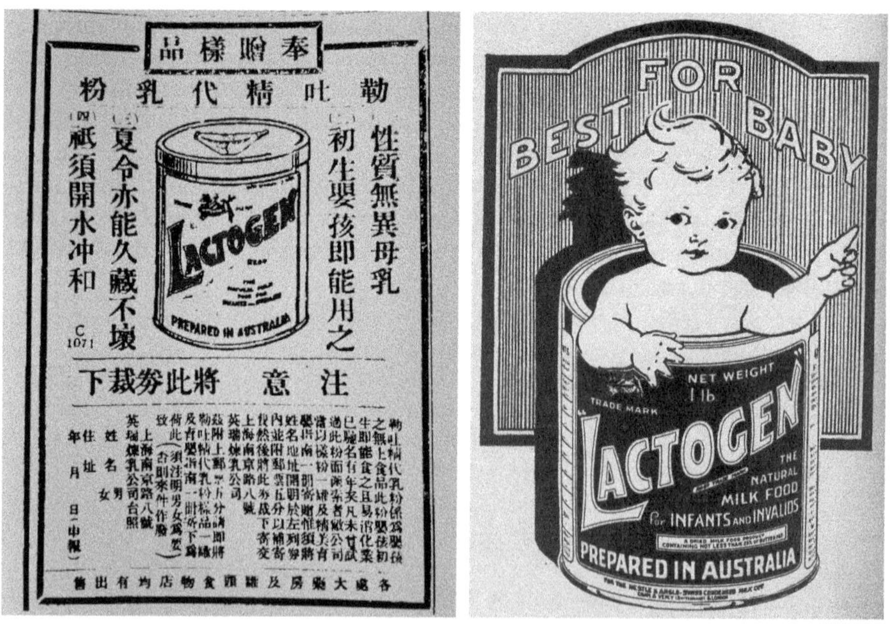

Figure 5.1 Advertisements for Lactogen in English and Chinese

Credit: *China Journal of Science and Arts* 1928, 9(2): n.p. and *Shenbao*, 12 August 1922, p. 5

Similar presentation techniques were used in Momilk campaigns of the time. Bold headlines in Chinese characters described the product as "pure, nutritious milk powder," while the image of the company's milk powder was topped with the English heading "The Vitamine Milk," which highlighted its vitamin-rich characteristics and the power of Western science. Momilk advertisements also drew upon recent scientific and medical studies to emphasise that milk powder was the best form of milk because it could be stored for a long time. Furthermore, the production process preserved the nutritious value of milk because Momilk adopted the sophisticated technique of roller processing to produce its powder. This made Momilk "virtually identical" to human milk in terms of cleanliness, purity, hygiene and vitamin content (*Shenbao*, 10 October 1924).

The heavy-text characteristics of Chinese advertisements for milk powder in the Republican era (1912–1949) demonstrated that milk powder was new to Chinese consumers and, thus, in-depth product descriptions were preferred. As manufacturers strived to provide as much information as possible, advertisements began to resemble informative articles that explained the production procedures and characteristics of powdered milk. These advertisements also served as a platform for the populace to learn basic scientific knowledge about milk powder.

The advertisements for milk powder firms also made extensive use of space to instruct consumers on how to request a trial sample. The higher price of milk powder likely put parents off starting a new infant feeding plan. Milk powder companies, therefore, generously provided trial samples to anyone who wanted to try artificial feeding. Such a practice further supports the argument that both dairy products and bottle-feeding were unfamiliar to Chinese people, thereby leading manufacturers to offer a range of incentives for consumers to try.

Apart from textual information, advertisements for milk powder often included photos and drawings as visual elements to enhance their appeal. To ensure that consumers would remember the companies and their items, advertisements typically featured visual representations of the products. Moreover, the advertisements used unique graphic styles to make these images more eye-catching. A case in point is a 1929 advertisement in *Shenbao* for Vitamilk (Figure 5.2), which shows a "good wet nurse" with a feeding bottle in her right hand. She is physically fused into the tin, implying that Vitamilk is a substitute for an actual wet nurse. According to the advertisement, many wet nurses are unable to feed newborns because they are out of breast milk, which causes the babies to cry nonstop throughout the day. The "Vitamilk wet nurse," on the other hand, has a variety of benefits, including (1) no need for a paycheck; (2) abundant in nutrition; (3) free of infectious diseases; (4) no need for dressing or eating; and (5) diligent women.

Vitamilk's criticism of wet nursing was reasonable to some extent. A laboratory test, conducted by the Public Health Bureau of the Shanghai Municipal Government in late 1934, indicated that 59 out of 257 wet nurses (or about

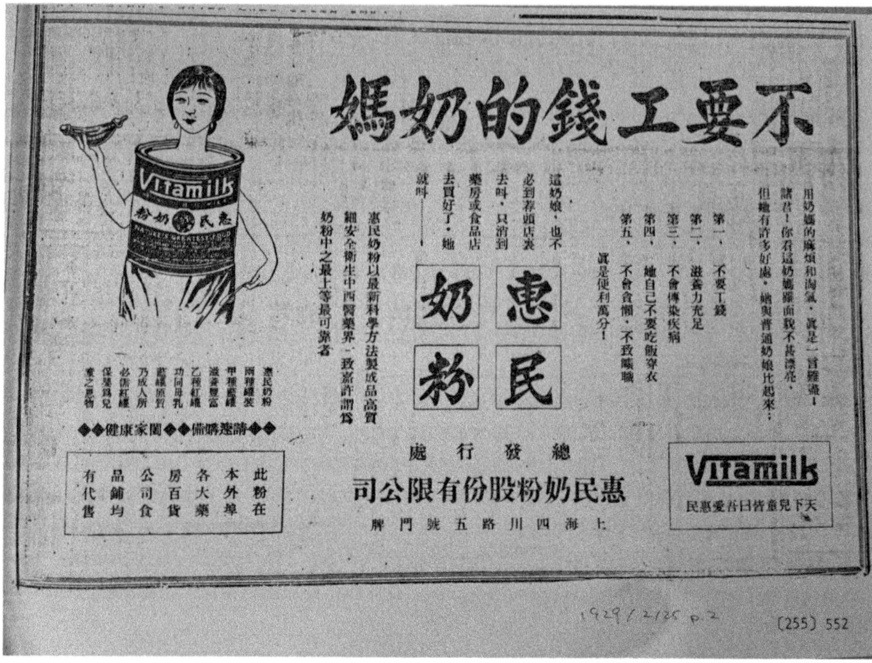

Figure 5.2 Vitamilk 1929 Advertisement

Credit: *Shenbao*, 25 February 1929, Local Supplement 2.

25%) had syphilis (*Shenbao*, 18 January 1935). As a syphilis test amounted to nearly half of their monthly salaries, many wet nurses were unwilling or unable to pay. As a result, the number of infected wet nurses was underestimated. Additionally, wet nurses were frequently involved in criminal activities, such as theft, fraud and adultery, according to *Shenbao* (Lo, 2018:128, 131). To highlight the disadvantages of wet nurses, milk powder companies, such as Vitamilk, made attempts to persuade parents to switch to artificial feeding.

Scientific Discourses and the "Healthy" Image of Powdered Milk

This section outlines some of the key strategies that Lactogen, Momilk and Vitamilk used in their advertisements to convince consumers that their products were best for babies. Both domestic and international brands commonly made scientific claims so as to highlight the benefits of their products and the drawbacks of their rivals. These claims, to a certain extent, misinterpreted Western scientific knowledge. Some even combined scientific concepts with other traditional Chinese medical ideas in novel ways to disseminate their messages.

Appropriation of Scientific Ideas: in order to convince consumers to adopt artificial feeding, milk powder companies needed to prove that their products were almost identical to breast milk. Consequently, a comparison in chemical composition between powdered milk and human milk was a common feature in advertisements, with the amount of fat (butter) in the milk being a focus of discussion. Lactogen regularly presented tables in its advertisements, which gave "proof" that its chemical composition was almost identical to that of human milk (*Shenbao*, 20 December 1926c). Momilk adopted a similar strategy, yet used a completely different argument regarding milk fat. It emphasised that oil (butter) was not the most important ingredient of milk powder and that excessive milk fat could, in fact, harm the digestive system of babies, causing many diseases (*Shenbao*, 29 October 1926d). Momilk stated that it was, of course, low in fat. This was not a case of the company trying to cut corners because Momilk made a significant capital investment in oil purifying technology (*Shenbao*, 28 October 1926c). Responding to criticisms, Lactogen claimed that certain brands of milk powder claiming to be light in fat and cheaper in price contained insufficient nutrients and were harmful to babies' health (*Shenbao*, 30 October 1926b).

Modification of cow's milk for infant feeding purposes started in the early 1910s. As infants, especially newborns, could not digest the fat in cow's milk, scientists attempted to replace animal fat with vegetable oils while still keeping the milk safe and palatable. In 1915, Dr Henry J. Gerstenberger and Dr Harold O. Ruh developed Synthetic Milk Adapted (SMA), which was non-fat cow's milk along with lactose, oleo oils and vegetable oils. Throughout the subsequent three years, 385 infants of varying ages and conditions were fed SMA as part of clinical studies.[7] The research findings showed that SMA provided infants with a sufficient amount of nutrients and did not cause rickets, spasmophilia or anaemia (Gerstenberger and Ruh, 1919:1–37). SMA, thereafter, became one of the popular, modern commercially manufactured infant formulas (Fomon, 1993:11). In short, the quality and quantity of fat had a significant role in determining the quality of milk powder in the early twentieth century. It also explained the reasons behind the disputes over milk fat between Lactogen and Momilk.

The controversy between Lactogen and Momilk over milk fat seemed to be based on scientific knowledge. Neither of them, however, gave empirical data to support their arguments. Lactogen claimed that its chemical composition was virtually identical to that of human milk if one followed the reconstitution instructions and used the right ratio of water to dried milk. Lactogen's data, however, was misleading. According to the laboratory analysis of Shanghai Municipal Council, the percentages of fat and protein in human milk should be 3.8% and 1.7%, respectively (*SMCR*, 1913:85A). Lactogen presented deceiving information about human milk by deliberately decreasing the fat content to 3.1% and increasing the percentage of protein to 2.0% (Table 5.1). Such tactics aimed to narrow the gap between human milk and Lactogen, forming an illusion that their chemical make-up was almost the same.

Both Lactogen and Momilk used limited information to make sweeping generalisations. Cow's milk consists of various chemicals, including proteins, fats, carbohydrates, minerals (calcium in particular), vitamins and water.

Table 5.1 Comparison of the Chemical Compositions of Human Milk and Reconstituted Lactogen or Cow's Milk

Chemicals	*Human milk*		*Reconstituted lactogen/cow milk*	
	Lactogen's advertisement (%)	*Shanghai Municipal Council's analysis (%)*	*Lactogen's advertisement (%)*	*Shanghai Municipal Council's analysis (%)*
Water	88.1	-	87.07	-
Fat	3.10	3.8	3.13	3.6
Protein	2.00	1.7	2.80	3.8
Lactose	6.60	6.6	6.38	4.5
Minerals	0.20	0.2	0.62	0.7

Credit: Author's own image compiled from information in *Shenbao*, 20 December 1926c, Local Supplement 3; *SMCR*, 1913:85A

However, these two companies highlighted only fat and protein in their comparisons, drawing a misleading conclusion as to the similarity between powdered milk and breast milk.

Momilk also became involved in a controversy over vitamins. High cooking temperatures or extended cooking times can lead to the breakdown of vitamin C because it is easily damaged by heat and light. Milk, nonetheless, can only be made into powder by being heated to the temperature near to its boiling point (135–150°C), where it solidifies. As a result, milk powder has a low vitamin C content. Physicians, therefore, suggested feeding babies orange juice or fruit juice once a day if they were artificially fed (Mi, 1927:72). Contradicting medical opinions, Momilk argued in its advertisements that its products were rich in nutrients due to its sophisticated manufacturing methods; thus, infants fed with Momilk did not need any extra supplements (*Shenbao*, 9 July 1926a; 26 September 1926b). In addition, the company stressed that medical professionals never recommended that breastfed infants took supplements because breast milk was already full of all the nutrients infants required. This justification was provided by Momilk as "proof" that it was "absolutely the same as breastmilk" (*Shenbao*, 7 November 1926e).

Furthermore, Momilk claimed that its product's ability to maintain vitamin C was due to its use of the roller process—an advanced production technique—while other companies, such as Lactogen, continued to employ an outdated spray methodology (*Shenbao*, 10 October 1924). This was false because whatever technique was used, milk had to be heated until it was near to the boiling point and solidified. As a result, it caused some of the vitamin C in milk powder to be destroyed, regardless of the production method adopted. Momilk sounded authoritative and convincing, however.

The abovementioned examples demonstrate how milk powder companies adopted pseudoscientific discourses to present their products in a scientific light, only highlighting scientific ideas that favoured their products. Some even showed inaccurate or improper information intentionally. In addition, advertisements often presented many figures and technical terms alongside professional images of the products that were hard for the general public to understand. Such promotional tactics skewed the public's understanding of breastfeeding and artificial feeding while providing them with false information.

Hybrid Interpretations

Another strategy used by milk powder companies was to appropriate traditional Chinese medical theories to explain the characteristic of their products, thereby making them more easily comprehended by the general public. Momilk, for example, criticised other brands for adopting antiquated manufacturing techniques, claiming that other brands of milk powder contained excessive fat and "heaty" properties (*reqi*) that were more likely to cause skin rashes and constipation in infants. Babies who consumed these brands would need to take supplements, such as orange juice, to alleviate their illnesses (*Shenbao*, 26 September 1926b).

Advertisements such as these used two arguments. First, milk powder was "heaty" in nature. Food, according to traditional Chinese medicine, is classified into "four natures and five flavours" (*sixing wuwei*). The basic nature of a food can be changed through different cooking and storage methods. Cooking techniques, such as stewing, baking, braising, deep-frying, roasting and simmering, can change a food's cooling properties into "heaty" ones (Xu, 2005:90). Cow's milk, according to the *Compendium of Materia Medica* (*Bencao gangmu*),[8] is non-toxic in nature with slight cooling properties that can nourish the heart, lungs and skin (Li, 1987 [c. 16th century], *juan* 50, Part II). Its cooling properties are replaced by hot ones when the milk transforms into dried milk. According to Momilk, this problem was avoided because of their sophisticated manufacturing technique.

The second argument was that the "heaty" nature of milk powder, with the exception of Momilk again, resulted in various health problems, such as skin rashes and constipation. There were many causes of rashes and digestive problems, and milk's "heaty" properties were not given much thought by Western scientists and medical professionals. Furthermore, milk had to be heated in order to turn into its solid form, regardless of the production techniques applied. It was neither fair nor scientific that Momilk solely accused outdated manufacturing processes as the reason for the hot properties of milk powder and the cause of skin and digestion problems in infants. Nonetheless, the argument was one likely to be understood more clearly by Chinese consumers.

This hybrid interpretation of the properties of milk powder reveals the responses of Chinese people to new knowledge and material cultures. Both science and milk powder were novel to the Chinese in the early twentieth century. Therefore, some milk powder companies used Western scientific knowledge together with traditional Chinese medical beliefs to explain the advantages of milk powder. In doing so, they helped make complex scientific ideas more palatable to their target audience. While these justifications might not have been entirely false, they were certainly heavily biased.

From Chinese Formula Milk to National Goods

Some brands of milk powder, especially those made in China, stressed their tailor-made characteristics. Vitamilk is an important example in this regard, its Chinese name being *Huimin Naifen*, which literally meant that it benefitted people. This brand intentionally emphasised that its product benefitted not just Chinese people, but also the nation as a whole. Skilfully making use of national discourse, Vitamilk criticised the fact that almost all milk powders in China were imported goods. Chinese consumers had never had a say in the manufacturing process nor did they ever request formula specifically adapted for Chinese babies. It was only when Vitamilk was put on the market that Chinese babies obtained their own tailor-made formula milk (*Shenbao*, 2 October 1927).

The Chineseness of Vitamilk further evolved to include the recommendation that Chinese consumers purchased Chinese milk powders in order to support the national economy. In 1930, Vitamilk was promoted as the most cost-effective product according to the following factors: (1) less expensive; (2) of great quality; (3) nourishing to the body; and (4) best for babies. Thus, for the benefit of Chinese commerce, customers were encouraged to purchase Vitamilk, which was "medically proven" to be the most suitable powdered milk for Chinese infants (*Shenbao*, 14 May 1930).

It is arguable whether Vitamilk was tailor-made or suitable for Chinese babies. The raw materials of the brand came from the United States, Canada or Australia and were then packaged in China (*Huimin Gufen Youxian Gongsi Zhaogu Zhangcheng* 1927:n.p.; *Shenbao*, 27 September 1927). This implies that the main manufacturing procedure for Vitamilk was still under the control of foreigners. Furthermore, Vitamilk's advertisements never gave any details regarding the Chinese formulas, such as what the key ingredients required by Chinese babies were. Consumers, thus, lacked the information necessary to evaluate the distinctiveness of Vitamilk in comparison to other imported milk powders.

Moreover, it is questionable whether the national milk powder would be able to protect Chinese commerce. Before the outbreak of the War of Resistance against Japan (1937–1945), few Chinese businessmen were involved in the milk powder manufacturing industry. This was mainly due to technological backwardness and a shortage of essential commodities, namely dairy cattle. This only changed in 1935 when Xiao Jiaqian of the West Lake Condensed Milk Factory invented a milk powder manufacturing machine and Chinese-made milk powder was put on the market (*SSCYDYL, n.d.*, vol. 2). Despite customers' willingness to buy national milk powders, the dairy industry and business in China did not change significantly. As for Vitamilk, its Chinese characteristics were merely a marketing gimmick.

Medical Authorities

Citing medical authorities was another way to prove the benefits of milk powder. This could be in the form of medical consultations or simply recommendations from famous or well-known figures. Lactogen was the first milk powder company to provide medical consultations to consumers. Its advertisements identified medical consultation as a company obligation:

> Obligation
>
> Our company employs several famous Chinese and Western nurses, who are experts in infant feeding. If guidance is needed, please contact us for a home visit. Our nurses offer outreach medical consultations free of charge. We shall reply in detail by mail if you live far away [out of Shanghai].
>
> (*Shenbao*, 21 August 1926a)

Lactogen emphasised that it was the company's obligation to care for both parents and babies and that free medical consultations were, therefore, provided. Such services helped construct a responsible image for Lactogen, demonstrating it to be a conscientious enterprise. As a successful image-building strategy, other milk powder manufacturers, such as Momilk, also provided similar services (*Shenbao*, 26 September 1926b).

One may wonder whether such medical consultations really helped both mothers and babies. The experience of Ms. G (a fictitious name)—a nurse working for a milk powder company— illustrates the reality. Her regular tasks were listed as follows:

> My working hours are from 9:00 am to 12:00 pm, and from 2:00 pm to 5:00 pm. I have to visit six or seven families every day before reporting to the company. I have two major duties. First, I need to approach physicians and ask for information on newborns. Second, I have to visit those babies at home and promote milk powder.
>
> (Qian, 1935:133)

These so-called medical consultations were, according to Ms. G, marketing strategies. She was ostensibly addressing hygiene, but in reality, she was a saleswoman. In order to collect information about newborns in Shanghai, Ms. G was required to approach physicians every working day. Dairy companies also took the initiative to approach relevant government departments, requesting information about newborns.[9] She would then visit the infants and persuade their parents to adopt artificial feeding. If the infants were already being fed artificially, she would ask to take photos (ibid). These photos might be published in the periodicals or booklets of the brand.[10]

Employing lactation nurses to provide baby nursing guidance, Lactogen fostered the idea that even medical professionals supported artificial feeding and branded milk powder, convincing customers that this brand was trustworthy, reliable and healthy. From an economic perspective, recruiting female nurses instead of physicians could reduce costs. Above all, female lactation nurses were approachable to mothers and easily convinced them to change their infant feeding practices. They also formed an illusion that Lactogen would offer medical support for any sickness caused by artificial feeding during their home visits with infants and mothers.[11]

Featuring positive product reviews from medical professionals reinforced the healthy image of milk powder. Vitamilk, for example, invited Dr Wu Lien-Teh—a famous plague fighter who founded the Manchurian Plague Prevention Service in China in 1912—to comment on its products.[12] According to the advertisement (*Shenbao*, 4 December 1928), Wu stated that Vitamilk had been proven to be a healthy diet good for the human body, especially the brain, bones and muscles. The modified milk powder in the red can (*hongguan naifen*) was "as good as breastmilk and most suitable for babies." The endorsement of Wu helped increase the sales volumes of Vitamilk in northeastern China (*SSCYDYL, n.d.*, vol. 2).

The recommendation of Vitamilk given by Wu was debatable. It was no doubt that Wu was a famous medical professional across East Asia, not just China, but he was not a paediatrician. His advice, as shown in the advertisement, was not just limited to infants. He also suggested that adults, including doctors and laboratory technicians in northeast China where plague had ravaged, drink Vitamilk every day. Wu most probably recommended Vitamilk due to his partnership with William Yinson Lee, the brand's founder. Lee marketed his business by engaging in community service and charitable activities (Fitzgerald and Kuo, 2017:85). His milk powder business seemed to follow this track. He set up The Chinese Mission to Lepers in 1926 and served as the first chairman of the organisation. Meanwhile, Wu was one of the honorary vice-chairmen of the organisation (Du, 2013:616). Lee most likely took advantage of his partnership with Wu, seeking help from him to recommend Vitamilk.

The "Politics" of Scientific Marketing

Not all milk powder advertisements presented biased and misleading scientific knowledge. Under the Advertisement Regulations of 1930 (*Shenbao*, 12 June 1930), newspaper advertisements were prohibited from presenting false descriptions of medicines. However, there was not enough manpower to execute the law. It was also difficult to determine whether an advertisement was purposefully misleading. Government authorities, medical societies and the media, for instance, were present in Britain and Japan to control the quality of medical advertisements for milk powder. China, however, lacked all these components before the War of Resistance (Huang, 1988:159).

While clearly deceptive in some cases, the advertisements presented still convinced many as to the benefits of powdered milk in infant feeding. This was due to the fact that advertisements were a significant source of scientific ideas. Many Chinese people were unable to obtain scientific information from books and magazines. Newspaper advertisements providing detailed accounts of the characteristics of milk powder, thus, became a popular platform for businesses to advertise their goods, as well as for the general public to learn the fundamentals of science. Advertisements for milk powder might not have been based on empirical research and might even have included biased arguments and exaggerated or inaccurate data; nevertheless, they constructed an image that milk powder was a medically sound substance that was helpful for babies' health.

The popularisation of milk powder was also closely related to the political background of modern China. The quest by Chinese intellectuals for a strong nation and strengthening race had been advocated since the end of the nineteenth century in order to resist foreign invasions. Various strategies have been used to accomplish this goal, including female education. Equally, powdered milk, which was "scientifically proven" to be nutrient-rich and comparable to human milk, could nourish healthy babies, which was a big step towards a strong nation, even though artificial feeding was not explicitly advised.

There were also additional reasons why powdered milk was chosen for infant feeding. Cow's milk was a symbol of modernity (Li, 2010; Wang, 2011; Sabban, 2014), widely accepted by the Chinese in the early twentieth century, but few people could afford it. Mothers, who fed their infants powdered milk, were portrayed as modernised, trendy, intelligent, educated and liberated middle-class women. Some of them, who were working or still enrolled in schools, also fed their babies powdered milk to reduce the burden of motherhood. In short, powdered milk gave freedom to nursing mothers (Lo, 2018).

Conclusion

In response to the national salvation movement, the May Fourth intellectuals advocated the study of science. But how did science permeate the everyday life of Chinese people? Consuming powdered milk was one method. Using scientific theories, milk powder was marketed as an ideal infant food which was healthy and nutrient rich. Above all, it echoed the literati's quest for a strong nation and strengthening race. The scientific claims of milk powder, however, were usually misleading and even presented biased or false information.

Although Chinese demand and consumption of powdered milk increased in the first half of the twentieth century, the three milk powder companies under study in this chapter underwent different developments, even before the outbreak of the War of Resistance. After 1933, neither Momilk nor Vitamilk ran product advertisements in *Shenbao*. Momilk's business was affected when William Yinson Lee quit in 1927 and launched Vitamilk. After a long period of absence, its advertisements returned to *Shenbao* in 1931. However, after the Shanghai Incident broke out in late January 1932 (a conflict between China and Japan), Momilk no longer posted advertisements in *Shenbao*.[13] The reason for its absence and final withdrawal from the Chinese market is unknown, yet the Japanese invasion, followed by the worldwide economic depression, probably played a significant role. At the same time, Vitamilk saw a sharp decline in sales in northeast China because of Japan's attack on Mukden in September 1931. This resulted in another firm reorganisation in 1932 (*SSCYDYL, n.d.*, vol. 2).

Throughout wartime, the demand for milk in China kept rising. Owing to its higher price and fraud-resistant nature, milk powder had become a common commodity for hoarding and speculative activity (Chen, 2001:29). It was most likely a reason why Vitamilk's business still operated normally in 1939 (*SSCYDYL, n.d.*, vol. 2). After the war, China's milk consumption continued to rise due to the United States' donations of tons of skimmed milk powder to Chinese refugees (DuBois, 2019:196–197). Since 1949, the Chinese economic system has undergone changes that have affected the production and consumption of milk. Lactogen as a foreign commodity was not available on the Chinese market in the early 1950s, for example. The long and complicated story of the supply and demand of milk powder in China is certainly worth further examination.

Over a century has now passed since China began using cow's milk for infant feeding, but little has changed in the way that milk powder is marketed (see Chapter 8 in this volume). Advertisers of today continue to think in the same ways as those of a century ago. Milk powder marketing still frequently uses the strategy of medical authority. In numerous advertisements, medical practitioners expertly quote medical research studies, discussing the benefits of milk powder. Moreover, milk powder companies continue to emphasise that their products either are intended for infants born by Caesarean section or contain ingredients like AHA, DHA, prebiotics and probiotics that make them equivalent to breast milk. As the amount of chemicals and nutrients became an indicator of the quality of cow's milk, some farmers added melamine to boost the tested protein level of watered-down milk, which resulted in the milk scandal of 2008.

In addition to containment of powdered milk, many countries have put restrictions on the production and circulation of powdered milk advertisements, with the aim of encouraging breastfeeding. The legislation governing the marketing of formula milk to infants under the age of six months is one of the key distinctions between milk powder advertisements today and those from a century ago (Health Bureau & Department of Health, 2022). However, the most crucial duty in regulating milk powder advertising seems to be to emphasise the value of breastfeeding rather than give accurate presentations of the product and its effects.

Note

All copies of *Shenbao* were accessed via the Green Apple Shen Pao Database: http://www.huawenku.cn/html/huawenkuguihua/ruxuanbaokan-201303212453.html

Abbreviations

MCSR:	Municipal Council of Shanghai Report
RTTR:	*Returns of Trade and Trade Reports*
SMCR:	*Shanghai Municipal Council Report*
SSCYDYL:	*Shanghai Shangye Chuxu Yinhang Diaocha Yanjiu Lei*

Notes

1 Originally, *Shenbao* had approximately 42.7% of space reserved for advertisements, but this gradually increased to 60% in the mid-1920s (Ge, 1927:227). The newspaper's circulation also grew over time: from 1,200 daily copies in 1875 to 30,000 in 1920 and 150,000 in 1937 (Wang, 2007:69). It ceased publication in May 1949 when the Chinese Communist Party liberated Shanghai as part of the Chinese Civil War (Milter, 2004).

2 Established in Worcester (MA), Brewer & Co. Inc was a drug company dealing with pharmaceuticals and patent medicines. The company also manufactured vitamin products, ampuls and private formulas, such as milk powder (Trade Catalogs from Brewer & Co. Inc., 2023).

3 Lee's business card once indicated that he was a co-director of Brewer & Co. Inc. (Fitzgerald and Kuo, 2017:84).

4 There is a lack of information regarding the creation and production of advertisements for these three companies. However, in early twentieth-century China, advertisements tended to be produced by either advertising agencies or the advertising units of newspapers. Some local enterprises had their own departments for the production of advertisements (Huang, 2009:114).

5 The Canton System was a trading pattern that developed between Chinese and foreign (particularly British) merchants in the mid-seventeenth century. It dictated that all foreign trade coming into China was confined to Canton, while foreign traders were subject to regulations by the Chinese government. It remained in force until 1842.

6 Approximately, 30%–45% for men and 2%–10% for women (Rawski, 1979:149–154).

7 74 of the 385 infants were removed from the trial within six weeks.

8 Complied by Li Shizhen (1518–1593), a herbalist and physician, *Compendium of Materia Medica* is the most complete and comprehensive medical book published in the mid-Ming Dynasty (1368–1644).

9 In 1936, the Anglo-Swiss Condensed Milk Company sent a letter to the Director of the Public Health Department of the Shanghai Municipal Council, asking for information on newborns registered in the International Settlement (*Ertong Fuli Hui De Ertong Fuli Ji Zhaokai Jiankang Yinger Bisai Hui Deng Shiyou* 1934–1939).

10 In the late nineteenth and early twentieth centuries, many American dairymen distributed free childcare guides to attract middle-class families to try artificial feeding. Similar promotional strategies were applied when these international brands entered the Chinese dairy market in the 1920s. Lactogen, for example, published *Yuying Zinan* [Baby Care Guidelines], while Momilk compiled *Niunai Yu Muzi Zhi Guanxi* [Relationships Between Milk and the Mother and Child].

11 Baby nursing guidance offered by milk powder companies was still in use in Southeast Asia and Africa in the 1960s and 1970s. Milk powder enterprises employed lactation nurses at hospitals and clinics to give parents advice on nursing, but were in reality persuading mothers to change to artificial feeding (Chetley, 1983 [1979]).

12 Wu's letter was written in English. It was the advertiser who selectively translated the letter into Chinese.

13 Momilk continued to run advertisements in another Chinese newspaper entitled *Sin Wan Pao*, where its final advertisement appeared on 5 June 1935.

References

Adachi, H. 1908. *Yuer Tan* [Talks on Childcare]. Translated by D. Fubao. Shanghai: Yixue Shuju.

Apple, R. 2006. *Perfect Motherhood: Science and Childrearing in America*. New Brunswick: Rutgers University Press.

Ceng, P. 1991 [1904]. *Niehai Hua* [Flower in a Sea of Sin]. Shanghai: Shanghai Ancient Books Press.
Chen, C.R. 2001. *Kangzhan Shidai Shenghou Shi* [History of Life During the War of Resistance]. Shanghai: Shanghai People's Publishing House.
Chen, L. 1926. Niuru Zhi Xin Yanjiu (San Xu) [New Research on Cow Milk (Part 3)]. *Zhongwa Nongbao* [China Agriculture News] 34:1–3.
Chetley, A. 1983 [1979]. *The Baby Killer Scandal: War on Want Investigation into the Promotion and Sale of Powdered Baby Milks in the Third World*. Translated by S.C. Chau. Sunbeam: Hong Kong.
Chou, C.Y. 2010. Xiong Bu Yu Ping Bu–Jindai Zhongguo Buru Guannian De Bianqian (1900–1949) [Breastfeeding Versus Bottle-Feeding: The Transformation of Nursing Concepts in Modern China (1900–1949)]. *Jindai Zhongguo Funu Shi Yanjiu* [Research on Women History in Modern China] 18:24–37.
Du, D.K. 2013. Mafeng Jikan De Bankan Zongzhi Yu Bianji Tese [The Objectives and Editorial Features of *Lepers Quarterly*]. *Zhongguo Keji Qikan Yanjiu* [Chinese Journal of Scientific and Technical Periodicals] 24(3):616–618.
DuBois, T.D. 2019. "China's Dairy Century: Making, Drinking and Dreaming of Milk" in *Animals and Human Society in Asia: Historical, Cultural and Ethical Perspectives*, edited by R. Kowner, G. Bar-Oz, M. Biran, M. Shahar and G. Shelach-Lavi (Cham: Palgrave MacMillan), pp. 179–212.
Ertong Fuli Hui De Ertong Fuli Ji Zhaokai Jiankang Yinger Bisai Hui Deng Shiyou [Children Welfare and Healthy Baby Contest Organised by the Children Welfare Association] (1934–1939). Shanghai Archives: U1-16-996.
Fitzgerald, J. and Kuo, M.F. 2017. Diaspora Charity and Welfare Sovereignty in the Chinese Republic: Shanghai Charity Innovator William Yinson Lee (Li Yuanxin, 1884–1965). *Twentieth-Century China* 42(1):72–96.
Fomon, S.J. 1993. *Nutrition of Normal Infants*. St. Louis: Mosby.
"Gail and Bordon Condensed Milk Advertisement." 1920. *Shenbao* (23 May), 19.
Ge, G.Z. 1927. *Zhongguo Baoxue Shi* [History of Chinese Press]. Shanghai: Shanghai Bookstore.
Gerstenberger, H.J. and Ruh, H.O. 1919. Studies in the Adaptation of an Artificial Food to Human Milk. *American Journal of Diseases of Children* 17(1):1–37.
Glosser, S.L. 2003. *Chinese Visions of Family and State, 1815–1953*. Berkeley and Los Angeles: University of California Press.
Goossaert, V. 2005. "The Beef Taboo and the Sacrificial Structure of Late Imperial Chinese Society" in *Of Tripod and Palate: Food, Politics and Religion in Traditional China*, edited by R. Skerckx (New York: Palgrave MacMillan), pp. 237–248.
Hattori, S. 1908. *Qingguo Jiating Ji Xuetang Yong Jiazheng Xue* [Home Economics for Families and Schools in Qing China]. Japan: Toyama Bo.
Health Bureau & Department of Health. 2022. *Hong Kong Code of Marketing of Formula Milk and Related Products, and Food Products for Infants & Young Children*, rev. ed. Hong Kong: Government of the Hong Kong Special Administrative Region.
Huang, K.W. 1988. Cong Shenbao Yiyao Guanggao Kan Min Chu Shanghai De Yiliao Wenhua Yu Shehui Shenghuo [Medical Culture and Social Life in Shanghai: A Study Based on the Medicine Advertisements in *Shen Pao*, 1912–1926]. *Bulletin of Institute of Modern History, Academia Sinica* 117 (Part II):141–194.
Huang, W. 2020. "How China Got Milk." *Six Tone* (21 February). Available at https://www.sixthtone.com/news/1005211 (Accessed: 7 July 2023).
Huang, Y.T. 2009. *Minguo Shiqi Shangye Guanggao Yanjiu* [Research on Commercial Advertisement in Republican China]. Xiamen: Xiamen University Press.
Huimin Gufen Youxian Gongsi Zhaogu Zhangcheng [Prospectus of Vitamilk Company Limited] (1927). Shanghai: Vitamilk Company Limited.
Hunter, W. 1882. *The "Fan Kwae" at Canton Before Treaty Days, 1825–1844*. London: Regan Paul, Trench, & Co.

Lee, L.O. and Nathan, A. 1985. "The Beginnings of Mass Culture: Journalism and Fiction in the Late Ch'ing and Beyond" in *Popular Culture in Late Imperial China*, edited by D. Johnson, A.J. Nathan and E.S. Rawski (Berkeley: University of California Press), pp. 360–395.
"Lactogen Advertisement." 1922. *Shenbao* (12 August), 5.
"Lactogen Advertisement." 1926a. *Shenbao* (21 August), 11.
"Lactogen Advertisement." 1926b. *Shenbao* (30 October), 7.
"Lactogen Advertisement." 1926c. *Shenbao* (20 December), Local Supplement 3.
"Lactogen Advertisement." 1928. *China Journal of Science and Arts* 9(2):n.p.
Levenstein, H.A. 1988. *Revolution at the Table: The Transformation of the American Diet*. New York: Oxford University Press.
Li, S.Z. 1987 [c. 16th century]. "Bencao Gangmu" [Compendium of Materia Medica] in *Siku Quanshu* [Complete Library in the Four Branches of Literature] vol. 774. Shanghai: Shanghai Classics Publishing House.
"Li Yunxin Zuozi Naifan Gongsi" [Lee Yinson Establishes Milk Powder Company]. 1927. *Shenbao* (27 September), 15.
Li, Z.P. 2010. Cong Jindai Niuru Guanggao Kan Zhongguo De Xiandai Xing–Yi 1927–1937 Nian *Shenbao* Wei Zhongxin De Kaocha [Modernity of China Viewed from Milk Advertisements in *Shanghai Post* Issued from 1927 to 1937]. *Anhui Da Xue Xue Bao (Zhexue Sehui Kexue Ban)* [Journal of Anhui University (Philosophy and Social Sciences Edition)] 3:106–113.
Lo, S.Y. 2018. *Muru Yu Niunai: Jindai Zhongguo Muqin Juese De Chongsu (1895–1937)* [Breastmilk and Cow's Milk: The Reshaping of Motherhood in Modern China (1895–1937)]. Hong Kong: Chungwah Bookstore.
McCollum, E. 1918. *The Newer Knowledge of Nutrition: The Use of Food for the Preservation of Vitality and Health*. New York: Macmillan.
McCollum, E. 1920. Milk as a Factor in Race Development. *The China Medical Journal* 32(1):98–99.
Mi, A. 1927. "Yinger De Siyang Fa" [Methods of Infant Feeding] in *Jiating Wenti Taolun Ji* [Discussion on Family Issues] (Shanghai: National Association of Chinese Young Women's Christian Association Editorial Department), pp. 67–87.
Milter, B. 2004. *A News for China? Power, Identity and Changes in Shanghai News Media*. Cambridge: Harvard University Asia Center.
"Momilk Advertisement." 1924. Shenbao Guoxing Jinian Zengkan [National Day Commemorative Supplementary of *Shenbao*], *Shenbao* (10 October), 11.
"Momilk Advertisement." 1926a. *Shenbao* (9 July), 18.
"Momilk Advertisement." 1926b. *Shenbao* (26 September), 18.
"Momilk Advertisement." 1926c. *Shenbao* (28 October), 11.
"Momilk Advertisement." 1926d. *Shenbao* (29 October), 16.
"Momilk Advertisement." 1926e. *Shenbao* (7 November), 12.
"Momilk Advertisement." 1935. *Sin Wan Pao* (5 June), 16.
Municipal Council of Shanghai Report for the Year Ending 31st March, 1873 and Budget for the Year Ending 31st December, 1874. 1874. Shanghai: The North-China Herald Office.
Municipal Council of Shanghai Report for the Year Ending 31st March, 1898 and Budget for the Year Ending 31st December, 1899. 1899. Shanghai: The North-China Herald Office.
Nestlé's Management of Dairy Supply Chain in China. 2008. Nestlé. Available at https://www.nestle.com/media/pressreleases/allpressreleases/nestlemanagementofdairysupplychaininchina (Accessed: 17 May 2023).
Qian, J. 1935. Huoyue Zai Shi Yejie Shang De Nu Zhanshi [Active Female Warriors in the Industrial Sector]. *Funu Shenghuo* [Women's Life] 1(2):125–133.
Rawski, E.S. 1979. *Education and Popular Literacy in Ch'ing China*. Ann Arbor: University of Michigan Press.

Reichardt, R. 1989. "Print: Images of the Bastille" in *Revolutionary News: The Press in France, 1789–1799*, edited by R. Darnton and D. Roche (Berkeley: University of California Press), pp. 223–251.
Returns of Trade and Trade Reports for the Year 1894: Part II—Reports and Statistics for Each Ports with Report on Foreign Trade of China. 1895. Shanghai: The Statistical Department of the Inspectorate General of Customs.
Sabban, F. 2014. "The Taste for Milk in Modern China (1865–1937)" in *Food Consumption in Global Perspective: Essays in the Anthropology of Food in Honour of Jack Goody*, edited by J.A. Klein and A. Murcott (New York: Palgrave MacMillan), pp. 182–208.
"Shanghai Huojia Jikan" [Shanghai Price Quarterly]. 2005 [1924]. *Zaoqi Shanghai Jingji Wenxian Huibian* [A Compilation of Early Shanghai Economic Information] vol. 19. Beijing: China National Microfilming Centre for Library Resources.
Shanghai Municipal Council Report for the Year 1912 and Budget for the Year 1913. 1913. Shanghai: Kelly & Walsh, Ltd.
Shanghai Shangye Chuxu Yinhang Diaocha Yanjiu Lei: Niunai Naifen Diaocha Ziliao n.d. [Survey and Research of the Shanghai Commercial & Savings Bank: Milk and Milk Powder Materials]. vol. 2. Shanghai Archives: Q275-1-2007-2.
Shimoda, U. 1902. *Xinbian Jiazheng Xue* [New Edition Home Economics], Translated by Wu Rulun. Shanghai: Zuoxin She.
"Shi Zhengfu Qudi Baozhi Qian Deng Weijin Guanggo" [The Municipal Government Outlawed Prohibited Newspaper Advertisements]. 1930. *Shenbao* (12 June), 14.
Trade Catalogs from Brewer & Co. Inc., National Museum of American History. 2023. Available at https://americanhistory.si.edu/collections/search/object/SILNMAHTL_35326 (Accessed: 16 January 2024).
Valenze, D.M. 2011. *Milk: A Local and Global History*. New Haven and London: Yale University.
"Vitamilk Advertisement." 1927. *Shenbao* (2 October), 6.
"Vitamilk Advertisement." 1928. *Shenbao* (4 December), 13.
"Vitamilk Advertisement." 1929. *Shenbao* (25 February), Local Supplement 2.
"Vitamilk Advertisement." 1930. *Shenbao* (14 May), 1.
"Vitamilk Advertisement." 1935. *Shenbao* (18 January), 12.
Wang, R.N. 2007. *Yuwang De Xiangxiang: 1920-1930 Niandai "Shenbao" Guanggao De Wenhua Shi Yanjiu* [The Imagination of Desire: A Cultural History of *Shenbao* Advertisements, 1920s-1930s]. Shanghai: Shanghai People's Publishing House.
Wang, S. 2011. Buyu Zhongguo: Jindai Zhongguo De Niuru Xiaofei–Ershi Shiji Ersanshi Niandai Shanghai Wei Zhongxin De Kaocha [Feeding China: Milk Consumption and Changes in Health Concepts in Modern China: Investigation by *Shenbao* During the Period 1920–1939]. *Zhongguo Yinshi Wenhua* [Journal of Chinese Dietary Culture] 7(1):207–239.
Wong, T. ed. 2020. *Xiaer Guanzhen Xianggang Shiliao* [Historical Materials about Hong Kong in *Chinese Serial*]. Hong Kong: Chungwah Bookstore.
Wu, Y.R. 1977 [1933]. *Ershi Nian Mudu Zhi Guai Xianzhuang* [The Strange State of the World Witnessed Over 20 Years]. Shanghai: Shanghai Ancient Books Press.
Xu, B.Y. 1995. "Lao Shanghai Guanggao Fazhan Guiji" [Development of Old Shanghai Advertisements] in *Lao Shanghai Guanggao* [Old Shanghai Advertisements], edited by Y. Bin, L. Youming and G. Zhenhu (Shanghai: Shanghai Pictorial Press), pp. 3–10.
Xu, W.Y. 2005. *Zhongguo Yinshi Wenhua Gailun* [Introduction to Chinese Food Culture]. Beijing: Qinghua University Press & Beijing Jiaotong University Press.
Yu, Z.Q. 1935. Yuying Yu Rufang [Baby Care and Breasts]. *Xiandai Fumu* [Modern Parents] 3(10):22–24.
Zhang, S.R. 2020. *Suzao Jindai Zhongguo De Niunai Xiaofei: Dui Jindai Shanghai Ruye Shuchang Fazhan Ji Qi Guanli De Kaocha* [Shaping Milk Consumption in Modern China: An Examination of the Development and Management of the Dairy Market in Modern Shanghai]. Shanghai: Shanghai Academy of Social Sciences Press.

6 "The Great Natural Health Drink of Our Time"

Health, Gender and Nutrition in British Advertisements for Ribena Blackcurrant Drink

Daniel Ewers

Introduction

On 6 April 2018, the Soft Drinks Industry Levy—known colloquially as the "Sugar Tax"—came into effect in the United Kingdom with the intention of encouraging manufacturers to reformulate their soft drinks in response to growing concerns surrounding public health and childhood obesity. The measures were intended to reduce the consumption of Sugar-Sweetened Beverages (SSBs) in both adults and children, with public discussions centred around risks of tooth decay, obesity, Type 2 diabetes and cardiovascular disease (*British Medical Journal*, 2021). The introduction of the "Sugar Tax" resulted in the manufacturers of several high-profile sugary drinks, including the blackcurrant soft drink Ribena (the focus of this chapter), adjusting their formulas to reduce the total amount of sugar per litre so as to avoid paying additional charges.

Reactions from consumers to the news of Ribena's reformulation were reportedly mixed. On 16 March 2018, *The Guardian* published a tongue-in-cheek "interview" article entitled "Why Ribena Fans Have Been Left with a Bad Taste in Their Mouths." One of the two voices in the interview described the new taste as being "like a robot's armpit," in direct contrast to the old formulation of Ribena which had combined "the natural sharpness of blackcurrants with the natural sweetness of a lorryful of sugar." Equally, in the *Daily Record*, consumers described the reformulated Ribena as "vile," "disgusting" and "like drain cleaner," and even started a petition to bring back the original full-sugar recipe (Burnside, 2018). In another article appearing on the BBC News website (2018), it was reported that some consumers were stockpiling the blackcurrant drink in their homes for fear that the new, lower-sugar formula would drastically alter the taste of the product.

One element that repeatedly featured in reports on Ribena's reformulation was the longevity of the product's original formula. Ribena had first appeared in the British marketplace in 1938 and, by 2018, had been available for purchase in the United Kingdom for 80 years in various forms, including its fruit concentrate bottled drink, ready-to-drink cartons and in several different flavour variations and lower-sugar offerings. Throughout Ribena's history, the

DOI: 10.4324/9781003450276-10

drink was frequently marketed to consumers as a "health" drink due, in part, to the high vitamin C content of the blackcurrant fruit it contained. Therefore, the fact that Ribena featured so prominently in discussions over high levels of sugar found in soft drinks—and the impact that sugar consumption had on especially younger consumers—is in many ways unsurprising. Given Ribena's repeated emphasis on the role of its vitamin C content in maintaining and optimising consumers' health, studying historical Ribena advertisements can offer important insights into the origin of this scientific claim and how it evolved over time in response to broader sociocultural trends.

To this end, the current chapter surveys advertising materials for Ribena, selectively analysing prototypical examples of advertisements throughout the mid-twentieth century that speak to broader motifs found in the brand's overarching advertising strategy. By deploying a qualitative historical analysis of the Ribena advertisements—both print and televisual—it enables an examination of the history of the brand's image in the British marketplace. Specifically, it identifies three core periods in the brand's history, each outlined by a different approach: (1) framing the blackcurrant drink and its vitamin C content as a supplemental food product reserved for "vulnerable" groups (the Second World War period); (2) rebranding Ribena as a "great natural health drink of our time" suitable for the whole family (postwar period); and (3) repositioning Ribena's public image to appeal to the shifting cultural conditions provided by the arrival of commercial television (from the mid-1950s onwards).

The advertisements under study have been systematically collected using a keyword search for "Ribena" on the websites of the British Newspaper Archive (for printed advertisements in both regional and national newspapers) and the History of Advertising Trust (for televisual advertisements). Additionally, the History of Advertising Trust's archival collection houses a repository of administrative files within the J Walter Thompson (JWT) Archive relating to advertising and marketing campaigns for Ribena conducted on behalf of JWT's client, Beecham Food, which provide insights into the development of advertising campaigns.

The Origins of Ribena

The origins of "Ribena Blackcurrant Syrup" can be traced back to the work of Dr Vernon L.S. Charley and research staff in the Fruit Products Section of the Long Ashton Research Station near Bristol. Founded in 1903, The National Fruit and Cider Institute (later renamed the Long Ashton Research Station after formal association with the University of Bristol in 1912) was responsible for conducting research into the cultivation of fruits and vegetables for use in the production of cider, perry, other alcoholic drinks and fruit juices (Wallace and Marsh, 1953). Alongside providing technical knowledge to local manufacturers of fruit products, the Station also conducted research into mycology, plant pathology and horticultural methods, and research staff regularly collaborated with staff at the University of Bristol through an exchange of scientific knowledge, technical expertise and teaching opportunities (Wallace and Marsh, 1953). According to Dr Charley, the product which would later be known as Ribena was first made in 1933 by staff at the Long Ashton Research Station as part of a scheme carried out by the University of Bristol conducting research into the use of fruit syrups as milkshake flavourings (*Ribena: Its Properties and Applications in Medical Practice*, n.d.).

Following biochemical analysis, it was discovered that the blackcurrant syrup had retained a considerable proportion of its natural vitamin C content after processing, thus identifying the syrup as a potentially suitable vessel for the delivery of vitamin C to vulnerable groups in the British population. From 1936, H.W. Carter & Co. Ltd—a Bristol-based manufacturer of soft drinks including tonics, fruit syrups and cordials—collaborated with the Long Ashton Research Station to begin experiments in the commercial production of blackcurrant syrup, with the company providing "the necessary equipment, while the Research Station furnished scientific guidance and technical control" (*The Development and Medical Uses of Ribena*, n.d.). The product, named "Ribena" after the Latin for blackcurrant—*Ribes nigrum*—was first available on the British marketplace in 1938 and, by the end of the first season, reportedly "more than 100,000 gallons of syrup had been processed and had found a ready sale" (*The Development and Medical Uses of Ribena*, n.d.).

It is notable that Ribena's introduction onto the British marketplace coincided with the tail end of the period characterised by "vitamania," as described by Rima D. Apple (1988, 1996, 2000) in her work on vitamins in nutrition and popular culture—a period which witnessed the elucidation of the vitamin concept within scientific and popular arenas. The early twentieth century saw a series of scientific discoveries surrounding the role of vitamins in human diets, resulting in the identification, isolation and synthesisation of several vitamin compounds, of which vitamin C formed a central strand (Carpenter, 1986, 2012). This was also to have important implications for the ways the "healthfulness" of foodstuffs was assessed, as the quantification of micronutrient levels across different foodstuffs contributed to the early stages of a nutritional paradigm that Gyorgy Scrinis (2008, 2013) has termed "nutritionism," whereby the relative values of foodstuffs were ideologically reduced to the quantifiable nutrient levels they contained. As the vitamin concept became increasingly stabilised across scientific and popular discourses, food manufacturers and advertisers drew upon the potent cultural symbol that vitamins offered and often appropriated scientific knowledge of the compounds' role in healthy human diets to position their products at the cutting edge of scientific and nutritional knowledge (Kamminga, 2000). Indeed, concerns surrounding vitamin deficiency on a wide scale across populations were to become of considerable concern with the outbreak of the Second World War in 1939—one year after Ribena's arrival on British shelves—and the resulting disruption to food supply lines and production.

Ribena at War: Blackcurrants, Vitamin C and the War Effort

Following the introduction of food rationing in Britain in January 1940, staff at the Fruit Products Section at the Long Ashton Research Station were asked by the Ministry of Food to take charge of large-scale production of blackcurrant syrup with a guaranteed minimum vitamin C content to be distributed to identified priority groups (Wallace and Marsh, 1953:83–84). As a result, two "shadow factories" were established to protect the production of blackcurrant syrup at the H.W. Carter Factory, given the "vulnerability of the Bristol premises to air-raid damage" (Wallace and Marsh, 1953). With the subsequent introduction of the Vitamin Welfare Scheme in December 1941, which was established to ensure the dietary nutritional needs of the British population were met, the vitamin consumption of young children and expectant and nursing mothers became a matter of political concern (Ministry of Food, 1951). Blackcurrant syrup, alongside cod liver oil, was provided free of charge to children under the age of two until, in 1942, Lend-Lease orange juice replaced the blackcurrant syrup on offer through the scheme (Ministry of Food, 1951). Following a decision by the Ministry of Food in 1940, Ribena was made available on medical prescription from chemists in plain, unbranded packaging, later described as a "wartime 'battledress'" in a booklet produced by Ribena on the therapeutic qualities of the product (*The Development and Medical Uses of Ribena*, n.d.). According to the booklet, it was only in 1944 that Ribena was seen again in British shops and, even then, the product "was sold only for children or on a doctor's recommendation" (*The Development and Medical Uses of Ribena*, n.d.).

Following a similar approach to those highlighted in David Clampin's (2013) and Angela Loxham's (2016) work on the history of commercial advertising, with the outbreak of the Second World War, advertisements for "Ribena Blackcurrant Syrup" in British newspapers frequently assimilated the product within broader wartime food conditions and government propagandistic messaging campaigns. Advertisements frequently drew upon conditions of food scarcity and fears of declining general health in the British population to position Ribena as central to the national war effort. Ribena advertisers also often evoked the dual authorities of the Ministries of Food and Health to present the product as sanctioned by the decisions of government ministries. They also appealed directly to the impact that conditions of food scarcity could have on following a balanced diet and emphasised the vital role of vitamin C in ensuring the good health of the most vulnerable members of the British population.

One of the earliest examples of an advertisement for Ribena carried the headline "Message to Doctors" and appeared in several regional newspapers with its headline adjusted to match the geographical region of publication. The advertisement announced that "by arrangement with the Ministries of Health and Food, chemists are receiving increased supplies, made from this season's blackcurrants, of Ribena Blackcurrant Syrup for children, invalids and any others for whom it may be medically prescribed" (*Yorkshire Post and Leeds Intelligencer*, 10 November 1942). The rationale behind this decision was that "this blackcurrant syrup is a rich source of vitamin C, containing not less than 20 mgms. ascorbic acid (vitamin C) per fluid ounce – together with the associated nutritional factors of a *natural* product" [emphasis in original] (*Yorkshire Post and Leeds Intelligencer*, 10 November 1942).

The advertisement then emphasised the digestibility of the product, claiming that "Ribena is usually well tolerated by old people and in cases of intestinal ulceration," before outlining the availability, price and manufacturer's information. The emphasis placed on the ease of digestion and the invocation of nature to imbue certain "associated nutritional factors" upon the product resonates with recent historical work on the role of digestion in the framing of "nerve food" and "invalid food" and the invocation of a "mythical nature" within commercial advertising sources (Lyon and Kautto, 2021; O'Hagan and Eriksson, 2022). The interaction between "science" and "mythology," as is the case here in the juxtaposition of scientised and quantified language with the emphasis on nature, forms a central element in Ribena's wider advertising strategy. Science and nature, in many ways, were in almost constant dialogue in many advertisements for Ribena throughout its history (cf. O'Hagan and Eriksson, 2022).

The notice blurred the line between government pronouncement and commercial advertisement, drawing authoritative credence from the decisions of the Ministries of Food and Health in reserving blackcurrant syrup for those deemed most at risk of vitamin deficiency. The advertisements addressed doctors in various regions directly, presenting a "Message to Doctors" concerning the reported scientific and medical benefits of Ribena for health through a notice that employed a layout that mirrored that of articles appearing in newspapers at the time. This urged readers to draw intertextual links between wider news reporting and the commercial advertisement itself (O'Hagan, 2021). The use of technical and precise terminology, wherein advertisers opted for the scientific-sounding "ascorbic acid" before explaining to readers that this was an alternative term for the more widely known "vitamin C," further contributed to the advertisement's authoritative tone regarding the nutritional needs of a population at war.

Further print advertisements for Ribena during wartime frequently highlighted the need for Ribena to be supplied to those deemed most at risk of vitamin C deficiency. One advertisement, published in the *Yorkshire Post and Leeds Intelligencer* on 2 December 1942, carried the headline "Natural Vitamin C for Children, Invalids, etc," while its copy emphasised that "doctors and parents will feel a sense of satisfaction that the Ministries of Health and Food have released greatly increased supplies of blackcurrants and sugar to be made into Ribena Blackcurrant Syrup" (*Yorkshire Post and Leeds Intelligencer* on 2 December 1942). The copy continued, stating that "in so doing, the Ministries give recognition to the therapeutic qualities of the blackcurrant in this form, in particular its high content of vitamin C together with the associated nutritional factors of the vitamin from a natural source." Again, policy decisions taken by government ministries in response to conditions of wartime scarcity were invoked to lend authority to the health claims made in the advertisement for Ribena and to satisfy both doctors and parents of the scientifically justified benefits that Ribena reportedly delivered to those who consumed the drink.

One recurrent motif in wartime Ribena advertisements was the comparison drawn between the respective vitamin C contents of blackcurrants and oranges following scientific testing, especially given restrictions to the importation of fresh fruit into Britain during the early years of the war. Scientific fruit research was often deployed in the advertising copy to give superlative comparisons in favour of blackcurrant consumption, rhetorically placing "Ribena Blackcurrant Syrup" on the cutting edge of nutritional research and as a superior alternative to orange juice. In one such example, printed in the *Western Morning News* on 12 February 1943, the advertisement's copy explained the substitution of the two fruits, wherein it updated consumers that "previously the succulent orange was available to meet this need. In present conditions the place of the orange is very amply filled by another well-known source of natural vitamin C, viz., Ribena Blackcurrant Syrup." Advertisers explicitly tied wartime food conditions—namely the scarcity of citrus fruits—to the need for the substitution of alternative supplemental foodstuffs to meet dietary requirements for vitamin C and, thus, stave off deficiency conditions and ill health. This was amplified by the explicit link drawn between "another well-known source of natural vitamin C" and "Ribena Blackcurrant Syrup" in another invocation of the mythical status of "nature" to imbue a symbolic potency to the product and the vitamin C it contained (O'Hagan and Eriksson, 2022).

The supplantation of the orange with the blackcurrant as the superior source of vitamin C appeared again in an advertisement published in *The Scotsman* on 16 April 1943 (Figure 6.1). Under the headline "A Blackcurrant Vitamin Tonic," the advertisement copy opened with "Vitamin C used to be known as the 'orange vitamin' – until recent research showed the homegrown blackcurrant to be a far richer source of this precious vitamin." The text continued in its exposition of the value placed on blackcurrant syrup, again invoking the authority of the two government Ministries of Food and Health: "The Ministries of Food and Health welcomed this great nutritional discovery and took steps to secure the provision of large supplies of Ribena Blackcurrant Syrup for children, invalids and others in special need of vitamin C." Here, the interaction between scientific research and policy decisions was explicitly mobilised by advertisers to fortify the claims of the "tonic uplift" that Ribena reportedly offered to those at risk of vitamin deficiency and ill health: scientific research's "great nutritional discovery" was framed as directly influencing national food policy. A year later, in an advertisement which appeared in the *Belfast News Letter* on 12 April 1944, the role of scientific and nutritional research was again mentioned alongside the recognition that had been given to

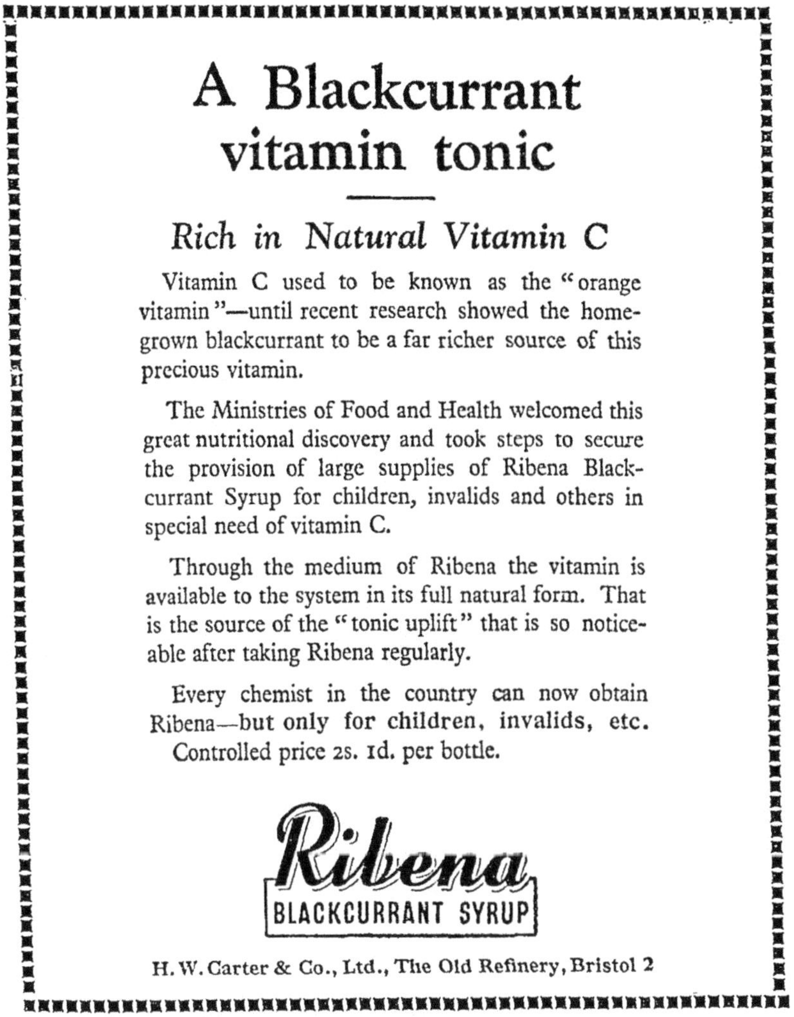

Figure 6.1 "A Blackcurrant Vitamin Tonic"

Credit: *The Scotsman*, 16 April 1943, p. 3. With thanks to Suntory for permission and the British Newspaper Archive, on behalf of Reach, to reprint

blackcurrant juice as a supplemental foodstuff, wherein a box on the left-hand side of the advertisement contained a copy which explained that:

> Modern research workers place blackcurrant juice in the forefront as a provider of natural vitamin C. At the request of the Ministries of Food and Health, priority in obtaining Ribena is accorded to those who are most in need of vitamin C

"Ribena Fights Fatigue": Postwar Print Advertisements for Ribena

With the cessation of the Second World War in 1945 and the final removal of food rationing restrictions in Britain in 1954, Ribena's brand image in advertising materials slowly underwent a transformational shift away from that of a governmentally sanctioned foodstuff for the delivery of vitamin C to specific vulnerable individuals and towards that of a family-centric health drink suitable for all but aimed primarily at children. Mentions of continuing conditions of austerity and material scarcity persisted into the immediate postwar period in Ribena advertisements, including in several advertisements calling for consumer assistance in alleviating critical raw material shortages, namely the shortage of glass bottles which restricted the supply of Ribena to chemists who were unable to provide the drink to vulnerable individuals in need of vitamin C. Advertisements appeared in several newspapers during the immediate postwar period, urging consumers to search their cupboards for empty glass bottles and return them to their local chemists to ensure that vulnerable infants and babies could receive the vitamin C they so desperately needed. Ribena's manufacturers were, thus, able to appeal directly to consumers through their advertising materials and continue to present their product as an essential foodstuff for the most vulnerable individuals in the British population. This resonates with what Lauren Alex O'Hagan (2021) has shown occurred during the Spanish Flu pandemic (1918–1920), which saw canny marketers capitalising on shifting socioeconomic conditions to position their products alongside prevailing crises and concerns.

The postwar period also saw Ribena's advertising materials increasingly incorporate images and photographs with progressively elaborate advertisement layouts. Images of families who consumed Ribena regularly featured in such advertisements, either pictured in a group consuming the drink together or in campaigns that singled out one member of the family in particular. This was typically the children, with a particular emphasis on the responsibility of older family members in providing daily Ribena to ensure children's continued good health. By doing so, these advertisements resonated with broader discourses around what Rima D. Apple (1995, 1999) has termed "scientific motherhood"—the increasing sociocultural pressure on mothers to seek out the latest scientific and medical advice, often from their doctor, on the best way to raise their children healthfully and in line with the latest scientific knowledge.

One particular advertising campaign, appearing in 1952 in the *Daily Herald*, saw individual members of an imagined family (father, mother, son and daughter) each represented in their own advertisement which extolled the danger that fatigue presented to the individual featured. The headline "Too tired for overtime?" was accompanied by an image of a tired-looking man in overalls (*Daily Herald*, 6 May 1952), while "Does *your* son sleep on his way to work?" [emphasis in original] was displayed next to an image of a boy asleep, head propped up on his hand (*Daily Herald*, 3 January 1952). Similarly, "Does *your* daughter yawn at her work?" [emphasis in original] was showcased alongside an image of a young girl yawning, her head resting in her hand (*Daily Herald*, 13 October 1952), while "Mother, are you too tired to care?" (Figure 6.2) overlaid an image

Figure 6.2 "Mother, Are You Too Tired to Care?"

Credit: *Daily Herald*, 8 July 1952, p. 4. With thanks to Suntory for permission and British Newspaper Archive, on behalf of Reach, to reprint

of a mother, head in hands, looking crestfallen and exhausted. All examples featured copy extolling the virtues of Ribena's vitamin C in making "all the difference between feeling slack and being on top of the world." Also mentioned in all cases were Ribena's three different types of sugars—"cane sugar, fruit sugar *and* glucose"—which offered the consumer "energy and vitality." Lack of energy and fatigue featured prominently in these advertisements, with sleeping and tiredness at irregular times being presented as impacting upon an individual's engagement with social, educational and work responsibilities. In the headlines, "Does *your* daughter yawn at her work?" and "Does *your* son sleep on his way to work?" advertisers directly appealed to parental viewers of the advertisement by placing emphasis on the pronoun "*your*." By asking viewers directly whether "*your* child" slept at school or work, advertisers played directly into the anxieties of parents surrounding their children's performance in school, their general state of health and the disruptive threat that fatigue posed.

Another series of Ribena advertisements from the mid-1950s provided testimonials from British families on the apparent benefits that drinking Ribena had brought to them or their children. One such example, printed in the *Coventry Evening Telegraph* on 13 April 1955 (Figure 6.3), carried the headline "We're making doubly sure"—a quote from a Mrs Gillmore of Ebury Bridge Road, London—in what the advertisement reported was "a true story about Ribena." The advertisement carried a large image of two young children drinking from glasses of Ribena; just below were four panels, each appearing

Figure 6.3 "We're Making Doubly Sure"

Credit: *Coventry Evening Telegraph*, 13 April 1955, p. 8. With thanks to Suntory for permission and British Newspaper Archive, on behalf of Reach, to reprint

alongside rhyming headlines ("Another Rest!," "Healthy Chest!," "Extra Zest!," "Ribena Best!"). Each panel contained a short caption outlining the associated benefits of restfulness, freedom from coughs or colds, extra energy and vitality before the advertisement finally extolled the superlative nature of Ribena in fortifying against flu and infection. When read from left to right, the panels tell the story of a young "Wednesday's child all right – full of woe – and always taking time out from play with her friends" who is taken to see a male doctor, pictured listening to her chest with a stethoscope. The doctor recommends Ribena consumption, which gives the young girl the "extra zest" she needs to brush away the fatigue and constant colds, before the final panel outlines the health benefits of Ribena as well as suggested serving options.

Other Ribena advertisements from the period had a similar stylistic layout, designed to resonate with established conventions found in comic strips and cartoons, and telling the "story" of one family's Ribena consumption and the health benefits that the drink has conferred. Comic vignettes were a common feature of many newspaper advertisements during this period, often offering a storyline involving the consumption of the advertised product in a panelled comic format (Eriksson and O'Hagan, 2021; O'Hagan, 2022, 2023). In this vein, Ribena advertisements which employed a comic-style layout usually traced a similar story: a mother or her child is taken ill or is suffering from fatigue; a visit is undertaken to a (typically male) doctor or similar medical authority who recommends Ribena consumption; the child or the wider family is pictured playing outside with renewed energy and vigour; and, lastly, the consumption of Ribena is emphasised in the final panel, often reinforcing the user testimonials presented in the headline of the advertisement.

The use of testimonials from supposedly "real" families was employed by advertisers to lend an air of role model authority to the advertisements' claims: by presenting a testimonial from an example family in the advertisement copy—intended to resonate with consumers who were also looking for information and guidance on how best to look after their own children—Ribena was able to foreground the benefits that consumption of the product would bring to British families. Indeed, some mothers even wrote letters to J Walter Thompson—the advertising agency responsible for the management of Beecham Food's advertising campaigns for Ribena in the 1950s and 1960s—to espouse the benefits that the consumption of Ribena had brought to their children and to enquire whether the agency would be interested in featuring their children in future advertisements. Some letter writers even attached photographs of their children for the convenience of JWT staff to consider when devising upcoming campaigns in the hopes that their children would be featured (JWT Client Files, History of Advertising Trust).

That these consumers wrote into JWT to offer their experiences with Ribena indicates a dynamic dialogue between consumer and advertiser in which consumers were able to participate in the shaping of product development and advertising materials through the expression of their user testimony. A letter from a Mrs Gillmore of Ebury Bridge Road, as quoted in the *Coventry Evening Telegraph* advertisement (Figure 6.3), survives in the JWT London Client Files currently held in the archives of the History of Advertising Trust, in which she writes that her "two young children were very low and dispirited after a succession of colds, now only after a few weeks of 'Ribena', the difference in their vitality is amazing." However, the phrase "we're making doubly sure," as appeared in the headline of the Ribena advertisement, does not appear (although it is unclear whether correspondence was later established between the two parties). Correspondence containing testimonials from mothers appears to have continued throughout the twentieth century, with consumers writing about the impact that Ribena had on their children and other family members and asking JWT to consider their children when casting actors in future advertisements following the arrival of a new advertising medium for Ribena to reach consumers: commercial television.

"The Great Natural Health Drink of Our Time": Television Advertisements for Ribena

The emergence of commercial television in the United Kingdom, following the passage of The Television Act in 1954, presented a new technological medium through which advertisers could reach audiences in Britain. From 1955, regional commercial television companies were systematically established across Britain to broadcast the new independent commercial service, which would later be named "ITV" (Nevett, 1982:176–203). In his work on the evolution of commercial television in Britain, Rob Turnock (2007) has charted an expansion in the 1950s and 1960s in not only consumer television but also in British consumer culture, as technological and cultural innovations brought new commodities and cultural forms to British consumers. Similarly, Renée Dickason (2000) has highlighted that the early years of British television advertising represented a considerable consumer boom, as well as a normative and formative phase whereby "the medium established itself in the public mind, set its own standards and principles and became a part of everyday life in the context of an ever changing social and economic background" (31). It is within this context that the advertisements presented in this section appeared.

In a similar approach to that deployed in the previously discussed print advertisements, advertisers alluded to Ribena's role as a wartime supplement in early postwar television advertisements for the blackcurrant drink. In one television advertisement from 1956 entitled "Evacuees," footage of children returning home after having been evacuated to the countryside during the Second World War was overlaid with a voiceover which asked, "Do you remember ten years ago, the children coming back to the town from the countryside where they'd been evacuated?" The advertisement then highlighted one particular little girl, shown getting into a vehicle, while the voiceover asked, "What are these children like today? Children like this little girl, for instance." The advertisement then conducted an "interview" with "a young lady of nineteen now" and her mother about how the girl had been given Ribena when she was evacuated in the countryside and how continued daily consumption had benefited her health.

The advertisement then closed with a Ribena packshot accompanied by a voiceover that reminded viewers to "Remember Ribena: the blackcurrant vitamin C health drink." The advertisement, thus, explicitly tied Ribena's wartime role as a supplemental vitamin C foodstuff to the health of children evacuated during wartime and, later, to adults who had grown up to be healthy owing to their consumption of the blackcurrant drink in their youth. In this advertisement, Ribena was explicitly situated by advertisers in a substantial event in British history and recent public memory: the evacuation of young children out of metropolitan centres during the aerial bombardments of the Blitz.

One prevalent motif from postwar Ribena advertising, both print and televisual, was how the consumption of the blackcurrant drink and the vitamin C it contained allowed for greater participation in the activities that modern postwar lifestyles so often demanded. Advertisements frequently mentioned the impact that the lost time from having to recover from colds, flu and chills would have on participation in school, sports, work and leisure activities and emphasised how the vitamin C in Ribena could fortify consumers' immune systems and stave off infections. In one television advertisement entitled "Rugger," which aired on British television in 1961, a young boy was pictured playing a game of rugby, before a brief shot of him turning away teammates visiting his house, presumably to ask him to play a game of rugby with them. The male voiceover stated, "When I think back to last winter, what a difference. Just one cold after another," subsequently describing how the boy's mother had discovered the benefits of vitamin C and given her child Ribena every day because it was "made from blackcurrants and they're full of vitamin C." As a result, over footage of a group of children playing rugby with the same young boy taking a kick, the voiceover claimed that there "isn't a healthier boy in the school." Here, Ribena was directly attributed not only to the young boy's continued participation in school sports but for his ultimate sporting and personal victory as the "healthiest boy" in his school.

In another similar television advertisement entitled "Diving," which aired on British television in 1964, a young girl was pictured sitting down, looking despondent on the side of a swimming pool, while her peers were shown diving into the pool as they competed in a swimming competition. Emulating the voice of the girl's mother, the accompanying female voiceover explained how "last year, Pat missed the local swimming gala – another bad cold," before describing her discovery of the benefits of vitamin C and Ribena, overlaid over footage of a book being turned to a page on the scientific and nutritional benefits of vitamin C and a packshot of the Ribena bottle. The mother's voice explained how "vitamin C, as many doctors agree, helps to protect us against colds and chills. So I gave Pat Ribena every day." The benefits of daily consumption of the drink appear to have been considerable: accompanying footage of "Pat" diving from a diving board into the swimming pool, the mother's voice explained how "this year, Pat won the trophy for her school. She never seems to catch colds now. And how she's grown lately!" The advertisement ended with a final packshot of a Ribena bottle and an accompanying glass of the blackcurrant drink, overlaid with the words "the great natural health drink of our time."

In these advertisements, the advertisers positioned Ribena as the means to maintain optimal health in children and, thus, maintain their participation in active, healthful lifestyles in which sports and leisure comprised a vital part. In these examples, the mother's "discovery" of the science of vitamin C and Ribena's high content of the named vitamin, alongside her decision to give the blackcurrant drink to her child on a daily basis in a pseudo-emulation of a medical "dosage," was figured to have had a direct impact on the health of her child who was now reportedly not only strong but also victorious in the sports in which they participated. Ribena, therefore, provided protection from seasonal illnesses but also enabled the child to go on to outperform their peers in their chosen sport. Again, this encouragement for mothers to seek out the most current scientific and nutritional knowledge in order to best look after their children resonates with broader discourses surrounding "scientific motherhood" that were prevalent during the early twentieth century (Apple, 1995, 1999). In these advertisements, which depicted how mothers who sought out scientific and nutritional knowledge could ensure that their children were not only healthy but as optimally healthy as they could be, the purchasing and consumption of Ribena were aligned with the broader ideological commitment to scientific motherhood. This ideological alignment saw conscientious parenthood intertwined with the desire to seek out knowledge of the benefits of regular vitamin C consumption and the value of vitamin consumption in children's diets, all of which was provided within Ribena, "the great natural health drink of our time."

Children frequently appeared in television advertisements for Ribena, often depicted being given the drink by older family members, typically mother and grandmother figures. During the 1960s, Ribena advertisements repeatedly emphasised the generational role of the passage of knowledge about Ribena and vitamin C consumption along maternal lines. Mothers and grandmothers were regularly shown talking to younger children about the benefits of taking daily Ribena and how the drink aided in helping them to grow up with strong bones and teeth. Whenever fatherly figures appeared in television advertisements for Ribena, they were typically depicted as either engaging in activities outside of the home, such as sailing with their son as their wife and daughter watched on from the riverbank, in the garden tending to plants or collecting their son from school in the family car.

Familiar domestic settings also appeared frequently in early Ribena television advertisements, often depicting domestic kitchen or living room scenes in which the drink was prepared either hot or cold. Typical scenes included family members gathered around the kitchen table discussing the taste or health benefits of Ribena or sitting outside in the garden, with sunshine featuring most prominently (although some advertisements also featured snow or rain, seasonal weather associated with increased prevalence of colds and flu). One advertisement even drew parallels between the milk prepared for the family cat, Mr Tiddles, the tea prepared for the parents in the household and the Ribena prepared for their son, Jamie, who had been given the blackcurrant drink since he was a baby ("Jamie," 1966).

The recurrent slogan "the great natural health drink of our time" appeared in both printed and televisual advertisements for Ribena throughout the postwar period. The slogan drew the listeners'/readers' attention to several of the key elements of Ribena's overall marketing strategy: that the drink contained natural ingredients, was healthy due to its vitamin C content and was perfect for the health-conscious consumer living a modern lifestyle. The slogan tended to feature at the very end of Ribena's television advertisements, thereby drawing particular attention to the phrase, often displayed over a packshot of the Ribena bottle in order to reinforce the association between the two. The importance of this slogan was such that, in 1963, one draft television advertisement was even sent back to JWT for the soundtrack to be re-recorded, following concerns that the shortening of the slogan to omit the words "of our time" had diluted the advertisement's overall message (JWT Client Files, Beecham: Ribena, History of Advertising Trust).

There is evidence that the "great natural health drink of our time" slogan was occasionally met with some scepticism, however, as evidenced in one review which appeared in *The Stage and Television Today* on 1 October 1959. Appearing under the headline "This is Ridiculous," the review, written by Alan Abbott as part of his "Alan Abbott Reviews Commercials" series, stated that:

> Ribena: It's one thing for a detergent to be described not merely as white, but whitest of all. However, for the manufacturers of Ribena (an unquestionably good product) to describe it as 'the great natural health drink of our time' surely smacks of excessive self-glorification.

Abbott continued, criticising the "altogether badly conceived and even ridiculous script [...] showing a number of children scenes selected to re-cap the growing-up stages of a baby born in war time." Then, he unpicked select lines of dialogue from the voiceover about how the viewer had supposedly grown up on Ribena and "your Uncle Harry told you about vitamin 'C' which made your teeth strong." Finally, in response, Abbott asked in the final line of his review "how on earth does she know?" For Abbott here, Ribena's marketing approach, which brought together its self-appointed position as the "great natural health drink of our time" and an overfamiliarity with an assumed shared memory of wartime Britain, prompted a response of suspicion and disbelief in his highly sceptical review of the television advertisement's messaging.

Conclusion: The Great Natural Health Drink of Our Time?

Abbott's scepticism regarding the scientific and nutritional claims made in Ribena's marketing materials was echoed in many ways by the prevailing discourse surrounding Ribena at the end of the twentieth century and the beginning of the twenty-first century. This period saw Ribena embroiled in two public controversies that were to have a considerable impact on the way health claims were framed and the ways the drink was advertised to consumers in light of public backlash.

The first of these controversies saw Ribena's ToothKind[1] product facing complaints made to the Advertising Standards Authority (ASA) by the political pressure group Action and Information on Sugars (Brabbs, 2000). The group's chairman, J.T. Winkler later outlined in a 2005 article the fallout that the controversy had for the soft drinks industry at large and how, for GlaxoSmithKline:

> the consequences of the false claim had been severe: public shame, falling sales and now withdrawal; all the research and promotional expenditure wasted [...] the moral of the story is: if you make a claim, it had better be true
>
> (189)

The second controversy saw Ribena's health claims coming under widespread international scrutiny after two schoolgirls in New Zealand, Anna Devathasan and Jenny Suo, conducted an experiment in 2004 to test the levels of vitamin C found in Ribena's "Ready to Drink" cartoned product and found that the drink contained almost no detectable trace of vitamin C, contrary to prominently displayed claims on the product's packaging that it contained "four times the vitamin C of oranges" (Jaques, 2008). The news was reported in the *British Medical Journal* by Trisha Greenhalgh (2009) as "a splendid David and Goliath story about how two 14 year old girls exposed a false claim by the pharmaceutical giant GlaxoSmithKline." The schoolgirls' discovery led to GlaxoSmithKline pleading guilty before the Auckland District Court, receiving a fine of $227,500 NZD and being ordered to print advertisements in major New Zealand newspapers to correct the mistakes, which GSK attributed to "incorrect labelling."

Both public controversies spoke, to some extent, to the reported health benefits of Ribena consumption, especially in relation to health claims which appeared upon the product's advertising and packaging materials. As this chapter has shown, the construction of Ribena's brand image as a vitamin C health drink, full of "natural" blackcurrants and "energy-giving" sugars, has a long history both on the British marketplace and globally. Thus, the two controversies stood in stark contrast to the health benefits that Ribena's marketing strategy so often espoused. Although the controversies somewhat threatened Ribena's longstanding status as a "health" drink, the brand won back consumers' trust by targeting the health-conscious market with its Ribena Light variants (Roderick, 2016), launching campaigns that focused on its rich heritage (Fleming, 2019) and producing new eco-friendly bottles (Langley, 2020). Today, an estimated 3.8 million people consume Ribena per year, with annual revenues of £445 M.

Thus, we see how, over its 86 years of production, Ribena has repeatedly been positioned at the intersection of food and medicine, with advertisers deploying rhetorical appeals to the agreement of doctors and government agencies on the medical benefits of adequate vitamin C consumption in maintaining optimal nutritional health and advocating for the "pseudo-dosage" of daily consumption of Ribena to afford the maximum benefits to consumers. Ribena's advertising materials have typically invoked images of happy families and active children, all of whom are able to participate widely in social spheres, such as schooling, the workplace, sport, leisure and the broader natural world. Regular consumption of Ribena has also been repeatedly figured as a means to ensure that consumers are able to continue this participation through the fortification of their bodies' immune systems with vitamin C, which enables them to ward off colds, flu and other seasonal infections. By doing so, consumers could avoid the withdrawal from social life inherent in periods of illness due to the time required for recovery and convalescence, as well as benefit from the energy and vitality Ribena reportedly provided, which was figured as a vital requirement for leading active and healthy lifestyles. Ribena advertisements have also frequently emphasised the generational aspects of both Ribena consumption and the passing down of health and nutritional knowledge through depictions of older female family members handing Ribena to younger children and through rhetorical appeals to Ribena's suitability "for you, your children, and your children's children." By drawing upon prevailing discourses surrounding health, nutrition and family, Ribena has repeatedly been framed by advertisers as not only a "healthful" and "natural" drink but also as a vital element in sustaining optimal health through the superlative slogan "the Great Natural Health Drink of Our Time."

Contemporary Ribena advertisements continue to place a strong emphasis on the drink's blackcurrant content, with television commercials often including personified blackcurrant characters, such as in one commercial for the blackcurrant drink that was first screened in 2014 and was updated to reflect the drink's 85th anniversary in 2023 (Green, 2023). At the time of writing, the vitamin C content of the drink continues to appear on the packaging of the product, while the drink's history on the British marketplace is featured on the Ribena brand's website. Such marketing strategies demonstrate the way in which Ribena's brand image has constantly shifted and redefined itself against prevalent social, economic and cultural conditions since its commercialisation in 1938, yet health and well-being discourses have always remained at its core.

Acknowledgements

Many thanks to Professor James Stark, Dr Adrian Wilson, and Alistair Moir and Eve Read at the History of Advertising Trust for their guidance. Thanks also to Suntory for granting permission to include images of the Ribena advertisements in this chapter and to the British Newspaper Archive for providing the high-resolution images.

This work was supported by the Arts & Humanities Research Council (grant number AH/R012733/1) through the White Rose College of the Arts & Humanities.

Note

1 ToothKind was a cartoned drink accredited by the British Dental Association and advertised as being better for consumers' teeth by not encouraging tooth decay.

Bibliography

Abbott, A. 1959. This Is Ridiculous. *The Stage and Television Today* (1 October), 13.

Apple, R.D. 1988. "They Need it Now": Science, Advertising and Vitamins, 1925–1940. *Journal of Popular Culture* 22(3):65–83.

Apple, R.D. 1995. Constructing Mothers: Scientific Motherhood in the Nineteenth and Twentieth Centuries. *Social History of Medicine* 8(2):161–178.

Apple, R.D. 1996. *Vitamania: Vitamins in American Culture*. New Brunswick: Rutgers University Press.

Apple, R.D. 1999. "Scientific Motherhood" in *Women's Studies Encyclopedia*, edited by H. Tierney (Westport: Greenwood Press), pp. 953–954.

Apple, R.D. 2000. "Vitamins Win the War: Nutrition, Commerce, and Patriotism in the United States During the Second World War" in *Food, Science, Policy and Regulation in the Twentieth Century: International and Comparative Perspectives*, edited by D.F. Smith and J. Phillips (London & New York: Routledge), pp. 135–150.

Brabbs, C. 2000. Ribena Fights ASA in Dental Health Row: ToothKind's Ads for Its Children's Fruit Juice Range Has Resulted in a Warning from the UK's Advertising Watchdog. *Campaign Live* (13 July). Available at https://www.campaignlive.co.uk/article/ribena-fights-asa-dental-health-row-toothkinds-ads-its-childrens-fruit-juice-range-resulted-warning-uks-advertising-watchdog-cordelia-brabbs-reports/67584 (Accessed: 27 September 2022).

Burnside, A. 2018. Don't Mess with Ribena – Soft Drink Fans Furious at Recipe Change and Petitioning for the Original to be Brought Back. *Daily Record* (17 March). Available at https://www.dailyrecord.co.uk/lifestyle/food-drink/low-sugar-ribena-causes-outrage-12202057 (Accessed: 16 September 2022).

Carpenter, K.J. 1986. *The History of Scurvy and Vitamin C*. Cambridge: University Press.

Carpenter, K.J. 2012. The Discovery of Vitamin C. *Annals of Nutrition and Metabolism* 61(3):259–264.

Clampin, D. 2013. *Advertising and Propaganda in World War II: Cultural Identity and the Blitz Spirit*. London: Tauris.

"Consumption of Sugar from Soft Drinks Falls Within a Year of UK Sugar Tax." 2021. *British Medical Journal* (11 March). Available at https://www.bmj.com/company/newsroom/consumption-of-sugar-from-soft-drinks-falls-within-a-year-of-uk-sugar-tax/ (Accessed: 20 March 2023).

Dickason, R. 2000. *British Television Advertising: Cultural Identity and Communication*. Luton: University of Luton Press.

Eriksson, G. and O'Hagan, L.A. 2021. Selling "Healthy" Radium Products with Science: A Multimodal Analysis of Marketing in Sweden, 1910–1940. *Science Communication* 43(6):740–767.

Fleming, M. 2019. Ribena Pins Hopes on Heritage to 'Future Proof' the Brand, *Marketing Week* (17 April). Available at https://www.marketingweek.com/ribena-pins-hopes-on-heritage-to-future-proof-the-brand/ (Accessed: 16 January 2024).

Green, W. 2023. Ribena Brings Back Berries Ad for 85th Birthday. *Campaign Live*. Available at https://www.campaignlive.co.uk/article/ribena-brings-back-berries-ad-85th-birthday/1825319 (Accessed: 16 January 2024).

Greenhalgh, T. 2009. The Ribena Girls. *British Medical Journal* 339, https://doi.org/10.1136/bmj.b4136

Jaques, T. 2008. When an Icon Stumbles: The Ribena Issue Mismanaged. *Corporate Communications* 13(4):394–406.

JWT London Archive, Client Account Files: Beecham, Ribena. n.d. *The History of Advertising Trust*. Raveningham, Norfolk.

Kamminga, H. 2000. "'Axes to Grind': Popularising the Science of Vitamins, 1920s and 1930s" in *Food, Science, Policy and Regulation in the Twentieth Century: International and Comparative Perspectives*, edited by D.F. Smith and J. Phillips (London & New York: Routledge), pp. 83–100.

Langley, J. 2020. Biffa Helps Redesign Ribena Botte, *Lets Recycle* (10 November). Available at https://www.letsrecycle.com/news/biffa-helps-redesign-ribena-bottle/ (Accessed: 16 January 2024).

Loxham, A. 2016. Profiting from War: Bovril Advertising During World War II. *Journal of Macromarketing* 36(2):198–214.

Lyon, P. and Kautto, E. 2021. Half the Battle is Fought in the Kitchen: Convalescence and Cookery in 1920s and 1930s Britain. *Food, Culture & Society* 24(3):345–367.

Ministry of Food. 1951. *The Urban Working-Class Household Diet 1940 to 1949: First Report of the National Food Survey Committee*. London: Ministry of Food.

Nevett, T.R. 1982. *Advertising in Britain: A History*. London: Heinemann.

O'Hagan, L.A. 2021. Commercialising Public Health During the 1918–1919 Spanish Flu Pandemic in Britain. *Journal of Historical Research in Marketing* 13(3–4):161–187.

O'Hagan, L.A. 2022. All That Glistens Is Not (Green) Gold: Historicising the Contemporary Chlorophyll Fad Through a Multimodal Analysis of Swedish Marketing, 1950–1953. *Journal of Historical Research in Marketing* 14(3):374–398.

O'Hagan, L.A. 2023. From Fatigue Fighter to Heartburn Healer: The Evolving Marketing of a Functional Beverage in Sweden. *Journal of Food Products Marketing* 29(1):19–40.

O'Hagan, L.A. and Eriksson, G. 2022. Modern Science, Moral Mothers, and Mythical Nature: A Multimodal Analysis of Cod Liver Oil Marketing in Sweden, 1920–1930. *Food and Foodways* 30(4):231–260.

"Ribena Advertisement." 1943a. *The Scotsman* (16 April), 3.

"Ribena Advertisement." 1943b. *Western Morning News* (12 February), 3.

"Ribena Advertisement." 1942a. *Yorkshire Post and Leeds Intelligencer* (10 November), 5.

"Ribena Advertisement." 1942b. *Yorkshire Post and Leeds Intelligencer* (2 December), 6.

"Ribena Advertisement." 1944. *Belfast News-Letter* (12 April), 3.

"Ribena Advertisement." 1952a. *Daily Herald* (3 January), 1.

"Ribena Advertisement." 1952b. *Daily Herald* (6 May), 2.

"Ribena Advertisement." 1952c. *Daily Herald* (8 July), 4.

"Ribena Advertisement." 1952d. *Daily Herald* (13 October), 4

"Ribena Advertisement." 1955. *Coventry Evening Telegraph* (13 April), 8.

Ribena. 1956. *Evacuees* (1 min) [Television advertisement], J Walter Thompson. History of Advertising Trust, Raveningham. Available at https://www.hatads.org.uk/catalogue/record/cc640c8e-bf24-4c43-a39c-36323d24c26b (Accessed: 22 September 2022).

Ribena. 1961. *Rugger* (30 secs). [Television advertisement], J Walter Thompson. History of Advertising Trust, Raveningham. Available at https://www.hatads.org.uk/catalogue/record/531f131e-8be8-417a-933b-c97d1c377628 (Accessed: 22 September 2022).

Ribena. 1964. *Diving* (30 secs). [Television advertisement], J Walter Thompson. History of Advertising Trust, Raveningham. Available at https://www.hatads.org.uk/catalogue/record/cdb5b12c-d15e-46a0-9047-13cefb146121 (Accessed: 22 September 2022).

Ribena. 1966. *Jamie* (30 secs). [Television advertisement], J Walter Thompson. History of Advertising Trust, Raveningham. Available at https://www.hatads.org.uk/catalogue/record/fa3aae34-0f91-49d5-99c4-570e2d51feef (Accessed: 22 September 2022).

Ribena: Its Properties and Applications in Medical Practice. n.d. *The Royal Forest Laboratory*, Coleford: H.W. Carter & Co. Limited.
Roderick, L. 2016. Ribena Attempts to Wake 'Sleeping Giant' and Target Health Conscious Consumers with Ribena Light Push, *Marketing Week* (2 March), Available at https://www.marketingweek.com/ribena-attempts-to-wake-sleeping-giant-and-target-health-conscious-consumers-with-ribena-light-push/ (Accessed: 16 January 2024).
Scrinis, G. 2008. On the Ideology of Nutritionism. *Gastronomica* 8:39–48.
Scrinis, G. 2013. *Nutritionism: The Science and Politics of Dietary Advice*. New York: Columbia University Press.
"Sugar Tax Revolt: Meet the Ribena Stockpilers." 2018. *BBC News* (27 April). Available at https://www.bbc.co.uk/news/av/uk-43843614 (Accessed: 1 September 2022).
The Development and Medical Uses of Ribena. n.d. *The Royal Forest Laboratory*, Coleford: H W Carter & Co. Limited.
Turnock, R. 2007. *Television and Consumer Culture: Britain and the Transformation of Modernity*. London & New York: Tauris.
Wallace, T. and Marsh, R.W. eds. 1953. *Science and Fruit: Commemorating the Jubilee of the Long Ashton Research Station, 1903–1953*. Bristol: J. W. Arrowsmith Ltd.
"Why Ribena Fans Have Been Left with a Bad Taste in Their Mouths." 2018. *The Guardian* (16 March). Available at https://www.theguardian.com/lifeandstyle/shortcuts/2018/mar/16/why-ribena-fans-have-been-left-with-a-bad-taste-in-their-mouths (Accessed: 16 September 2022).
Winkler, J.T. 2005. Controversial Claims. *British Dental Journal* 199(4):188–189.

7 A Cheap and Tasty Way to Health

Advertising Coffee Substitutes in Sweden, 1870–1914

Leif Runefelt

Introduction

Throughout the 1890s, the marketing of coffee substitutes increased significantly in Sweden. Spurred on by fierce competition between producers, coffee substitutes represented a growing consumer market. There were several factors that facilitated this growth. One was the extensive Swedish coffee consumption, which has always been—and still is—higher than in most other countries. Coffee drinking was an important part of the Swedish middle-class way of life, while also a widespread practice among the working classes. A second factor was a century-old perception that coffee was harmful to consumers, which was given new impetus by late nineteenth-century hygienism, medicalisation and promotion of healthy lifestyles. Added to these factors were urbanisation, which encouraged the use of goods such as coffee, and industrialisation, which facilitated the development of technology in the food industry. Finally, the often-high international price of coffee made this ritualised habit expensive.

In this chapter, I analyse the arguments in Swedish coffee substitute advertisements, focusing mainly on the decade around the turn of the twentieth century and on the three major advertisers on the market: the German company Kathreiner KFN and the two Swedish companies Skandinaviska Kaffeförädlings Aktiebolag (Kronkaffe) and Stockholms Kaffe-Aktiebolag (Intubikaffe). Their main arguments can be divided into four distinct but interrelated themes: medical arguments referring to the harmfulness of real coffee and the alleged scientifically proven healthiness of substitutes; economic arguments appealing to rational housewives that substitutes were cheaper than coffee; arguments of equal experience, that is claims that a specific substitute could indeed replace coffee in terms of taste and smell; and protectionist or nationalist arguments based on coffee being an imported commodity that drained the country of money and, thus, it was a Swede's duty to avoid such goods.

The study is based on an analysis of claims made in texts and images in press advertisements for coffee substitutes from 1870 to 1914. An inventory of the material shows that advertisers had a clear intended readership: middle-class women. It was women who controlled the household purse and ensured that their families lived up to expected standards. Women were also responsible

DOI: 10.4324/9781003450276-11

for their children's choice of beverages. At this time, publications aimed at female audiences could have several different coffee advertisements in each issue, while publications aimed at male audiences had far fewer. The analysis is based on a broad inventory of the press, but I mainly use examples of advertisements from the larger daily newspapers in Stockholm, such as *Dagens Nyheter*, *Aftonbladet* and *Svenska Dagbladet*, and weekly magazines for women, such as *Damernas Värld* and *Idun*.

For many years, advertising and consumption were understudied in Sweden. Recently, however, a number of studies have changed this and there is now much research on Swedish advertising from the 1920s onwards (Arnberg, 2018; Arnberg and Husz, 2018; Åström Rudberg, 2019; O'Hagan, 2022, 2023a, 2023b) and on the eighteenth and early nineteenth centuries—including coffee and coffee substitutes (Runefelt, 2015; Lundqvist, 2016; Knutsson and Hodacs, 2021; Hodacs, 2023). However, the food industry has been less examined and, in general, the decades around the turn of the twentieth century are still poorly researched, despite the fact that they seem to represent a crucial period of study in order to understand the impact of modern consumer culture from a European perspective (Runefelt, 2019; Nilsson, 2020).

One of the aims of this chapter is, therefore, to focus on a small part of the ongoing commercialisation in Sweden by studying the advertising of coffee substitutes (1870–1914) and to show how arguments connected to contemporary discourses on health, nation and rationality. These advertisements contained an element of scaremongering, whereby companies first presented a threat (in the form of coffee and caffeine) and then placed the responsibility for avoiding the threat on consumers (by choosing the right substitute). Already at the turn of the twentieth century, the responsibility for making wise and rational choices was granted to individuals and a fundamental argument was that these choices could be made without any real sacrifice on the part of consumers. In this way, arguments were put forward that are today associated with the neoliberal ideology of our time (Jovanovic, 2014).

The Importance of Coffee in Late Nineteenth-Century Sweden

To understand the breakthrough of commercialised coffee substitutes as advertised products, it is necessary to first reflect on Swedish coffee culture and the country's social and economic development during the late nineteenth century. For centuries, coffee consumption in Sweden has been high in relation to many other countries (Lindgren, 1993:96). Today, Sweden is among the top six most coffee-drinking nations in the world. From the end of the eighteenth century, coffee had a strong cultural significance within the Swedish bourgeoisie. Being able to afford, drink and indeed have the time for coffee (a sign that one did not spend one's days performing manual labour) became an essential part of Swedish middle-class respectability. During the nineteenth century, coffee spread to the urban and rural working classes. The intense struggle against high alcohol consumption among Swedes—the temperance movement—drove the spread of coffee among the lower classes, being seen as an alternative to spirits (Lindgren, 1993; Ahlberger, 1996:90–99; Runefelt, 2015:218–227).

From this point onwards, coffee consumption in Sweden increased continuously (a development in stark contrast to its steady decline in Britain—see Burnett 1999:81). However, there were differences in how the working and middle classes consumed their coffee. While workers drank coffee in a hurry, often outside of their homes and (according to some social commentators) as a substitute for food, ritualised coffee consumption remained an important reference point in the social life of the middle class: not drinking coffee (or tea) in particular circumstances was tantamount to no longer being middle class. Being able to drink coffee in this way was also a gateway to middle-class life for the growing urban population (Lundqvist, 2016). Thus, coffee was an essential commodity in Swedish social life at the end of the nineteenth century.

Already one century earlier, excessive coffee drinking had led to a critical debate in which coffee was attacked for two different but interrelated reasons: medical (it hurt individual health) and economic (it hurt the national economy) (Runefelt, 2015:220–223). I will return to this criticism below, only to make clear at this point that there was an opening in late nineteenth-century Sweden for coffee substitutes due to three core factors: the high demand for coffee, the widespread perception of its harmfulness and the public debate in favour of domestic production of alternatives. Although this had been the case throughout the nineteenth century and indeed even earlier, the component that enabled the product's expansion in the 1890s was Sweden's late industrialisation and related commercialisation.

From the 1870s, Sweden was rapidly transformed from a country whose prosperity was based on agriculture and mining to one where engineering was seen as the noblest of activities. Over time, industrialisation led to mass urbanisation which, in turn, created a growing urban middle class who embraced the middle-class lifestyle and a large urban working class that towns were unable to accommodate and who were believed to have poor nutritional intake. As a result, two different movements—both reactions to modern urbanity—came to emphasise the harmfulness of coffee and provide at least a discursive basis for coffee substitutes.

The first was the entry of new ideals about health into the middle-class way of life. Nervousness—the classic cultural disease of late nineteenth-century Sweden, particularly among women—was now to be combatted through a healthy lifestyle: movement and exercise, fresh air, good hygiene and a well-considered nutritional intake based on scientific evidence (Johannisson, 1994:141–149; Gijswijt-Hofstra, 2005). Inspiration was drawn from the German *Lebensreform* movement and the emerging fields of social medicine and nutritional science, which emphasised the importance of lifestyle choices for an individual's health (Johannisson, 1991:145–160; Qvarsell, 2005:222–226; Eklöf, 2005:245–248). There was a firm belief that middle-class women, who so easily fell victim to nervous breakdowns, consumed large quantities of coffee at their coffee parties (*Idun*, 22 February 1895; N–a, 1898:284; K-dt, 1912:68).

The second was discussions around working-class diets, whereby coffee was presented as a major problem (Johannisson, 1991:140; Lindgren, 1993:99–107). There was a perception that workers—both men and women, and by extension children—consumed large amounts of coffee as an appetite suppressant (*Kaffemissbruket bland barnen*, 1910; Johannisson, 1991). Thus, they traded healthy, nutritional foods for a product that was perceived as both nutrient-poor and toxic (Fru H., 1898:33; J.W., 1899:2–3; Cassel, 1903:262; F-zon, 1905:4–5).

Malt Coffees, 1870–1890: Early Scientific Arguments

Nineteenth-century Swedish food advertisements were long underdeveloped in comparison to other European countries. Both producers and distributors were locally based; thus, the need for marketing was considered low. In the 1870s, the number of advertisements in the Swedish press increased due to the onset of industrialisation. Now, not only were there more producers acting on a national level and, therefore, a greater need to spread awareness of their products, but there was also a growing range of competing commodities. Although the food industry remained local for many years and advertised less than other sectors, from the 1870s onwards, there was a notable growth in the number of advertisements for processed and industrially refined food. This included coffee substitutes (Jonsson, 2009:208–214).[1]

One of the first coffee substitutes was created by the German engineer E. Beckman-Olofson, who obtained Sweden's first patent for malt coffee in 1871. The patent application, reprinted in the press, describes a complicated roasting process, whereby 9/12 of rye malt was roasted in the same way as regular coffee and then 1/12 of coffee and 2/12 of barley malt were added and roasted separately. A small amount of burnt sugar or syrup was also put into the mix, after which roasted bitter almonds or hops were added. The end product was consumed instead of regular coffee and had, according to the patent (but without any evidence supporting the claim), significant advantages, being more nutritious and not sleep-disturbing. It was particularly recommended for the weak, sickly and elderly, as well as for children (*Post- och Inrikes Tidningar*, 1871).

The Swedish retailer, Aug. Norman, advertised this malt coffee for over a decade, using simple advertisements without images and just a few lines of text. The main argument was twofold: compared to real coffee, malt coffee was cheap and healthy. Health benefits were highlighted in some advertisements (*Dagens Nyheter*, 26 January 1872), but the normal practice was to include recommendations only, from anonymous doctors. An advertisement in *Dagens Nyheter* on 6 February 1879, for example, stated that Beckman-Olofson's award-winning coffee was recommended by "Mr:s Scientists and Doctors." The substitute's real unique selling point was that it was considerably cheaper than real coffee; in early 1872, Aug. Norman sold it to consumers for half the price of coffee (*Dagens Nyheter*, 26 January 1872; *Dagens Nyheter*, 20 March 1872; *Bohusläns Tidning*, 2 April 1872).

Beckman-Olofson, thus, tried to give his product legitimacy by referring to physicians. It was less important to explain *why* doctors found malt coffee so healthy. This may have been because there was abundant criticism of coffee dating back to the late eighteenth century on which advertisers could fall back. The criticism was summarised by physician Magnus Huss in his pamphlet *Om Kaffe: dess bruk och missbruk* [*About Coffee: Its Use and Abuse*, 1865]. Huss wrote that coffee consumption was increasing rapidly, causing a range of medical problems, such as gastric acidity, nervous disorders and malnutrition (Huss, 1865).

Criticism of this kind was often repeated in the press and in popular works on medicine (Lindgren, 1993:99–100). One standard example was an article printed in *Westerwiks-Posten* on 19 December 1885 entitled "Kaffeförbrukningen" [Coffee Consumption]. According to the anonymous writer, it was the power of habit that made Swedes drink a lot of coffee. This was unfortunate; coffee temporarily revitalised body and mind, but lacked nutrients and instead acted as an appetite suppressant, which caused malnutrition. Furthermore, coffee led to physical weakness, chronic gastritis, loss of appetite, vomiting after proper meals and nausea that could only be relieved with more coffee. On top of that came an economic criticism. Coffee was supposed to be a major expense for Swedish households and detrimental to the Swedish balance of trade. According to both Huss and *Westerwiks-Posten*, it would be best to replace coffee with milk, bread and gruel, but that was not practical; instead, coffee substitutes were the way forward, particularly malt coffee.[2]

However, Beckman-Olofson's substitute faced competition from other malt coffees, such as the German firm Gebrüder Behr's "Sundhets-Kaffe." The Behr brothers emphasised the scientifically controlled manufacturing process used to produce their coffee. Additionally, a chemist was said to carry out "permanent chemical analytical control" at the site of production. The result was a beverage "similar to Indian coffee" (i.e. genuine coffee) that could be drunk on its own or added to coffee (*Dagens Nyheter*, 13 January 1880). The scientific rhetoric served to highlight the recognised health benefits of the product, but perhaps also its authenticity, purity and controlled production conditions. Later, in the twentieth century, this was part of the standard repertoire in Swedish advertising for healthy foodstuffs, but at this time, it was rather innovative (Eriksson and O'Hagan, 2021; O'Hagan and Eriksson, 2022). Emphasising authenticity and purity offered a way to counteract a well-established perception that fraud was common within the retailing of grounded products, especially real coffee (*Nya Wermlands-Tidningen*, 7 July 1881).

Intensified Advertising at the Turn of the Twentieth Century

In the 1890s, several new producers began advertising coffee substitutes. In most cases, producers were small and local, such as Frihamns Kaffebränneri in Malmö, Pehr Frick's factories (also in Malmö) and Cederroth's St Bravo malt coffee in Gävle. In the following section, I focus on the arguments in advertisements from the three major players: Kathreiner FKN, Skandinaviska Kaffeförädlings Aktiebolag and Stockholms Kaffe-Aktiebolag.

By far the most advertised product on the Swedish market was Kathreiner Kneipp, introduced in the autumn of 1894. It was a malt coffee first produced in Munich by Kathreiner FKN ("Franz Kathreiners Nachfolger"), a large German food retailer. With Kathreiner Kneipp, the company entered the coffee substitute market. The raw material was barley malt roasted in a complicated process patented in Sweden in 1892. In accordance with a protectionist rhetoric, the product for the Swedish market was also claimed to be made in Sweden (Svenskt Patent no. 4272, 1892). Kneipp coffee became a successful product in Germany that survived well after the First World War, before production was incorporated into larger companies under different names. In Sweden, Kneipp coffee was extensively marketed from 1895, ceasing only in the late 1920s.

The health benefits of Kathreiner Kneipp were at the heart of its marketing campaign, with the name itself giving the product a scientific and healthy basis well known in Sweden. "Kneipp" came from an agreement between the company and the famous German health entrepreneur Sebastian Kneipp, who lent his name to the product (Spiekermann, 2018). Kneipp was best known for his teachings on bathing, reflected in Sweden, for example, by the Kneippen district in Norrköping, which grew in the 1890s around a spa based on Kneipp's principles. Malt coffee was easily incorporated into Kneipp's broader view of health, according to which coffee was a harmful product lacking nutritional value (Kneipp, 1897:251). *Idun* pushed for the merits of Kneipp coffee in an 1895 article, highlighting its manufacturing process. According to the article entitled "Damernas älsklingsdryck" [Ladies' Favourite Drink], Kneipp was a revamped version of the roasted malt coffee, consisting of "specially selected" malt, roasted in whole grains impregnated with a strong coffee essence, which added to the grain "the flavour and aroma of real coffee and that which is the essence of coffee, the 'soul' of coffee, so to speak: the caffeine." The latter was a complete misunderstanding; on the contrary, a key part of Kathreiner Kneipp's marketing was that the product was caffeine free.

In advertisements, Kathreiner Kneipp was often referred to as a "coffee additive," meaning that it was a substitute that could be drunk as it was or mixed with real coffee. The slogan was "The best coffee additive! The only coffee substitute!" (*Svenska Dagbladet*, 12 November 1894). The scientific production process and its health benefits were guaranteed by different professors. In an 1895 advertisement in *Svea*, three professors gave their opinions. Ernst Almquist of the Karolinska Institute in Stockholm said that Kathreiner Kneipp should be welcomed both in families and in public institutions, and that it was better for children and the sick than ordinary coffee. Ernst Edvard Sundvik of the Imperial Alexander University in Helsinki confirmed that Kathreiner Kneipp was already widely available, which was only to be recommended. "C. Hammarsten" at Uppsala University wrote that it was highly "deserving the attention and confidence of both doctors and the general public" (*Svea*, 1895). There was no Professor C. Hammarsten at Uppsala University; it was a misspelling of O. (Olof) Hammarsten. In 1894, he certified that Kathreiner Kneipp, being a malt coffee, was cheaper than ordinary coffee, while lacking the irritating effect of caffeine on the nervous system (Ottosson, 2020:81).

Hammarsten's and Almquist's testimonials were still used in advertisements ten years later, but were supplemented by an appeal from Professor Torsten Thunberg of Lund University: "Cut down on coffee drinking!" The advertisement, placed in the weekly newspaper *Hvar 8 dag* in May 1907, carried the headline "The Swedish national wealth can be increased by 20 million each year." However, in addition to coffee being detrimental to the wealth of the nation, the "dangerous stimulant" was also considered to corrupt health. This scaremongering rhetoric was used in other advertisements, such as one in *Idun* in 1908a, where Thunberg described what real coffee led to: "Nerve weakness, gastritis, anaemia, digestive disorders and poor appetite." In *Svensk Damtidning*—about to become the leading weekly magazine for women—similar opinions were instead given by a Professor Lewin in Berlin, and later by Dr Martin Mendelsohn in the same city (1908b, 1909b).

The scientific authority could also be bestowed by a completely fictitious or imaginary doctor, such as in a 1911a advertisement in *Svensk Damtidning*. It was headlined "The Doctor," symbolised by a drawing of a bald, elderly man with a well-trimmed beard and small, round glasses—an image that signalled authority and knowledge. The doctor was depicted holding a pack of Kathreiner with the headline stating: "The doctor has been recommending Kathreiner's malt coffee for 20 years" (Figure 7.1).

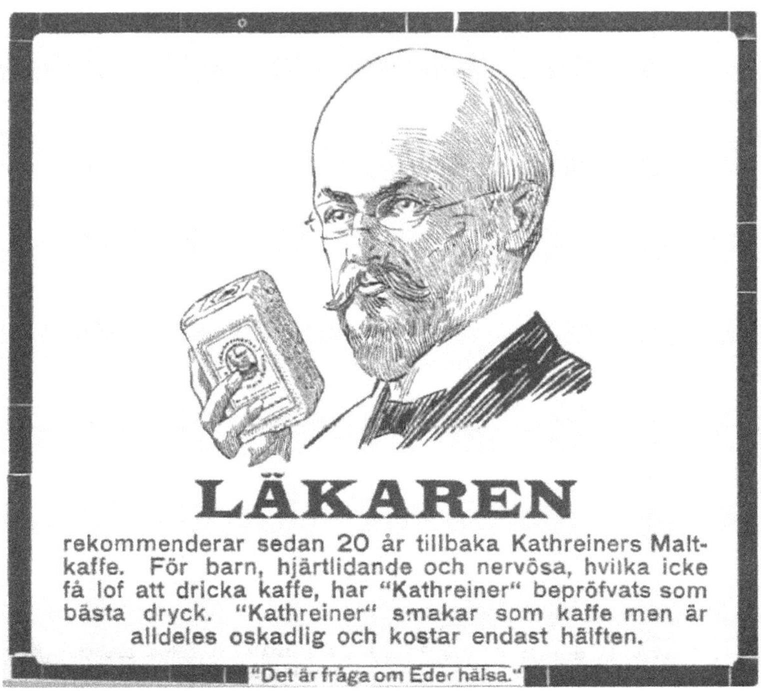

Figure 7.1 "The Doctor" in Advertisement for Kathreiner's Malt Coffee

Credit: *Svensk Damtidning*, 1911a, p. 122

Neurasthenia and nervousness came up in several of the physicians' opinions. Magnus Huss had already highlighted the negative effects of caffeine on the nerves (Huss, 1865). The relationship between caffeine and nervous disorders was also at the heart of Kathreiner's argument. In an advertisement published in *Dagens Nyheter* on 14 February 1909a, the headline was a question: "Can nervous people drink coffee?" A long text followed, with the opening words: "Anyone interested in this question should read 'Arzneimittellehre' [*Education in Pharmaceuticals*] by Professor Med. Dr Binz." Carl Binz, a member of the German National Health Council and the director of the Pharmacological Institute in Bonn, was quoted on the harmfulness of coffee: "Binz calls caffeine 'a poison for the nerves, of which fractions of a gram are already sufficient to cause palpitations, ringing in the ears, dizziness, excitement, vomiting and similar signs of an attacked brain.'"

Therefore, according to the advertisement, everyone should "curtail coffee consumption before it is too late." The advertisement exaggerated the effects of coffee, while encouraging consumers to listen to both science and their own desire to stay healthy. Such scaremongering was not unique to Kathreiner, but a method used by many advertisers marketing healthy foods or other health products, both at the turn of the century and much later (Jovanovic, 2014; Runefelt, 2019:163–176; O'Hagan, 2023b). As shown below, the growth in coffee consumption indicates that, in the case of coffee substitutes, it was probably not successful.

From the very beginning and for a long time afterwards, Kathreiner targeted women, the sick and the elderly, claiming to be the cheapest morning drink "for all social classes" (*Svea*, 1895), but it was particularly aimed at mothers with children. Kathreiner was the best and healthiest drink "for everyone, especially children" (*Stockholms-Tidningen*, 12 January 1895a). Women were, of course, the obvious target group: they drank the most coffee, while also being responsible for the household budget and the well-being of their children. Appealing to mothers with scientific and health arguments to look after their children's best interests was a common method; Rima D. Apple calls it the argument of scientific motherhood, and it was also used for other products in Sweden (Apple, 1997; O'Hagan and Eriksson, 2022; O'Hagan, 2023b). It was an argument that combined rationality and morality. An 1897 advertisement in the fashion magazine *Freja* stated that "The best children's drink is obtained from one half Kneipp malt coffee and one half boiled milk." Why would a mother give anything but the best to her children?

An important part of the mother's and housewife's duties was the rational use of household funds. This, along with the health argument, was the main argument in Kathreiner's marketing. Kathreiner Kneipp was not only healthy but also cheap. "The thrifty housewife" was the title of an advertisement in *Idun* in 1911a: she "wants to provide the family with a daily drink, which firstly must be cheap and secondly completely harmless and tasty." In her study of the history of advertising, Ellen Gruber Garvey has shown that marketing to working-class women emphasised thrift and high morals while marketing to middle-class women tended to emphasise the maintenance of status and the realisation of ideals (Garvey, 1996:8; Jonsson, 2009:222). This difference did not exist in the Swedish coffee substitute advertisements: instead, a central argument was that middle-class status and ideals could be maintained at a lower cost than with regular coffee, while also improving the family's health.

O'Hagan (2023a) has shown that the Swedish margarine industry, established at this time as a result of industrialisation, used the same arguments. Margarine and coffee substitutes were similar in that they were both cheaper products designed to replace well-established foods (i.e. butter and coffee). This put them at risk of being labelled as food for the poor. Avoiding this was important, and manufacturers wanted to show middle-class women that they would not lose anything in terms of lifestyle and quality of life by switching their coffee or butter. Overall, Kathreiner's underlying arguments for malt coffee were similar to other advertisements focusing on homes, health and beauty at this time in Sweden (Runefelt, 2019). The key message was that, while the consumer had to make choices with limited means, in modern society, the right choice was easy to make: a cheap, healthy and scientifically proven coffee substitute that did not threaten women's social status nor their ritualised coffee moments. It was, thus, the individual's own fault if he/she was sick, poor and still drinking real coffee.

When intensified its marketing in 1895, another producer began an aggressive advertising campaign: Intubikaffe (Kathreiner, 1895a, 1895b, 1895c, 1895d). Intubikaffe differed from Kathreiner Kneipp in that it was a substitute based on roasted chicory, the name deriving from its Latin name *Cichorium intybus*. Chicory had been promoted as a coffee substitute at least since the early nineteenth century (*Åbo Tidning*, 1802). In 1883, a company in Gävle started selling "Scandinavian Intubi-Coffee" (*Norrlandsposten*, 19 March 1883), while in the 1890s, several companies from around the country marketed chicory substitutes under the name "intubi coffee": Winborg's Intubi, Per Frick's Intubikaffe and Heiner Busck's Intubikaffe, to name but a few examples.

Stockholms Kaffe-Aktiebolag sold Intubi Coffee with arguments about good health and with doctors' alleged testimonials. The marketing was much vaguer than Kathreiner's. There were no named physicians or experts nor any substantiated scientific arguments. Instead, they used scientific prose, with words such as "organism" (*Förgätmigej*, 1896), and claimed that "drowsiness and sluggishness" could be avoided (*Svea*, 1895) and "coffee poisoning" prevented (*Allehanda*, 11 January 1902). The company did not refer to any specific physicians or professors, merely stating that Intubikaffe "is recommended by prominent professors and doctors" (*Förgätmigej*, 1896) or that "professors and doctors" recommended the product as the most suitable and healthy coffee additive (*Svea*, 1895). Intubi coffee could be consumed as it was, but advertisements emphasised that a cup of coffee mixed with Intubi had "a good effect on the human organism," facilitating muscle work, sharpening the mind and eliminating fatigue (*Svea*, 1895).

Moreover, Intubi coffee was cheap. The basic argument was the same as for Kathreiner Kneipp: the consumer should know to choose health first, especially since it was cheap and easy to obtain with coffee substitutes. "Everyone knows," the company said, that coffee was unhealthy and ruined the stomach. However, adding a large amount of Intubi coffee, which lacked all the unhealthy elements of coffee while close to coffee in taste and appearance, neutralised the harmfulness of coffee. Thus, the line of argumentation was similar to Kathreiner's, pointing to the low price, while using phrases such as "Everyone knows" to place responsibility on the individual. Scaremongering was also a major part of these advertisements, regarding not only real coffee but also competing products within the substitute business. Intubi warned consumers about "the too strongly nourishing coffee additives," likely referring to Kathreiner Kneipp which, unlike Intubi coffee, was marketed as nourishing and filling (*Svea*, 1895).

The third major player in the wave of coffee substitutes at this time was Skandinaviska Kaffeförädlings Aktiebolaget with its product Kronkaffe [*Crown Coffee*], also made from chicory (Marklin, 2018). Unlike Intubi Coffee, whose name revealed its chicory base, Skandinaviska Kaffeförädlings Aktiebolaget never mentioned its components. Even the two patents that the company took out on its methods do not reveal the crop on which the substitute was based, as they only concerned technical improvements and the addition of large amounts of fat, such as fresh tallow, peanut oil, pure butterfat and olive oil (Svenskt Patent no. 8098, 1896; Svenskt Patent no. 9176, 1897).

The founder of the company was chemical entrepreneur Erik Taflin. He was also the founder of the company Tekniska Fabriken Röda Korset, which he still ran, producing, among other things, maltose products (Ring, 1894–1907:201–203). The fact that Taflin had built up a range of maltose products, including maltose bread for children and a "maltose-cannabis" health beverage, but now chose to market a coffee based on chicory indicates that maltose coffee was not seen as a viable product. The most common advertisement stated that the company sold "an epoch-making kind of coffee-saving agent, which we call Kronkaffe" (*Aftonbladet*, 28 June 1897a), said to have the taste, aroma and stimulating effect of coffee. The latter meant that the product contained what other coffee substitutes lacked: caffeine. Moreover, it was nourishing and healthy, with no negative effects associated with real coffee. Finally, it was cheap (*Aftonbladet*, 28 June 1897). The name was clever, the Swedish word *Krona*—"Crown"—relating both to royalty (i.e. exclusive quality) and the Swedish currency (i.e. *krona*) and, thus, to good housekeeping.

The company's use of experts was questionable. Like Kathreiner, Kronkaffe used named experts to legitimise arguments of health and taste, relying on Dr Carl Setterberg and trade chemist John Landin. Landin certified in advertisements that the coffee retained both the taste and the stimulating effect of real coffee in a way that far exceeded all previous competitors' products. This was due to the specific production method, which involved impregnating the coffee substitute not only with coffee aroma extract but also with chemically obtained caffeine. Thus, one company (Kathreiner) could rely on experts who vouched for the absence of caffeine as a benefit, while another (Skandinaviska Kaffeförädlings Aktiebolaget) could rely on other experts vouching for the presence of caffeine as a benefit. However, what John Landin did not say in the advertisements was that he was the holder of said patent of 1896 and that Landin, indeed a trade chemist, was also Taflin's business partner (Svenskt Patent no. 8098, 1896; Marklin, 2018:13). Furthermore, Carl Setterberg was not a doctor. He was a pharmacist and commercial chemist who was involved in several chemical companies at the time. Such fraudulent claims were easy to make, as advertising remained almost completely unregulated in Sweden until after the First World War (Björklund, 1967:886–888; Åström Rudberg, 2019).

Skandinaviska Kaffeförädlings Aktiebolaget excelled in innovative marketing at the General Art and Industrial Exposition of Stockholm in 1897. In connection to the pavilion of Taflin's other company, Röda Korset, the so-called Moorish Coffeehouse was erected—an oriental fairy-tale pavilion and a major success among visitors—in which Kronkaffe was served. The company also sold or handed out tens of thousands of coffee cups with saucers—a pioneering act and one of the most extensive marketing campaigns at this time in Sweden. Women were a target group also for Kronkaffe: "Thrifty housewives are the clientele we have calculated for our Kronkaffe" (*Aftonbladet*, 28 June 1897). The company had a slogan, "3 cups of coffee for 1 öre," which was very cheap (*Dagens Nyheter*, 25 September 1897b). Thus, Kronkaffe's unique selling point was that it was cheap while not decaffeinated like other coffee substitutes. Since caffeine was widely believed to be the basis of coffee's harmfulness, the company's health arguments remained unclear in relation to contemporary medical opinions.

The three competitors developed differently after the turn of the twentieth century. Kathreiner remained a frequent advertiser well into the 1920s, with modern advertisements adapted to the trends of the time, often with a children's theme. In *Idun* in 1913, for example, the company depicted young scouts—a new and popular phenomenon in Sweden (Figure 7.2): "The best drink for hiking in the forest and countryside is Kathreiner's malt coffee" (*Idun*, 1913). The advertisement is a beautiful example of how Kathreiner tried to connect its substitute to a healthy and active childhood, showing two well-ordered scouts hiking, facing the reader's gaze with confidence while pointing to the pack of Kathreiner Kneipp. The focus on children also worked well in relation to Kneipp's teachings, which highlighted malt coffee as particularly suitable for children (Kneipp, 1897:245).

Chicory suffered from a bad reputation. For instance, an article on coffee published in *Aftonbladet* on 4 June 1901 stated that chicory coffee was the most common substitute, but also the worst, as it was harmful to the consumer's health. This led Stockholms Kaffe-Aktiebolag to change the name of its product to Arla-Kaffe in 1903. "Intubikaffe" was not trademarked and was used by many other companies. Thus, perhaps Stockholms Kaffe-Aktiebolag found it best to disconnect the name from the main ingredient, intubus being another

Figure 7.2 Boy Scouts in Advertisement for Kathreiner's Malt Coffee
Credit: *Idun*, 1913, p. 418

word for chicory. There were cases where companies advertised that they sold "genuine intubi coffee" (*Sydsvenska Veckobladet*, 15 August 1895; *Malmötidningen*, 21 January 1905). This could indicate that fraud occurred and that chicory products could be of low quality, but it could also have been a rhetorical effort to raise the status of a product with the reputation of being a poor family's alternative.

Instead, "Arla" in Swedish was a positively charged word that characterised the early morning (etymologically, "arla" and "early" are related): productive, healthy individuals were up at the crack of dawn drinking their coffee additive. Stockholms Kaffe-Aktiebolag continued to market Arla-Kaffe until the First World War, albeit to a lesser extent than Kathreiner. An advertisement in *Idun*'s popular Christmas issue of 1911 read: "If you want to drink coffee and avoid being nervous or otherwise nauseated by it, and get a real coffee, which is good, cheap and completely harmless, you should always blend coffee and Arla-Kaffe." The advertisement also stated that "the most prominent Swedish and foreign professors and physicians have certified that Arla-Kaffe is the best and most suitable coffee substitute." This was clearly a lie used by the company for over 15 years, since no such certifying physicians and professors were ever presented to consumers.

After 1902, Kronkaffe disappeared from the market, but its place was swiftly taken by other competitors making chicory coffees. One of these was Victoria coffee, produced by Per Frick's factories. Although the product had existed since the 1880s (*Dagens Nyheter*, 30 March 1887), its advertising in the press was extended around 1910 (*Svensk Damtidning*, 1911b). Its arguments were similar to other brands: Victoria coffee was cheaper and healthier. The advertisements generally featured women—either housewives drinking or maids serving—emphasising coffee consumption as a middle-class habit (*Idun* 1913; *Dagens Nyheter*, 22 October 1911b). There were also new substitutes of a more ephemeral character, such as Ido—or "Plant Coffee Ido" as it was called in advertisements. Ido claimed that it was made "from guaranteed healthy and stimulating plant substances with very low caffeine content" (*Idun*, 1911). However, an article in *Dagens Nyheter* on 22 August 1911 revealed that Ido was made of coffee, rye, beans and cocoa bean shells and, thus, no positive health effects could be established.

Another coffee substitute to enter the market in 1914 was Brana-Kaffe, a malt coffee developed by the Brana Company. An early advertisement described "How Coffee Abuse Undermines Sweden's Independence" (*Dagens Nyheter*, 26 April 1914a) and represented a new, nationalistic tone. As Figure 7.3 shows, it was adorned with a picture of Mother Svea—the allegorical Sweden (drawn by the well-established artist Gunnar Widholm)—dressed in a Viking-style outfit. She held a smoking hot and haloed cup of coffee in one hand, making an inviting gesture with the other. In this way, she became an allegory not only of Sweden but also of the Swedish housewife, always ready to generously offer a cup of coffee. This generosity was emphasised by the headline "Mother Svea gives Brana Coffee to all her inhabitants." At her side was a sword and a shield reading "Sweden for the Swedes."

Below the picture was a series of one-liners answering three brief questions, pedagogically explaining the relationship between Brana Coffee, Sweden as a nation, Swedish nationalism and the health of the individual Swede. The first question, "How does coffee abuse undermine Sweden's independence?" was answered by stating that it destroyed public health, weakening the nerves and the moral strength of the people, and that 45 million Swedish crowns were spent annually on coffee imports, which undermined

Figure 7.3 Mother Svea in Advertisement for Brana Coffee

Credit: *Dagens Nyheter*, 26 April 1914a, p. 4

Sweden's economic strength. The second question—"What does Sweden's independence consist of?"—was followed by the answer: "a healthy and vigorous race. In a strengthened moral force; in a solid economic power," while the final question asked, "How does Brana contribute to maintaining Swedish independence?" Again, there were three answers: Brana Coffee did not undermine public health, it did not corrupt the nervous system and it did not take money out of the country.

This protectionist and nationalist rhetoric should not be confused with state-sanctioned "buy national" campaigns that occurred in several Western countries in the twentieth century (Kühschelm, 2020). Instead, it was about companies embracing a current theme in politics and public debate—the issue of coffee abuse—to which middle-class audiences could relate, much like Kathreiner's advertisement with the Boy Scouts. Just a few weeks later, Brana Coffee used a completely different rhetoric: the headline "Take good advice!" and a text appealing to housewives. Coffee destroyed one's health and was expensive: "if you need to look at your expenses and reduce household spending, Brana Coffee offers the benefit of great affordability" (*Dagens Nyheter*, 17 June 1914b). The image spoke a different language. It showed a beautiful, fashionable woman breathing in the smell of Brana Coffee, eyes closed, indulging in pleasure. This woman served as an ideal for housewives and an object for the male gaze. However, she did not have to think about cutting expenses. The image, thus, connected Brana Coffee with beauty, fashion and a bourgeois lifestyle. Such advertisements highlight the fickleness of companies in striving to retain consumer interest, having no problem reconciling a nationalist rhetoric based on civic duty with a more consumerist approach.

Substitutes Versus the Real Thing: The Dilemma of the Coffee Substitute Industry

Although the early twentieth-century market for coffee substitutes in Sweden was clearly dynamic, with many competitors large and small, the consumption of genuine coffee increased at a fast pace, suggesting that Swedes in general were unwilling to replace their coffee with anything else. In the years before the First World War, perceived coffee abuse even became a political issue. In 1911, trade statistics revealed that Sweden had become the world's biggest per capita consumer of coffee and, according to statistics produced by the Swedish Parliament, coffee consumption had quadrupled from the mid-nineteenth century to 1910 (Berg and Santesson, 1917:37–48; *Bihang till Riksdagens protokoll* 1911, 1:2:2c, motion AK285).

In 1911, the politician Carl Lindhagen introduced a motion in the Swedish Parliament to curb coffee abuse through political means. The motion failed, but the National Swedish Board of Health—*Medicinalstyrelsen*—issued an opinion on the issue of coffee abuse. In 1912, Lindhagen renewed his motion, which now passed and led to a missive from Parliament to the government "concerning measures to counteract coffee abuse" (*Bihang till Riksdagens protokoll* 1912, motion AK258, 13). The National Swedish Board of Health made a further statement on the matter in the summer of 1914. This later led physician Henrik Berg and professor of pharmacology, Carl Gustaf Santesson, to publish a popular pamphlet to educate Swedes on the dangers of their copious coffee drinking, entitled "On Coffee Abuse Among the Swedish People" (Berg and Santesson, 1917). Berg was one of the country's most ardent advocates for coffee surrogates (as long as they were not made of chicory) and, in 1913, had published a translation of an article by the German physician F. Mendel on coffee abuse and its harmful consequences in a magazine for popular medicine, *Hälsovännen* (Mendel, 1889).

This political debate with its central concept of "coffee abuse" was picked up by coffee substitutes, such as Brana and Kathreiner. When Kathreiner claimed in an advertisement in 1911 that "provincial doctors report unanimously that coffee contains absolutely no nutritive elements but (caffeine) poison" (*Idun*, 1911), the company had not asked any such doctors. Instead, they fell back on the opinion of the National Swedish Board of Health, presented to Parliament in 1911, which contained a long list of statements from provincial doctors (Bihang till Riksdagens protokoll 1911, 9:2:2, utlåtande 2.7; Eklund, 2022:40). In 1914, Kathreiner also published an advertisement which recycled Professor Ernst Almquist's recommendation for Kneipp coffee. It was then claimed that Kathreiner was "by far the most effective weapon in the fight against serious coffee abuse" (*Dagens Nyheter*, 10 December 1914).

Despite these marketing claims, a fundamental problem that coffee substitutes had to (and indeed failed to) overcome is the totality of coffee as a product: a surrogate must look, smell and taste like the real thing as much as possible. However, nothing could change the fact that, for most Swedish consumers, real coffee was superior and, thus, no substitute managed to establish itself as a realistic option. Coffee substitutes not only lacked the desired stimulating effects, but they also smelt and tasted worse. For Berg and Santesson (1917:64), these characteristics were an advantage: substitutes tasted so bad that they would never be overconsumed like coffee. However, Swedes in general paid little attention to this message. As coffee consumption increased during the early twentieth century, there is no evidence that average consumers were worried about or scared of caffeine. Scaremongering, therefore, did not work and neither did economic arguments; the price of coffee did not convince any mass of Swedish consumers to switch to cheaper substitutes. In the face of coffee, all basic lines of argumentation were weak.

Nonetheless, the coffee substitute market has been resilient. O'Hagan, for example, demonstrates the very similar marketing techniques of the substitute brand Postum in mid-century Sweden (O'Hagan, 2023b), while today, several coffee substitutes are available on the Swedish market, such as the chicory-based Chicca Roast and Chikko Not Coffee, mushroom-based Four Sigmatics and KoRo, made from roasted lupins. To take one example, Chicca Roast was launched by the Swedish company Womensync in 2022 as an "organic decaffeinated alternative to coffee with no toxins." Womensync's basic idea is to sell products that synchronise a woman's life with her cyclical biology. Like Intubi Coffee 130 years earlier, the name Chicca Roast reveals that it is a chicory product.

Comparing the past and present marketing of coffee substitutes reveals some similarities and differences. First, in both cases, companies seek to make their products mimic coffee as much as possible. Equally, companies aim to promote the health effects of their products with the same central consumer argument: we want coffee, but it contains toxins, especially caffeine, and should be avoided;

thus, there is a need for something similar to coffee. A further similarity is the use of experts to create legitimacy. Womensync, for example, uses a team of experts in the marketing of its entire product range. Given the company's name and business concept, all authority figures are female (as of October 2023). The website highlights the Womensync experts: a specialist nurse, a nutritionist and coach and a licensed psychologist specialising in women's health. Some experts are more reflective of our zeitgeist: a "herbal specialist" and a "holistic reproductive health practitioner."[3] We may find it telling of our time, but Kronkaffe did exactly the same thing because "trade chemist" was a very contemporary and rather vague term in 1900, often used in marketing to give legitimacy to products.

In terms of differences, arguments about nation and duty are no longer present. Furthermore, the focus is on the individual woman's well-being, not on her role as a bearer and caregiver of children in the service of Sweden. Protectionist or economic nationalist arguments are also absent. No one should buy Chicca Roast to improve the Swedish trade balance and reduce coffee imports. The well-being of the individual—and nothing else—takes centre stage. However, the key difference between contemporary and historical coffee substitutes relates to private housekeeping. In the health sector today, frugality no longer seems to be an argument. It is almost shameful to say that a product is cheap, as if suggesting that those who buy cheap products do not take their own health seriously. In contrast, the primary argument for all coffee substitutes around 1900 was frugality. As coffee substitutes were cheaper than coffee, they allowed housewives to manage their household budgets wisely, while at the same time upholding a good and healthy life and an acceptable social lifestyle. In a society where prosperity was relatively low, it was logical to advertise products with the argument that consumers could choose a healthier life without having to pay extra and even save money. Today, in contrast, the famous slogan "because I'm worth it" applies. The choice has a higher cost, but consumers are worth it, and the choice gives them more than just health, making them part of an active, conscious and successful lifestyle too. At the beginning of the twentieth century, the argument was the opposite: you can be part of a successful lifestyle and save money at the same time. You are uneducated, lazy *and* wasteful if you make a different choice.

In August 2022, an article in *Svenska Dagbladet* highlighted that a cup of Chicca Roast was three times more expensive than a cup of regular coffee (Helander, 2022). Although I am not an entrepreneur, as a historian, I imagine that the product will have a difficult future. Chicca Roast is essentially the same product as Intubi coffee of the late nineteenth century: roasted chicory root. Despite being much cheaper than coffee in 1900 and despite heavy advertising arguing for its health benefits, chicory was never able to compete with coffee on a large scale. Since the eighteenth century, Swedes have considered coffee to taste good and have positive stimulating effects, while not being harmful enough to be avoided. This is likely to continue being the case. If the famous slogan "because I'm worth it" was ever relevant and true, then it applies sincerely to the Swedes' relationship with coffee.

Notes

1 While "Health Coffee" (SV: *sundhets-kaffe*)—different types of substitutes made from roasted malt, chicory or other plants, sometimes blended with real coffee—had been advertised locally ("Sundhets-Caffe," *Aftonbladet*, 1 February 1838) since at least the 1830s, it was not until 1870 that a marked increase in advertisements for coffee substitutes occurred.

2 It should be clarified that Beckman-Olofsson used roasted *malt*, not to be confused with the various *maltose*-based products that were on the market at the same time. Maltose was said to be the most effective remedy for coughs, shortness of breath, hoarseness and throat, chest, intestinal and lung disorders, as well as anaemia. Between 1870 and 1900, several companies launched various maltose products using the same health-related and economic arguments as Beckman-Olofson. However, no maltose coffee was ever put on the market. Perhaps it was too difficult to make it mimic coffee.

3 See https://womensync.se/pages/om-oss for more details.

References

Ahlberger, C. 1996. *Konsumtionsrevolutionen 1: Om det moderna konsumtionssamhällets framväxt 1750–1900*. Göteborg: Humanistiska fakulteten vid Göteborgs universitet.

"Annonser." 1871. *Post- och Inrikes Tidningar* (22 December), 4.

Apple, R.D. 1997. "Constructing Mothers. Scientific Motherhood in the Nineteenth and Twentieth Centuries" in *Mothers and Motherhood: Readings in American History*, edited by R.D. Apple and J. Golden (Columbus: Ohio State University), pp. 161–178.

"Arla-Kaffe." *Idun*, 1911 (Christmas issue), 34.

Arnberg, K. 2018. Beyond Mrs Consumer: Competing Femininities in Swedish Advertising Trade Publications, 1900–1939. *Scandinavian Economic History Review* 66 (2):153–169.

Arnberg, K. and Husz, O. 2018. From the Great Department Store with Love: Window Display and the Transfer of Commercial Knowledge in Early Twentieth-Century Sweden. *History of Retailing and Consumption* 4(2):126–155.

Åström Rudberg, E. 2019. *Sound and Loyal Business. The History of the Swedish Advertising Cartel 1915–1965*. Stockholm: Stockholm School of Economics.

"Aug. Norman." 1872. *Dagens Nyheter* (26 January), 4.

"Aug. Norman." 1879. *Dagens Nyheter* (6 February), 4.

Berg, H. and Santesson, C.G. 1917. *Om kaffemissbruket bland Svenska folket*. Stockholm: P.A. Norstedt & Söners Förlag.

Bihang till riksdagens protokoll vid lagtima riksmötet år 1911. 1911. Stockholm: Riksdagen.

Bihang till riksdagens protokoll vid lagtima riksmötet år 1912. 1912. Stockholm: Riksdagen.

Björklund, T. 1967. *Reklamen i svensk marknad 1920–1965: Band 2*. Stockholm: P.A. Norstedts & Söners Förlag.

"Brana-Kaffe." 1914a. *Dagens Nyheter* (26 April), 4.

"Brana-Kaffe." 1914b. *Dagens Nyheter* (17 June), 5.

Burnett, J. 1999. *Liquid Pleasures: A Social History of Drinks in Modern Britain*. London & New York: Routledge.

Cassel, J. 1903. Något om Stockholms klädsömmerskor och deras arbetsförhållande. *Idun* (18), 261–262.

"Damernas älsklingsdryck: Några ord om kaffet, dess tillagning, surrogater m.m." 1895. *Idun* (22 February), 62.

"Den 27 Mars 1872." 1872. *Bohusläns Tidning* (2 April), 2.
Eklund, M. 2022. *Upp till allvarlig kamp mot kaffemissbruket! Kaffemissbruksfrågan i svensk dagspress 1910–1940*. Unpublished undergraduate dissertation, Jönköping University.
Eklöf, M. 2005. Vegetarisk (rå)kost och det reformerade livet: Maximilian Bircher-Benner och de svenska hälsokoströrelserna. *Lychnos* 70:245–272.
Eriksson, G. and O'Hagan, L.A. 2021. Selling "Healthy" Radium Products with Science: A Multimodal Analysis of Marketing in Sweden, 1910–1940. *Science Communication* 43(6):740–767.
"F.J. Kahn." 1872. *Dagens Nyheter* (20 March), 4.
Fru H. 1898. "Liten socialogi [sic]." *Svensk Damtidning* (5), 33.
F-zon. 1905. "Sömmerskor." *Morgonbris* (4), 4–5.
"För hemmet." 1901. *Aftonbladet* (4 June), 3.
Garvey, E.G. 1996. *The Adman in the Parlor: Magazines and the Gendering of Consumer Culture, 1880s to 1910s*. New York: Oxford University Press.
"Gebrüder Behr." 1880. *Dagens Nyheter* (13 January), 4.
Gijswijt-Hofstra, M. 2005. "Introduction: Cultures of Neurasthenia" in *Cultures of Neurasthenia: From Beard to the First World War*, edited by M. Gijswijt-Hofstra and R. Porter (Amsterdam: Rodopi), pp. 1–31.
"Heiner Busck." 1905. *Malmötidningen* (21 January), 22.
Helander, I. 2022. Chicca-roast-skaparnas ord visar sig inte hålla, *Svenska Dagbladet* (24 August). Available at https://www.svd.se/a/QydV3R/chicca-roast-skaparnas-ord-om-kaffe-faller-platt (Accessed: 18 January 2024).
Hodacs, H. 2023. Substituting Coffee and Tea in the Eighteenth Century: A Rural and Material History with Global Implications. *Journal of Global History* 18(3):461–480.
Huss, M. 1865. *Om kaffe: dess bruk och missbruk. En folkskrift, Rikets hushållningssällskaper tillegnad*. Stockholm: Beckman.
"Idokaffet." 1911. *Dagens Nyheter* (22 August), 4.
"Intubikaffe." 1895. *Svea* (2), appendix, 1.
"Intubikaffe." 1896. *Förgätmigej* (2), 1.
"Intubikaffe." 1902. *Allehanda* (11 January), 1.
Johannisson, K. 1991. Folkhälsa: Det svenska projektet från 1900 till 2:a världskriget. *Lychnos* 56:139–195.
Johannisson, K. 1994. *Den mörka kontinenten: Kvinnan, medicinen och fin-de-siècle*. Stockholm: Norstedts.
Jonsson, P. 2009. "Följ de omtänksamma husmödrarnas exempel…" Livsmedelsannonsering i en svensk dagstidning, 1875–1965. *Historisk Tidskrift* 129(2):205–234.
Jovanovic, M. 2014. Selling Fear and Empowerment in Food Advertising. A Case Study of Functional Foods and Becel® Margarine. *Food, Culture & Society* 17(4):641–663.
J.W. 1899. "Våra tobaksarbeterskor." *Idun* (50), 2–3.
"Kaffeförbrukningen." 1885. *Westerwiks-Posten* (19 December), 5.
Kaffemissbruket bland barnen. 1910. Uppsala: Lärares nykterhetsförbund.
"Kathreiner." 1894. *Svenska Dagbladet* (12 November), 1.
"Kathreiner." 1895a. *Stockholmstidningen* (12 January), 3.
"Kathreiner." 1895b. *Svea* (1), appendix, 1.
"Kathreiner." 1895c. *Svea* (2), appendix, 1.
"Kathreiner." 1895d. *Svea* (14), 1.
"Kathreiner." 1897. *Freja. Illustrerad modetidning* (4), inside front cover.
"Kathreiner." 1907–08. *Hvar 8 Dag* (19), appendix, 5.
"Kathreiner." 1908a. *Idun* (2), 28.

"Kathreiner." 1908b. *Svensk Damtidning* (48), 483.
"Kathreiner." 1909a. *Dagens Nyheter* (14 February, B edition), 3.
"Kathreiner." 1909b. *Svensk Damtidning*(2), 23.
"Kathreiner." 1911a. *Idun* (7), 113.
"Kathreiner." 1911b. *Svensk Damtidning* (10), 122.
"Kathreiner." 1913. *Idun* (25), 418.
"Kathreiner." 1914. *Dagens Nyheter* (10 December), 4.
K-dt, A. [pseud. for Amanda Kerfstedt]. 1912. "En önskvärd reform?" *Svensk Damtidning* (7), 68.
Kneipp, S. 1897. *The Care of Children in Sickness and Health*. Kempten: Jos. Koesel Publisher.
Knutsson, A. and Hodacs, H. 2021. When Coffee Was Banned: Strategies of Labour and Leisure among Stockholm's Poor Women, 1794–1796 and 1799–1802. *Scandinavian Economic History Review* 59:1–23.
"Kontroll öfwer födoämnen." 1881. *Nya Wermlands-Tidningen* (7 July), 1.
"Kronkaffe." 1897a. *Aftonbladet* (28 June), 4.
"Kronkaffe." 1897b. *Dagens Nyheter* (25 September), 3.
Kühschelm, O. 2020. Buy National Campaigns: Patriotic Shopping and the Capitalist Nation State. *Journal of Modern European History* 18(1):79–95.
Lindgren, S. 1993. *Den hotfulla njutningen. Att etablera drogbruk som samhällsproblem 1890–1970*. Stockholm/Stehag: Symposion Graduale.
Lundqvist, P. 2016. Taste for Hot Drinks: The Consumption of Coffee and Tea in Two Swedish Nineteenth-Century Novels. *History of Retailing and Consumption* 2(3):171–192.
Marklin, T. 2018. Erik Taflins fantastiska liv. *Sundsjökrönikan* 59, 11–15.
Mendel, F. 1889. Die schädlichen Folgen des chronischen Kaffeemissbrauchs. *Berlin Klin. Wochenschrift* 26(40):877–880.
N–a. 1898. "Öfveransträngning." *Idun* (36):283–284.
Nilsson, C. 2020. *En förbindelse med en större värld: Postorder i Sverige under tidigt 1900-tal*. Lund: Mediehistoriskt Arkiv.
O'Hagan, L.A. 2022. Modernity, Beauty, and the Swedish 'Way of Life': Lifestyle Marketing in Stomatol Toothpaste Advertisements, 1910–1940. *Journal of Historical Research in Marketing* 14(4):424–452.
O'Hagan, L.A. 2023a. "Classifying" Margarine: The Early Class-Based Marketing of a Butter Substitute in Sweden (1923–1933). *Global Food History* 9(1):20–46.
O'Hagan, L.A. 2023b. The Golden Path to Health: Marketing Postum as a Cure for Coffee Abuse in Early Twentieth-Century Sweden. *Food, Culture and Society*. https://doi.org/10.1080/15528014.2023.2191103
O'Hagan, L.A. and Eriksson, G. 2022. Modern Science, Moral Mothers, and Mythical Nature: A Multimodal Analysis of Cod Liver Oil Marketing in Sweden. *Food and Foodways* 30(4):231–260.
"Om Brunswigs handel med cichoriekaffe." 1802. *Åbo Tidning* (104), 2.
Ottosson, M.O. 2020. *Lärdomsstadens grand old man. Olof Hammarsten i Uppsala*. Uppsala: Uppsala universitet.
Qvarsell, R. 2005. Maten och vetenskapen. Näringslära, kostvanestudier och socialpolitik. *Lychnos* 70:219–244.
Ring, H.A. 1894–1907. *Sveriges industri, dess stormän och befrämjare*. Stockholm: P.B. Eklunds Förlag.
Runefelt, L. 2015. *Att hasta mot undergången: Anspråk, flyktighet, förställning i svensk debatt om konsumtion 1730–1830*. Lund: Nordic Academic Press.
Runefelt, L. 2019. *Den magiska spegeln: Kvinnan och varan i pressens annonser 1870–1914*. Lund: Nordic Academic Press.
"Rörsjöns äkta Intubi-Kaffe." 1895. *Sydsvenska Veckobladet* (15 August), 4.

"Skandinaviskt Intubi-Kaffe." 1883. *Norrlandsposten* (19 March), 1.
Spiekermann. U. 2018. Dominantes Heißgetränk – Die Anfänge von Kathreiners Malzkaffee, Available at https://uwe-spiekermann.com/2018/05/25/dominantes-heissgetraenk-die-anfaenge-von-kathreiners-malzkaffee/ (Accessed: 18 January 2024).
"Sundhets-Caffe." 1838. *Aftonbladet* (1 February), 4.
Svenskt Patent no. 4272, June 4, 1892, Svensk patentdatabas. Available at https://tc.prv.se/spd/search?lang=sv (Accessed: 18 January 2024).
Svenskt Patent no. 8098, November 10, 1896, Svensk patentdatabas. Available at https://tc.prv.se/spd/search?lang=sv (Accessed: 18 January 2024).
Svenskt Patent no. 9176, October 25, 1897, Svensk patentdatabas. Available at https://tc.prv.se/spd/search?lang=sv (Accessed: 18 January 2024).
"Victoria-Kaffe." 1887. *Dagens Nyheter* (30 March), 1.
"Victoria-Kaffe." 1911a. *Svensk Damtidning* (2), 24.
"Victoria-Kaffe." 1911b. *Dagens Nyheter* (22 October), 3.
"Victoria-Kaffe." 1913. *Idun* (12), 195.
"Växtkaffet Ido." 1911. *Idun* (45), 738.

8 "Unveil Your Inner Youth"

Science, Gender and Anti-Ageing Milk Marketing in a Chinese Society

Veronica Sau-Wa Mak

Introduction

In 2021, the number of people in China aged 60 or above reached 264 million—a figure that accounts for 18.7% of the country's total population and which is set to reach 25% by 2035. The growing number of elderly people has resulted in a "grey-hair economy," with the anti-ageing formula milk market seen particularly to have huge untapped economic potential (Li, 2022). Although cow's milk consumption was not widespread in traditional Chinese society, anti-ageing formula milk has recently become one of the most popular new milk products offered by most dairy and pharmaceutical companies. China Mengniu, for example, reported an outstanding growth rate of 76% for adult milk sales in 2021 (China Mengniu Dairy Company Limited, 2022). In addition, China is swiftly becoming the largest and most important formula milk market in the world, with the value of such products predicted to reach 216.3 billion yuan by 2024 (Wang, 2019; Euromonitor International, 2020). Yet, the fact that ethnic Chinese people are known for being lactose intolerant begs the question: what is driving the popularity of anti-ageing formula milk in Hong Kong society? With this in mind, the current chapter uses adult formula milk as a lens to understand how science is being used in the gendered marketing strategy of pharmaceutical companies to sell anti-ageing functional food in Hong Kong and how this whole phenomenon intertwines with dietary change, age discrimination and gender inequality faced by the elderly.

Anti-ageing formula milk is a science-driven food because science has changed how we produce, understand and consume it over the years. Given advancements in food science and technology, current nutrition-enriched adult formula milks, which are mostly in powder form, do not necessarily contain cow's milk; instead, to lower production costs, they are made from a combination of soy protein isolate, milk protein isolate and protein whey. Since these formulas have significantly reduced amounts of lactose, they are suitable for people with lactose intolerance (Abbott Laboratories, 2022). In addition, the development of anti-ageing formula milk products has been led by a growing awareness of "new" illnesses, such as osteoporosis, and the discovery of the medicinal functions of nutrients, including calcium to prevent bone loss, the

DOI: 10.4324/9781003450276-12

cholesterol-lowering effects of phytosterol-enriched milk (Clifton et al., 2004), the ability of Omega-3 fatty acids to prevent heart disease, the benefits of glucosamine to prevent knee osteoarthritis (Chan and Ng, 2011) and the muscle-rebuilding benefits of beta-hydroxy-beta-methylbutyrate (HMB) (Wilson et al., 2008). These new products include Anlene Total High-Calcium Low Fat Milk Powder, Nestlé Carnation High Calcium Joint Low Fat Milk Powder and Abbott Ensure NutriVigor, most of which are sweetened with glucose syrup or corn syrup and enriched with flavourings like cocoa powder.

Given the growing popularity of anti-ageing functional foods and medicines, there is a burgeoning body of research in the area. Current studies have focused on consumer perceptions of anti-ageing products (Niva, 2006), the marketing of anti-ageing food (Heasman and Mellentin, 2001) and the political economy of anti-ageing medicine (Petersen and Seear, 2009) and food (Mak, 2021a). Curiously, despite the growing importance and ubiquity of anti-ageing foods in Chinese societies, there are limited studies of their advertising and websites from a (multimodal) critical discourse perspective. Through a chronological study of the changing brand positioning and advertising strategies of anti-ageing formula milk in Hong Kong, this chapter seeks to understand what draws elderly Chinese people to this new category of pricey and specially formulated nutrient-dense milk products and how this process reinforces ageism and gender inequality.

Milk Consumption in Ancient and Modern China

Although cow's milk was not part of the traditional Chinese diet, Chinese people have a long history of consuming dairy products from a wide variety of mammals as medicinal food. Based on ancient texts such as the *Compendium of Materia Medica* by Li Shizhen, written during the Ming dynasty (1368–1644), milk was intimately related to health and consumed as medicine (Li, 2003). The text contains clear instructions on how milk from different mammals—including water buffaloes, cows, yaks, sheep, goats, donkeys, horses, dogs and pigs—can be used to cure illnesses. It also outlines how different types of milk need to be taken at particular times and in certain ways depending on one's medical condition. For the elderly, who mostly had "cold" bodies, goat's milk was the perfect choice as it was "warm" and could nurture a cold and weak body. Furthermore, it nourished the heart and lungs and quenched thirst, while *bu*-ing ("nourishing") the *qi*[1] of the kidneys and small intestine. In addition, Chinese butter, known as *su* in ancient texts and made from sheep's milk, was considered "warm" and deemed suitable for consumption by the elderly, especially those who were sick or "cold." Last but not least, *tihu* (which resembles clarified butter) was used as a powerful tonic for bones and marrow and was considered conducive to a long life (Li, 2003).

The introduction of Western cow's milk into China occurred in the early nineteenth century, following the arrival of a small number of English and North American Protestant missionaries who established 166 hospitals and 241 dispensaries across coastal and inland areas (Swislocki, 2001). Their arrival coincided with the maturity of Western nutrition science and the advocacy of using Western nutrition science to build national strength in China (Lo, 2009; Fu, 2018; Mak, 2021b). Until the early twentieth century, the use of cow's milk (mostly in the form of condensed milk) was limited to hospital patients and babies whose mothers could not breastfeed or did not have a suitable wet nurse available (see Chapter 5 in this volume).[2] This began to change following the discovery of vitamins—a term first coined in 1912 by biochemist Casimir Funk—along with the proof of their importance in preventing and curing diseases, which fundamentally altered the relationship between food and the human body (Baigent and Kenneth, 2022). From that point onwards, the benefits of food to health started to be analysed based on different food components (Valenze, 2011). Some nutritionists also began to relate dietary habits to the strength of a nation: white people drank milk and were, therefore, stronger and more advanced in science, literature, arts and politics, while Chinese and Japanese people, who did not drink milk, were seen as weaker and less advanced (cf. McCollum, 1918).

This period in global history also saw a rise in imperialism and multinational invasions, which led to the signing of many unequal treaties that resulted in territories becoming occupied and governed by Western powers (Schrecker, 1971). In China, there was a particular fear that the country's military and technological weakness might leave it open to such threats. In response, authors like Wu Xinfa suggested that adopting scientific dietary habits, such as drinking cow's milk, was a prerequisite to building healthy babies and strong citizens, thus building a solid nation that would prevent China from being invaded by foreigners (Wu, 1937). The diffusion of Western nutrition science from the West to the East and its association with national strength also led to women's education reform in China at the time, with a growing focus on home economics in which nutrition science was taught (Schneider, 2011). The nutritional benefits of drinking milk, thus, became further localised and expanded, consolidating the belief that milk would build not only children's health but national strength too.

These beliefs were reflected in advertisements, which drew increasingly on science and evoked sentiments of nationalism. An advertisement for Momilk, published in *Liangyou Huabao* [強國必先強民 強民必先] on 15 December 1926, for example, has the tagline: "Strengthening the nation must begin with strengthening the people; strengthening the people must begin with strengthening the children." The emphasis on children's health, nation-building and cow's milk drinking was further evidenced by the Shanghai government's invitation for the top local dairy companies, including Huimin and Shengsheng, to sponsor a children's health competition in 1937 (Lo, 2009).

Methodology

In this study, I used multimodal critical discourse analysis [MCDA] (Ledin and Machin, 2018, 2020) to study how marketers embed anti-ageing milk in scientific and medical discourses and how these discourses are made to appear true and scare consumers into taking action to protect their health. My data was collected from many forms of media, including a sample of 37 advertisements from historical newspapers (e.g. 1920s editions of *Shenbao*[3] and *Singtao Daily*[4]), television programmes (principally from the 1980s and 1990s), together with online resources (collected between January 2018 and March 2021), including nine pharmaceutical company websites, five Hong Kong government websites and social media samples.

The CDA generates insights into the social production of texts, providing a linguistic approach to understanding the relationship between language and ideology. It focuses on how theories of "reality" and relations of power are encoded in aspects of language, such as syntax, style, rhetorical devices and semiotics within texts (Lupton, 1992). MCDA adds an additional layer to CDA, exploring the following multimodal elements of texts: (1) language (e.g. vocabulary, grammar and the use of metaphor); (2) image (e.g. people, actions, perspectives, angles and distance); (3) colour, particularly meaning potentials in terms of emotions, attitudes and values; (4) typography, especially the cultural connotations of certain typefaces; (5) materiality in terms of their physical and symbolic meanings (e.g. liquidity, viscosity and density); and (6) layout and composition (e.g. salience, framing and hierarchies) (cf. O'Hagan, 2023).

The collected advertisements were split into groups based on recurring themes and patterns in their arguments and their use of language and other semiotic resources. My data showed that early milk product advertisements highlighted the dangers of wet nurses for babies and weak national bodies for China during wartime. After entering into the postwar period, the strategy of milk drinks changed, specifically targeting undernutrition and insomnia (1930–1970). Lastly, in the 1980s, new formula milk specialised for older adults (>50) was developed, emphasising the dangers of osteoporosis, declining energy and losing a youthful appearance. It is this latter finding that will be the main focus of my analysis in this chapter.

Localisation of Western Milk Drinks, Chinese Medical Principles and Rapid Social Change (1930s–1970s)

The practice and health beliefs surrounding Western formula milk drinks among the elderly would probably not have developed in Asian countries had there not been a surplus of military food supplies, including milk powder drinks and canned milk, in Western countries in the immediate postwar era. One successful example is Horlicks—a blend of milled malted barley, wheat flour and dairy powders, which was first patented as an artificial infant formula milk drink in the United States in 1873 by the Horlick brothers, who were immigrants from Gloucestershire (United Kingdom). This novel malted milk powder was then fortified with vitamins and minerals, lending some credence to its claim to being a healthy evening drink for good sleep. It was consumed largely by the British army and was promoted as a dietary supplement endorsed by Western medical doctors in many British colonies in Asia. In Pakistan, for example, Horlicks was prescribed by medical doctors as a food supplement for the elderly (Latif et al., 2016).

In Hong Kong, Horlicks was localised by W.S. Sherly & Co. (the sole agent) who combined Chinese medicinal terms and the Western science of nutrition. Throughout the 1950s and 1960s, Horlicks was specifically positioned as a scientific dietary supplement for boosting *jingli* (精力the essence of life, such as mental and sexual energy) and *tili* (體力physical energy) (Zhang, 2002). At this time, Hong Kong was rapidly changing from an entrepôt to an industrialised city. Therefore, advertisements targeted ageing office ladies, young children and the elderly, with the constant tagline, "Please drink Horlicks frequently, develop good *jingli* and *tili*." One such example told the story of a middle-aged office lady who always feels tired, resulting in repeated typing mistakes, while another advertisement outlined the story of an elderly man who risks losing a table tennis competition because he is facing younger competitors (Wong, 1999:124–127).

In these advertisements, the social issues of an overloaded working environment and ageism in sports are translated into individual health problems (declining energy levels), which can be resolved by Horlicks. After consulting with Western doctors, both the middle-aged office lady and elderly man learn that the root of their illness is a lack of nutrition. They, thus, take Horlicks as a prescribed dietary supplement, which results in the lady outperforming her colleagues and the man winning his table tennis competition. Horlicks, in this case, was promoted similarly to what O'Hagan (2020) describes as a "nerve food," which guards against nervous breakdown that results from overwork, worry and mental concentration in a rapidly industrialising society where highly productive labour is in demand. Capitalising on increasing urban health problems, such as endless tiredness reflecting a psychological state of powerlessness and engulfment among the elderly and the working class, Horlicks and other similar dairy products flourished in Hong Kong and China throughout the 1930s–1970s. Even today, Horlicks is still regarded by many elderly people as a localised Western product that indicates a modern identity (Ehlert, 2021) and a healthy alternative to coffee and tea.

Gendered Nutrition Benefits, Body and Customer Needs (1980s–2020s)

The 1980s marked a turning point for pharmaceutical companies, which started to launch new specialised adult formula milk because of two cardinal reasons: (1) the pressing need to develop new market segments; and (2) the technological advancement in measuring illness and the discovery of nutrition's functions for specific parts of the human body.

Although osteoporosis is not a new disease, it obtained global attention in the late 1980s when bone mass could be measured for the first time with new medical equipment, such as dual-energy X-ray absorptiometry (DXA) scanners. This new capacity to quantify bone mass density pushed raging discussion (e.g. Mazess, 1987; Nordin, 1987; Melton III and Wahner, 1989) and, consequently, the development of a densitometric definition of osteoporosis.[5] Osteoporosis is widely categorised as a gendered disease because many scientists believe that its leading cause is postmenopausal oestrogen deficiency (Albright et al., 1941; National Institutes of Health, 1984). As osteoporosis is a condition characterised by the decrease in bone mass with attendant decreased density and enlargement of bone spaces—resulting in fractures that have costly human and economic consequences—it is now recognised as one of the major public health concerns affecting the geriatric community (Becker et al., 2010). This new scientific definition, coupled with novel devices to measure osteoporosis, has created a pool of osteoporosis patients who need to be treated, representing a sizeable portion of the aged population.

Recognising a significant business opportunity, Anlene—a brand designed for the Asian market under the Fonterra Co-operative Group Limited—was probably the first milk brand to change its original positioning of low-fat content milk (as implied in its original name "Anlean") to a new one: the "expert in bone nutrition." During the early period of its product launch in the 1990s, Anlene specialised in promoting the high calcium content in adult milk drinking for osteoporosis prevention, targeting both women and men. Throughout its Asian promotion campaign, instead of showing idyllic images of healthy cows frolicking on the rolling green pastures, Anlene used fear appeal to raise people's need for calcium. In a television advertisement from 1995, for example, we see a couple in their late 30s suddenly turned into two skeletons with hunchbacks due to their lack of calcium. The image is accompanied by the following narrative (TPB HK CM, 2018):

> As we start ageing, we will lack calcium, resulting in brittle bones. Anlene High Calcium Non-Fat milk is rich in calcium. Sufficient calcium can prevent osteoporosis. In addition, each glass of Anlene powdered milk has only 0.1% fat. Drinking two glasses of Anlene powdered milk can provide you with sufficient calcium you need for a day.

As the market expanded in the 2000s, however, pharmaceutical companies began to change their marketing strategy, targeting women specifically, with a focus on healthy bones and sociability, and strong hearts and care. Since the late 2010s, there has been yet another change, this time towards a male market, with a growing focus on energy and control.

Healthy Bones and Sociability

The early twenty-first century saw a clear construction of osteoporosis as a gendered illness and, thus, adult milk started to be framed as a scientific, modern solution for women specifically. This new targeting strategy affected how scientific data was collected and interpreted. A two-year random study of 400 Asian women conducted in Hong Kong by the Chinese University of Hong

Kong (Lau et al., 2001) and in Malaysia (Chee et al., 2003) found that women who drank two glasses of Anlene High Calcium Low Fat milk powder were able to prevent bone loss by 90% compared to those who did not. This gendered research study provided evidence for Anlene products to be claimed as the only milk products tested on female humans that were clinically proven to prevent osteoporosis among women.

Once scientifically "proven" to prevent osteoporosis, the benefits of adult milk for women were then translated into gaining vigour and love. These gendered physical, behavioural, aesthetic and social goals of anti-ageing milk were spelt out clearly in both television and print advertisements throughout the 2000s. A television commercial in Hong Kong, for example, showed a young woman, who used to dance happily with different men, growing a hunchback and no longer being able to dance beautifully. After drinking Anlene milk powder, she miraculously regained her agility and was able to dance again (Cannationnest, 2010). In 2016, another advertisement for Anlene featured an old woman in her garden, who suddenly shed her old skin like a snake and became young again. Her older husband, seeing her dancing happily like a young girl in the rain, lovingly passes her a towel to dry herself. The end of the commercial shows the old woman drinking a glass of milk happily (Anlene Hong Kong, 2017a, 2017b).[6]

My findings support the notion that the marketing of a product targeting women can serve very specific ideological purposes by bringing about a neoliberal governance where individuals are interpellated and constructed as entrepreneurial and responsibilised subjects invested in self-transformation (Gill, 2021). Subsequently, many advertisements constantly address women with images and messages that suggest that their bodies are always at risk of "failing" (Gill, 2007) and in need of continuous improvement.

Strong Hearts and Care

In addition to meeting consumers' desires for sociability and love by selling mobility through high-calcium-content adult milk, pharmaceutical companies also sell the fantasy of care capacity through heart disease prevention. In recent years, scientists have discovered the cholesterol-lowering effects of plant sterol (Clifton et al., 2004), as well as the ability of Omega-3 fatty acids to prevent heart disease and glucosamine to repair and renew cartilage tissue. All these nutritional elements are formulated into Anlene's new product, emotionally named as "Heart Care" (護心佳), which is promoted as having multi-functions. In addition to its heart-protecting function, the "Heart Care" formula is also said to protect bones and joints. It also claims to be the only adult nutritional milk powder in Hong Kong which can help curb three hypers: hypertension (high blood pressure), hyperlipidemia (high blood cholesterol) and hyperglycaemia (high blood sugar).

In these advertisements, consuming heart-protecting adult milk is presented as a positive, empowering choice for older women to increase their care capacity so as to gain love and maintain their conjugal relationship. In one Anlene "Heart Care" advertisement, Gigi Leung, a 41-year-old Hong Kong singer, states (Cannationnest, 2017):

> If you want to do what you like with your loved one [image shows a heterosexual middle-aged couple jogging and the female protagonist gazing at her male partner frequently], you need to have a strong heart. If you want to stay with your loved one to enjoy life [close-up of a woman doing a boxing workout with her partner], you need to start with your heart. Anlene can prevent the 3 hypers [image of plant sterols to lower bad cholesterol]; maintain bone, joint and muscle health, and strengthen your heart.

Anlene advertisements featuring Gigi Leung can also be found on the side of buses in Hong Kong (Figure 8.1). Marketers in Asia frequently use celebrity endorsements to attract consumers and encourage purchase decisions (Bergkvist and Zhou, 2016; Chan and Fan, 2022). My data supports current studies, which argue that the use of older celebrities in advertising promotes new discourses about ageing in which older women's sexuality is presented as a form of power (Kenalemang, 2022). In this commercial, although the main female actor is pictured in an athletic context (hiking and working out), she pays full attention to her male partner.

Figure 8.1 Gigi Leung in Anlene Advertisement

Credit: Image licensed under the Creative Commons Attribution-Share Alike 4.0 International license (Author – LN9267)

The importance of women keeping a young and beautiful appearance to gain love from their significant other is also evidenced in the product design and website of another adult milk offered by Quaker Oats, which has ventured into the adult milk market with its Collagen Pearl Non-Fat milk powder (Quaker Milk Powder, 2023). As explained on its official website, the "Beauty Foundation Formula" of this specialised milk powder, which targets older Chinese women in Hong Kong and the Philippines, includes (1) collagen, which "helps increase skin elasticity"; (2) pearl powder, which can "help erase age spots and dark skin due to ageing, and create clear and bright skin"; and (3) high iron content, which helps replenish blood and obtain pink cheeks. These promoted functions of anti-ageing adult milk are in line with previous findings that ageing is undesirable (e.g. Calasanti, 2007) and supports scholars' arguments that women are expected to look young and, thus, attractive and visible, even in the later stages of life. This, therefore, reproduces and legitimises sexist and ageist expectations about women's appearances (Coupland, 2007).

Current studies on anti-ageing functional food consumption usually associate such consumption with the influence of neoliberal health policies, which stress self-responsibility and self-care (e.g. Crawford, 1980; Katz and Marshall, 2003; Cardona, 2008). However, there is one cardinal difference in my findings from previous Western studies: the motives for consuming anti-ageing formula milk are not only for self-care—that is achieving a younger, prettier, healthier, more energetic and sportier version of the self as the ultimate goal—but also for attaining a stronger body to care for others, especially significant others (husband/wife), members of extended families (grandson/granddaughter) and/or friends. The provision of care to senior family members is an important familial duty in traditional Confucian family values and practices. Yet, childcare provided by ageing parents in modern Chinese societies now alters this relationship. Goh (2009) discovered that providing childcare for the middle generation is considered one of the "reminders" of the requirement to perform filial piety. In Hong Kong, it is estimated that two-thirds of children are cared for by grandparents (Hampshire, 2015). According to advertisements, this social goal of childcare can be achieved by consuming adult milk. For example, in one advertisement for Anlene anti-ageing formula milk, an old lady, while playing with her grandchildren, suddenly sheds her skin and dances vigorously, gaining applause from them (Anlene Hong Kong, 2017b).

Many of these advertisements use emotive words, such as "enjoying life with your beloved one," which dramatise the important function of anti-ageing adult formula milk in enhancing physical mobility, facilitated by healthy bones and joints, thus empowering customers to gain love, respect and happiness. These advertisements also reflect hierarchical and fragile conjugal relationships in which men dominate (Tam, 1996) and wives and grandmothers are obliged to provide care to them, their children and grandchildren (Mak, 2021a). The morality of self-care and care provision is clearly conveyed and reinforced by media discourses under the context of modern neoliberal, patrilineal and hierarchical Chinese societies.

The most critical message communicated through advertisements is the designation of anti-ageing formula milk as possessing special properties that enhance physical mobility and youth due to the consumption of extra quantities of nutrients, such as collagen, pearl powder, calcium and glucosamine. These nutrients are said to transform an imperfect face into a more desirable one and make bodies more energetic with a higher physical capacity, so as to maintain a conjugal relationship, take care of grandchildren and keep pace with men in middle-class leisure activities in a society where gender inequality (woman as the inferior caretaker) is institutionalised and socially reinforced (Ng and Chakrabarty, 2005). The ways in which women are to defy old age and recast themselves as attractive and caring are, thus, based on idealised gender and family relations that prevail among middle-aged men and women in Chinese societies. Pharmaceutical companies have a long history of targeting women by capitalising on female insecurities. O'Hagan (2023), for example, notes that at the end of the 1930s, the Swedish health drink Samarin promoted the link between stomach upsets and a "nasty effect on the skin," which was "particularly unpleasant for women." With this bold (and unsupported) claim, Samarin suggests that women need to discipline and reshape their bodies in accordance with expected norms of beauty. Equally, with anti-ageing formula milk, the emphasis on women's allure and caring behaviour tells ageing women that femininity and productivity are based on a younger body. In this way, to avoid old age, they must preserve their bodies and change their behaviour by consuming adult formula milk.

Energy and Control

Although adult formula milk mainly targets women, the late 2010s saw the emergence of a product targeting "young old" men (around 60–65 years old), capitalising on their sense of insecurity during this transitional life stage. While advertisements for ageing women sell hope to maintain young and beautiful for the "good" of their families, ageing men are provided with a gendered and age-based image concerning how they should defy old age by building their muscle, physical energy and mental capacity so as to display both their primitive and civilised masculinity (Bederman, 1995), superiority and power.

In the advertisements and website of Abbott Ensure NutriVigor, for example, the demand for life energy (*huoli*活力), which usually includes *jingli* (sexual and mental energy) and *tili* (physical energy), is associated with male masculinity, with sexual performance anxiety often covertly implied. In a 2018 television and online commercial, Francis Ng—a 57-year-old Hong Kong actor—surprises a young woman by picking her up in a deluxe private plane (Abbott Nutrition Hong Kong, 2018). Upon arrival, Francis contends that there are lots of unpredictable things in the world: flying, the weather and declining energy levels. Stepping out of the plane, the couple walk to Francis's large and modern house. While he is sitting on his designer sofa looking tired, the young woman hands him a glass of milk and says, "Ensure Low Sugar milk is suitable for your age." This claim is supported by the next shot, which shows a series of bubbles labelled with different names of nutrients (Omega-3, vitamins B6, E and D, calcium, protein and 11 types of heart-protecting nutrients). This shot is accompanied by a voiceover: "Drinking Ensure daily for two weeks can increase your *jìngli*." Francis then finishes the glass of drink quickly and, in the next shot, the couple return to the plane. The young woman seems impressed and states, "You have added sufficient oil (full of energy)." Francis replies that it is due to Ensure. In another scene, he meets the lady accidentally in a pharmacy, where he is picking up a can of Ensure adult formula milk. "It [Ensure] is so good that I have to drink it every day," he says. Just as with the Anlene advertisements featuring Gigi Leung, Abbott Ensure advertisements featuring Francis Ng can also frequently be found on the side of buses in Hong Kong (Figure 8.2).

In addition to life energy, mobility provided by muscle-building is another important theme highlighted in the anti-ageing advertisements that target men, particularly since the formal categorisation of "locomotive syndrome"[7] by medical scientists in the mid-2010s (Nakamura and Ogata, 2016). In a series of advertisements from 2020 to 2022, entitled "Testing your muscles in a second," Ensure uses an emotive tagline—"Do you want to know whether you can still walk in your 70s?"—to stir up fear among the audience and urge them to take time for a muscle test, which is also a test of physical strength, mobility and male masculinity (Abbott Nutrition Hong Kong, 2021). In these advertisements, Francis Ng appears in a high-tech computer-produced background. In white body-tight sportswear, Francis performs a single-leg sit-to-stand test

Figure 8.2 Francis Ng in Abbott Ensure Advertisement

Credit: Image licensed under the Creative Commons Attribution-Share Alike 4.0 International license (Author – LN9267)

flawlessly, creating a sense of anxiety around immobility for those who cannot perform as suggested. Immediately, the advertisement states the benefits of Ensure: "With its high-quality protein and vitamins, Abbott Ensure helps maintain and strengthen your muscles." The credibility of Ensure as the solution to regain *jingli* and *tili* is claimed to be due to science. According to Wilson et al. (2008), new scientific findings on the muscle-rebuilding benefits of HMB are responsible for this increased focus on male mobility in new anti-ageing formula milk products.[8]

Similarly, Nestlé Carnation High Calcium Joint Low Fat Milk Powder also uses a 48-year-old well-known actor, Chilam, to promote their specialised milk by acting like a teacher who lectures on bone-and-joint health and mobility (Nestlé Carnation, 2019). These advertisements are supported by scientific facts about the benefits of glucosamine to prevent knee osteoarthritis and vitamin C to aid normal collagen synthesis for the normal function of cartilage and to maintain body agility (Nestlé Carnation, 2021). Using an emotive product name, this formula milk links up its benefits with masculinity, control and power, thus "maximising life enjoyment" (Nestlé Carnation, 2021).

Another recurring theme in website and television commercials targeting men is better work performance and, thus, better control of one's life. For example, an Abbott television commercial portrays a man in his late 50s feeling exhausted during a social gathering with his colleagues after a long workday, evoking a fear of losing one's job, social network and self-esteem due to a decline in energy levels (Abbott Nutrition Hong Kong, 2019). In addition to the advertisement, over half of the testimonials from male customers on the Abbott Hong Kong website (2021) mention that an improvement in their work performance was an important reason for them to continue drinking Ensure, compared with less than 10% of female customers who mentioned work. As two of the male customers explain:

> I work 12 hours a day. My work is so hectic that I have irregular mealtimes. In order to protect my stomach, I drink a cup of Ensure milk before continuing my work. I am always energetic, having a healthy heart and good quality of sleep. (Mr. Mak, Ensure consumer for over 10 years)
>
> I am accustomed to drinking a glass of Ensure for breakfast and before going to bed. I often feel full of energy, high spirit, and sleep well at night. I need to work from home, and sometimes I delay eating due to busy work. So, I will drink Ensure to replenish my *tili* (physical strength).

While the advertisements targeting women mostly link to nature, youth, vigour, attractiveness, agility and family-caring capabilities, men's anti-ageing formula milk advertisements are related to technology (e.g. planes, laboratories), professionals (e.g. pilots, teachers) and focus on life energy, physical strength, mobility and performance. Based on scientific research sponsored by pharmaceutical companies, men and women are not only socially but biologically different but also have different nutritional needs and goals. However, to be successful, men and women must both avoid growing old physically and psychologically, thereby seeking different brands of expensive adult milk in order to return to gendered health. My data also shows that the advertisements and webpages of anti-ageing formula milk display little variation by social class. They generally take middle-class or upper-class lives as a standard, based on the leisure activities, style of dress and environments depicted. These advertisements, thus, reinforce the hierarchical social structure of men and women in Chinese society, as well as the idea that it is the differences between middle- and working-class lifestyles that make them unequal. Finally, they create the allusion that gender implies youth and old age, therefore implying unfortunate social and job market exclusions.

Concluding Discussion

In recent years, a growing body of research has paid attention to the impact of the global hegemony of multinational, Euro-American-centric, science-driven food and pharmaceutical industries in shaping the human diet (Sunder, 2017; Nestle, 2018; Mak, 2021b). Such studies allude to how these industries, by localising Western nutrition science using Chinese medicinal terms and gendered marketing strategies, work to institutionalise some forms of dietary governance and transform the lifestyle of people worldwide, all primarily benefitting their own interests. By providing a longitudinal study of the advertisements and marketing activities of anti-ageing formula milk in Hong Kong, this chapter contributes to the fields of critical science, the political economy of food and gender and gerontology studies by showing the pivotal role of pharmaceutical and dairy companies in changing the dietary patterns of elderly Chinese consumers—from leading a dairy-free diet to ingesting cow's milk as an everyday anti-ageing medicinal drink. This dramatic dietary change in Chinese society has created a number of social, ethical and health issues.

First, by providing an MCDA of the advertisements and websites in Hong Kong, this chapter has shown how the messages delivered by the marketing materials of anti-ageing formula milk reinforce the social norm of ageism. Given that "[w]e respond to the representation of an old person as much as we respond to old people" (Laws, 1995:116), the gerontophobia that these anti-ageing advertisements express justifies the exclusion of old people from many occupational, sports and other social networks (Calasanti, 2007; Walsh et al., 2017). When we combine the belief that we should and can "unveil our inner youth" by controlling ageing (read: disease) with promises from the science of slowing or altering it (Anlene Hong Kong, 2022), the pressure not to "appear old" exacerbates. The popular belief that ageing can be controlled through lifestyle and dietary changes can justify the ageism heaped upon those who do not "choose" to manage ageing. This imagination of the possibility of not ageing strikes the bell for the elderly in a neoliberal society, which adopts health policies stressing self-responsibility and self-care (Crawford, 1980; Katz and Marshall, 2003; Cardona, 2008). Following this view, the elderly are no longer people entitled to the same rights as younger middle-aged people.

Second, the anti-ageing advertisements convey an underexamined message: what constitutes being old—the basis for discrimination—varies by gender. In these television commercials, advertisements and websites, male and female bodies are presented as different, and such differences dictate both the physical and social aspects of masculinity and femininity. The social inequality that accrues to being a powerful man or an attractive woman is, thus, rooted in biology; to unveil inner youth, then, one must maintain this hierarchy. Appearances and youthful-looking bodies account for larger shares of women's social capital than they do for men. The stress on appearance, mobility and vigour is exacerbated by ageing. Thus, anti-ageing formula advertisements and websites dictate that Chinese women's bodies should approximate younger bodies by looking youthful, being energetic, lean, fit and alluring to men and strong enough to care for themselves and their extended families. Here, we see the intersection of ageism and sexism with other social indicators: the hegemonic ideal of women's erotic and vigorous bodies is inscribed with age (i.e. youth), as well as other privileged statuses (heterosexuality and upper-middle-class status). Nutrition science seeks to rescue ageing women from this marginalised position by casting them as alluring and caring sexual partners and helpful family members.

Third, by using trustworthy images of celebrities, the anti-ageing advertisements, websites and marketing activities, which suggest that adult milk consumption is *the* solution to health and social problems, may, in fact, have negative health impacts. As noted by several scholars, the trend of nutritionism—understanding food in terms of its nutrients (Scrinis, 2008)—has led to the marketing of unhealthy foods by highlighting a single healthy component (e.g. antioxidants in chocolate), thereby resulting in unhealthy dietary practices in certain modern societies. Nutritionism creates a problematic blind spot: by diverting attention away from the overall "lack" of nutrients in certain traditional foods for a single healthy component, emerging issues such as obesity and overnutrition have become overlooked. In Hong Kong, the Consumer Council has warned the public that, except for the purported benefits of Omega-3, other health claims regarding anti-ageing formula milk lack scientific evidence, such as the consumption of glucosamine to promote joint recovery and knee strength, probiotics to improve intestinal health and calcium absorption and choline to improve memory. As noted by the Hong Kong Consumer Council, for ordinary people, the long-term consumption of anti-ageing formula milk can lead to an excessive intake of calories and fats, thereby aggravating obesity-related health problems, such as the risk of cardiovascular diseases, lower extremity joint problems and blood sugar control (Choice, 2020). The youth ideal embedded in the marketing campaigns of anti-ageing functional food encourages consumers to spend ever more money, time and effort on not ageing, penalising them for the inevitable failure and increasing their guilt for not being able to do so. Such an ideal ultimately adds pressure to the aged, and women in particular, to drink adult milk, which, in fact, may not improve health.

Notes

1 Traditional Chinese medicine believes that *qi* is the basic substance that constitutes the human body and maintains basic functions (Xu and Zhang, 2020).
2 As Lo (2019) points out, two brands of condensed milk from America—Eagle (鷹牌, founded in 1853 by Gail Borden) and Carnation (三花, founded in 1899 by Elbridge Stuart)—had been represented by the American trading firm of Connell Brothers (公利洋行) in Hong Kong since the early 1900s and had a significant market share.
3 *Shenbao* was founded by British businessman Ernest Major (1841–1908) in Shanghai in 1872 and closed in 1949 when the Communist Party came into power. It was one of the most influential newspapers in the late Qing Dynasty (1901–1911) and the Republic of China (Milter, 2004).
4 Founded in 1938, *Singtao Daily* is one of Hong Kong's oldest and second-largest Chinese language newspaper.
5 Osteoporosis is defined as a reduction of bone mineral density by 2.5 standard deviations or more from the peak bone mass in early adulthood (WHO, 1994).
6 Advertisements in Hong Kong are regulated by specific legislation and codes of practice, such as the Telecommunications Ordinance and the Public Health and Municipal Services Ordinance. Such legislation prohibits misrepresentations or false, misleading or deceptive claims in advertisements. In the two advertisements I described, there is no direct linkage between drinking the adult formula milk and the cure of a particular disease and, thus, they are not considered as misleading advertisements.
7 Locomotive syndrome is a condition of reduced mobility due to impairment of locomotive organs.
8 The effects of HMB on human skeletal muscle were first discovered by Steven L. Nissen at Iowa State University in the mid-1990s (Nissen and Abumrad, 1997). HMB is a naturally produced substance in humans that is used as a dietary supplement and was originally used to promote wound healing and provide nutritional support for people with muscle wasting due to cancer or HIV/AIDS. As of 2017, HMB has found widespread use as an ergogenic supplement among young athletes (Cruz-Jentoft, 2018).

References

Abbott Hong Kong. 2021. Low-Sugar Ensure. Real Users' Testimonials. Available at https://www.abbottnutrition.com.hk/ensure/experience.php (Accessed: 24 January 2024).

Abbott Laboratories. 2022. *Annual Report 2021*. Available at https://www.abbottinvestor.com/financials/annual-reports/ (Accessed: 20 June 2022).

Abbott Nutrition Hong Kong. 2018. *[One Click to Experience It for Yourself!] Free Sample Pack [After Flying Up to an Altitude of 20,000 Feet, He Will Make a Cup…]* (30 secs) [Television advertisement]. Available at https://www.facebook.com/AbbottAdultNutritionHK/videos/%E4%B8%80click-%E8%A6%AA%E8%BA%AB%E9%AB%94%E9%A9%97%E5%85%8D%E8%B2%BB%E8%A9%A6%E9%A3%B2%E8%A3%9D/10155345724171020/?locale=zh_HK (Accessed: 22 January 2024).

Abbott Nutrition Hong Kong. 2019. *Abbott Low Sugar Plus Nutritional [How Energetic Are You at This Age? Are You Sure? Ensure Can Help You!]* (45 secs) [Television advertisement]. Available at https://www.youtube.com/watch?v=AYMLQOwPVa4 (Accessed: 22 January 2024).

Abbott Nutrition Hong Kong. 2021. *Abbott NutriVigor® Francis Ng: Have You Ever Thought That You Might Not Be Able to Walk at the Age of 70?* (20 secs) [Television advertisement]. Available at https://www.youtube.com/watch?v=Bs10IHc3Dv4 (Accessed: 22 January 2024).

Albright, F., Smith, P.H. and Richardson A.M. 1941. Postmenopausal Osteoporosis: Its Clinical Features. *Journal of the American Medical Association* 116:2465–2474.

Anlene Hong Kong. 2017a. *Anlene Enables You to Live Vigorously Beyond Your Age – Husband and Wife* (15 secs) [Television advertisement]. Available at https://www.youtube.com/watch?v=H1GOai4QCKs&list=PLOiN35n0lXPMqoDPyLmn-71WtsHKtXevQ (Accessed: 22 January 2024).

Anlene Hong Kong. 2017b. *Anlene Enables You to Live Vigorously Beyond Your Age – Grand-Mother and Grand-Children* (15 secs) [Television advertisement]. Available at https://www.youtube.com/watch?v=5MhtzHM3Wb4. Accessed 22 January 2024.

Anlene Hong Kong. 2022. *Unveil Your Inner Youth*. Available at https://www.anlene.com/hk/zh/events.html (Accessed: 27 September 2022).

Baigent, M.J. and Kenneth, C. 2022. Vitamin, *Encyclopedia Britannica*. Available at https://www.britannica.com/science/vitamin (Accessed: 23 July 2022).

Becker D.J., Kilgore, M.L. and Morrisey, M.A. 2010. The Societal Burden of Osteoporosis. *Current Rheumatology Reports* 12:186–191.

Bederman, G. 1995. *Manliness and Civilization: A Cultural History of Gender and Race in the United States, 1880–1917*. Chicago: University of Chicago Press.

Bergkvist, L. and Zhou, K.Q. 2016. Celebrity Endorsements: A Literature Review and Research Agenda. *International Journal of Advertising* 35(4):642–663.

Calasanti, T. 2007. Bodacious Berry, Potency Wood, and the Ageing Monster: Gender and Age Relations in Anti-Ageing Ads. *Social Forces* 86:335–355.

Cannationnest. 2010. *Anlene High Calcium Formula Milk Advertisement* (30 secs) [Television advertisement]. Available at https://www.youtube.com/watch?v=ZrIgbySaEMY (Accessed: 22 January 2024).

Cannationnest 2017. *Anlene Heart Plus x Gigi Leung 2017 Advertisement* (30 secs) [Television advertisement]. Available at https://www.youtube.com/watch?v=NkxEPQBpR2A (Accessed: 22 January 2024).

Cardona, B. 2008. "Healthy Ageing" Policies and Anti-Ageing Ideologies and Practices: On the Exercise of Responsibility. *Medicine, Health Care, and Philosophy* 11(4):475–483.

Chan, K. and Fan, F. 2022. Perception of Advertisements with Celebrity Endorsement Among Mature Consumers. *Journal of Marketing Communications* 28(2):115–131.

Chan, O.W. and Ng, Y.F. 2011. A Review on the Effects of Glucosamine for Knee Osteoarthritis Based on Human and Animal Studies. *Hong Kong Physiotherapy Journal* 29(2):42–52.

Chee, W.S.S., Suriah, A.R., Chan, S.P., Zaitun, Y. and Chan, Y.M. 2003. The Effect of Milk Supplementation on Bone Mineral Density in Postmenopausal Chinese Women in Malaysia. *Osteoporosis International* 14(10):828–834.

China Mengniu Dairy Company Limited. 2022. *Annual Results 2021*. Available at https://media-mengniu.todayir.com/20220331073020173106O656_en.pdf (Accessed: 1 July 2022).

Choice. 2020. Drinking Formula Milk for Middle-Aged or Older People May Lead to Obesity. Available at https://echoice.consumer.org.hk/article/455-4053 (Accessed: 21 September 2022).

Clifton, P.M., Noakes, M., Sullivan, D., Erichsen, N., Ross, D., Annison, G., Fassoulakis, A., Cehun, M. and Nestel, P. 2004, Cholesterol-Lowering Effects of Plant Sterol Esters Differ in Milk, Yoghurt, Bread and Cereal. *European Journal of Clinical Nutrition* 58:503–509.

Coupland, J. 2007. Gendered Discourses on the "Problem" of Ageing: Consumerized Solutions. *Discourse and Communication* 1:37–61.

Crawford, R. 1980. Healthism and the Medicalization of Everyday Life. *International Journal of Health Services: Planning, Administration, Evaluation* 10(3):365–388.

Cruz-Jentoft, A.J. 2018. Beta-Hydroxy-Beta-Methyl Butyrate (HMB): From Experimental Data to Clinical Evidence in Sarcopenia. *Current Protein & Peptide Science* 18(7):668–672.

Ehlert, J. 2021. Food Consumption, Habitus and the Embodiment of Social Change: Making Class and Doing Gender in Urban Vietnam. *The Sociological Review* 69(3):681–701.

Euromonitor International, 2020. *Dairy in China, Country Report*. Available at https://www.euromonitor.com/dairy-in-china/report (Accessed: 1 September 2022).

Fu, J. 2018. *The Other Milk: Reinventing Soy in Republican China*. Seattle: University of Washington Press.

Gill, R. 2007. Postfeminist Media Culture: Elements of a Sensibility. *European Journal of Cultural Studies* 10(2):147–166.

Gill, R. 2021. "Neoliberal Beauty" in *The Routledge Companion to Beauty Politics*, edited by M. Leeds Craig (New York: Routledge), pp. 9–16.

Goh, E.C. 2009. Grandparents as Child Care Providers: An In-Depth Analysis of the Case of Xiamen, China. *Journal of Ageing Studies* 23(1):60–68.

Hampshire, A. 2015. Why Hong Kong is Failing Its Young Families. *South China Morning Post—Post Magazine* (31 October). Available at https://www.scmp.com/magazines/post-magazine/article/1873679/why-hong-kong-failing-its-young-families (Accessed: 19 May 2023).

Heasman, M. and Mellentin, J. 2001. *Functional Foods Revolution*. London: Earthscan Ltd.

Katz, S. and Marshall, B.L. 2003. New Sex for Old: Lifestyle, Consumerism, and the Ethics of Ageing Well. *Journal of Ageing Studies* 17(1):3–16.

Kenalemang, L.M. 2022. Visual Ageism and the Subtle Sexualisation of Older Celebrities in L'Oréal's Advert Campaigns: A Multimodal Critical Discourse Analysis. *Ageing & Society* 42(9):2122–2139.

Latif, A.A., Sibghatullah, A. and Siddiqui, K.A. 2016. Repositioning Horlicks in Pakistan. *Journal of Marketing Management and Consumer Behavior* 1(2):44–53.

Lau, E.M., Woo, J., Lam, V. and Hong, A. 2001. Milk Supplementation of the Diet of Postmenopausal Chinese Women on a Low Calcium Intake Retards Bone Loss. *Journal of Bone and Mineral Research* 16(9):1704–1709.

Laws, G. 1995. Understanding Ageism: Lessons from Feminism and Postmodernism. *The Gerontologist* 35(1):112–118.

Ledin, P. and Machin, D. 2018. *Doing Visual Analysis: From Theory to Practice*. London: SAGE.

Ledin, P. and Machin, D. 2020. *Introduction to Multimodal Analysis*. London: Bloomsbury.

Li, J 2022. "Gray-Hair Economy" Has Huge Untapped Potential. *China Daily* (7 March). Available at https://www.chinadaily.com.cn/a/202203/07/WS622572b9a310cdd39bc8ad81.html (Accessed: 2 August 2022).

Li, S.Z. 2003 [1578]. *Compendium of Materia Medica: Bencao Gangmu*. Beijing: Foreign Languages Press.

Lo, S.Y. 2009. *Mother's Milk and Cow's Milk: Infant Feeding and the Reconstruction of Motherhood in Modern China, 1900-1937*. Unpublished PhD thesis, Chinese University of Hong Kong.

Lo, Y. 2019. Live Long and Prosper: Longevity Condensed Milk, Black and White Evaporated Milk and Friesland Ice Cream, *The Industrial History of Hong Kong Group* (25 November), Available at https://industrialhistoryhk.org/live-long-and-prosper-longevity-condensed-milk-%e5%a3%bd%e6%98%9f%e5%85%ac%e7%85%89%e5%a5%b6-black-and-white-evaporated-milk-%e9%bb%91%e7%99%bd%e6%b7%a1%e5%a5%b6-and-friesland-ice-cream/ (Accessed: 19 May 2022).

Lupton, D. 1992. Discourse Analysis: A New Methodology for Understanding the Ideologies of Health and Illness. *Australian Journal of Public Health*, https://doi.org/10.1111/j.1753-6405.1992.tb00043.x

Mak, S.W.V. 2021a. Technologies and Dietary Change: The Pharmaceutical Nexus and the Marketing of Anti-Ageing Functional Food in a Chinese Society. *Food and Foodways* 29(4):309–330.
Mak, S.W.V. 2021b. *Milk Craze: Body, Science and Hope in China*. Honolulu: University of Hawaii Press.
Mazess, R.B. 1987. Bone Density in Diagnosis of Osteoporosis: Thresholds and Breakpoints. *Calcified Tissue International* 41:117–118.
McCollum, E.V. 1918. *The Newer Knowledge of Nutrition: The Use of Food for the Preservation of Vitality and Health*. MacMillan Company: New York.
Melton III, L.J. and Wahner, H.W. 1989. Defining Osteoporosis. *Calcified Tissue International* 45:263–264.
Milter, B. 2004. *A News for China? Power, Identity and Changes in Shanghai News Media*. Cambridge: Harvard University Asia Center.
"Momilk Advertisement." 1926. *Liangyou Huabao* (15 December), 11.
Nakamura, K. and Ogata, T. 2016. Locomotive Syndrome: Definition and Management. *Clinical Reviews in Bone and Mineral Metabolism* 14(2):56–57.
National Institutes of Health. 1984. Consensus Conference on Osteoporosis. *Journal of American Medical Association* 252:99–802.
Nestle, M. 2018. *Unsavory Truth: How Food Companies Skew the Science of What We Eat*. Basic Books: New York.
Nestle Carnation. 2019. *Want to Take Care of Your Health? Nestlé Carnation Low Glycemic Golden Model Can Help You!!* (30 secs) [Television advertisement]. Available at https://www.facebook.com/100075996393424/videos/772745213157104/ (Accessed: 22 January 2024).
Nestlé Carnation. 2021. Brands. Available at https://www.nestle.com.hk/zh/brands/milk/carnation (Accessed: 19 May 2023).
Ng, C.W. and Chakrabarty, A.S. 2005. Women Managers in Hong Kong: Personal and Political Agendas. *Asia Pacific Business Review* 11(2):163–178.
Nissen, S.L. and Abumrad, N.N. 1997. Nutritional Role of the Leucine Metabolite B-Hydroxy-B-Methylbutyrate (HMB). *Journal of Nutritional Biochemistry* 8:300–311.
Niva, M. 2006. Can We Predict Who Adopts Health-Promoting Foods? Users of Functional Foods in Finland. *Scandinavian Journal of Food and Nutrition* 50(1):13–24.
Nordin, B. 1987. The Definition and Diagnosis of Osteoporosis. *Calcified Tissue International* 40:57–58.
O'Hagan, L.A. 2020. Packaging Inner Peace: A Sociohistorical Exploration of Nerve Food in Great Britain. *Food & History* 17(2):183–222.
O'Hagan, L.A. 2023. From Fatigue Fighter to Heartburn Healer: The Evolving Marketing of a Functional Beverage in Sweden. *Journal of Food Products Marketing* 29(1):19–40.
Petersen, A. and Seear, K. 2009. In Search of Immortality: The Political Economy of Anti-Ageing Medicine. *Medicine Studies* 1(3):267–279.
Quaker Milk Powder. 2023. Collagen Pearl Non-Fat Milk Powder – Beauty Foundation Formula. Available at http://www.quakermilkpowder.com/milk-powder-1.php (Accessed: 24 January 2024).
Schneider, H.M. 2011. *Keeping the Nation's House: Domestic Management and the Making of Modern China*. Vancouver: UBC Press.
Schrecker, J.E. 1971. *Imperialism and Chinese Nationalism*. Cambridge: Harvard University Press.
Scrinis, G. 2008. On the Ideology of Nutritionism. *Gastronomica* 8(1):9–48.
Sunder, R.K. 2017. *Pharmocracy: Value, Politics and Knowledge in Global Biomedicine*. Durham: Duke University Press.

Swislocki, M.S. 2001. *Feast and Famine in Republican Shanghai: Urban Food Culture, Nutrition, and the State*, Unpublished PhD thesis, Stanford University.

Tam, S.M. 1996. Normalization of "Second Wives": Gender Contestation in Hong Kong. *Asian Journal of Women's Studies* 2(1):113–132.

TPB HK CM. 2018. *Hong Kong Classic Advertisement 1995. Anlene High Calcium Formula Milk* (30 secs) [Television advertisement]. Available at https://www.youtube.com/watch?v=nLRuZl38vvg (Accessed: 22 January 2024).

Valenze, D.M. 2011, *Milk: A Local and Global History*. New Haven: Yale University Press.

Walsh, K., Scharf, T. and Keating, N. 2017. Social Exclusion of Older Persons: A Scoping Review and Conceptual Framework: Correction. *European Journal of Ageing* 16(1):129.

Wang, Z.Q. 2019. Nestle Launches New High-End Milk Powder Products for Adults in China, *China Daily* (22 August), Available at https://www.chinadaily.com.cn/a/201911/22/ (Accessed: 10 July 2022).

WHO. 1994. Assessment of Fracture Risk and Its Application to Screening for Postmenopausal Osteoporosis. Report of a WHO Study Group. *World Health Organization Technical Report Series* 843:1–129.

Wilson, G.J., Wilson, J.M. and Manninen, A.H. 2008. Effects of Beta-Hydroxybeta-Methylbutyrate (HMB) on Exercise Performance and Body Composition Across Varying Levels of Age, Sex, and Training Experience: A Review. *Nutrition & Metabolism* 5(1), https://doi.org/10.1186/1743-7075-5-1

Wong, S.Y. 1999, *Guanggao Wenhua Shenghuo 1945–1970* [*Advertising, Culture and Daily Life 1945-1970*]. Hong Kong: Yuewen Shudian.

Wu, X.F. ed. 1937. *Niuru Ji Qi Zhipin [Cow Milk and Milk Products]*. Shanghai: Zhenzhong Shuju.

Xu, J. and Zhang, Y. 2020. Traditional Chinese Medicine Treatment of COVID-19. *Complementary Therapies in Clinical Practice* 39, https://doi.org/10.1016/j.ctcp.2020.101165

Zhang, Z.C. 2002. *Huangdi Nei Jing*. Hangzhou Shi: Zhejiang Gu Ji Chu Ban She.

Part 3

Promoting "Pure" and "Authentic" Foods

9 Selling Motherhood through Science

Advertisements for Dalda Cooking Oil in India, 1940s to the Present

Saurabh Mishra

Introduction

This chapter focuses on the commodification and consumption of science and scientific products related to health and womanhood in post-colonial India. It focuses specifically on Dalda, a brand of hydrogenated oil that was pitched as a replacement for ghee (or clarified butter), which has long occupied a privileged place in North Indian cuisine. This chapter will use the advertisements for Dalda to study issues related to consumerism, science and motherhood. Such links have been made for other products by some scholars in the South Asian context (Saha, 2017), but the post-colonial period has been largely overlooked by historians of science and medicine. This has led to an elision of the various ways in which food marketing continued and/or broke with colonial days. Furthermore, scholars have also tended to focus on "traditional" medical products or cures, such as ayurveda or unani, whilst ignoring everyday commodities that carried medical and scientific meanings.

This is not to say that post-colonial developments have been completely ignored. Indeed, several scientific studies have looked at the Nehruvian notion of "scientific humanism" (Prakash, 1999; Arnold, 2013), the idea of "big science" and the massive investments in "big science" by a relatively resource-poor state (Abraham, 1998; Roy, 2007; Subramanian, 2013). Studies have also been conducted on the much broader links between rationality, science and religion (Thomas, 2021). Scholars, writing from more interdisciplinary perspectives, have further produced historically grounded critiques of science as "the reason for state" (Nandy, 1988) and as facilitating the creation of a "laboratory state" (Vishwanathan, 1988). Sunil Amrith's (2009) research has brought to light some fascinating aspects that show the deep continuities between colonial and post-colonial health policies. These works, however, explore the relationship between the state and science, not on popular (or even middle-class) perceptions of science. There are some exceptions to this rule, such as Nandy (1988) who argues in his landmark study that, after the 1960s, scientists—especially those working on "big sciences"—came to be seen as "god-kings" by the middle classes, enabling them to work in complete secrecy

DOI: 10.4324/9781003450276-14

and without any sense of accountability. However, for Nandy, the question of reception of "big science," rather than the everyday consumption of scientific products, appears to be of greater significance. This chapter shifts the focus to the latter by exploring advertisements of a popular scientific product and by viewing the advertisements for these commodities as dynamic and informed mediators between scientific discourse and the larger consumer base.

Before we move further into our discussion, it might be useful to explain the choice of motherhood as the subject around which these consumption and mediation practices have been explored. First, this is because most Dalda advertisements directly appealed to the mother, invoking her duty to look after the health of the family. Second, a closer look at "scientific motherhood" (Apple, 1995) and "wifehood" allows us to investigate the type of language and symbolism that was mobilised to harness the extremely pro-natalist middle-class families in India. The commodity that this chapter focuses on became extremely popular all over India by the 1950s and advertisements focused sharply on the link between science and motherhood or "wifehood." My work takes a long-term view of changes in relation to vegetable ghee over the late-colonial and post-colonial periods in India, which is important, as historians have often shown a tendency to lump the entire post-colonial period together, without noticing the slow accretion of changes, or even rapid transformations, that might have occurred. Such an investigation shows, among other issues, the fact that the discourse around scientificity has strengthened massively in recent years. Additionally, spatiality has also played a huge role, as the way in which Dalda has been marketed or commodified has varied significantly depending on regional or provincial contexts.

Purity, Adulteration and Ghee

Before we go into a discussion of advertisements for vegetable ghee—or vanaspati, as it was popularly called—we need to understand its popularity against the broader canvas of rapid urbanisation at the end of the nineteenth century, and the huge population growth in sprawling cities like Calcutta. For example, in the relatively short period between 1891 and 1911, the population of Calcutta leapt from 682,000 to nearly 895,000 (O'Malley, 1913); by 1921, it had become the first city in India to hit the million mark (Prasad, 2006). This rapid growth can largely be explained by the rapid influx of people from rural areas in Bengal, Bihar and other regions. Indeed, it would not be incorrect to see Calcutta as a city of migrants, to which even established inhabitants had moved in the relatively recent past. Srirupa Prasad (2006:247) notes, in this context, that:

> Many of [the *bhadralok*[1]], who were working as educated professionals or clerks or in mercantile establishments under the British in Calcutta, were recent immigrants to the city (after the disintegration of the *zamindari* system[2]) and still had families in the villages.

In fact, most inhabitants continued to live in the in-between space between city and village and retained a connection with the countryside, either through possession of land or through continued familial links. A parallel can be seen here between developments in Indian cities and those that E.P. Thompson (1968:445) describes in the English context, where he notes that the city was not fully urban nor was the countryside completely rural. One of the consequences of this development was a sense of dystopia, especially in cities where the population was growing very rapidly, and a feeling that these urban spaces were bursting at their seams due to problems such as unemployment, overcrowding and urban decay. This feeling was further strengthened by frequent reports in newspapers about the rising cost of living, disease, famines and epidemics that appeared to occur with much greater frequency than ever before (Prasad, 2006:247).

Such a sense of decay was palpable in almost every walk of life: not just in the outer or public domain where momentous developments had been wrought by colonialism but also in the domestic sphere as Sumit Sarkar (1992) and others have shown. Matters related to food began to be seen in similar ways, with certain food items like milk and ghee—seen as integral parts of the internal domain—receiving much attention from all quarters. Ghee, in particular, was at the centre of a number of public discussions as it was considered an extraordinarily healthy food that was linked to masculinity, vigorous physical sports (e.g. wrestling) and restorative bodily functions (Alter, 1992:40). Unfortunately, it was also seen as being especially susceptible to adulteration by unscrupulous dealers and shopkeepers (Mishra, 2015).

The striking thing about public discomfort over adulteration was that it was acknowledged as a genuine concern even by colonial officials, who went to unusual lengths to assuage the ruffled sentiments of the middle classes. The promulgation of several anti-adulteration regulations is a testament to this, as is the appointment of food inspectors and the practice of spot-checking of ghee at major transit points, such as railway stations (Mishra, 2015; for similar developments in the British context, see O'Hagan, 2020). Calcutta became the first city to receive an anti-adulteration law in 1866, perhaps due to its proximity to the seat of British power. This was followed exactly two decades later by another bill, based on the template of the British Food and Drug Act 1872, with a somewhat larger jurisdiction. In the years to come, similar bills were passed for Bombay (1899), the United Provinces (1912, amended in 1916 and 1930), Madras (1918 and 1928), Central Provinces (1919 and 1928), Bengal (1919 and 1925) and the Punjab (1919 and 1929).

The feeling against adulteration of ghee ran particularly high in Punjab, where it was considered an absolutely indispensable part of regular diet. One of the members of the legislative assembly, Sayad Muhammad Husain, noted that, "There is no denying the fact that we, Punjabis, live upon ghi [sic]. Our life, our character, our physique and indeed everything is dependent upon this article of food that we consume…" (Legislative Proceedings, 1929). Despite the greater sense of urgency in Punjab, though, the state appears to have responded much more promptly to the cries emanating from Calcutta. This is explained by the closer interaction between a burgeoning anglophone middle class and colonial officials, leading to a sense of class-based empathy on certain issues that were also of great concern to the middle classes back in Britain. The importance of different colonial attitudes towards various subjects and various regions has been emphasised by scholars like Carole McGranahan (2019:519), who notes that "even in the most authoritarian of periods, people rarely [respond to] or experience colonialism in a singular way," and we need to explore the range of experiences to which various sections of people were subjected.

Despite prompt action by colonial officials, the furore around adulterated ghee refused to die down, especially as sellers constantly found ways of circumventing regulations. For example, retailers often created posters that admitted to impure ghee being sold in their shops, but these were safely tucked away into corners of their shops so that they could not be noticed by customers. When the food inspector came visiting, shopkeepers freely admitted that they were selling mixed/adulterated ghee, thus gaining immunity from a law which, in most provinces, was applicable only if mixed ghee was being hawked off to unsuspecting consumers under the guise of pure ghee (Joshi, 1916:3–4). Such avoidance of regulations finally led to the eruption of a scandal in Calcutta in 1917, when rumours began to coalesce and spread about Calcutta becoming the centre of ghee adulteration. In fact, it was suspected that animal fat—an anathema to orthodox Hindus and vegetarians—was used to carry out the adulteration. Responding to these suspicions, the Marwari Association—a group established to promote the interests of Marwaris (primarily a business community)—took it upon itself to assuage customers' fears and organised an examination of random samples of ghee from all over the city.

The results showed that nearly every sample that was tested contained animal fat; indeed, out of the 67 samples tested, only seven were found to be pure, and one sample contained no ghee at all (Hardgrove, 2013:204). This revelation led to strong protests led by upper-caste Hindus across the city, who demanded that all offending merchants be apprehended and punished without delay (*The Singapore Free Press and Mercantile Advertiser*, 4 September 1917). The matter acquired such importance that priests from Banaras were consulted regarding the best means of atoning for the sin of consuming animal fat. When they recommended fasting and praying on the banks of the Ganges as an acceptable solution, this was promptly followed by a large number of upper-caste Hindus who gathered by the riverside. The Governor of Bengal noted that "the result of this edict was electrifying. Three thousand Brahmins gathered on the banks of the Hooghly forthwith… by the morning of 19 August there was a vast concourse of between four and five thousand undergoing purification" (cited in Moorhouse, 1994:184). The situation settled down only after the Marwari Association accepted responsibility and imposed a fine on culprits.

A more lasting solution, however, presented itself when certain Dutch firms (like Van den Berghs, Jurgens, Verschure Creameries and Hartogs) began to export vegetable ghee to India in the 1920s and the commodity became instantaneously popular. For the more prosperous sections, though, this growing popularity represented a threat to their health because, to them, vegetable ghee was a vastly inferior product compared to "real" ghee. Such opposition notwithstanding, vegetable ghee continued to grow in popularity, to the extent that most Dutch firms were bought out by Indian entrepreneurs in the 1930s, and it began to be manufactured almost solely in India. The one way in which Dalda differed from other brands of vegetable ghee was that it took the opposite route: instead of an indigenous firm buying a foreign brand, this was a case of a foreign multinational buying an Indian brand. Indian firm or not, two things worked in favour of vanaspati in general: its lower price and the advertising campaign that was launched from the 1940s onwards (including the campaign for Dalda), which proved to be highly successful in converting even the more sceptical consumers. During its initial years, the industry was also given a boost by government subsidies as the state was concerned about promoting cheap and plentiful food during the war years. The rest of this chapter will focus on the advertising campaign launched by Dalda—the brand that became the undisputed leader in the field from the 1940s onwards.

Positioning Novelty Food: Motherhood and Science in Dalda's Marketing

Dalda had an interesting journey as a brand. As mentioned above, it was run by an Indian entrepreneur and its market was, initially, mostly confined to the province of Bengal. However, there was a change in ownership when it was bought by Hindustan Unilever Limited, which replaced its earlier name Dada—a respectful term for "elder brother" in Bengali—to the more neutral Dalda, the additional letter standing in for "Lever" in the firm's title (Singh, 2022). Right from its initial days of acquisition, Unilever made it clear that it had great ambitions for the product and wanted to turn it into a commodity that was consumed across the country. A nationwide advertising campaign—the first of its kind—which required resources that only a prosperous multinational corporation like Unilever could afford was launched. It proved to be considerably successful as, by the 1960s and 1970s, Dalda became a household name, both in India and Pakistan. This was despite continuous criticisms regarding its nutritional value and its undesirable symbolic status as a poor man's substitute for ghee. The firm's advertising campaign countered such negative perceptions using a multi-pronged strategy, within which science and the idea of motherhood played a major role, as I shall demonstrate below.

One of the prominent strands in these advertisements, in line with my earlier discussion of the rather dystopian and bleak contemporary perceptions of urbanisation, was that Dalda was impervious to any attempt at adulteration since it came in sealed tins that were untouched by human hands. This trope was quite visible until the 1960s, after which the discourse over the nutritional value of Dalda became more predominant, although the idea of purity continued to make its presence felt. An example of the earlier set of advertisements that focused on the issue of adulteration can be seen below (Figure 9.1). It appeared in the newspaper *Indian Express* on 6 February 1942, making it one of the earliest advertisements of Dalda commissioned by Unilever.

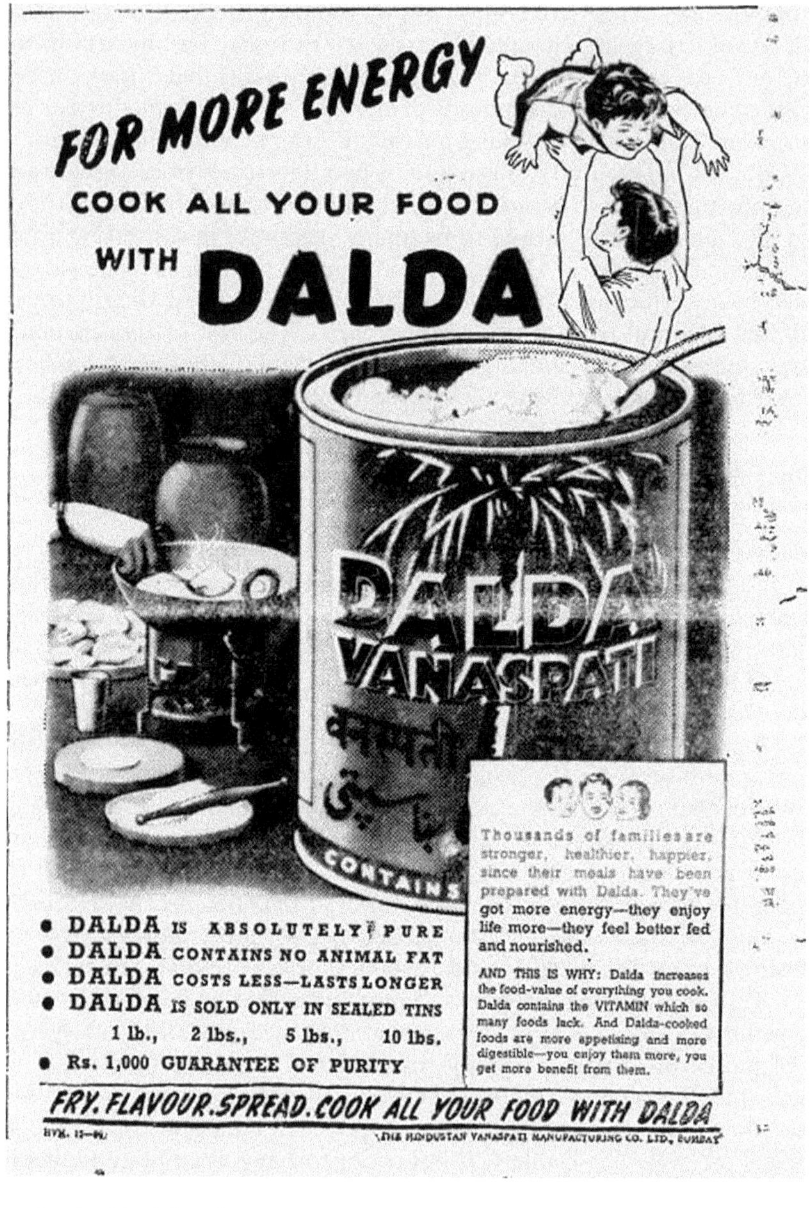

Figure 9.1 Dalda Advertisement Expressing Purity

Credit: *Indian Express*, 6 February 1942, p. 7

The advertisement highlighted the energising qualities of the product, together with its nutritional value, but it heavily underlined the fact that it was "absolutely pure," "contain[ed] no animal fat" and was sold "only in sealed tins."

A couple of other aspects stand out in this advertisement. One of these is that the tin featured the name of the brand in three different languages (English, Hindi and Urdu), but not Bengali, which was the language in which it was exclusively marketed in its earlier avatar as Dada. In line with its change in name, the brand also embraced a multimodal visual discourse that appealed at a number of levels to various kinds of consumers. For example, the image of the father lifting the child was used to signify happiness and positivity, while the phrase "more energy" in bold font and ascending upwards right at the top of the advertisement reinforced the same idea. Additionally, the open tin with the spoon invited readers to partake in the product and become a part of the affective community of "thousands of [happy] families." Other visual tropes included the use of bullet points to convince the reader that all communication was based on facts, while the vague use of certain terms such as "thousands of families" and the emphasis on vitamins conveyed a sense of reliability. As Ledin and Machin (2016) note, bulleted lists and tables present a picture of quasi-quantifiable data, which is a powerful tool for legitimation.

While the advertisement above did not focus much on adulteration, or indeed on motherhood (apart from the disembodied hand doing the cooking), other advertisements around the same time focused almost exclusively on this aspect. A particularly interesting example, published in *The Times of India* on 27 April 1940, showed sketches of hypothetical "ordinary women" with speech bubbles next to them ventriloquising the benefits of Dalda for readers. As Marlis Schweitzer (2003) notes in the American context, advertisements featuring "ordinary women" were often considered more reliable than those featuring celebrities, especially as the latter began to endorse products rather indiscriminately, including those that were in direct competition with each other. The advertisement also reflects a trend towards "technologisation" (Fairclough, 1992) as it relied on visuality rather than text, especially during an era when short, classified advertisements with no images were the norm in India. The messages contained in speech bubbles dominated the advertisement and would have stayed with readers for far longer than the content in smaller print at the bottom. Another noticeable feature is the announcement of a reward of Rs 1000—more than the annual salary of a prosperous middle-class person at the time—for anyone who could prove (presumably through scientific means) that Dalda contained any signs of adulteration.

However, merely showing that Dalda was a healthier, safer and cheaper option compared to ghee was not enough; the real test was whether it came close to ghee on the question of taste. Calcutta presented an urban climate where links with the countryside were still intact, and nostalgia regarding idyllic lifestyles in the past became conflated with life in contemporary villages. In other words, temporal and spatial dimensions of people's lives were perceived as being fused together. Acharya Chatursen Shashtri (1932:238) thought, for example, that in ancient times "an ordinary householder had thousands of cows." Perhaps recognising that readers might see this as an exaggeration, he added that "this might be difficult to grasp in the modern age, when a single cow costs no less than a hundred rupees," but that this was indeed true. Even dealers played upon this nostalgia for villages from an idyllic rural past, some of them even hiring the services of villagers and sending them to the city to sell ghee. This, according to contemporary observers, was done to create the "false impression to many consumers that the *ghee* being brought by village producers must be unadulterated" (Appadurai, 1988), thus implying that it was an "authentic" and "pure" product.

While such narratives are interesting, food historians like Arjun Appadurai have argued that this search for authenticity, where certain ethnic characteristics or spatial features can play a big role in defining the idea, can lead to tendencies akin to colonialism; others like Monica Perales (2016) have highlighted the fact that the notion of traditional/authentic food can, in fact, be dated back to relatively recent times—an argument that has echoes of the notion of "the invention of tradition" that Hobsbawm and Ranger (1984) have famously discussed. Such a view of authenticity also privileges the choices, tastes and preferences of the middle classes and higher castes, while marginalising the dietary habits of the working class and lower castes. In an anthropological survey in a "vegetarian Brahmin village" carried out by McKim Marriott in 1968, he noted how certain dietary contrasts (and the avoidance of certain "impure food items") constituted differential attributes of castes (135; see also Illiah, 2004). As the advertisements for Dalda responded to middle-class notions of "proper food," they reflect many of these propensities.

Apart from emphasising the idea of authenticity and taste, Dalda advertisements could also be distinctly patriarchal in their tone and imagery—perhaps because they were, most likely, designed by men. One example, published in *Janata* on 10 June 1954, shows a cartoon strip where a woman shares her anxiety with her friend about cooking flavoursome food, and her friend helpfully recommends Dalda to her. The strategy seems to have worked because the final frame depicts three immaculately dressed men seated at a table praising the woman's delicious food, while she stood at a distance—as if she is waiting on them—sharing her sense of relief with her friend. The anxiety created in the female consumer due to patriarchal expectations is supplemented with other types of anxieties that were palpable at the time. One of these was the anxiety regarding dearth of food during the inter-war years and the years of the Great Depression (1929–1937), and the consequent adulteration of food to a greater degree. The advertisement subconsciously plays upon these fears while offering Dalda as a quick and easy remedy. Lori Anne Loeb (1994) notes, in her pioneering study titled *Consuming Angels*, that advertisers often amplified fears and anxieties of their consumers, while also offering a quick and simple remedy in the form of their product. Indeed, in this advertisement, the woman makes direct eye contact with the consumer, encouraging them—in a helpful and inviting way—to buy the product and solve their dietary problems.

The advertisement also shows the ability of the firm to modify its images and symbols depending on the region it was targeting. It appeared in *Janata*, the readership of which was mostly confined to the province of Bombay. This partly explains why the women were shown wearing *salwar kurtas* instead of the usual *sari*, as was the case with the other advertisements that have been explored until now. However, since *saris* were also a common sartorial choice for women in Bombay, possibly the *salwar-kurta* was also inserted as a marker of a newly fashioned pan-Indian modernity, or even a sense of youthfulness. This impression is reinforced by the absence of some other "traditional" symbols, such as *bindis* (coloured adornments on the forehead) or vermillion. These advertising strategies worked during a time when the larger notion of modernity was rather ambiguous. A final interesting feature of the advertisement is that the brand's name was inscribed on its tin not just in the Roman script but also in Urdu and Marathi, once again reflecting the capacity of the pan-Indian advertising campaign to be flexible enough to factor in local conditions.

These strategies proved to be effective, as the demand for Dalda—and vanaspati ghee in general—grew exponentially during the 1940s. This growth was so remarkable that the total production of the product across the country trebled during the three years between 1947 and 1950, while 40 new factories were established, producing 450,000 tonnes per annum (Subrahmanyan and De, 1942:242). As mentioned earlier, with the flooding of the market came the suspicion that vanaspati was not only being used to adulterate ghee but that it contained very little nutritional value. This was treated very seriously by the colonial government, which instituted animal experiments at premier laboratories across the country, including the University College of Science (Calcutta), the Indian Dairy Research Institute (Izatnagar) and the Indian Institute of Science (Bangalore)—research projects that aimed to compare the relative impact of diets rich in ghee, vegetable ghee and vegetable oil (Subrahmanyan and De, 1942:244) on animals and humans. Additionally, a Food Technical Panel was set up in 1946, headed by Dr Rajendra Prasad (the future first President of independent India) to adjudicate on the matter and to compare the results obtained from various institutions (Subrahmanyan and De, 1942:243).

While the Food Technical Panel adopted a scientific-technical approach and relied completely on the results obtained from the above-mentioned research projects, the sense of suspicion amongst the middle classes regarding the deleterious effects of vanaspati was more difficult to manage. Recognising this, firms such as Hindustan Unilever launched a new advertising campaign that used scientific terminology to instil the idea that their product had health-giving qualities and that its benefits were scientifically validated and widely recognised as "modern." These advertisements also targeted the idea of motherhood more frequently, often implying that it was the mother's primary duty to ensure the good health of her family. The advertisement below (Figure 9.2), which intends to appeal to the sensibilities of "modern" anglicised mothers in post-independent India, is a clear example of this. It was published in *Indian*

Figure 9.2 Dalda Advertisement Expressing Scientific Motherhood

Credit: *Indian Express*, 17 July 1961, p. 8

Express on 17 July 1961. The modernity of this family is reflected in the clothing worn by the children, as well as the confident visage of the mother, who appears to have used cosmetics to highlight her facial features. While this might seem to be a rather superficial way of defining what was modern, westernised products, ideas and sartorial choices were often seen as synonymous with the idea of modernity (Chatterjee, 1997). The advertisement also assumes—as mentioned earlier—that such a modern, anglicised family should have been naturally attracted by scientific ideas of nutrition, vitamins and the special requirements of growing children.

The visuality and the quality of language used in the advertisement also warrant some commentary. While the previous example explicitly highlighted, using a substantial amount of text, the central role of mothers or wives in ensuring the health of the family, this particular advertisement portrays the idea visually, with the most prominent aspect being the amount of space devoted to the mother's face, which looms large over the entire image. The extreme close-up of her face is able to capture expressions of happiness and satisfaction at the fact that her children are healthy and happy. More importantly, though, they are playfully fighting over the food that has been cooked using Dalda. This image was obviously an invitation to other mothers to embrace modernity and novel food items in order to ensure the happiness of their children. Finally, the reduction in the textual aspect (despite the continued use of deeply affective words or phrases, such as "mother's world of love," "mothers who care," "pure, quality cooking fat," and scientific terms like "vitamins") reflects a shift—by the 1960s—towards semiotically dense, technologised and visually rich advertisements.

While the use of scientific language in this advertisement was somewhat limited, other advertisements that were published around the same time employed much more scientific language. One such advertisement, published in *Indian Express* (11 September 1955) was headlined by the assertion that the vitamin A content in Dalda had been raised to 700 international units per ounce—a figure that would not have been intelligible to most readers, but looked impressive enough to leave a positive impact on them. Assertions in the rest of the text were also couched in scientific language, including the claim that Dalda contained Vitamin D, which was, supposedly, good for bones and teeth. It also ended with the punchline that "[Dalda is] more than a cooking medium – A Food," implying that the nutrients that it contained did not lead to a compromise with taste and that it also had health-giving qualities. Despite this emphasis on scientific language, there was a point of similarity with the earlier advertisement in the way that it was directly aimed at mothers and/or wives, telling them that "when they cook[ed] the family's meals in Dalda, [they were] giving them good food."

Before concluding this section, I must also discuss one final advertisement for Dalda, published in *The Times of India* on 25 August 1958, which combines tropes of informed motherhood, affective ties and scientificity. It featured a healthy, happy girl who displayed many of the insignias of modernity, including her clothing, her short, cropped hair and even the fact that she was very comfortable with the idea of playing outdoors. However, the child's name (Munni) is a very traditional pet name that has no hint of anglicisation about it, while the expectation that her mother should know what was best for her child was certainly in line with "traditional" notions of motherhood. Arguably, these pointers show that makers of the advertisement were trying to appeal to a form of modernity that, in their view, was formed out of an amalgam of various modes of living and conducting oneself—a lived form of modernity rather than modernity that was imported from the "West" (Eisenstadt, 2000). The advertisement also contains very strong scientific elements; though, as it not only made the usual reference to vitamins but also claimed that Dalda conformed to the nutritional standards set by doctors (although no details are provided of what these "nutritional standards" are).

Reinventing Dalda in the Present Day

Following its initial runaway success, Dalda began to gather a slightly negative reputation due to the furore over the idea that it was being used to adulterate ghee. In fact, the brand completely fell out of favour during the 1950s and 1960s. However, it was able to resurrect itself to a large extent in the ensuing decades using the twin discourses of motherhood and science/nutrition. After the 1960s, its journey was an uninterruptedly upward one, until it found a place—by the 1980s—in almost every middle-class home, both in India and Pakistan. In the 1990s, though, when the economy in both countries was opened up to foreign investment, a whole range of alternative products became available that were more desirable because they were of distinctly foreign origin, and because they could claim to have been manufactured using natural (and therefore healthier) products, such as groundnuts—a claim that Dalda certainly could not make. In the last decade, however, Dalda has been trying to re-enter markets, using a wide range of glossy print and televisual advertisements that attempt to harness the appeal of celebrities to its own cause.

In perhaps the most striking example of the use of celebrities, Fawad Khan—undoubtedly the most popular superstar in Pakistani films and television—is shown in a 2023 commercial, dressed immaculately in a suit and tie, sitting at an airport while munching on some food prepared by his mother. He appears to be an extremely modern individual and a high-flyer, one of the indicators of which is an aeroplane that occupies a lot of the space in the background. It is also quite possible that Khan himself has been depicted as a pilot, judging by the colour and design of his clothes, as well as by the presence of an illegible label on his chest. Interestingly, the only text in the advertisement is "Jahan Mamta Wahan Dalda" [or "where there's mother's love, there's Dalda"]. The light use of text might be due to the fact that copywriters wanted to capitalise upon the incredible celebrity status of Khan, not wanting people to be diverted from the fact that an actor of such calibre and popularity was endorsing the product. The expression on Khan's face is also fascinating, as it reflects satisfaction and happiness, and the fact that he is totally at ease consuming a supposedly traditional meal made by his mother at an airport—a space that is seen as the epitome of modernity in South Asia, as frequent air travel has become affordable for the middle classes only in the last couple of decades. Echoing earlier Dalda advertisements, Khan also makes direct eye contact with the reader while lifting some food with his spoon, inviting readers to partake in delicious Dalda-made food. Besides encashing on Khan's popularity, the advertisement also conveys the idea of motherhood or that of "mother knows best" in a new hyper-modern context.

While in the Pakistani case the brand has gone all out by roping in superstars with a huge mass appeal (Khan is not the only star they have used in their advertisements), in the Indian case the advertisers have decided to rely on a single face that certainly does not have the same seductive appeal as Khan's. This is the celebrity chef Sanjeev Kapoor, whose television shows have been watched all over the country since the 1990s. Once again, the advertisements featuring Kapoor are more visual than textual, with him sporting his trademark beaming smile while dressed in his chef's uniform, also indicating with a hand gesture that the food items laid out before him—no doubt prepared with Dalda—are absolutely delicious. A 2021 advertisement shows the slogan, "Saalon ke swaad par mera vishwas" [or "I trust something that has delivered tasty food for aeons"], drawing upon the 75-year legacy of the product. Perhaps the use of this legacy is avoided in the case of Pakistani advertisements since it has not been completely uncontroversial in that country. Indeed, some of the Indian advertisements not only invite the reader to "discover the legacy" but also directly pose the question, "Why has Dalda Vanaspati been trusted for 75+ years?"

While in its most recent reincarnation Dalda appears to rely on both the appeal of its legacy and of celebrities, it has also not let go of its scientific claims. Just like the advertisements from the 1940s to 1960s that have been presented above, contemporary advertisements also draw upon the language of nutrition and vitamins. In fact, Dalda in India has now launched a whole new range of healthy oils, including refined soya bean oil, which is even packaged differently, that is in the same way as other vegetable oils, not in the trademark yellow Dalda plastic jar. The advertisements for these oils prominently feature the fact that the oil contains vitamins A, D and E, has zero cholesterol and contains Omega 3 and Omega 6. Packages for Dalda in Pakistan also note that it is cholesterol free and "virtually trans-fat free" and also contains vitamins A and B. All this is an acknowledgement of the fact that "diseases of affluence" have been on the rise in India and Pakistan in the last few decades, and that the use of inappropriate cooking oil is often viewed as the primary contributor to the issue.

Conclusion

The trajectory of Dalda over the last 75 years, as this chapter has shown, has been fraught with a number of controversies and setbacks, but it has also seen a fair amount of success, becoming the first choice of cooking oil in middle-class households by the 1980s. However, since its initial days, it had to face a number of criticisms, including the criticism that it was contributing to the growing problem of adulteration in sprawling urban areas by lending itself easily to being mixed with ghee. As a result of this scrutiny and doubt, the product began to fall out of public favour by the 1950s and 1960s. Its resurrection a little later was not completely unchallenged either, for in the 1990s—with the influx of foreign investors due to the opening up of the Indian and Pakistani economies—its popularity saw such a massive dip that it was almost completely replaced in middle-class households with other, supposedly healthier, options.

In the present day, as we have seen above, Dalda's owners have been attempting to build the brand once again, using celebrity appeal and playing upon the tropes of legacy, health and scientificity. This most recent attempt has achieved significant success, though from a cursory look at the figures, it seems that Dalda is enjoying greater success in Pakistan compared to India. Indeed, Dalda has become the largest player in Pakistan's edible oil industry. When it wanted to go public and launch its IPOs [Initial Public Offering] in September 2023, it was noted that the company expected to "raise between Rs 3.3 billion to Rs 4.6 billion in a share sale… which would account for 15% of shares in Dalda." The same report went on to note that, "At Rs 4.6 billion, [it] could prove to be the largest ever IPO by a consumer staple company" (Riaz, 2023).

While the language, tone and visuality of Dalda advertisements have changed to a large extent over the last several decades—from being very text-heavy to being predominantly visual in the present day—one of the things that has remained constant is the appeal to motherhood. One of the best examples of this is the advertisement from 1961 (referred to above) where the mother's satisfied and happy visage dominated the advertisement. However, even in the present day, advertisements (such as the one featuring Fawad Khan at an airport) draw upon the idea of a mother's love. This is not surprising in heavily pro-natalist regions like South Asia where achieving motherhood is often seen as the pinnacle of achievement in a woman's life. Such a stance can be clearly seen when flipping through the pages of popular women's magazines, such as *Grihshobha*, whose primary function appears to be to train and instruct women into performing the duties of the ideal wife, mother or family member. While the question of whether the advice is heeded or not is a separate one altogether—one suspects that there would be substantial resistance to it—there is little doubt that instructions are being constantly hurled at women with great vehemence. It is inevitable that some of these ideas will end up being internalised by both women and men (since the readership consists of a substantial number of men too), reinforcing pre-existing ideas of motherhood.

Overall, it seems that, despite various changes in the way in which Dalda has been advertised over the years, certain aspects have remained constant, particularly the idea of scientific motherhood. However, certain aspects of advertisements have also changed, as they appear to have become more semiotically dense while letting go of the heavy textual aspect of earlier times.

The attempt to create catchphrases that stick with the reader or viewer and the desire to appropriate some of the appeal of popular celebrities are new developments and it is yet to be seen whether they will be successful in resurrecting Dalda to its former days of glory. Its 75-year trajectory is, however, instructive in showing how brands negotiate the various challenges that they encounter over time, some of them successfully and others not so successfully.

Acknowledgements

I am extremely thankful to Lauren Alex O'Hagan for her wonderful suggestions on an earlier draft of this paper, which have improved it immeasurably.

Notes

1 The new class of "gentlefolk" who arose during British rule in India in the Bengal region.
2 The zamindar was an autonomous or semi-autonomous ruler of a province in India.

Bibliography

Abraham, I. 1998. *The Making of the Indian Atomic Bomb: Science, Secrecy and the Postcolonial State*. London: Zed Books.

Alter, J. 1992. *The Wrestler's Body: Identity and Ideology in North India*. Berkeley: University of California Press.

Amrith, S. 2009. Health in India since Independence. *BWPI Working Paper* 79. Available at https://hummedia.manchester.ac.uk/institutes/gdi/publications/workingpapers/bwpi/bwpi-wp-7909.pdf (Accessed: 29 January 2014).

Appadurai, A. 1988. How to Make a National Cuisine: Cookbooks in Contemporary India. *Comparative Studies in Society and History* 30:3–24.

Apple, R. 1995. Constructing Mothers: Scientific Motherhood in the Nineteenth and Twentieth Centuries. *Social History of Medicine* 8(2):161–178.

Arnold, D. 2013. Nehruvian Science and Postcolonial India. *Isis* 104(2):360–370.

"Brahmin's Hunger Strike." 1917. *The Singapore Free Press and Mercantile Advertiser* (4 September), 8

Chatterjee, P. 1997. *Our Modernity*. Rotterdam: SEPHIS.

Dalda. 2023. *Watch #FawadKhan feature once again as #Dalda Maamta story continues!* (30 secs). [Television advertisement]. Available at https://www.youtube.com/watch?v=mSioYleha8M (Accessed: 5 February 2024).

"Dalda Advertisement." 1940. *The Times of India* (27 April), n.p.

"Dalda Advertisement." 1942. *Indian Express* (6 February), 7.

"Dalda Advertisement." 1954. *Janata* (10 June), n.p.

"Dalda Advertisement." 1955. *Indian Express* (11 September), 5.

"Dalda Advertisement." 1958. *The Times of India* (25 August), n.p.

"Dalda Vanaspati Ropes in Sanjeev Kapoor as Brand Ambassador." 2021. *Brand Equity* (10 March). Available at https://brandequity.economictimes.indiatimes.com/news/marketing/dalda-vanaspati-ropes-in-sanjeev-kapoor-as-brand-ambassador/81432971 (Accessed: 5 February 2024).

Eisenstadt, S.N. 2000. Multiple Maternities. *Daedalus* 129(1):1–29.

Extract from the Proceedings of the Meetings of the Punjab Legislative Council on 25th November, 3rd, 5th, 6th, 9th and 14th December 1929. 1929. British Library, Asia, Pacific and Asia Collection, file no. L/E/7/1540.

Fairclough, N. 1992. *Discourse and Social Change*. Cambridge: Polity.
Hardgrove, A. 2013. "The Politics of Ghee Adulteration and its Public Resolutions in Calcutta, c. 1917" in *Commodifying Everything: Relationships of the Market*, edited by S. Strasser (New York: Routledge), https://www.taylorfrancis.com/chapters/edit/10.4324/9781315023601-13/politics-ghee-adulteration-public-resolutions-calcutta-1917-anne-hardgrove
Hobsbawm, E. and Ranger, T. 1984. *The Invention of Tradition*. Cambridge: Cambridge University Press.
Illiah, K. 2004. *Buffalo Nationalism: A Critique of Spiritual Fascism*. Kolkata: Samya.
Joshi, L.L. 1916. *Milk Supply of Indian Cities – with Reference to Bombay*. Bombay: Tarporewala & Sons.
Ledin, P. and Machin, D. 2016. Strategic Diagrams and the Technologization of Culture, *Journal of Language and Politics* 14(3):322–336.
Loeb, L.A. 1994. *Consuming Angels: Advertising and Victorian Women*. New York: Oxford University Press.
Marriott, M. 1968. "Caste Ranking and Food Transactions: A Matrix Analysis" in *Structure and Change in Indian Society*, edited by B.S. Cohn and M. Singer (Chicago: Aldine Publishing), Available at https://www.taylorfrancis.com/chapters/edit/10.4324/9781315130361-8/caste-ranking-food-transactions-matrix-analysis-mckim-marriott
McGranahan, C. 2019. "Afterword: Chinese Settler Colonialism: Empire and Life in the Tibetan Borderlands" in *Frontier Tibet: Patterns of Change in the Sino-Tibetan Borderlands*, edited by S. Gros (Amsterdam: Amsterdam University Press), pp. 518–539.
Mishra, S. 2015. *Beastly Encounters of the Raj: Livelihood, Livestock, and Veterinary Health in North India, 1790–1920*. Manchester: Manchester University Press.
Moorhouse, G. 1994. *Calcutta: The City Revealed*. Delhi: Penguin Books.
Nandy, A. 1988. "Introduction: Science as the Reason of State" in *Science, Hegemony, Violence: A Requiem for Modernity*, edited by A. Nandy (Delhi: Oxford University Press), pp. 1–16.
O'Hagan, L.A. 2020. Pure in Body, Pure in Mind? A Sociohistorical Perspective on the Marketisation of Pure Foods in Great Britain, *Discourse, Context & Media* 34, https://doi.org/10.1016/j.dcm.2019.100325
O'Malley, L.S.S. 1913. *Census of India, 1911*, Vol. VI, Part I. Calcutta: Bengal Secretariat Press Depot.
Perales, M. 2016. The Food Historian's Dilemma. *The Journal of American History* 103(3):690–693.
Prakash, G. 1999. *Another Reason: Science and the Imagination of Modern India*. Princeton: Princeton University Press.
Prasad, S. 2006. Crisis, Identity, and Social Distinction: Cultural Politics of Food, Taste, and Consumption in Late Colonial Bengal. *Journal of Historical Sociology* 19(3), https://doi.org/10.1111/j.1467-6443.2006.00281.x
Riaz, N. 2023. The Company that Cried IPO. *PT Profit* (3 September). Available at https://profit.pakistantoday.com.pk/2023/09/03/the-company-that-cried-ipo/ (Accessed: 13 December 2023).
Roy, S. 2007. *Beyond Belief: India and the Politics of Postcolonial Nationalism*. Durham: Duke University Press, Durham.
Saha, R. 2017. Milk, Mothering & Meanings: Infant Feeding in Colonial Bengal. *Women's Studies International Forum* 60:97–110.
Sarkar, S. 1992. "Kaliyuga", "Chakri" and "Bhakti": Ramakrishna and His Times. *Economic and Political Weekly* 27(29):1543–1566.
Schweitzer, M. 2003. Uplifting Makeup: Actresses' Testimonials and the Cosmetics Industry, 1910-1918. *Business and Economic History* 1:1–14.

Shashtri, A.S.C.S. 1932. *Arogya Shashtra*. Delhi: Sanjivni Institute.
Singh, R. 2022. Kaise Shuru Hua Lagbhag 85 Saal Puraane Dalda Brand Ka Safar, *Navbharat Times* (29 January). Available at https://navbharattimes.indiatimes.com/business/business-news/story-of-dalda-brand-how-dalda-gained-and-lost-its-popularity-and-monopoly/articleshow/89187929.cms (Accessed: 25 June 2023).
Subrahmanyan, S. and De, S.S. 1942. The Vanaspati Problem. *Current Science* 16(8):242–245.
Subramanian, T.S. 2013. Every Rupee Spent Benefits People. *The Hindu* (6 November), Available at https://www.thehindu.com/news/national/every-rupee-spent-benefits-people/article5318298.ece (Accessed: 20 June 2023).
Thomas, R. 2021. *Science and Religion in India: Beyond Disenchantment*. Delhi: Routledge.
Thompson, E.P. 1968. *The Making of the English Working Class*. London: Penguin.
Vishwanathan, S. 1988. "On the Annals of the Laboratory State" in *Science, Hegemony, and Violence*, edited by A. Nandy (Delhi: Oxford University Press), pp. 257–290.

10 The Rhetoric of Unadulterated Wholemeal

Thomas R. Allinson and the Natural Food Company, 1892–1918

Amber Hinde

Introduction

> Food is essential to life, and essential to our health. Food also shapes the substance and texture of our lives in countless ways: it is linked to pleasure, escape, friends and family time, cultural traditions and rituals; it is both intimate and communal; and it has accrued a great deal of symbolic, moral, and transformative meanings.
>
> (Hanganu-Bresch, 2021:114)

Food and diet are inescapably social and, as such, rhetorical in nature. Aligning with Hanganu-Bresch (2021), quoted above, Gerhardt (2013:4) argues that "[f]ood is not only sustenance and language not only a tool to transmit information […] [s]ince both do more than cater for bare necessities, they represent perfect sites for social studies." One foodstuff which has a complex history—wrought with social meaning, scientific authority and persuasion—is bread.

At the centre of transhistorical discourses surrounding bread is the competition between white and brown bread, which Fouser (2021:37) refers to as a "colour line" in "a battleground for bread" in Victorian Britain (1837–1901). This sentiment has carried through history, with ongoing discussions of bread in terms of purity and health-giving properties. Zweiniger-Bargielowska (2017:145) notes that "[t]he debate on the nutritional deficiencies of white bread has a long history." Individual brands provide fruitful textual evidence of the rhetorical complexities of bread marketing at specific points in history.

This chapter focuses on one such example: Thomas R. Allinson's Natural Food Company. In 1892, the same year Allinson was struck off the medical register for infamous professional conduct, he purchased a flour mill in Bethnal Green. In doing so, he launched the Natural Food Company, the legacy of which remains rooted in Allinson's Bread today. While Allinson's is a recognisable brand name, the historical roots of the company show Allinson to have been a central figure in the alternative health movement, being an outspoken critic of orthodox approaches to diet and writing prolifically to communicate his views to the public. It was Allinson's belief that abiding by certain "laws of health" would keep people healthy and allow them to avoid unnecessary drugs

DOI: 10.4324/9781003450276-15

or surgery (Bae, 2022:4). In this regard, Allinson was one of many competing voices advocating for prevention over cure at this time—a sentiment which remains prevalent in modern health discourses.

Cauvain (2020:726) asserts that "[b]read has a long history of contributing to human nutrition," and analysing the marketing of bread by individual market leaders—in this case, Allinson's—can support a deeper understanding of how nutrition science and authority contributed to highly rhetorical discourses of bread consumption at the turn of the twentieth century. Through analysis of a rich sample of Natural Food Company bread advertisements and original archival research, insights can be gained regarding the rhetoric used to sell Allinson's lifestyle ideas to the public. The inherently rhetorical nature of food communication sees individuals choose to represent their suggested diet in socially significant ways. As argued by Hanganu-Bresch (2021:115), "[i]nsofar as food is associated with health, it necessarily relies on a rhetoric of control and selection." Thus, in order to examine the rhetorical strategies used, this study is driven by the following interrelated research questions, pertaining to a sample of bread advertisements printed in *Reynolds's* newspaper between 1913 and 1915:

1 How did the Natural Food Company draw on contemporary discourses of science and well-being to legitimise Allinson's Wholemeal Bread?
2 How was Allinson constructed as a credible authority on diet in Natural Food Company advertisements for wholemeal bread?

In order to address these research questions, the analysis draws on theoretical concepts from the field of critical discourse analysis (CDA), namely van Leeuwen's (2007, 2017) model of legitimation. Encouraging individuals to invest their time and energy in a lifestyle change inevitably involves the need to legitimise what is novel for audiences. It is argued by van Leeuwen (2007:91) that, in attempting to establish any kind of legitimacy, "language is without doubt the most important vehicle." Legitimation strategies "seek to give meaning to social practices" (van Leeuwen, 2017:219) and, in doing so, persuade at the intersection between text and society. When attempting to legitimise new approaches to lifestyle or certain health food products, a variety of communication mediums can be drawn upon, including both text and image (van Leeuwen, 2017). This potential for multimodality makes CDA a useful model with which to approach advertisements. Ultimately, this study aims to contribute a historical case study of rhetorical strategies used to promote wholemeal bread as a health food in Edwardian (1901–1914) advertisements. In doing so, this study also aims to demonstrate the value of CDA approaches to understanding historical food discourses.

Thomas R. Allinson, Hygienic Medicine and the Natural Food Company

Thomas Allinson's name is well-known in relation to Allinson's Bread, which can still be found on British supermarket shelves today. Rich historical evidence points to Allinson's activity and influence within the burgeoning wellness market of the late nineteenth and early twentieth centuries being far-reaching (Pepper, 1992; Bae, 2022). Central to Allinson's messaging was the notion that his wholemeal bread was unadulterated; he argued that, when grinding wheat to make bread, "nothing must be taken from it, nor must anything be added to the flour" (Allinson, 1889:5–6). Allinson also contributed to the growing number of branded foods towards the end of the nineteenth century, including "speciality and patent breads" (Collins, 1976:28), which "evolved in response to the anarchy of the marketplace with its multiplicity of products of unknown origin and doubtful quality" (Collins, 1976:108). Allinson attempted to instil trust in buyers by including his signature on all packaging, drawing on a variety of rhetorical strategies to construct a brand identity which promised a high quality and healthy product for consumers. In this respect, Allinson's Natural Food Company was part of the pure food movement (O'Hagan, 2020), which gained traction towards the end of the nineteenth century.[1]

Alongside Allinson's advocation of wholemeal bread, he was a vegetarian, teetotaller and non-smoker. He advised his readers to consume a diet of simple, natural foods "at a time when opportunities for a more varied diet were widening for all sections of the population" (Pepper, 1992:34). Prior to 1891, Allinson had given lectures at Vegetarian Society events, but a disagreement with Arnold Hills, the then president of the society, saw Allinson removed on 20 February 1891 (Scott, 2010:135). Influenced by the ideas of famous naturopaths such as Sylvester Graham, who believed in a "system of medicine which avoids the use of drugs and the consumption of anything but natural foods" (Scott, 1999:258), Allinson's work was underpinned by hygienics—or "the science of maintaining health"—rather than treating the immediate symptoms of disease (Pepper, 1992:31). Allinson laid out his core health philosophy in *A System of Hygienic Medicine* (1904), which is the only text in which he "purposefully delivered his whole philosophy in the form of a monograph" (Bae, 2022:10). Committed to prevention over cure, Allinson (1904:26) argued:

> Therefore it behoves all persons who would be well, to carefully study the conditions of health for themselves. It needs no special intelligence to understand these laws; anyone who can read and think and observe, will soon lay down for himself a code of laws regarding health; by following which he will keep in a good state of health, avoid much suffering, and live to a ripe old age.

Not only does this demonstrate Allinson's commitment to preventative medicine but it also evokes the medical individualism which was implicit in such holistic approaches, emphasising individual agency in health matters (Bae, 2022). This was part of a growing genre of self-help which was heavily populated by alternative health texts, resisting orthodoxy and instead promoting health foods which would enable individuals to be more self-sufficient in terms of their mental and physical health. This self-help genre was also rooted in the

Victorian sentiment of *mens sana in corpore sano*, which entailed unity of the self through mind-body wholeness (Haley, 1978); individuals were increasingly responsible for ensuring their own health and happiness. Haushofer (2018:171) also recognises the link between self-help and prevention, arguing "[b]ehind these calls to more responsible health behavior was a conception of sickness as an avoidable burden on the national economy." In this regard, Allinson's Natural Food Company was advertising health food products at a time when preventative health measures were increasingly being couched in terms of national duty, with concerns surrounding the physical fitness of the nation being prominent at the turn of the century.

Allinson's surviving legacy as a "rebel baker" (Allinson's Bread, 2023) includes his removal from the medical register for "infamous conduct in a professional respect" in 1892 (Brahams, 1987:3). Endorsing and selling products with his name and credentials, as well as condemning his medical colleagues in the press, was considered by the General Medical Council (GMC) to be too commercial and unprofessional for a registered doctor. It is important to note that being struck from the medical register "did not mean Allinson could not practise medicine, only that he could not sign birth and death certificates or hold public office, and that the collection of his fees could not be enforced by the courts" (Scott, 1999:259–260). In fact, Allinson went on to explicitly refer to his separation from the mainstream medical community by using "ex-L.R.C.P." after his name.[2] In a study of the Atkins diet, Shapin (2007:181) notes that "[o]ne of the most pervasive tropes one finds in the popular dietetic literature is a studied disavowal of credentialed expertise." These counterculture notions have a long history in food discourses, with Atkins and Allinson similarly distancing themselves from traditional forms of expertise in favour of foregrounding experience and identity. Allinson's separation from the orthodox medical community makes his use of rhetoric particularly interesting, given his professional and commercial success through the Hygienic Hospital and the Natural Food Company. Crowe (2021) has recently asked similar questions about the rhetoric of actress Gwyneth Paltrow and her lifestyle company Goop.[3] This is relevant to a discussion of Allinson as both figures are seen as controversial in terms of the advice they endorse, with some overlapping ideas about natural and holistic approaches. As such, by exploring the rhetoric of a similar wellness guru a century earlier, this study contributes an important transhistorical perspective to current discussions of rhetoric, identity and wellness culture.

The proliferation of mass media and rising literacy levels in the late nineteenth and early twentieth centuries fuelled a culture of communication which was embraced by Allinson in his approach to disseminating his health ideas. Pepper (1992:34) argues that "it seems unlikely that Allinson would have achieved either the commercial success or the notoriety that he did, had it not been for the emerging opportunity for mass communication afforded by the period." She further notes that "Allinson enthusiastically embraced mass advertising as a way of promoting his essentially individualist approach to health and physical welfare" (Pepper, 1992)). Allinson was the medical editor for the *Weekly Times and Echo* from 1885, "writing a weekly column and answering readers' questions; in all he wrote more than 1,000 articles on health" (Scott, 1999:259). Allinson's column possessed seriality which has been identified as harmonising the new with the old at this time (Mussell, 2009), introducing new ideas to society with both regularity and familiarity. His column allowed him to gain heightened fame as a dietary authority, which then enabled him to use his signature on his products with greater power. Allinson was also writing at a critical time when journalism was becoming more personal in nature, with editors and authors having a more explicit personality and even engaging with readers (Jackson, 2000). Alongside his *Weekly Times and Echo* column, Allinson also lectured on "Scientific Food Reform" across the country and began holding bread-baking competitions in 1909. His ideas about health also formed the basis for the Hygienic Hospital that he opened in London in 1890, made possible by contributions from readers of his regular column (Scott, 1999:259).

In the same year that Allinson was struck off the medical register, he launched his Natural Food Company by purchasing a mill in Bethnal Green. Despite wholemeal bread being their most famous product, the Natural Food Company produced a wide variety of health foods, including Dr. Allinson's Food for Babies and the stimulant-free drink, Brunak. Though the Natural Food Company produced a wide variety of different products, the marketing of these products was rooted in repeated notions of the pure and natural, alongside Allinson's personal authority by virtue of his medical experience. Allinson is described by Bae (2022:11) as having "a certain similarity with the famous market-friendly medical thinkers who established themselves as authors or preachers rather than as medical doctors in the mid-nineteenth century." In this sense, Allinson's relationship with the health food market is comparable to that of Dr John Harvey Kellogg, who played a pivotal role in the formation of breakfast cereals in the United States and "helped to popularise the science of applied dietetics" (Collins, 1976:31). Similarly, Charles Post, who was the "inventor of Grape Nuts and Post Toasties," instigated a trend of using "symptom-inducing advertising techniques" to market health foods (Collins, 1976:32). Breakfast cereal foods produced by Kellogg and Post in the United States "had become an established part of the British diet by the 1930s as a result of 'vigorous promotion'" (Zweiniger-Bargielowska, 2017:155). Allinson's command of both the health food marketplace and medico-scientific knowledge makes him a rich source of legitimation strategies for this analysis.

Allinson's Bread

Allinson's Bread was at the heart of the Natural Food Company's range of health foods and, in focusing their marketing efforts on this particular foodstuff, the Natural Food Company contributed to the growing discourse surrounding bread production and consumption. Towards the end of the nineteenth century, bread and flour "were the most adulterated foodstuffs," with alum being used to whiten the bread and "meet the obsessive public demand" (Collins, 1993:97). In *The Advantages of Wholemeal Bread* (1889), Allinson (11) argued, "[t]o banish the white flour loaf from his home is the duty of every good citizen." This sentiment was expressed by Allinson at a time when "[w]hite bread was perhaps the single most important material object in the lives of Victorian Britons" (Fouser, 2021:35). When such public opposition is present, the legitimation of the product is of utmost importance. How was Allinson's Bread marketed to a public who preferred white bread? On a wider scale, Allinson faced the task of marketing a natural and vegetarian diet to a British public who invested national identity and pride in the consumption of meat (Waddington, 2011:55).

In the early twentieth century, the intersection of science, health and food marketing manifested in the "standard bread campaign" pursued by the *Daily Mail* (Weatherall, 1995:181). The messaging for the campaign emphasised the importance of having a "legal standard for the purity of bread," citing the poor quality and negative health consequences associated with white bread (Weatherall, 1995:183). The campaign rose amid concerns surrounding the practice of flour bleaching, and Page (2023:156) notes that "[t]his was the first time the white bread issue had received so much coverage in the press and in medical circles." This highlights the prominence of the bread debate at the beginning of the twentieth century, with discourses of purity and health being central to the arguments posed by the standard bread campaign.

Alongside Allinson's Bread, a popular market leader of brown bread was Hovis, which specialised in producing "wheat germ bread" (Zweiniger-Bargielowska, 2017:145). Like Allinson's, Hovis was marketed as a health food to a public who favoured white bread. To market their bread, Hovis issued "special baking tins" to bakers, which featured the Hovis logo (Collins, 1976:30). Both Allinson's and Hovis engaged in the practice of wrapping loaves with a branded paper band in order to promise the consumer an authentic and trustworthy product (Collins, 1976). Furthermore, both the Natural Food Company and Hovis held bread-baking competitions, with a focus on quality bread-baking and the popularisation of the products. In 1910, the trophy for Allinson's competition was described by the *Baker's Record* as "one of the handsomest ever seen in connection with the trade" (Allinson Papers, MS 3186), thereby pointing to the potential influence that these competitions could have within the baking trade.

Despite the lower status of brown bread, when compared with its white counterpart, Allinson's "sold well in the health food market and it became Britain's best-selling wholemeal loaf in the interwar years" (Zweiniger-Bargielowska, 2017:145). Writing on the "brown bread experience," Collins (1976:38) suggests that "the potential of new products is weak where the benefits are intangible and the incentives are not deeply grounded socially or dietetically in the 'consumer revolution'." As such, Allinson's Bread advertisements represent an important site for analysis, given the combination of his medical experience and his entrepreneurship in the health food market. In comparison to competitors such as Hovis, Allinson's Bread is a valuable case study, given the foregrounding of Allinson's identity in the marketing of the product, calling into question issues of science and authority.

Data Collection and Approach to Analysis

For this study, I collected a sample of 22 advertisements from the Allinson Papers collection (henceforth, AP), which is an expansive collection of Allinson's personal papers held by the Centre for Research Collections at the University of Edinburgh. The sample was collected by photographing every Natural Food Company advertisement appearing in the folder of *Reynolds's* newspapers within the Allinson Papers collection, with the newspapers spanning the years 1913–1915. This study forms part of a wider doctoral research project on the rhetoric of food reform in the Edwardian era, meaning that the analysis is also informed by this larger research context.

This study is underpinned by the principles of CDA, which sees language as a "form of 'social practice'" (Fairclough and Wodak, 1997:258). CDA "is very much about making connections between social and cultural structures and processes on the one hand, and properties of text on the other" (Fairclough and Wodak, 1997:277). Given the interrelationship between food and society, CDA approaches are particularly beneficial for analysing historical food advertisements. For this analysis, I draw on van Leeuwen's (2007, 2017) model of legitimation, questioning the ways by which Allinson attempted to legitimise his claims in order to sell his wholemeal bread. van Leeuwen (2007:93) argues that legitimation "adds the answer, sometimes explicitly, sometimes more obliquely, to the question 'Why' – 'Why should we do this?' and 'Why should we do this in this way?'" It is, therefore, to be expected that individuals and companies will draw heavily on legitimation strategies when trying to sell healthy lifestyles, with "the persuasive role of legitimation" being foregrounded "when new or changed practices are proposed" (van Leeuwen, 2017:219).

According to de Boer and Aiking (2021:1), "proposals for a diet shift will fall short without broad social legitimation, aimed at a change in social norms." When studying legitimation, "attention must therefore be paid, not only to language, but also to the other forms of expression that combine with language [...] in short, to multimodality" (van Leeuwen, 2017:218). Particularly with mediums like advertising, legitimation can be visually realised, making it important to attend to both text and image when considering the legitimation strategies at work. The potential for legitimation to be realised in both text and image makes it a valuable theoretical underpinning for discussing persuasion in advertisements, which combine textual and visual mediums in their persuasive efforts.

For the purposes of this analysis, the key aspects of the legitimation model are authorisation and moral evaluation, given the dual importance of both Allinson's authority and his manipulation of moralised discourses. van

Leeuwen (2007, 2017) outlines several different subcategories of authorisation or authority legitimation; in this study, the construction of both expert and role model authority is considered in the advertisements. van Leeuwen (2007:94) notes that, "in the case of expert authority, legitimacy is provided by expertise rather than status," whereas "in the case of role model authority, people follow the example of role models or opinion leaders." Alongside authorisation, "moral evaluation legitimation is based on moral values" (van Leeuwen, 2007:97), with moralised discourses being invoked through the use of contextually rooted adjectives such as "pure" and "natural." In these cases, adjectives can be seen as "the tip of a submerged iceberg of moral values" (van Leeuwen, 2007:97). This form of legitimation can, hence, be employed persuasively in advertising by implicitly triggering socially relevant values; for example, in the late nineteenth and early twentieth centuries, the adjective "pure" was linked to moralised discourses surrounding recent food adulteration scandals and concerns about the integrity of food products (O'Hagan, 2020). Hanganu-Bresch (2021:114) explains that "[t]erms used to describe healthy food, such as pure, clean, natural, or organic are deeply contested" and have been of notable interest to scholars across disciplines. It is important to highlight that moral evaluation legitimation strategies cannot be identified based on linguistic evidence alone, but they are rather entrenched in the social conditions of the time and, therefore, require historical context to make "explicit what was lost over time" (van Leeuwen, 2017:227). Due to the fact that "the same practices may be legitimated differently in different social contexts, or by different groups of people" (van Leeuwen, 2017:219), a case study approach, rooted in sociohistorical context, is of great value.

Pure, Natural and Honest: Discourses of Moral Value

In Britain, purity gained rhetorical significance towards the end of the nineteenth century and into the early twentieth century, triggered by widespread food adulteration and the 1875 Sale of Food and Drugs Act, which initiated "the development of a code of practice in commercial relationships, with food companies now trading on their reputation for honesty, integrity and quality" (O'Hagan, 2020:2). This combined with concerns about achieving good health and harnessing a strong nation amid social factors such as record military rejections and poor infant welfare. The promotion of purity, alongside associated values such as "natural" and "simple," was also part of prolific life reform discourses which were present at the time. Life reform is "shorthand for a wide range of practices including vegetarianism, fasting, reducing or high-fibre diets, care of the skin, sun- and air-bathing, nudism, breathing and sex reform" (Zweiniger-Bargielowska, 2010:2). Central to life reformers' rhetoric was "a critique of the artificiality of modern urban lifestyles" (Zweiniger-Bargielowska, 2010). Thus, the use of purity as a rhetorical device can also be seen to fit into a larger persuasive agenda which worked to create a "celebration of the pastoral idyll" (Zweiniger-Bargielowska, 2010:8). The use of purity in the branding of the

Natural Food Company is apparent through the use of the word "natural" in the brand name, alongside the use of "unadulterated wholemeal" as a subheading in the "Allinson Bread" logo featured at the bottom of each advertisement.

One core element of Allinson's portrayal of his bread as "pure" and "unadulterated" was the branding of the loaves to reassure customers that they were buying a genuine and high-quality product: "[t]o protect buyers, every genuine Allinson loaf bears the name 'Allinson' in raised letters on both sides and is wrapped in a paper band bearing the portrait and signature of the world-famous food specialist—T. R. Allinson" (AP, MS 3195). Collins (1993:108) points out that the advent of branded foods, coupled with industrialisation and the depersonalisation of the buyer–seller exchange, "offered the assurance of consistent quality from a trusted source." This was evidently deemed a valuable aspect of Allinson's branding, given the images of branded loaves which were featured on Natural Food Company advertisements. As will be discussed in the next section, this was also a visual representation of Allinson's personal authority.

The idealisation of nature and use of purity as a rhetorical device can be seen throughout the sample of advertisements for this study. Loaded adjectives are employed to trigger relevant moral concepts, as in the featured examples below:

> "Ere long you will realize also a wonderful improvement in health, for Allinson Bread is beyond comparison **pure**, **wholesome**, and **digestible**" (AP, MS 3195) [bold mine]
>
> "You will not miss meat if you eat this **honest** all-of-the-wheat Bread; it supplies all the nourishment your brain and body require and, in addition, keeps you in **natural** health" (AP, MS 3195) [bold mine]
>
> "In a word Allinson Bread is *true to Nature*—being **pure** wholemeal of the **choicest** wheat, **unadulterated** and **unspoiled**" (AP, MS 3195) [bold mine]

These adjectives relate to broader concepts which were socially significant at the time. Though purity is explicitly signalled by the use of the adjective "pure" in the first and third examples, it is also implicit in the use of "honest" and "natural" in the second example. As discourses of purity were directly linked to concerns about food adulteration—and, therefore, food quality—these moralised discourses are also present in adjectives such as "wholesome," "choicest," "unadulterated" and "unspoiled." Widespread concerns about common medical complaints at the time, such as indigestion and constipation, are also triggered by adjectives such as "digestible." It is, thus, evident that, situated in their social context, the adjectives used in these examples linked to much wider discourses of moral value, aiming to legitimise Allinson's Wholemeal Bread by aligning it with these values.

Moreover, in terms of moral evaluation legitimation, van Leeuwen (2017:227) points out that this persuasive strategy can also be realised through use of analogy, arguing that "comparisons in discourse almost always have a legitimating or critical function." The Natural Food Company advertisements feature such use of analogy in order to legitimise Allinson's Bread in a contextually relevant way, as in the example below:

> Windmills are a frequent feature of the War in Flanders, scouts of both armies utilizing them as posts of observation. In peace, as in War, the Windmill fulfils an important duty—that of supplying the food of the nation. The Windmill is familiarly identified with Allinson Bread—the all-of-the-wheat bread made from flour stone-ground in the good old way.
> (AP, MS 3195)

In the above example, taken from an advertisement entitled "The Windmill in War," an analogy is drawn between the use of windmills during World War One and the use of windmills in food production, aiming to legitimise Allinson's Bread by investing in it a necessary function and notions of national duty. On the persuasive function of analogy, Mulholland (1994:37) argues:

> When used to persuade A. [audience] to take a desired attitude about one matter, C.s [communicators] should choose a matter for comparison about which A. already holds the desired attitude, and suggest that since the two resemble each other, they should be accepted in the same way.

Assuming that the audience accepts the value of the windmill in the war, in terms of the national duty involved in the activities of soldiers, they are thereby implicitly asked to ascribe similar importance to Allinson's use of the windmill in bread production. The example also draws on what van Leeuwen (2007:96) terms the "authority of tradition," which aims to legitimise by suggesting that "this is what we have always done." The use of the phrase "good old way" works towards this end, drawing on widespread concerns about modernity by idealising the past. In the example, abiding by the old ways is linked with the production of "all-of-the-wheat bread," equating the "pastoral idyll" (Zweiniger-Bargielowska, 2010:8) with the wholesome and natural loaves produced by Allinson's.

Speaking on modern vegetarianism, Hanganu-Bresch (2023:2) argues that one significant pole of the rhetoric used is the ongoing legitimation of "a 'traditional' way of doing things." This notion is also drawn upon in an advertisement titled "Our Sturdy Forefathers" (Figure 10.1), which claims that "[t]he stalwart 'yeomen of England' were strangers to white bread; their bone and muscles were nourished on bread made as Allinson bread is made, *from the whole of the wheat*" (AP, MS 3195). The authority of tradition, and the notion that prior generations had higher fitness levels, is reinforced by an accompanying image picturing a "yeoman" with muscular arms—one of which is raised to highlight the muscular form—holding a sickle. In the background, fields of wheat can be seen, alongside the signature Allinson's windmill and the rising sun. Providing this

Figure 10.1 "Our Sturdy Forefathers" Allinson Bread Advertisement from *Reynolds's Newspaper*, 1914

Credit: Allinson Papers (AP, MS 3195), University of Edinburgh Archive

ode to agricultural labour of the past invests the brand with authority steeped in tradition, drawing parallels between "the old way" and Allinson's use of the "whole of the wheat." The advertisement also states that "Allinson gives you the WHOLE of the wheat, including those elements which are so important to the healthy working of your system" (AP, MS 3195). As will also be shown in a later example (Figure 10.3), Allinson offers the reader his product as a microcosm of health, using synthetic personalisation to bridge the gap between references to the past and the modern consumer viewing the advertisements. In referring to what the body needs, Allinson underpins his argument with modern nutrition science, representing a tension between the old and the new. Allinson's Bread is rhetorically constructed as the antithesis to modernity, as in the following example, "**Constipation, Indigestion, Anaemia**, etc., only became so prevalent since people gave up eating the old-fashioned wholemeal bread, some 80 years ago. Wherever Allinson Wholemeal Bread is regularly eaten these complaints are practically unknown" (AP, MS 3195). Listing these common medical complaints, such as indigestion, and linking them explicitly to modern lifestyles, encourages the audience to value the "back to nature" approach advocated by life reformers in order to counter the effects of modernity on their bodies.

Considering the persuasive potential of multimodality (van Leeuwen, 2017), the repeated use of images, such as Allinson's signature windmill and fields of wheat, visually employs moral evaluation by playing into the rhetorical construction of purity and working to conjure the "pastoral idyll" (Zweiniger-Bargielowska, 2010:8) desired by life reformers. A case in point is Figure 10.2, which shows a branded loaf of Allinson's Wholemeal Bread in the foreground, with a wheat field and Allinson's signature windmill in the background. The drawing of these images together equates Allinson's wholemeal loaf with nature by suggesting a field-to-table approach to food production. Given concerns surrounding food production—and particularly bread production—at the time, these images visually legitimise Allinson's product by drawing on moralised discourses of purity and "back to nature" sentiment. The foregrounding of nature and simultaneous diminishment of the modern "production process" is a "paradoxical strategy" (O'Hagan and Eriksson, 2022:248) which serves to market the product as pure and untouched by the negative aspects of modernity.

Capturing notions of the pure and natural, Allinson's Bread is characterised as being "perfect" throughout the sample of advertisements, for example: "ALLINSON BREAD gives you the perfect food in its perfect form—with ALL of the elements provided by Nature for the nourishment AND HEALTH of the human system" (AP, MS 3195) and "[i]f you would be certain that your diet, however simple, contains the full nourishment necessary to perfect health, be sure of ALLINSON the perfect bread at every meal. See the band on every loaf" (AP, MS 3195). In context, perfection appears to relate to the bread being scientifically balanced, with health-giving properties. Haley (1978:4) points out that health "has long been used analogically to represent various kinds of perfection or excellence." In the Natural Food Company advertisements, perfection is used as a rhetorical device to link to discourses of purity, nature and positive health. Evaluative adjectives such as "best" further tie into these notions: "[n]ature's best food in its best form" (AP, MS 3195). Chen and Eriksson (2019:2) argue that "[t]he vagueness of healthy food allows producers to position themselves as solution providers and emerge as actors doing good for individuals and the society at large." This relates to the rhetorical potential for food discourses to draw on socially relevant values in order to align healthy food with key concerns of the time, appearing to be driven by the best interests of audiences.

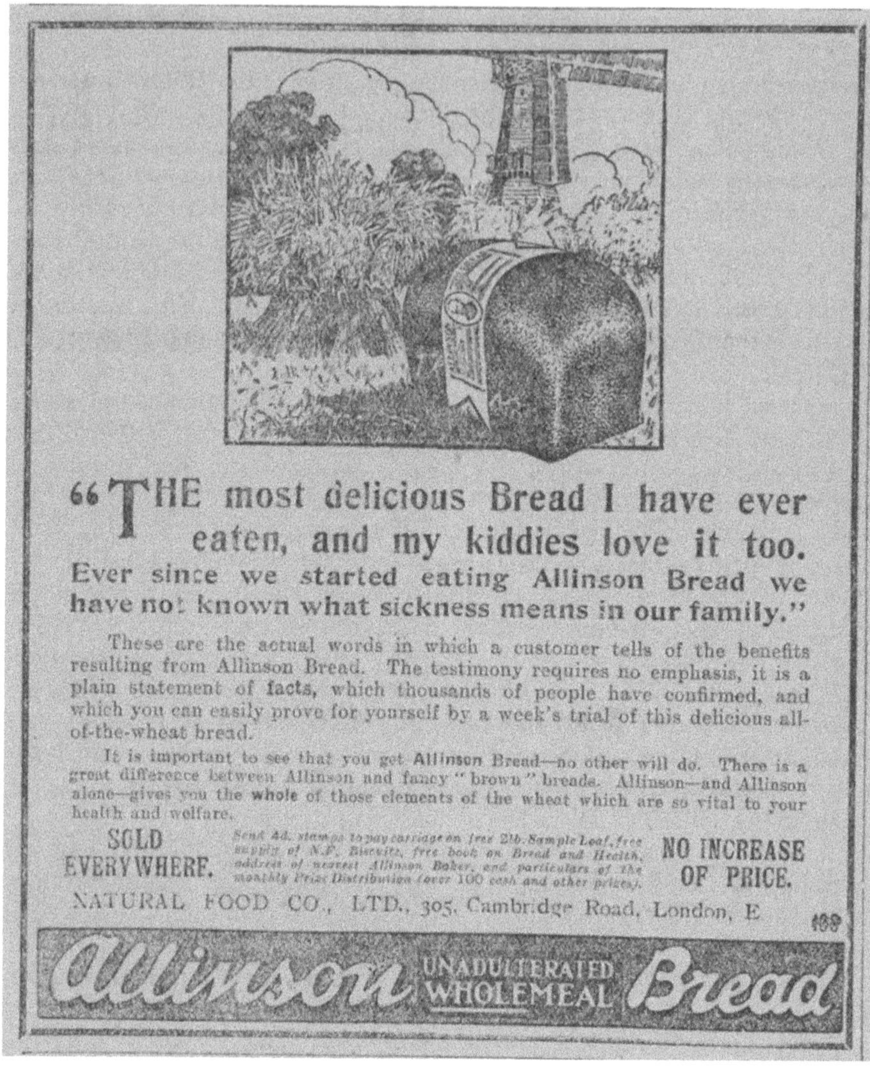

Figure 10.2 "The Most Delicious Bread..." Allinson Bread Advertisement from *Reynolds's Newspaper*, 1914

Credit: Allinson Papers (AP, MS 3195), University of Edinburgh Archive

"Dr. T. R. Allinson, The Great Diet Specialist": Constructing Authority and Selling Expertise

When attempting to sell natural wholemeal bread—framed as a health food—to the public, the Natural Food Company drew on rhetorical strategies to portray Allinson as a credible authority on diet and health matters. Van Leeuwen (2017:223) notes that expertise:

> is frequently used in the media, which play a key role in translating science [...] into legitimate practices, especially in areas that are not formally regulated and yet play a significant role in social life – health, beauty, relationships, and so on.

The rhetorical manipulation of expertise is combined with the use of moralised discourses in order to persuade readers to buy Allinson's Bread, attempting to convince them not only of its purity but also of Allinson's identity as an authority on diet.

In an advertisement entitled "Health by Food," the following extract appears below the title:

> Dr. T. R. Allinson, the great diet specialist, says: - "During 30 years of the busiest medical practice I have restored many thousands of people to health, chiefly by the aid of the Wholemeal Bread which bears my name"
> (AP, MS 3195)

In terms of expert authority, van Leeuwen (2007:95) notes, "[t]ypically, expert legitimation takes the form of 'verbal process clauses' or 'mental process clauses' (e.g. 'Professor so-and-so believes...') with the expert as subject." As shown in Figure 10.3, the advertisement also provides visual legitimation by showing Allinson himself engaged in the act of "offering" consumers his branded loaf (Kress and van Leeuwen, 2006). This visual endorsement and manifestation of expert authority is furthered by the accompanying quote from Allinson, which explicitly signals his expertise and experience as a medical professional. The headline "I give you health" works alongside the image of Allinson looking towards the reader, further fostering a relationship with the viewer through synthetic personalisation, with Allinson himself claiming to offer the reader the abstract concept of health through his wholemeal bread. Allinson's expertise is further visually legitimised through his general appearance, being a middle-aged male pictured in smart, formal dress and glasses, signifying knowledge and experience. The use of both Allinson's portrait and personal pronouns within the quotations gives Allinson an explicit presence in the text, which Hyland (2005:181) argues is a deliberate feature in order to "adopt a particular stance and disciplinary-situated authorial identity." Though van Leeuwen (2007:95) notes that expert authority can be signalled by credentials, he also recognises that "if the expert is well-known in the given context, it may be taken for granted." Thus, the mere presence of Allinson in the advertisement, both visually and textually, draws on expert authority as a legitimation strategy.

Alongside Allinson's status as an expert, the advertisements also draw on role model authority by showing Allinson to be consuming his own bread. It is noted that "role models legitimate practices by engaging in them or endorsing them" (van Leeuwen, 2017:224), with this kind of authority being of significance in "advertising and lifestyle media" (van Leeuwen, 2017). The use of role

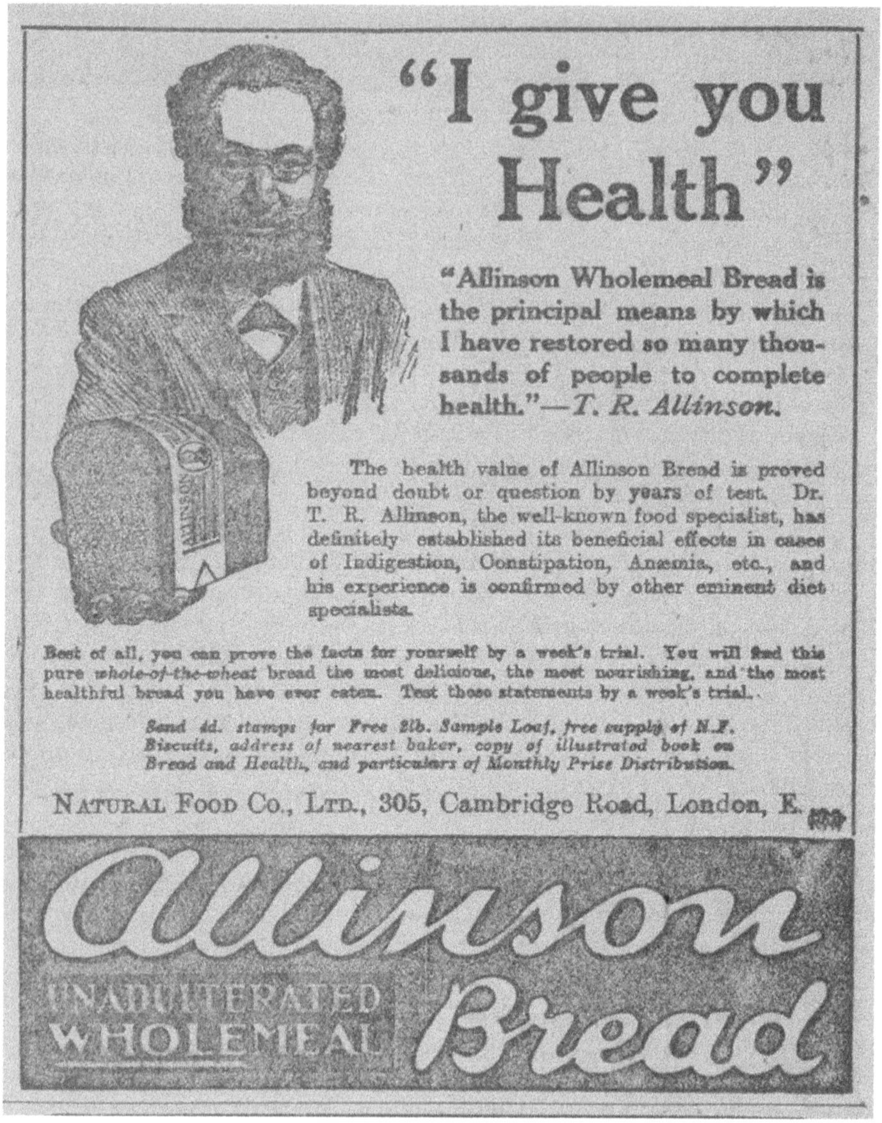

Figure 10.3 "I Give You Health" Allinson Bread Advertisement from *Reynolds's Newspaper*, 1914

Credit: Allinson Papers (AP, MS 3195), University of Edinburgh Archive

model authority can still be seen today with influencer and celebrity culture, with dieticians being able to show internet audiences what they eat on a day-to-day basis in order to support their claims about diet. It is important to recognise that this sample of advertisements is taken from *Reynolds's* newspaper, in which Allinson had a regular medical column from 1912, carrying readers of his *Weekly Times & Echo* column when the two publications amalgamated. As such, it is possible that viewers of these particular advertisements may have also been reading Allinson's column within the same publication and, therefore, were pre-conditioned to Allinson's medical ideas.

Despite being an outcast of the mainstream medical community, and a controversial figure in the eyes of many, Allinson's authority is presented in no uncertain terms:

> The health value of Allinson bread is proved beyond doubt or question by years of test. Dr. T. R. Allinson, the well-known food speciality, has definitely established its beneficial effects in cases of Indigestion, Constipation, Anaemia, etc., and his experience is confirmed by other eminent diet specialists
>
> (AP, MS 3195)

In this example, the health-giving properties of Allinson's Bread are linked to scientific proof, rooted in evidence, that evidence being a supposed track record of positive results. In explicitly portraying the bread as healthy, the advertisement adopts high modality (Kress and van Leeuwen, 2006). Modality relates to "the truth value or credibility of (linguistically realized) statements about the world" (Kress and van Leeuwen, 2006:155) and the above extract makes claims with a high degree of certainty. Alongside the truth value attached to Allinson's Bread, the high modality of the above extract is furthered through reference to Allinson's experience as a doctor, which is said to be "*confirmed* by other eminent diet specialists" [italics mine].

In the sample, Allinson is not the only individual who is used to provide expert legitimation for the product. External expertise is also drawn on to legitimise the quality of Allinson's wholemeal bread:

> One of the greatest dietetic authorities of this generation, Sir Henry Thompson, F.R.C.S., said in his well-known book, "Food and Feeding," that all bread should be made from *entire* wheatmeal (*as Allinson Bread is made*). In the plainest language he states that bread which lacks the health-regulating elements (*which you get in Allinson Bread*) is mischievous and should not be eaten
>
> (AP, MS 3195)

The above extract is a further example of expert authority, being a verbal process clause "with the well-credentialed expert as subject" (van Leeuwen, 2017:223). The insertions within the brackets—added for the purpose of the advertisement—serve to explicitly signpost to the reader the ways in which Allinson's Bread aligns with Thompson's expert opinions. The expert legitimation is also conveyed visually, with a portrait of Sir Henry Thompson and his accompanying credentials being displayed. O'Hagan (2021:9) notes that "the use of science was fairly innovative in the early twentieth century," with audiences not so aware of "subtle marketing strategies" as a result. This strategy is similarly adopted by modern lifestyle marketers such as Gwyneth Paltrow who, alongside her own voice, "creates space for other expert voices to provide a marketplace of voices and solutions" (Crowe, 2021:204). By drawing on different expert voices across the advertisements, Allinson's authority is bolstered by this multitude of opinions and credentials, aligning him with others who possess an expert right to speak on the topic. This is further shown by the use of political expertise in one of the sampled advertisements:

> "Wheat would go 50% further if the modern milling process did not remove from it far and away the most nutritious portion of the grain." Those were the words of Mr. Charles Bathurst, M.P. (House of Commons Debate, Feb. 17th), Chairman of the Central Chamber of Agriculture
>
> (*AP*, MS 3195)

This example works to reinforce the Natural Food Company's promotion of "the old ways" and consumption of the "whole of the grain."

Allinson's authority is constructed in the advertisements by reference to his medical practice and it is noted that "Dr. Allinson has completely proved in his practice that *Health* depends upon *Food*" (AP, MS 3195). Adelman and Haushofer (2018:128) argue that "science and medicine are crucial influences on past and modern conceptions of food," and Allinson stands as an example of how authority is entangled with this notion of food as medicine. In this instance, the connection between food and medicine is manipulated by Allinson's professional and commercial interests, underlined by the social conditions of the time.

Conclusion

The debate surrounding white versus brown bread in the United Kingdom has a long history which transcends modern health discourses. Considering the fact that "ads are parasitic upon their situation and other discourses" (Cook, 1992:29), this study has shown how the Natural Food Company's advertisements for Allinson's Wholemeal Bread drew on relevant discourses to market the product to the public. Thomas Allinson was a leading figure in the promotion of brown bread in the late nineteenth and early twentieth centuries, with his Natural Food Company using a variety of rhetorical strategies to legitimise the consumption of Allinson's Bread. Employing moralised discourses of purity, nature and good health, Allinson's Bread was marketed for an amalgamation of contemporary concerns.

This historical case study of legitimation strategies used in a sample of Natural Food Company advertisements has demonstrated the value of a socially situated analysis, building on important work at the intersection of food, health and communication. By subjecting historical texts to CDA approaches, scholars can explore the deeply interconnected nature of text and context. This analysis has shown how Allinson's Natural Food Company exploited key discourses of the time, capitalising particularly on concerns surrounding food quality and achieving good health. It has also shown how expert legitimation, grounded in the rhetorical construction of purity, was used to legitimise claims in a wellness market characterised by many competing voices. The manipulation of both moral discourses and different kinds of authority works to legitimise "the proposed changes" (van Leeuwen, 2017:219) which the Natural Food Company attempted to stimulate.

What is also apparent from this analysis is that modern sentiments surrounding health and diet, such as the desire for "organic" and "preservative-free" foods, have deep historical roots. Due to the fact that food is inherently sociocultural (Oddy and Miller, 1976), and language is the central medium with which to communicate about food, studies which focus on this connection between food and language can shed important insight on cultural values and rhetorical significance. I have also mentioned important parallels between historic food advertisements and modern influencer culture; future research could conduct a diachronic study of legitimation strategies across different brands to provide evidence of ongoing rhetorical strategies used to sell healthy lifestyles.

Following key events of the early twentieth century, such as the introduction of flour bleaching and the standard bread campaign, discourses surrounding bread consumption continued to be shaped by quality and health concerns with the "watershed" development of the Chorleywood Process[4] in the 1960s, which garnered "hostility" from "traditional craft (artisan) bakers" (Cauvain, 2020:722). This tension surrounding the colour of bread, alongside its ingredients, continues to be prevalent in the twenty-first century. The modern white sliced pan loaf, being mass-produced and packaged, is classed as an "ultra-processed food" (UPF) (see Chapter 3 in this volume). It is argued that these UPFs, which are "prolific in modern diets" (Elizabeth et al., 2020:1), are "highly profitable, intensely appealing and intrinsically unhealthy" (Monteiro et al., 2019:939). According to Monteiro et al. (2019), the nature of these UPFs is "not always immediately clear" and it is difficult for consumers when discerning the nature of modern breads. Considering the historical advertisements produced by the Natural Food Company to market Allinson's Bread, it can be argued that Allinson's promotion of "unadulterated" wholemeal bread in the face of unscrupulous bread production practices and public preference for white bread is strikingly relevant to ongoing discourses surrounding bread.

Notes

1 This focus on purity stemmed from widespread concerns surrounding food adulteration in the nineteenth century, with food advertisers capitalising on these concerns by emphasising the purity of their products (Collins, 1993; O'Hagan, 2020).

2 L.R.C.P. stands for Licentiate of the Royal College of Physicians.

3 Goop is a modern alternative health and wellness company founded by actress Gwyneth Paltrow. The website describes Goop as wellness pioneers who "operate from a place of curiosity and nonjudgment" (Goop, 2023). Paltrow is considered a controversial figure, accused of giving pseudoscientific advice to followers.

4 The Chorleywood Process is a method that made bread production possible on a large scale. It replaced slow mixing and kneading processes with more efficient dough production, thereby producing soft, fluffy loaves.

References

Adelman, J. and Haushofer, L. 2018. Introduction: Food as Medicine, Medicine as Food. *Journal of the History of Medicine and Allied Sciences* 73(2):127–134.

The Allinson Papers Collection. 1881–1928. Coll. 39, MS 3195. Edinburgh: University of Edinburgh Centre for Research Collections.

Allinson, T.R. 1889. *The Advantages of Wholemeal Bread*. London: The Natural Food Company.

Allinson, T.R. 1904. *A System of Hygienic Medicine, or the Only Rational Way of Treating Disease*. London: L.N. Fowler.

Allinson's Bread. 2023. Rethinking Bread Since 1892. Available at https://www.allinsonsbread.co.uk/about-us-story (Accessed: 10 April 2023).

Bae, M. 2022. Locating Hygienic Medicine within the Intellectual History of Hygiene: Cases of E. W. Lane and T. R. Allinson. *History and Philosophy of the Life Sciences* 44(4):1–25.

Brahams, D. 1987. The Meaning of Serious Professional Misconduct. *The Medico-Legal Journal* 55(1):3–5.

Cauvain, S.P. 2020. "The Future for Breadmaking" in *Breadmaking: Improving Quality*, edited by S.P. Cauvain (Cambridge: Woodhead Publishing), pp. 721–729.

Chen, A. and Eriksson. G. 2019. The Making of Healthy and Moral Snacks: A Multimodal Critical Discourse Analysis of Corporate Storytelling. *Discourse, Context & Media* 32, https://doi.org/10.1016/j.dcm.2019.100347

Collins, E.J.T. 1976. "The 'Consumer Revolution' and the Growth of Factory Foods" in *The Making of the Modern British Diet*, edited by D.J. Oddy and D.S. Miller (London: Croom Helm), pp. 26–43.

Collins, E.J.T. 1993. Food Adulteration and Food Safety in Britain in the 19th and Early 20th Centuries. *Food Policy* 18(2):95–109.

Cook, G. 1992. *The Discourse of Advertising*. London: Routledge.

Crowe, J.H. 2021. Toxically Clean: Homophonic Expertise, Goop, and the Ideology of Choice. *Rhetoric of Health & Medicine* 4(2):187–217.

de Boer, J. and Aiking, H. 2021. Favoring Plant Instead of Animal Protein Sources: Legitimation by Authority, Morality, Rationality and Story Logic. *Food Quality* 88:1–10.

Elizabeth, L., Machado, P., Zinöcker, M., Baker, P. and Lawrence, M. 2020. Ultra-Processed Foods and Health Outcomes: A Narrative Review. *Nutrients* 12(7):1–33.

Fairclough, N. and Wodak, R. 1997. "Critical Discourse Analysis" in *Discourse Studies: A Multidisciplinary Introduction*, edited by T. van Dijk (London: Sage), pp. 258–284.

Fouser, D. 2021. "Modern Food as Status: A Biography of Modern British Bread" in *Acquired Tastes: Stories About the Origins of Modern Food*, edited by B.R. Cohen, M.S. Kideckel, and A. Zeide (Massachusetts: The MIT Press), pp. 35–50.

Gerhardt, C. 2013. "Food and Language – Language and Food" in *Culinary Linguistics: The Chef's Special*, edited by C. Gerhardt, M. Frobenius and S. Ley (Amsterdam: John Benjamins), pp. 3–52.

Goop. 2023. What's Goop? Available at https://goop.com/whats-goop/ (Accessed: 27 April 2023).

Haley, B. 1978. *The Healthy Body and Victorian Culture*. Cambridge: Harvard University Press.

Hanganu-Bresch, C. 2021. The Rhetoric of Food as Medicine: Introduction to Special Issue on the Rhetoric of Food and Health. *Rhetoric of Health & Medicine* 4(2):111–125.

Hanganu-Bresch, C. 2023. "The Discursive Construction of Veg(etari)anism: A Polyphonic Rhetoric" in *The Rhetorical Construction of Vegetarianism*, edited by C. Hanganu-Bresch (Abingdon: Routledge), pp. 1–22.

Haushofer, L. 2018. Between Food and Medicine: Artificial Digestion, Sickness, and the Case of Benger's Food. *Journal of the History of Medicine and Allied Sciences* 73(2):168–187.

Hyland, K. 2005. Stance and Engagement: A Model of Interaction in Academic Discourse. *Discourse Studies* 7(2):173–192.
Jackson, K. 2000. "George Newnes and the 'loyal Tit-Bitites': Editorial Identity and Textual Interaction in Tit-Bits" in *Nineteenth-Century Media and the Construction of Identities*, edited by L. Brake, B. Bell and D. Finkelstein (Hampshire: Palgrave), pp. 11–26.
Kress, G. and van Leeuwen, T. 2006. *Reading Images: The Grammar of Visual Design*. London: Routledge.
Monteiro, C.A., Cannon, G., Levy, R.B., Moubarac, J.C., Louzada, M.L., Rauber, F., Khandpur, N., Cediel, G., Neri, D., Martinez-Steele, E., Baraldi, L.G. and Jaime, P.C. 2019. Ultra-Processed Foods: What They Are and How to Identify Them. *Public Health Nutrition* 22(5):936–941.
Mulholland, J. 1994. *Handbook of Persuasive Tactics: A Practical Language Guide*. London: Routledge.
Mussell, J. 2009. Cohering Knowledge in the Nineteenth Century: Form, Genre, and Periodical Studies. *Victorian Periodicals Review* 42(1):93–103.
Oddy, Derek J. and Miller, D. 1976. *The Making of the Modern British Diet*. London: Croom Helm.
O'Hagan, L.A. 2020. Pure in Body, Pure in Mind? A Sociohistorical Perspective on the Marketisation of Pure Foods in Great Britain. *Discourse, Context & Media* 34, https://doi.org/10.1016/j.dcm.2019.100325
O'Hagan, L.A. 2021. Flesh-Formers or Fads? Historicizing the Contemporary Protein-Enhanced Food Trend. *Food, Culture & Society* 25(5):875–898.
O'Hagan, L.A. and Eriksson, G. 2022. Modern Science, Moral Mothers, and Mythical Nature: A Multimodal Analysis of Cod Liver Oil Marketing in Sweden, 1920–1930. *Food and Foodways* 30(4):231–260.
Page, A. 2023. Pure White Bread? Bleached Flour, Contestations, and Regulation in Great Britain, 1900–50. *Technology and Culture* 64(1):149–171.
Pepper, S. 1992. Allinson's Staff of Life: Health without Medicine in the 1890s. *History Today* 42:30–35.
Scott, C.J. 1999. The Life and Trials of TR Allinson Ex-LRCP. *Proceedings of the Royal College of Physicians of Edinburgh* 29:258–261.
Scott, C.J. 2010. Ghandi and the "Struck-Off" Doctor, Thomas Richard Allinson (1858–1918). *Journal of Medical Biography* 18:133–137.
Shapin, S. 2007. "Expertise, Common Sense, and the Atkins Diet" in *Public Science in Liberal Democracy*, edited by J. Porter and P. Phillips (Toronto: University of Toronto Press), pp. 174–193.
van Leeuwen, T. 2007. Legitimation in Discourse and Communication. *Discourse & Communication* 1(1):91–112.
van Leeuwen, T. 2017. "Legitimation and Multimodality" in *The Routledge Handbook of Language and Politics*, edited by R. Wodak and B. Forchtner (London: Routledge), pp. 218–232.
Waddington, K. 2011. The Dangerous Sausage: Diet, Meat and Disease in Victorian and Edwardian Britain. *Cultural and Social History* 8(1):51–71.
Weatherall, M. 1995. "Bread and Newspapers: The Making of a Revolution in the Science of Food" in *The Science and Culture of Nutrition*, edited by H. Kamminga and A. Cunningham (Amsterdam: Rodopi), pp. 179–212.
Zweiniger-Bargielowska, I. 2010. *Managing the Body: Beauty, Health, and Fitness in Britain, 1880–1939*. Oxford: Oxford University Press.
Zweiniger-Bargielowska, I. 2017. "'Not a Complete Food for Man': The Controversy about White versus Wholemeal Bread in Interwar Britain" in *Setting Nutritional Standards: Theory, Policies, Practices*, edited by E. Neswald, D.F. Smith and U. Thoms (Rochester: University of Rochester Press), pp. 142–164.

11 Between Science and Tradition

Nutrition Epistemologies and Extractionist Logics in Chia Seed Development and Marketing

Jessica Loyer

Introduction: What Makes Food Healthy?

Over the past three decades, chia—the former Aztec staple grain—has been repositioned from a niche plant-based protein source to a celebrated omega-3 essential-fatty-acid-(EFA) rich superfood. This positioning is significant because of what the superfood label promises: energy, immunity, strength, vitality and beauty in a natural, whole, pure and clean form,[1] backed by the modern, empirical knowledge of science and ancient, innate wisdom of tradition. As a category of health foods, superfoods owe much of their popularity to this interaction between science and tradition in their representations, as they are doubly verified as healthy. Food marketing strategies blending science with tradition have a broad historical trajectory dating to the late nineteenth century, but grouping such products under the superfoods banner is an early twenty-first-century innovation (McDonnell and Wilk, 2020).

The interplay between the nutrient-reductionist discourse of nutritionism, "characterized by a reductive *focus* on the nutrient composition of foods as the means for understanding their healthfulness, as well as by a reductive *interpretation* of the role of these nutrients in bodily health" (Scrinis, 2013:2), and the quasi-nostalgic discourse of nutritional primitivism, "the pursuit of ostensibly simpler, more natural and authentic ways of eating as part of a quest for health" (Knight, 2015:442), is a defining characteristic of the superfoods category. Loyer and Knight (2018) examine the relationship between these discourses in superfoods books, tracing how, over time, nutritional primitivism evolved from a platform from which to demonstrate a superfood's scientifically proven health benefits into a knowledge framework in its own right. In superfoods books, these discourses exist side by side, as authors draw from both to confer superfood status on particular foods. Yet, despite the growing significance of nutritional primitivism as a measure of healthfulness, it has not displaced the prestige of nutritionism.

The give-and-take between nutritionism and nutritional primitivism in superfoods media is essentially an epistemological contest over how we "know" health through food (Loyer and Knight, 2018). If the healthfulness of a food can only be understood by measuring the quantities of nutrients it contains

DOI: 10.4324/9781003450276-16

and scientifically studying the effects of those nutrients on bodies—as the nutritionism ideology posits—then only nutrition scientists are able to know nutrition. The rest of us must take their word for it, making our knowledge of health through food second-hand and intellectual, rather than embodied or affective. Since the birth of nutrition science in the late nineteenth century, the notion that people could discern for themselves what foods are healthy for their own bodies has been dismissed. Praising the "exact" scientific approach to nutrition, a 1936 article in the *Medical Journal of Australia* clearly rejected such reliance on embodied knowledge, commenting that "it must always be remembered that people will eat what they like and not what they should. They must be taught to like the things that are good for them" (cited in Santich, 2005:153–154). Medical and public health professionals have increasingly emphasised the authority of knowledge created by the nutrition science discipline, exemplified in the proliferation of nutrient-focused dietary guidelines issued by government agencies and health promotion organisations, and the prevalence of "expert" endorsements in food marketing (Mudry et al., 2014). The unquestioning acceptance of nutrition science as the arbiter of nutritional truth by the medical establishment, government agencies, health promotion organisations, food manufacturers, media outlets and large public audiences contributes to the dominance of this way of knowing health through food and explains why Jessica Hayes-Conroy and Allison Hayes-Conroy (2013) term it "hegemonic nutrition."

Hegemonic nutrition also subjugates traditional ways of knowing health through food, which "are deeply embedded in cultural practices, environment, and belief systems" and "are personal but are also social and political processes" (Chen, 2009:xii). Throughout human history, diverse world cultures have developed nutritional knowledge systems that make sense of the ways in which edible substances heal and nourish bodies by "conceptualiz[ing] food and medicine on a continuum rather than as separate entities" (Mudry et al., 2014:31). For example, the Indian Ayurvedic system, Chinese dietetics and humoral theories of the Greco-Islamist tradition are based upon notions of maintaining or restoring balance, with foods and medicines classified according to their abilities to enact subtle shifts in the body's temperature and moisture levels. Each system also recognises that bodies vary in their intrinsic compositions and nutritional needs; thus, a patient's embodied knowledge is valued alongside practitioner expertise in determining how to eat therapeutically (Mudry et al., 2014). In many parts of the world, these nutrition traditions persist and influence both healthcare and culinary practices.

Superfood discourse seems to offer a "best of both worlds" solution in which various sources of traditional knowledge join with scientific knowledge as partners in a happy union. Like many marriages, however, tensions lie behind the rosy façade, and power imbalances plague the partnership. Through a case study of chia seed in Australia, this chapter explores the overlaps and tensions between nutritionism and nutritional primitivism in scientific research and superfoods media to reveal how these two seemingly competing discourses are co-constituted via a framework of extractionist logics applied at each stage of research, development and marketing. Ultimately, nutritional science retains its hegemonic position because tradition only comes to "matter" in superfoods discourse when it is verified by science. Consumers, thus, must still extract molecular knowledge to value chia as a foodstuff that promotes individual health.

This chapter draws upon a larger research project that adopted a case study methodology, "following" chia's gradual move into the commodity state that it currently inhabits, acquiring new meanings and values through scientific scrutiny, technological manipulation, media attention, marketing narratives and consumption practices (Appadurai, 1986). The methods used for this publication include observing physical objects and interrogating epistemic materials to understand how chia seed came to be positioned as a superfood (Rheinberger, 1997; Spackman, 2020). The physical objects were chia seed marketing materials, including packaging, advertisements and websites, collected by the researcher primarily in Australia from 2012 to 2016. The epistemic materials consist of an international body of media texts, scientific publications and regulatory policies that seek to "know" chia and/or the nutrients it contains.

Constructing and Marketing Chia Seeds

Chia seeds provide an ideal case study to examine the ways in which nutritionism interacts with nutritional primitivism in both the development and marketing of novel food products. Chia seed is native to Mesoamerica and was an Aztec staple grain, but was deliberately culturally and economically marginalised under Spanish colonial rule and its production and consumption were limited to remote rural communities along the Mexico–Guatemala border (Cahill, 2003). Over the past decade, chia has rapidly moved from relative obscurity to the health food limelight, following a trajectory both similar and different to those of other prominent superfoods. Like quinoa and açai, international development actors funded agronomic research into this potential "miracle crop" to bolster South American economies (Brondizio, 2020; McDonnell, 2020). However, unlike these examples, development projects never occurred in chia's place and culture of origin. Early commercial efforts to create more reliable supply chains were located even farther afield, in Australia, led by agribusinessman John Foss, founder of The Chia Co. (personal communication, 2014). The impetus behind these initiatives was chia seed's high content of omega-3 EFA, protein and fibre—three nutrients celebrated in contemporary nutritional discourse.

This chapter focuses on the latter factor, exploring how the nutrient-reductionist paradigm of nutritionism and the social environment in which nutritional science is practised and interpreted underpins both the scientific and popular valorisations of chia seed. However, it is not nutritional science alone that sells chia seeds; marketing materials emphasise "natural" and "traditional" qualities alongside scientifically substantiated health benefits. Thus, the knowledge framework of nutritionism intersects with nutritional primitivism as the two exist side by side on product packaging. While this discursive overlap is characteristic of superfoods media, it belongs to a broader patterned practice of use in historical marketing of foods such as cod liver oil (O'Hagan and Eriksson, 2022), Taroena (Hobart and Maroney, 2019) and the Swedish soft drink Pommac (O'Hagan, 2023).

Nutritional primitivism is a sub-branch of primitivism, a cultural pattern characterised by nostalgic longing for the lifestyles of pre-civilised peoples (Bell, 1972). Yet, rather than signify interest in understanding "primitive" cultures in their own right, this fascination serves as a mirror through which "modern" people might critically examine their own societies against the "primitive" foil (Torgovnick, 1990). While primitivism refers to a range of pre-industrial and ancient cultures, it makes little attempt to accurately portray these societies objectively; rather, it seizes on those aspects of primitive life that enable critical comparison with the present. Primitivism is, therefore, a reflective discourse, as the fetishising of the cultures of ancient or indigenous peoples speaks more about contemporary dissatisfaction with various aspects of modern life than about the nature and value of so-called primitive culture itself. The wide range of culinary cultures from which contemporary superfood products are drawn signifies the generalised nature of primitivism in this case.

Nutritional primitivism, a discursive phenomenon first observed by Christine Knight (2015) in relation to low-carbohydrate diets, applies the backward-looking sentiments of primitivism to ideas about food and health. Through valorisation of ancient, traditional or indigenous foodways, nutritional primitivism expresses dissatisfaction with contemporary food production practices and scientised ways of understanding nourishment. It would seem, therefore, that nutritional primitivism would be at odds with nutritionism. The former understands foods as healthy because of their natural, authentic and traditional qualities, while the latter defines healthy foods through their scientifically substantiated nutrient contents and effects on bodily functions. Yet, in the case of chia seed development and marketing, these seemingly competing discourses interact conversationally in influencing contemporary understandings of what makes food healthy. They are linked through a framework of extractionist logics.

Developed by Christy Spackman (2020) to explain the continuum between functional foods and superfoods, extractionist logics:

> refer to the way that nutritional reductionism activates the molecular imagination in researchers, policymakers, food producers, marketers, and eaters in a way that enacts a doubled extraction: first, the extraction of molecules from source ingredients/foods; and second, the transformation of eaters into micro-extractors of knowledge and value (energetic, health, social, cultural) from the food choices available to them.
>
> (58)

Spackman explores how scientific attention to antioxidants as anti-ageing molecules led to the development of the ORAC assay—a tool that enabled the quantitative comparison of disparate foods according to their antioxidant capacity and provided a shorthand for healthfulness embraced by political, industry and public actors. While a concept linking antioxidant activity to colour eventually replaced the ORAC assay, health communicators "continued to mobilize a molecular understanding of whole fruits and vegetables as carriers of health-promoting molecules" and consumers continued to "do the work of looking at something and extrapolating whether the food will contain biologically active molecules" (ibid:73).

In the case of chia seeds, extractionist logics underpin their positioning as carriers of functional nutrients, which relies on measuring and communicating the density of omega-3 EFA, protein and fibre in relation to other foods, as well as molecular understandings of how these dietary components work to promote bodily health. However, emphasis on naturalness and authenticity also pervade chia seed marketing, providing an indication of healthfulness that, while seeming to move away from reductive, molecular understandings of nutrition, nevertheless requires consumers to extrapolate the connection between these qualitative markers and the functional benefits within. Additionally, a further extraction underlies the superfood trajectory of chia seeds: the extraction of a foodstuff from its geographical and cultural context, from its place within broader dietary patterns of its historic consumers and from understandings of its culinary and medicinal values within indigenous nutrition epistemologies. Such extractions preclude traditional producers and consumers from both claiming authority about chia and benefitting economically from its increased demand, while also erasing its cultural identity among Global North consumers.

Researching Omega-3

Nutritionism and nutritional primitivism discourses interact via extractionist logics in discursively underpinning the development of chia seed as a health food. One of the major health claims regarding chia is that it contains large quantities of omega-3 EFAs. Indeed, omega-3 EFAs are the defining nutrients of chia seed and "the most celebrated macronutrients of the functional era" (Scrinis, 2013:168). But it is not given that omega-3 EFAs are desirable dietary components; rather, they had to be positioned as such by people with nutritional authority. Furthermore, the solution to the supposed dilemma of omega-3 deficiency via increased consumption of omega-3-rich foods is not obvious, as omega-3 competes in the body with omega-6 fatty acids found in many industrially processed foods. While it is nutritional science that has emphasised the role of omega-3 in the diet and the need for increasing its consumption, scientific interest in omega-3 stems from extractionist logic applied to nutritional anthropology research into the diets of Inuit people indigenous to Arctic regions.

In the 1970s and early 1980s, Danish medical researchers, driven by rumours of low rates of coronary heart disease among Greenland Eskimos, published epidemiologic studies attributing their heart health to diets high in whale, seal and fish fats (Harris et al., 2021). Instead of investigating holistic dietary patterns or indigenous nutritional epistemologies, these studies applied extractionist logics by emphasising the protective qualities of the omega-3 EFAs contained in animal fats (Bang and Dyerberg, 1972; Bang et al., 1976; Bang et al., 1980). Such extractionist logics fit within the particular vein of nutritional reductionism that characterised the era—that of "good-and-bad nutritionism"—in which nutrition science research focused on classifying nutrients (particularly types of fats) as beneficial or harmful and translating these findings into "eat more" and "eat less" public health messaging (Scrinis, 2013). They also demonstrate colonialist extractionist attitudes towards the knowledge systems of indigenous peoples as storehouses of raw information and materials to be exploited and developed by Western scientific knowledge systems.

Extracting omega-3 from its cultural milieu, researchers soon created knowledge about its importance not only for cardiac health but also for other bodily functions, including promoting brain and visual development, reducing inflammation-related diseases and protecting against some cancers (Dyerberg et al., 1978; Dusheck, 1985; Kromhout et al., 1985; Galli and Simopoulos, 1988; Lees and Karel, 1990; Nettleton, 1995; Simopoulos, 1998, 1999). Although there is scientific debate regarding the actual benefits of omega-3 consumption—in particular whether *increasing* consumption of omega-3 is preferable to *decreasing* consumption of the competing fatty acid omega-6, frequently found in processed oils and meats (Hooper et al., 2006; Danaei et al., 2009)—the publication of numerous studies reporting a range of benefits and the spread of this information via marketing and media led to both scientific and popular valorisation of omega-3 (Figure 11.1).

The ability of food manufacturers to make health benefit claims about omega-3 on product packaging solidified its positioning as an essential dietary component. In 2004, the United States Food and Drug Administration (2004) authorised a qualified health claim for foods containing omega-3 EFAs, linking consumption with reduced risk of heart disease. The European Union approach was more cautious, authorising only a "source of omega-3 fatty acids" claim in 2006, followed by two qualified health claims linking certain types of omega-3 EFAs with blood cholesterol and heart function maintenance in 2012 (Council of the European Union, 2006; European Commission, 2012). In 2013, Food Standards Australia New Zealand followed suit, authorising nutrient-content claims for omega-3 EFAs and a health claim connecting certain types of omega-3 EFAs and cardiac health. The media has latched onto the scientific, industry and government promotion of omega-3 EFAs, resulting in high consumer awareness of their health benefits and role in preventing heart disease (Worsley and Scott, 2000; Harel et al., 2001). One significant result of the omega-3 deficiency discourse, in combination with changes in health labelling regulation, has been to create a "strong demand and perceived

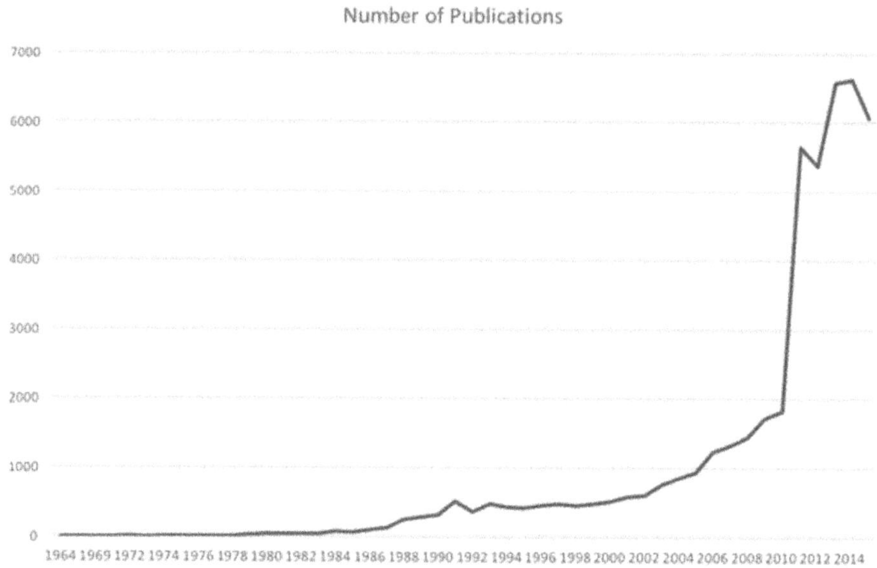

Figure 11.1 Articles with "Omega-3" in Title from Web of Science Database, 1964–2014
Credit: Author's own work

need for omega-3 fortified foods and nutritional supplements," which "has thereby been commodified and transformed into a range of convenient and accessible products" (Scrinis, 2013:170). This demand recalls that of vitamin D, which, following its identification, was commodified via cod liver oil, heavily marketed and transmitted to the public via media sources (O'Hagan and Eriksson, 2022); the main difference here is the codified government sanctioning of such marketing tactics.

As omega-3 has gained prominence in nutrition discourse, the traditional diets of Arctic peoples and the beliefs and knowledge that animate their food practices have been sidelined. Rather than consider broad dietary patterns situated within indigenous nutritional epistemology, scientists have instead undertaken molecular extraction, exposing omega-3 EFAs to increasing scrutiny, identifying various sub-types and exploring their isolated effects on human and non-human bodies. Likewise, chia seed's trajectory towards superfood stardom follows this pattern of scientific appropriation and eventual overshadowing of indigenous knowledge.

Researching Chia Seeds

Western science first took an interest in chia seeds in the mid-twentieth century within the domain of oil chemistry. As industrial development boomed in Mexico, studies focused on the commercial potential of chia production for use as an industrial oil (Baughman and Jamieson, 1929; Palma et al., 1947; Earle et al.,

1960; Earle and Jones, 1962; Hagemann et al., 1967). Scientists identified chia oil's superior drying properties, making it suitable for use in paint. The production of chia seed for the use of its oil in paint is one of the only traditional practices related to chia that did not decline after Spanish colonisation (Ayerza Jr and Coates, 2005). While scientists may have been inspired by this traditional use, the subjection of chia oil to chemical scrutiny was necessary to verify its usefulness within scientific epistemology and thereby encourage government and industry actors to consider the plant's potential.

Having begun outlining chia's chemical properties as an industrial oil, the field of chemistry retained a mild interest in chia into the second half of the twentieth century. Subsequently, several scholars began to investigate chia seed's nutritional properties as a human and animal food (Bushway et al., 1981; Ariffin, 1984; Bushway et al., 1984; Taga et al., 1984; Weber et al., 1991). Inspiration for nutritional studies came from the literature identifying properties of the oil, as well as a trend towards research on plant oil seeds driven by the "good and bad fats" paradigm of the era (Bushway et al., 1981), but not from observation of traditional food uses of chia, which are mentioned only in passing. It is unlikely that these authors had contact with traditional consumers, not only because of their small numbers and remote location but also because of the researchers' demonstrable indifference to non-scientific knowledge. These studies outlined the vitamin and mineral contents of chia seed and measured the seed's favourable fatty acid composition and protein content. They also explored how the oil and seed performed under different conditions as they evaluated their suitability for industrial food production.

A study by Weber et al. (1991) was the first to consider the possibilities of chia seed as a whole food, comparing its nutrient composition to other cereal grains and evaluating it against the World Health Organization's amino acid requirements. Reflecting a popular development narrative in which "underutilised" species are positioned as miracle crops (McDonnell, 2020), they observed:

> The chia seed has more than one and one-half to twice the protein concentration of other grains and approximately three to ten times the oil concentration of most grains. Its high protein and oil concentration makes it a very attractive grain source for developing countries which have a shortage of protein and energy.
>
> (Weber et al., 1991:125)

Thus, scientists began to consider chia seed as a valuable food source only when it was extracted from indigenous foodways and understood within the knowledge framework of nutritional chemistry. When traditional use was mentioned at all in these papers, it was as a sentence or two in the paper's introduction, where it functioned as a prelude to authoritative scientific epistemology demonstrated by pages of measurements and charts.

Agronomic research into chia seed's cropping potential blossomed in the 1990s and 2000s in response to increased scientific recognition of its nutritional properties. As part of the Northwest Argentina Project, University of Arizona agronomists Wayne Coates and Ricardo Ayerza Jr collaborated with American and Argentinian governments, universities and NGO partners to develop chia as a commercial crop. This project initially sought indigenous perspectives by conducting fieldwork among chia growers in the Jalisco region of Mexico—the only region in the world conducting commercial chia production at the time, albeit on a very small scale. However, this fieldwork did not seek to understand chia's place in Mayan knowledge frameworks; rather, the goal was to document, extract, transport and improve upon chia agronomy in other locations. These practices fit within a sustainable development paradigm popular since the 1980s in which scientific, industry and NGO actors have framed nature and biodiversity (largely in the Global South) "as a storehouse of valuable genetic resources" (Hayden, 2003:49) whose value can best be extracted by "mobiliz[ing] market economies to promote environmental conservation and economic development" (Spackman, 2020:61). This paradigm relies upon extractionist logics in two ways: first, by valorising the extraction of plants from their geographical and cultural contexts via the assumed superiority of Global North political economy and Western science, and second, by viewing nature as a source of untapped molecules with medicinal or nutritional potential that require technological scrutiny to unlock their value. These extractionist logics underpinned the further agronomic and nutritional research and development that laid the foundations for increased global supply and awareness of chia seed, which was taken up by industry actors in the early 2000s.

Marketing Chia Seeds

In chia seed marketing, discourses of nutritionism and nutritional primitivism further interact in positioning chia as a health food. A case study of the "chia pod," the signature product of Australian company The Chia Co.—the world's largest producer of branded chia (Dunn, 2015)—illustrates this discursive symbiosis. The chia pod is a ready-to-eat snack made with chia seed, coconut milk and fruit, which sits on dairy shelves of health and mainstream food retailers alongside single-serve yoghurts (Figure 11.2). The "pod" is a squat semi-circle of transparent plastic with a flat bottom, suggesting playfulness through its curves and convenience through its bowl-like shape (Ledin and Machin, 2018). It bears a bold orange logo—a colour associated with fruity flavours and used in branding to suggest simplicity and positivity; additional text in white associates the food with purity and softness (Ledin and Machin, 2018). The snack inside is, indeed, soft, with a creamy but lumpy texture reminiscent of tapioca, while the taste is mildly sweet, with flavour variations such as mango, blueberry, banana, chocolate, coconut and vanilla bean. Nutrient contents of omega-3, fibre and protein feature prominently and are constantly emphasised on product packaging and in marketing material. Alongside the pod's logo, the words "Fiber," "Omega 3," and "Protein" descend in distinctive white text, while the smaller print on the side states "Per 170g Chia Pod: 3g of

Figure 11.2 Chia Pods on Australian Supermarket Shelf

Credit: Photo taken by author, 2016

Omega 3, 5g of Fiber (20% DV)" (for the vanilla bean pod).[2] This is the core functional message: chia is high in these particular nutrients, suggesting that these contents make chia a healthy food.

To advance this message, the Chia Co. has worked with health professionals, including cardiac coaches, dietician groups, naturopaths and doctors, as well as employing an in-house dietician to whom consumers can pose questions via the company's website (personal communication with Chia Co. founder John Foss, 2014). The company has also associated its products with performance athletes by sponsoring sporting events, such as the US Open tennis tournament, the New York, Sydney and Melbourne Marathons and multiple surf events, and by partnering with celebrity athletes, such as champion surfer Kelly Slater and tennis player Joanna Konta as brand ambassadors (Korporaal, 2014; PA Sport, 2016). Engaging sport celebrities to promote health foods is a tried-and-true strategy with roots in the early twentieth-century marketing of protein-enhanced foods like Plasmon (Heffernan, 2020; O'Hagan, 2022a, Chapter 1 in this volume). Here, marketers have positioned chia as a healthy food not only because it contains high concentrations of celebrated nutrients but also because consuming it promises to enhance athletic performance. These communication and marketing strategies simultaneously construct credibility around chia as a "healthy lifestyle" food and play upon the needs of what Scrinis (2013) terms the "functional body."

Single nutrient research among scientists and dissemination about health benefits via media and marketing has a long historical trajectory, particularly evident in the vitamin craze of the early twentieth century (Apple, 1996). This pattern has accelerated since the mid-1990s as nutrition research, dietary advice and popular discourse have increasingly emphasised not only the nutrient composition of foods but also the role of "functional" nutrients on particular bodily functions and health outcomes as measured by biomarkers. Foods are represented as vehicles for nutrients—both naturally occurring and added through fortification—and nutrients are represented as a means of optimising both general health and specific bodily processes. In this era of functional nutritionism, the body, too, is represented and experienced as functional.

It is not just nutrition scientists whose attention has focused on the way in which molecules within foods impact bodily health, but the lay public as well, leading to increased individual focus on how foods and nutrients function within one's body. The individuals who inhabit these functional bodies are "nutricentric persons" and they "directly experience this functional body, in the sense that they identify with and internalize a functional approach to nutrients, foods, and bodily functions" (Scrinis, 2013:165). Building on a public nutritional consciousness nurtured with calorie-counting advice and vitamin advertising, both public health and commercial marketing campaigns have increasingly directed the popular gaze inward, using imagery such as the artery clogged with cholesterol or the gut full of competing "good" and "bad" microorganisms (Lupton, 1996). While this onslaught of scientific information may lead to confusion among some people, others feel empowered to engage with these concepts in shaping their diets not only to be generally "healthy," but also to optimise their bodies' functional performance by manipulating the nutrient profiles of their diets (Scrinis, 2008). Nutricentric consumers are invited to participate in extractionist logics, extrapolating how molecules in their foods function in their bodies to produce health.

The association between chia and athletic performance is linked to the book *Born to Run* (McDougall, 2009). A cult favourite among runners, it tells the story of the Tarahumara, a native Mexican people who run long distances rapidly and barefoot. They are reported to eat native chia seeds for energy during long-distance running. This association gives chia seed a primitive mystique, similar to associations with native Hawaiian bodies in early twentieth-century taro marketing (Hobart and Maroney, 2019). There is also a tribal element to the association with performance athletes, which is evident in the way chia is marketed in connection with surf culture. A television commercial aired in Australia features surf champion Kelly Slater slinging chia pods to blonde-haired, blue-eyed surfer babes at a pop-up beach bar bearing the sign "Kelly's Chia Shop." The campaign marks chia as a product linked with a healthy, wholesome, playful and laid-back lifestyle, while gaining chia some of the exotic neo-tribal mystique surrounding surf culture (Canniford and Karababa, 2013). There are parallels here to associations between cross-fit and low-carb or Paleo diets, which often draw on similar tribal tropes (Pekkanen et al., 2017; Gressier, 2018; Weedon and Patchin, 2022).

Another element of nutritional primitivism obvious in chia seed marketing is the focus on chia's "natural" qualities and the idea that the product is not "messed with" (personal communication with Foss, 2014). The transparent chia pod packaging suggests transparency of food processing and highlights the simplicity of the product's ingredients; as Ledin and Machin (2018:89) observe, "transparent plastic material [...] unmasks the content, allowing it to speak for itself." Each pod promotes its three ingredients in bold orange text beneath the large logo; for instance, the blueberry chia pod bears text proclaiming "Blueberry," "Coconut Milk" and "Chia." To the right of the logo, capitalised text emphasises the product's contents of "Nothing but sun ripened chia seed, coconut milk, and real blueberry," and below, "Cold Processed" and "Vegan." Echoing a long history of notions of purity in food marketing (O'Hagan, 2020), the words "nothing but," "sun ripened" and "real" emphasise the key message of chia's naturalness and transparency. Similar to Pommac marketing, allusions to sunshine further suggest associations with health and wholesomeness, while also communicating romanticised notions of traditional food production and minimal processing (O'Hagan, 2023). A chia pod print advertisement proclaims that the product contains no added sugar, further emphasising its health credentials by tapping into the vilification of sugar in contemporary nutrition discourse. In this "free from" vein distinctive to the "clean eating" nutrition trend, the pods also carry "gluten free" and "non GMO" certification logos that lend more weight to naturalness claims (Chrzan and Cargill, 2022).

Visual and textual communication on the company's website[3] deepens the message of naturalness and authenticity. Clicking on "Our Story" on the website's top navigation bar takes the reader to a page featuring stunning images of chia production in the Australian outback. One photo depicts Foss, dressed in the quintessential Aussie farmer outfit of khaki shirt and leather hat, standing amidst a field of green leaves and purple blooms, while another features neat rows of young chia stretching to a horizon marked by the distinctive red rock formations of the Kimberley region of Western Australia. The text about the company's "Sustainable Farming" describes the region as "pristine" and "the perfect environment," while expanding on how their "fully transparent supply chain" is "like a farmers [sic] market on a global scale." These images harness romantic ideals of the Australian outback as a place both of wild nature and of white settler utilisation and dominance of Australia's vast "wasted" spaces that belies an invisible extraction: that of indigenous people, flora and fauna who failed to mobilised extractionist logics (Lane, 2003). They also play on idyllic conceptions of farming as a natural partnership between man, land and plant, while ignoring the mechanised nature of contemporary farming and food processing by omitting images of machinery, processing plants and other technological devices and practices. Similarly misleading pastoral representations are found in other types of superfood marketing, such as cranberry (Loyer, 2017) and maca (Loyer, 2016), as well as historic marketing of health food products such as Biomin (O'Hagan, 2022b) and cod liver oil (O'Hagan and Eriksson, 2022).

While the Chia Co. never makes outright claims that chia is "the Aztec superfood," associations between chia and the Aztecs are firmly embedded throughout superfood marketing and media (e.g. *The Iron You*, 2011; Arnot, 2013; *The Hormone Zone*, 2022). Additionally, the association with ancient cultures is already in the public mind because the broader concept of superfoods was well, if ambiguously, entrenched in contemporary food and health discourse by the time chia seed hit the market, and consumers knew what to expect from the marketing of trailblazing superfood products like quinoa and goji berries (McDonnell and Wilk, 2020).

Conclusion: Maintaining Nutritional Hegemony

By examining the interaction of nutritionism and nutritional primitivism in chia seed's development and marketing, we see how these seemingly competing food-health discourses are co-constituted via extractionist logics. Extractionist logics justified the development of chia as a commercial crop beyond its historical area of cultivation and positioned it as healthy on the merits of its molecular contents. But chia is also valued because its omega-3 occurs in a "natural" and "authentic" food product. Like cod liver oil before it, chia marketing blurs the lines between different nutrition knowledge frameworks, making claims for healthfulness because of both its nutrient contents and its naturalness, authenticity and pristine origins. Associations with Aztec peoples, distance running, high-level athletic events and surf culture combine the ideals of the functional body primed for athletic performance through the consumption of the "right" nutrients with notions of "primitive" bodies fuelled by the ancient wisdom and "clean" nutrition elusive amidst the highly technological world of modern food production.

The interweaving of nutritionism and nutritional primitivism in both the development and marketing of chia seed raises the question of whether the emphasis on traditional knowledge in superfoods discourse represents a move away from the dominance of the nutrient-reductionist view of nutrition. According to the extractionist logic of the nutritionism paradigm, a food's healthfulness is measured by the nutrients it contains, and these nutrients can come in any form. Fish, flax seed, chia seed and omega-3 fortified eggs are, therefore, viewed similarly because of the fatty acids they contain, with little consideration for differences in the form of delivery or production history. Chia's success modestly challenges this reductionism, as its representation relies on communicating not only its nutrient contents but also its natural and authentic qualities. The emphasis on the simplicity of ingredients and the supposed transparency of production practices on chia pod packaging suggests a shift towards ingredient quality as a marker of healthfulness. However, the prominence of "fibre," "omega-3" and "protein" content claims indicate that, without the authority of nutritional science, The Chia Co. would struggle to peddle pods; the consumer is still required to activate her molecular imagination to know and value chia.

Furthermore, this chapter has illustrated how extractionist logics applied to Arctic foodways underpinned nutritional research into the importance of omega-3 EFAs in human diets; yet, the complexity of indigenous dietary patterns, beliefs and knowledge were ignored. Likewise, chia seeds were "rediscovered" by researchers who removed them from places where indigenous growers had continuously cultivated them, despite colonial violence, and created new knowledge and value within scientific knowledge frameworks with little regard for traditional ways of knowing their healthfulness. Both omega-3 EFAs and chia seeds were isolated from their indigenous culinary contexts and nutritional epistemologies, replicating a colonialist ideology that views Global South foods and knowledge as resources to be developed for Global North markets. This ideology enables biomedicine to co-opt traditional knowledge towards the end of optimising the individual healthy body. This focus on individual bodies is shared by both of the nutritional knowledge frameworks explored here. As Aya H. Kimura observes, "both [biomedicine and the alternative] create subjectivities in which coping with disease and disease potentials become conflated with efforts at self-improvement" (cited in Mudry et al., 2014:33). Nutritionism and nutritional primitivism are united by extractionist logics all the way down: logics that conceptually extract humans from nature, the rational mind from the physical body and the individual from the social body.

Notes

1 All these claims are found on chia seed products available in Australia.
2 This nutrient declaration is separate from the mandatory nutrition facts panel, as omega-3 and fibre are not nutrients that are mandated to be reported in Australia.
3 The Chia Co. website can be accessed at the following link: https://thechiaco.com/au/

References

Appadurai, A. ed. 1986. *The Social Life of Things: Commodities in Cultural Perspective*. Cambridge: Cambridge University Press.
Apple, R. 1996. *Vitamania: Vitamins in American Culture*. New Brunswick: Rutgers University Press.
Ariffin, R. B. 1984. *Proximate Analysis of Sonoran Desert Food Plants*. Unpublished MSc Dissertation, University of Arizona.
Arnot, B. 2013. *The Aztec Diet: Chia Power: The Superfood That Gets You Skinny and Keeps You Healthy*. New York: William Morrow.
Ayerza Jr., R. and Coates, W. 2005. *Chia: Rediscovering a Forgotten Crop of the Aztecs*. Tucson: University of Arizona Press.
Bang, H.O. and Dyerberg, J. 1972. Plasma Lipids and Lipoproteins in Greenland West Coast Eskimos. *Acta Medica Scandinavica* 192:82–94.
Bang, H.O., Dyerberg, J. and Hjorne, N.A. 1976. The Composition of Food Consumed by Greenland Eskimos. *Acta Medica Scandinavica* 200:69–73.
Bang, H.O., Dyerberg, J. and Sinclair, H.M. 1980. The Composition of the Eskimo Food in Northwestern Greenland. *American Journal of Clinical Nutrition* 33:2657–2661.

Baughman, W.F. and Jamieson, G.S. 1929. Chia Seed Oil, Oil and Fat Industries. *Journal of the American Oil Chemists' Society* 6(9):15–17.
Bell, M. 1972. *Primitivism*. London: Methuen.
Brondizio, E.S. 2020. "The Global Açaí: A Chronicle of Possibilities and Predicaments of an Amazonian Superfood" in *Critical Approaches to Superfoods*, edited by E. McDonnell and R. Wilk (London: Bloomsbury), pp. 149–168.
Bushway, A.A., Belya, P.R. and Bushway, R.J. 1981. Chia Seed as a Source of Oil, Polysaccharide, and Protein. *Journal of Food Science* 46:1349–1356.
Bushway, A.A., Wilson, A.M., Houston, L. and Bushway, R.J. 1984. Selected Properties of the Lipid and Protein Fractions from Chia Seed. *Journal of Food Science* 49:555–557.
Cahill, J.P. 2003. Ethnobotany of Chia, Salvia Hispanica L. (Lamiaceae). *Economic Botany* 57(4):604–618.
Canniford, R. and Karababa, E. 2013. Partly Primitive: Discursive Constructions of the Domestic Surfer. *Consumption Markets & Culture* 16(2):119–144.
Chen, N. 2009. *Food, Medicine, and the Quest for Good Health*. New York: Columbia University Press.
"Chia Seeds, the Aztec Superfood." 2011. *The Iron You* (5 June). Available at https://www.theironyou.com/2011/06/chia-seeds-aztec-superfood.html [Accessed: 1 March 2023].
"Chia: The Rediscovered Aztec Superfood." 2022. *The Hormone Zone*. Available at https://hormone-zone.com/chia-the-rediscovered-aztec-superfood/ [Accessed: 1 March 2023].
Chrzan, J. and Cargill, K. 2022. *Anxious Eaters: Why We Fall for Fad Diets*. New York: Columbia University Press.
Council of the European Union 2006. *Regulation (EC) No 1924/2006 of the European Parliament and of the Council*. Available at https://eur-lex.europa.eu/LexUriServ/LexUriServ.do?uri=OJ:L:2006:404:0009:0025:En:PDF [Accessed: 22 January 2024].
Danaei, G., Ding, E.L., Mozaffarian, D., Taylor, B., Rehm, J., Murray, C.J.L. and Ezzati, M. 2009. The Preventable Causes of Death in the United States: Comparative Risk Assessment of Dietary, Lifestyle, and Metabolic Risk Factors. *PLoS Medicine* 6(4):1–23.
Dunn, C. 2015. Is Chia the Next Quinoa?, *Sydney Morning Herald* (25 May). Available at https://www.smh.com.au/business/small-business/is-chia-the-next-quinoa-20150514-gh1mb2.html [Accessed: 21 December 2022].
Dusheck, J. 1985. Fish, Fatty Acids and Physiology. *Science News* 128(16):252–254.
Dyerberg, J., Bang, H.O., Stoffersen, E., Moncada, S. and Vane, J.R. 1978. Eicosapentaenoic Acid and Prevention of Thrombosis and Atherosclerosis. *Lancet* 2:117–121.
Earle, F.R., Glass, C.A., Geisinger, G.C., Wolff, I.A. and Jones, Q. 1960. Search for New Industrial Oils IV. *Journal of the American Oil Chemists' Society* 37(9):440–447.
Earle, F.R. and Jones, Q. 1962. Analyses of Seed Samples from 113 Plant Families. *Economic Botany* 16(4):221–250.
European Commission 2012. *Commission Regulation (EU) No 432/2012*. Available at https://eur-lex.europa.eu/LexUriServ/LexUriServ.do?uri=OJ:L:2012:136:0001:0040:en:PDF [Accessed: 22 January 2024].
Food Standards Australian New Zealand. 2013. *Australia New Zealand Food Standards Code – Standard 1.2.7 – Nutrition, Health and Related Claims*. Available at https://www.legislation.gov.au/F2013L00054/latest/text [Accessed: 22 January 2024].
Galli, C. and Simopoulos, A.P. eds. 1988. *Dietary Omega-3 and Omega-6 Fatty Acids*. New York: Plenum Press and NATO Scientific Affairs Division.
Gressier, C. 2018. *Illness, Identity, and Taboo Among Australian Paleo Dieters*. Cham: Palgrave Macmillan.
Hagemann, J., Earle, F.R., Wolff, I.A. and Barclay, A.S. 1967. Search for New Industrial Oils. XIV. Seed Oils of Labiatae. *Lipids* 2(5):371–380.

Harel, Z., Riggs, S., Vaz, R., White, L. and Menzies, G. 2001. Omega-3 Polyunsaturated Fatty Acids in Adolescents: Knowledge and Consumption. *Journal of Adolescent Health* 28(1):10–15.
Harris, W.S., Calder, P.C., Mozaffarian, D. and Serhan, C.N. 2021. Bang and Dyerberg's Omega-3 Discovery Turns Fifty. *Nature Food* 2:303–305.
Hayden, C. 2003. *When Nature Goes Public: The Making and Unmaking of Bioprospecting in Mexico*. Princeton: Princeton University Press.
Hayes-Conroy, A. and Hayes-Conroy, J. 2013. "Introduction" in *Doing Nutrition Differently: Critical Approaches to Diet and Dietary Intervention*, edited by A. Hayes-Conroy and J. Hayes-Conroy (Farnham: Ashgate), pp. 1–20.
Heffernan, C. 2020. Superfood or Superficial? Plasmon and the Birth of the Supplement Industry. *Journal of Sport History* 47(3):243–262.
Hobart, H.J. and Maroney, S. 2019. On Racial Constitutions and Digestive Therapeutics. *Food, Culture & Society* 22(5):576–594.
Hooper, L., Thompson, R.L., Harrison, R.A., Summerbell, C.D., Ness, A.R., Moore, H.J., Worthington, H.V., Durrington, P.N., Higgins, J.P.T., Capps, N.E., Riemersma, R.A., Ebrahim, S.B.J. and Smith, G.D. 2006. Risks and Benefits of Omega-3 Fats for Mortality, Cardiovascular Disease, and Cancer: Systematic Review. *British Medical Journal* 332(7544):752–755.
Knight, C. 2015. "We Can't Go Back a Hundred Million Years": Low-Carbohydrate Dieters' Responses to Nutritional Primitivism. *Food, Culture & Society* 18(3):441–461.
Korporaal, G. 2014. How Kelly Slater Helped John Foss Sow the Seeds of Chia Success, *The Australian* (19 September), Available at http://www.theaustralian.com.au/business/the-deal-magazine/how-kelly-slater-helped-john-foss-sow-the-seeds-of-chia-success/story-e6frgabx-1227060507238 [Accessed: 17 June 2015].
Kromhout, D., Bosschieter, E.B. and de Lezenne Coulander, C. 1985. The Inverse Relation Between Fish Consumption and 20-year Mortality from Coronary Heart Disease. *New England Journal of Medicine* 312:1205–1209.
Lane, R. 2003. "History, Mobility and Land-Use Interests of Aborigines and Farmers in the East Kimberley in North-West Australia" in *Landscape, Memory and History: Anthropological Perspectives*, edited by P.J. Stewart and A. Strathern (London: Pluton Press), pp. 136–165.
Ledin, P. and Machin, D. 2018. *Doing Visual Analysis: From Theory to Practice*. London: Sage.
Lees, R.S. and Karel, M. eds. 1990. *Omega-3 Fatty Acids in Health and Disease*. New York: Marcel Dekker.
Loyer, J. 2016. "Communicating Superfoods: A Case Study of Maca Packaging" in *Proceedings of the Oxford Symposium on Food and Cookery 2015*. Oxford, United Kingdom.
Loyer, J. 2017. The Cranberry as Food, Health Food, and Superfood: Challenging or Maintaining Hegemonic Nutrition? *Graduate Journal of Food Studies* 4(2), https://gradfoodstudies.pubpub.org/pub/4-2-the-cranberry-as-food-health-food-and-superfood/release/1
Loyer, J. and Knight, C. 2018. Selling the "Inca Superfood": Nutritional Primitivism in Superfoods Books and Maca Marketing. *Food, Culture & Society* 21(4):449–467.
Lupton, D. 1996. *Food, the Body and the Self*. London: SAGE.
McDonnell, E. 2020. "The Miracle Crop as Boundary Object: Quinoa's Rise as a Neglected and Under-Utilized Species" in *Critical Approaches to Superfoods*, edited by E. McDonnell and R. Wilk (London: Bloomsbury), pp. 95–117.
McDonnell, E. and Wilk, R. 2020. "Tracking Superfoods: An Introduction" in *Critical Approaches to Superfoods*, edited by E. McDonnell and R. Wilk (London: Bloomsbury), pp. 1–16.
McDougall, C. 2009. *Born to Run: A Hidden Tribe, Superathletes, and the Greatest Race the World Has Never Seen*. New York: Alfred A. Knopf.

Mudry, J., Hayes-Conroy, J., Chen, N. and Kimura, A.H. 2014. Other Ways of Knowing Food. *Gastronomica* 14(3):27–33.
Nettleton, J.A. 1995. *Omega-3 Fatty Acids and Health*. New York: Chapman & Hill.
O'Hagan, L.A. 2020. Pure in Body, Pure in Mind? A Sociohistorical Perspective on the Marketisation of Pure Foods in Great Britain. *Discourse, Context & Media* 34, https://doi.org/10.1016/j.dcm.2019.100325
O'Hagan, L.A. 2022a. Flesh-Formers or Fads? Historicizing the Contemporary Protein-Enhanced Food Trend. *Food, Culture & Society* 25(5):875–898.
O'Hagan, L.A. 2022b. Scam Science: The Case of Biomin, "Your Daily Energy Source". *Graduate Journal of Food Studies* 9, Available at https://gradfoodstudies.org/2022/10/24/scam-science-the-case-of-biomin/
O'Hagan, L.A. 2023. Selling Swedish Summer: The Marketing of Pommac, 1920–1960. *History of Retailing and Consumption* 8(2):171–199.
O'Hagan, L.A. and Eriksson, G. 2022. Modern Science, Moral Mothers, and Mythical Nature: A Multimodal Analysis of Cod Liver Oil Marketing in Sweden, 1920–1930. *Food and Foodways* 30(4):231–260.
PA Sport. 2016. Johanna Konta Reveals Culinary Secrets to Australian Open Success, *ESPN* (23 January), Available at https://www.espn.co.uk/tennis/story/_/id/14630271/johanna-konta-reveals-food-secrets-helped-reach-australian-open-last-16 [Accessed: 21 December 2022].
Palma, F., Donde, M. and Lloyd, W.R. 1947. Fixed Oils of Mexico: I. Oil of Chia - Salvia Hispanica. *Journal of the American Oil Chemists' Society* 24:27–28.
Pekkanen, A., Närvänen, E. and Tuominen, P. 2017. Elements of Rituality in Consumer Tribes: The Case of Crossfit. *Journal of Customer Behaviour* 16(4):353–370.
Rheinberger, H.J. 1997. *Toward a History of Epistemic Things: Synthesizing Proteins in the Test Tube*. Stanford: Stanford University Press.
Santich, B. 2005. Paradigm Shifts in the History of Dietary Advice in Australia. *Nutrition & Dietetics* 62(4):152–157.
Scrinis, G. 2008. On the Ideology of Nutritionism. *Gastronomica* 8(1):37–48.
Scrinis, G. 2013. *Nutritionism: The Science and Politics of Dietary Advice*. New York: Columbia University Press.
Simopoulos, A.P. 1998. *The Return of Omega-3 Fatty Acids in the Food Supply*. Basel: Karger AG.
Simopoulos, A.P. 1999. Essential Fatty Acids in Health and Chronic Disease. *American Journal of Clinical Nutrition* 70(3): 560s–569s.
Spackman, C. 2020. "Extractionist Logics: The Missing Link Between Functional Foods and Superfoods" in *Critical Approaches to Superfoods*, edited by E. McDonell and R. Wilk (London: Bloomsbury), pp. 57–76.
Taga, M.S., Miller, E.E. and Pratt, D.E. 1984. Chia Seeds as a Source of Natural Lipid Antioxidants. *Journal of the American Oil Chemists' Society* 61:928–931.
Torgovnick, M. 1990. *Gone Primitive: Savage Intellects, Modern Lives*. Chicago: University of Chicago Press.
United States Food and Drug Administration. 2004. FDA Announces Qualified Health Claims for Omega-3 Fatty Acids. Available at https://www.fda.gov/SiteIndex/ucm108351.htm [Accessed: 22 January 2024].
Weber, C.W., Gentry, H.S., Kohlhepp, E.A. and McCrohan, P.R. 1991. The Nutritional and Chemical Evaluation of Chia Seeds. *Ecology of Food and Nutrition* 26(2):119–125.
Weedon, G. and Patchin, P.M. 2022. The Paleolithic Imagination: Nature, Science, and Race in Anthropocene Fitness Cultures. *Environment and Planning E: Nature and Space* 5(2):719–739.
Worsley, A. and Scott, V. 2000. Consumers' Concerns About Food and Health in Australia and New Zealand. *Asia Pacific Journal of Clinical Nutrition* 9(1):24–32.

Part 4

Food and Emerging Technologies

12 "The Triumph of the New Over the Old"

Electric Restaurants, Health and Modernity

Lucy Jane Santos

Introduction

This chapter explores the emergence of "electric restaurants"—dining establishments that relied on electricity as their primary energy source for cooking, heating and lighting. This transformation took place in early twentieth-century Britain at a time when restaurants were experiencing a surge in popularity and diversity, catering to a wide range of tastes and budgets. Scholars, such as Walkowitz (2012) and McWilliam (2020), have traced the trends and changes that transformed eating out in Britain during this period. They highlight three key contributory factors: the birth of the middle class, the growth of the urban population and the changes in social attitudes towards dining out. The developing importance and ubiquity of restaurants can be clearly seen in historical London trade directories. While in 1840, *Kelly's* listed 106 restaurants in the capital, this number had increased to nearly 2000 by 1910, with 400 in the West End alone (Assael, 2018:37).

Such culinary changes had begun in the late nineteenth century when a new wave of French-style restaurants emerged, targeted at an affluent clientele. Although the exquisite food was a major draw, patrons were also enticed by the luxurious ambience and entertainment offered. Simultaneously, other types of eateries gained popularity, including refreshment rooms in department stores, tea rooms and the "commercial restaurant," which provided affordable, standardised meals in a clean and modern setting. These restaurants were often part of large chains, such as J. Lyons & Co., and offered a variety of dishes, such as the traditional staples of roast meats, as well as a growing number of international cuisines, including foods from India and Italy.

There were also establishments that catered for specific dietary requirements, such as vegetarianism, and ones that sought to enhance public health and nutrition through education and modelling of the basic principles of their movements. The latter is perhaps best typified by Eustace Miles' Food Reform restaurant in Charing Cross Road, which served vegetarian food and offered programmes in mental, physical and spiritual health, and the Vitamin Café in Oxford Circus, which proudly proclaimed that it served the "Best Salads in London."

DOI: 10.4324/9781003450276-18

These styles of eateries and their links to the broader dietary reform movement, which advocated proper eating habits through better nutrition, natural unprocessed foods and economy in food expenses, have been described by researchers such as Stuart (2006), Buckley (2009) and Zweiniger-Bargielowska (2010). However, despite the wealth of research into restaurants and healthy eating, scant attention has, thus far, been paid to their role in demonstrating and subsequently normalising advancements in technology that changed not only the restaurant space but also had significant outcomes for improving wider public health.

This chapter addresses this gap in the literature by exploring specifically the creation of "electric restaurants" and how they were used to demonstrate new principles in healthy living, particularly by introducing and popularising electric cooking in the home. The scope of this research required an interdisciplinary approach to the study of electrical consumables and the emergence of electricity in the domestic and leisure spheres. As such, the resources consulted were diverse and comprehensive, including government industry publications, consumer magazines, diaries, autobiographies and memorabilia. The author also drew from their personal collection, adding valuable insights through the ephemera that is so often lost. Key publications included the trade periodical *Electrician* and *Electrical Review*, which is available at the British Library, as well as the archives of The Brompton & Kensington Electricity Supply Company, which are housed in the London Metropolitan Archives. The company records of Tricity and the British Electric Transformer Company (their parent corporation) are housed at the National Archives, Kew.

All of these resources were used to build up a picture of the styles of electric restaurants, the companies that opened them and the marketing approaches that were used. Through a comprehensive examination, this chapter not only gives insight into the changing lifestyles of the period but also the transformation of ideas surrounding health and well-being within the home that continues to this day.

Popularising Electricity

The journey to understanding and harnessing electricity spans centuries and involves numerous scientists and inventors. Humans may have long been aware of electrical phenomena, but it was not until the nineteenth century that electricity brought about a transformative revolution in various aspects of daily life. It found practical applications in telegraphy, lighting, industry and medicine, which improved communication and enhanced productivity, while the electrification of trains and urban transport networks revolutionised transportation, making travel faster and more efficient. Thomas Edison is often credited with the commercialisation of electricity through his work on the electric light bulb and the establishment of the first electrical distribution system. This led to the widespread adoption of electricity for public lighting and mass entertainment venues, offering new forms of entertainment and leisure to the public.

During this rapid advancement in electrical engineering and technology, the public had mixed reactions towards the introduction of electricity as a power source. While some saw it as a remarkable new technology that could transform their lives, others were fearful of potential dangers. Many people believed that electricity was too powerful and unpredictable, and that it could cause serious harm to both individuals and society. Some even feared that electric lights could cause blindness or insanity, while others worried that electric currents could disrupt the natural balance of the body and lead to illness or death (Simon, 2004). The fear of electricity was also fuelled by several high-profile accidents and incidents involving electric shocks, fires and electrocution. The invention of the electric chair for use in capital punishment also contributed to public anxieties about the technology (ibid).

Throughout history, fears about new technologies have been a recurring phenomenon, whether it is the anxiety surrounding new machinery, transport or medicine. The introduction of trains, for example—though relatively slow compared to modern standards—was seen as a fast and noisy innovation, causing widespread anxiety. Mid-Victorian writers like Charles Dickens highlighted their hideous speed and noise, and others raised concerns about potential brain injuries caused by the jarring motion of the train, as well as "railway maniacs" threatening the safety of other passengers. Similarly, medical advancements could be met with distrust or, in the case of the clearly useful technology of X-rays, with uncertainty; in a tale recounted by Alan Archibald Campbell Swinton (a Scottish electrical engineer), when Edward VII—the then Prince of Wales—was shown an X-ray photograph that Campbell Swinton had taken of his own hand, he had simply responded, "How disgusting" (Santos, 2020:19).

Despite these fears, however, electricity continued to gain popularity and acceptance in everyday life. As electrical technology advanced, an array of innovative electrical products entered the market, further changing the way people lived and interacted with their environment. While the technology was available, the most pressing issue was to educate and familiarise the consumer to encourage its adoption into their homes, particularly for cooking and heating, which did not seem to offer as many immediately understandable practical benefits as its use in lighting. This marketing and public awareness challenge was addressed in a number of ways by the different stakeholders who had an interest in changing the perception of electricity and its use.

One such way was through popular discourse. This was spearheaded by campaigns in the "Electrical Press." On 5 January 1911, the *Electrical Times* published:

> the first part of what we believe to be a valuable and instructive article on electric heating and cooking. So far as we know, it is unique in that it sets forth the actual experience of an observant and competent user.

This series of in-depth customer reviews was the result of the writer spending 12 months using electricity in the home and was a powerful, but largely balanced, argument for the adoption of the new technology.

Appliance companies, such as the British Westinghouse Company, Tricity and General Electric Company of America, worked with authors and experts to produce books explaining the benefits of electricity in a domestic setting, as well as detailed accounts of how the technology actually worked both within the entire house and specifically in the kitchen. These books were often lavishly illustrated with images of the latest in electrical appliances and had a dual function as both educational and marketing publications. This format also allowed the companies to directly address the lack of understanding of electricity as a barrier to its adoption.

The clear target audience for these publications was women, who were seen as the "quarter masters" of this space, holding decision-making power while also shouldering the responsibility for economy and healthy living (Buckley, 2009:1). In the 1914 edition of *Electric Cooking, Heating, Cleaning, etc.*, for example, author Maud Lancaster begins with a chapter titled "A Brief Explanation of Electricity from a Woman's Point of View." By addressing women specifically, they also followed a tradition already established through domestic manuals and later publications produced by food reformers, which aimed to educate women about healthier food choices and improved cooking practices (Buckley, 2009:7). Additionally, these publications, which also included women's magazines and became popular from the late 1800s onwards, focused on promoting economic practices, with articles targeted at middle-class housewives, providing advice on money-saving strategies (Buckley, 2009:57). Apple (1997) refers to such practices as "scientific motherhood" because they perpetuated the belief that women required expert advice to look after their families, thereby discrediting their own intuition and knowledge.

Another method adopted by electrical companies was exhibitions and displays. During the nineteenth century, exhibitions were so widespread that the period earned the title of the "great age of the exhibition." These events covered various subjects, from specific themes to international expositions and world fairs showcasing the achievements of nations. Technology became a popular focus, and the Great Exhibition of 1851 set the precedent for subsequent displays of modern advancements, including household appliances (O'Hagan, 2021:164). The World Columbian Exposition of 1893, which was held in Chicago, featured an Electricity Building, for example, with thousands of electrical devices developed by commercial companies, including General Electric and Westinghouse, on display.

Before radio, television and even the widespread adoption of print advertising, showcasing and demonstrating new technologies became a powerful marketing tool, as it allowed companies to present their innovations to a wide audience and establish themselves as pioneers in their respective fields. Expositions offered an opportunity for companies to gain public attention, build brand recognition and persuade consumers to adopt the latest technologies. Amid the bustling crowds, visitors would marvel at the dazzling displays of electrical technology, which visually communicated abundance and crafted a consumerism mythology, linking the new products with progress and modernity (Loeb, 1994:53). These events played a crucial role in shaping public perceptions of new inventions and fostering excitement around technological progress during the era. At the same time, the specific setting of the fairs and expositions diluted anxieties surrounding the products by allowing visitors to view them in real life and, in some instances, witness them actually being used.

Cooked by Electricity

In June 1894, the City of London Electric Company Ltd executed a successful demonstration of a "Banquet Cooked by Electricity" for a number of dignitaries including the Lord Mayor of London. Among the delicacies on offer were soups, a selection of cooked meats, as well as sweets and coffee, all of which were prepared in full view of the attendees in a kitchen that had been installed at the Canon Street Hotel especially for the event. This demonstration was designed to showcase the new innovations of electric stoves and ovens, as well as the "absence of smoke, dust and fumes" when electricity was used for cooking (Lancaster, 1914:49).

The absence of smoke, dust and fumes was of particular note because late eighteenth-century kitchens—whether domestic or commercial—were traditionally dominated by wood and, then from the nineteenth century, by coal-burning stoves. The growth of urban populations and the need for affordable heating and cooking solutions contributed to the popularity of coal as a domestic fuel. Coal was the predominant source of energy for both domestic and industrial purposes throughout the nineteenth century. It played a crucial role in powering the Industrial Revolution and transformed society in many ways through its utilisation in steam engines, which led to a massive increase in production capacity and accelerated economic growth in industries like textiles, iron and steel production and transport.

With the advent of new technologies and an increasing market demand for coal, initially, the resultant high levels of smoke in major cities were not an immediate health concern. Instead, they were seen as a symbol of productivity and expansion of empire. As such, they were something to be tolerated in the cause of progress (Bell, 2021:161). Smoke, whatever its source, was also largely considered to have health benefits. It was commonly used for food preservation, and sulphur—found in coal—was even marketed as a disinfectant. The use of open fires was believed to contribute to the overall freshness of complexion among the people of the British Isles, and it was thought to reduce the need for spectacles among the young (Brimblecombe, 1987:116).

However, as the Industrial Revolution advanced, population growth and industrial activity had worsened air pollution. Several significant fog disasters, such as one in December 1892 that resulted in approximately 1,000 excess deaths, highlighted the hazards of air pollution caused mainly by factory smokestacks and the domestic use of coal for heating and cooking.[1] While the full extent of air pollutants' health effects was not yet fully understood nor its role in climate change by adding carbon dioxide to the atmosphere, it was known that the visible smoke and soot produced by coal burning could lead to respiratory issues like coughing and bronchitis. Poor air quality was also associated with high child mortality rates, especially during very severe episodes of air pollution.

In response to such growing concerns, in 1880, the first organised movement for smoke abatement emerged, largely led by the London-based Fog and Smoke Committee which advocated for the adoption of cleaner fuels (Brimblecombe, 1987:90). These concerns were raised at the highest levels of government and in the media. As awareness grew and the evidence mounted, attitudes towards smoke pollution began to change. However, despite early attempts at legislation, progress in smoke abatement was slow and enforcing the laws proved challenging. While industrialists and committees were involved, complications with local legislation often resulted in non-compliance.

In addition to tackling industrial pollution, the domestic use of coal was another target for campaigners. For this purpose, expositions were used as part of the smoke abatement campaigns to broadcast new technologies and grow public awareness. From the 1880s, large events were held, designed to raise awareness of the health benefits of cleaner air and to provide high-profile platforms for inventors and manufacturers to display smoke-abating devices, such as smokeless fire grates, less smoky fuels and cleaner technologies powered by gas or electricity.

Specific electrical expositions also became popular marketing tools for manufacturers of machinery and appliances. By the end of the first decade of the twentieth century, expositions would often feature an "All Electric Model House"—a fully functional show home featuring the latest in electrical technology. This is exemplified by the 1908 Manchester Electrical Exhibition, where a complete working model home was constructed and fitted with the latest technology from incandescent lightbulbs to "ingenious contrivances," which "will clean the knives in the kitchen, play the piano in the drawing room, provide heat for 'warming' pans in the bedroom and in a score of other ways add to domestic comfort" (*Manchester Guardian*, 27 August 1908). Appliances on display included electrical ovens, which had first been introduced for the general domestic market in the 1890s. The idea was that visitors could wander around these spaces, inspecting and interacting with the items.

Displays of electrical equipment were expanded further with the March 1912 International Smoke Abatement Exhibition, held at the Royal Agricultural Hall in London. Here, there was an Electricity Hall featuring exhibits of electrical appliances, but also a restaurant "housed under the auspices of the London Electric Supply Companies" (*Electrical Times*, 28 March 1912). This temporary dining space catered for up to 800 people a day during the course of the exhibition (*Electrical Times*, 4 April 1912).

Similarly, an electric restaurant was also presented at the 1912 Earl's Court Exhibition, with practically all the cooking done within sight of the diners—something which was presented as a new experience:

> Hitherto the kitchen of a restaurant has been rather like the stoke hole of a liner a place which most people are glad to ignore. The electric kitchen, however, is likely to be a permanent feature of the modern restaurant, and its best advertisement
>
> (*Wakefield and West Riding Herald*, 31 August 1912)

Stepping out of the confines of the exhibition, more permanent spaces were established around London, all within a short space of time. In July 1911 alone, the press reported an Electric Restaurant on Goldhawk Road, another one in Dagenham and the Electric Restaurant, Electric House in Finsbury. Companies spotted a new opportunity to differentiate and popularise their product in what was noted as being "an opportunity not to be missed" and "a splendid advertisement" for the electrical industry (Electrical Times, 16 February 1911). In particular, there were two permanent electric restaurants that warrant further study: The Tricity House and the B&K Restaurant.

The Tricity House

The Tricity House—a four-storey building located at 48 Oxford Street—opened its doors on 6 December 1912 to a select group of specially invited journalists. A few days later, it was opened to the general public. This restaurant was owned by Modern Kitchens Ltd—a business set up by the directors of the British Electric Transformer Company, early pioneers in transformers, as well as domestic cooking and heating apparatus. They were also the owners of the brand Tricity, who had launched their first electrical appliances on the British market in 1908.

The origin of the Tricity House experiment can be found within the context of the tradition of expositions; early showcases for Tricity products were on display at the 1911 Electrical Exhibition at Olympia. Here, the company had a stand in both the main hall and in the gallery section where they gave frequent demonstrations of the "Tricity System." The company also experimented with cookery demonstrations at their showrooms in Charing Cross House, London during 1910 (*Electrical Times*, 15 June 1911).

These temporary forays were noted in the trade press as being successful in "spreading the gospel of electric cookery," as well as establishing Tricity as a reliable and reputable brand that consumers could trust:

> Anyone who has been fortunate enough to taste an omelette prepared by Mr Grogan over the Tricity hot-plate, or sampled a rasher of bacon grilled by the same means, if not immediately converted, is at any rate convinced, and is in a state of mind to give a favourable reception to the canvasser who next calls upon him to suggest the adoption of electric cooking
>
> (*Electrical Times*, 11 April 1912)

Following these successful activities, it is clear that, from the outset, Tricity House was envisaged as a form of demand management, where the company used the various areas within the restaurant to mould and increase the profile of electricity in general and the desirability of the appliances in particular.

It is notable that Tricity House, despite the technological wonders within, was designed to look like a traditional British dining establishment with its

Figure 12.1 Tricity House Restaurant Interior

Credit: Author's own collection

exterior of small glass panels and green painted wood to its interior of oak-beamed ceilings, antique candelabra and red tile floors (Figure 12.1). The ambience and the decor were deliberate design choices by the owners in order to create a reassuring "country inn-like" atmosphere of "quiet simplicity," which would stand in contrast to the modernity of its innovative cooking methods (*London Daily News*, 9 December 1912).

That the space was "quiet" was also of importance as the displays held in expositions would have been accompanied by a cacophony of other activities and competing showcases. The sheer number of people in attendance, which often ran into hundreds of thousands of people per day, would also have impacted the experience. Likewise, demonstrations in showrooms were also a world away from domestic realities. By situating their displays in more intimate settings, like a restaurant space, the electrical marketers of Tricity were aiming to reassure customers about new technologies by presenting them in a familiar setting, making the experience less jarring.

At Tricity House, visitors could view the complete Tricity system, which comprised of:

> one or a number of circular hot plates or boiling discs, with two-heat control. These are made singly or in duplex form, the latter patterns having sockets at the ends to enable one or two additional discs being connected up to the main cooker. These extra or extension cookers may be

> used for boiling and grilling or, when inverted, for use as top heat to the Tricity oven. The latter is of polished sheet metal, with a circular hole at bottom and top to fit over the hot plate of the cooker and to take the extension disc respectively.
>
> (Lancaster, 1914:185)

There were also a number of other Tricity appliances, including coffee percolators, throughout the restaurant rooms and at a special demonstration counter.

Electric restaurants were more than just simple demonstrations of new technology. Viewing a working kitchen and catering for hundreds of people a day was an ideal way of showcasing the "remarkable absence of dust and dirt"—a day-to-day problem that would have been familiar to the majority of their customers who were used to cooking with coal (*Globe*, 7 December 1912). Underlining the cleanliness of the space was the presence of waitresses and cooks dressed in white. Here, not only would the light-coloured outfits highlight the smoke-free nature of the kitchen but also had a wider symbolism of purity and transparency. This technique was also utilised in the broader food market, with companies such as Heinz employing Margaret McLeod—"the girl in the white cap"—to demonstrate their products in stores (O'Hagan, 2020:13). In this example, white was used to symbolise the purity of their food, distinguishing Heinz from its competitors and reassuring their customers of its quality.

Whilst it is tempting to draw parallels with today's widespread practice of display kitchens in restaurants where you can watch your food being prepared or even a chef's table where customers sit inside the kitchen and eat, the ideology of an electric restaurant went beyond passivity to a more interactive experience. Visitors were not only able to view the food preparation but—unlike at expositions—were actively encouraged to inspect all areas of the building. These free inspections served a further purpose, which was to immerse consumers in their brand's identity and, as such, also had marketing principles in common with companies like Cadbury's, which offered tours of their Bournville factory. This technique aimed to build a bond with consumers, moving their customer base from pioneers to a mass market uptake (Bradley, 2008:90). It also meant that Tricity's owners could develop their marketing from merely showcasing the products and the health benefits of flame-free cooking to directly addressing specific concerns around cooking with electricity and promoting it as part of an overall healthy lifestyle.

In the early twentieth century, there was a growing concern for nutrition and its profound implications on public health and societal well-being. As industrialisation transformed food production and distribution, advocates of these food reform movements found themselves increasingly alarmed by what they saw as the degradation of dietary habits and the proliferation of processed foods. At the same time, understanding of the intricate relationships between nutrients and human health increased with pioneering research by figures like Casimir Funk, who determined that certain nutrients could prevent diseases, as well as a broader recognition of the importance of a balanced diet. Championed by scientists, nutritionists, social activists and progressive policy-makers, food reform movements sought to raise awareness about the vital link between diet and health.

Of particular concern were certain processes, such as cooking or storage, which could cause the degradation or breakdown of important vitamins, minerals, proteins or other essential nutrients. While overcooking food—particularly vegetables or meat—was something to guard against, in general, there were specific concerns that using electricity would lead to an excessive amount of liquid loss during the cooking process. This would not only render the food tasteless but would waste money and could result in nutrient loss.

The charge of tastelessness was easily dealt with and, indeed, an electric restaurant provided an ideal vehicle to do so. Journalists who were invited to the launch of Tricity House covered the taste of the food extensively in their reviews, making it clear that "there was manifest a distinct improvement in the appearance and flavour of the meat bought to the table at Tricity House yesterday" (*London Evening Standard*, 7 December 1912). Another wrote:

> What may be described as their "piece de resistance" is stewed apples, which, cooked by this method, preserve their bloom and colour in a wonderful way, looking exactly as if just taken from the orchard, while their delicacy and purity of flavour are fully maintained".
>
> (*Globe*, 7 December 1912)

The complexity of concerns related to wastage, whether it be financial or of valuable nutrients, added a layer of intricacy. Specifically, the fears around the loss of nutrients were also deflected away from electrical cooking to its rival, gas:

> Owing to the necessity of giving a supply of fresh air to the gas burners and getting rid of the poisonous gases and flames, it is necessary to have a large vent to the gas oven, through which these gases can be given off to the outside air [...] A large part of the savoury juices of the meat is thus carried away by the hot poisonous gases through the vent to the outside air
>
> (Lancaster, 1914:31)

Tricity emphasised their mastery of electrical technology through continued discussions about safety, modernity and the remarkable progress symbolised by the use of such a great power which had been "tamed" by "our great scientists" and made to "do the so-called menial work of preparing our food" (Sketch, 25 December 1912). By controlling this "lightening," food could be cooked "slowly with moderate and even temperature throughout" (Lancaster, 1914:33). This claim not only served to abate concerns around cooking by electricity but also highlighted its superiority to flame cooking, which was notoriously difficult to control and required constant attention.

In addition to asserting their mastery over cooking, Tricity also substantiated it scientifically. One particular demonstration was extensively covered in press editorials and reiterated in many guides to the use of electricity. It detailed how journalists "watched as an uncooked 11 lb 7 1/2 oz beef joint was placed in a Tricity oven. I then examined how much weight it had lost throughout the process, and the loss was merely 1 lb 1 1/2 oz" (*London Evening Standard*, 7 December 1912). This use of precise and careful measurements—which can also be found in food marketing of the period—drew upon the field of health and medicine. Providing accurate guidelines for doses or quantities, thus, established scientific authority, leaving very little space for customer doubt in the product's efficacy (O'Hagan and Eriksson, 2022:241).

That this new technology marked a break with old traditions of cooking, both literally and symbolically, is encompassed by one review which stated that, "The electric ovens, with the warning red light indicating the extent of the heat generated, symbolised the triumph of the new over the old" (*London Daily News*, 9 December 1912).

The B&K Restaurant

Following the model already established by Tricity, the Brompton and Kensington Electricity Supply Company opened their own electric restaurant—known as the B&K—in the adjoining premises of an already established showroom at 254 Earls Court Road, London in May 1913. With an overall seating capacity of 95 people, the B&K included a main restaurant, with eight tables, a balcony with seven additional tables and a "cosy tea room" on the ground floor (Lancaster, 1914:178). Like Tricity House, the space was very traditional in décor with dark oak panelling and an arched ceiling decorated with frescoes (Figure 12.2). Again, like Tricity, this reassuring style belied the technology that was within.

However, the B&K restaurant was not set up specifically to sell own brand appliances, but instead to help its parent company develop demand for electrical heating and cooking in their local area, as well as to sell a range of electrical appliances and apparatus in a way that was "intended to supplement and reinforce one another" (*Electrical Times*, 18 April 1912).

In the early twentieth century, the electricity supply industry in Britain was dominated by intense competition between a patchwork of large, mostly privately owned, companies that were responsible for generating, transmitting and distributing electricity to consumers. Some of the major players in London included the Metropolitan Electric Supply Company and the Westminster Electric Supply Company. The B&K had been incorporated in 1888 and opened their Generating Station on Richmond Road the following year (LMA 4278/01/474). They served an area that had around 9,000 homes and was primarily residential. It was noted in the *Electrical Times* (18 April 1912) that the character of the area was changing rapidly, with many large mansions

Figure 12.2 B&K Restaurant Interior

Credit: Author's own collection

being converted into "good class flats, inhabited by well to do people." Of the current residents, it was reported that the B&K supplied about 5,000 of them with light, but had struggled to expand into cooking and heating.

Addressing the need to increase their customer base and highlight the use of electricity outside of lighting, the B&K had already tried a number of different marketing strategies, the most effective of which was the establishment of a showroom and demonstration space, which opened in 1909. This particular challenge had also been recognised by other supply companies, who also established showrooms. For example, the Westminster Electric Supply Company opened a demonstration area at their head office with an electric kitchen in which:

> a lady expert gives practical cookery demonstrations, and every opportunity will be afforded for cooks to handle and use the apparatus. This lady expert will also call at consumers' houses to instruct and advise on the use of electrical cooking appliances
>
> (*Electrical Times*, 1 June 1912)

The use of experts and demonstrators was another crucial marketing component, and their purpose was to help customers envision these technologies in their own spaces and acclimatise customers to their use. Outside of the electrical industry, female demonstrators were also frequently utilised for showcasing new technologies and products. Mrs Fletcher and Miss Williams were to be found at Watt & Grant's Stores, demonstrating Radium-Vita Radio-Active Beauty Preparations and offering consultations for customers to try them (Santos, 2020:179). In the restaurant context, in-house professionals like the "Diet Expert" at the Vita Sun Café—a partnership between the food reformers, the New Health Society and J. Lyons & Co., based on the ground floor of Coventry Street Corner House in Leicester Square, London—provided guidance to diners. Specifically, they acclimatised them to make informed choices from a menu that was "the result of the latest medical and scientific research into the question of food and its sustainability to the human requirements and the nourishment of the human frame" (LMA ACC 3527/399).

While the B&K showroom was a success and had improved appliance sales, a different tactic was required to increase the market share among domestic householders in the Brompton and Kensington areas. The directors had realised that, by encouraging cooking, especially during the daytime hours, they could increase their profits without the necessity of investing in larger outputs at their generating station (Lancaster, 1914:23). Electric restaurants allowed for more interactive demonstrations and at the B&K, customers were not only invited to inspect multiple kitchen spaces but also to try various small appliances during the course of their meal. This enabled them to see the technology in action but also served to emphasise the convenience, taste and nutritional superiority of food cooked in this way. Reports highlighted that, "Of the superior virtues of a newly boiled or newly poached egg in comparison with those prepared even a few minutes before consumption, there is no question" (*London Evening Standard*, 12 May 1913). This style of "table cooking," where simple food could be prepared by the diners, was not only hailed as the freshest, healthiest and tastiest way of eating but also a vital consideration for the housewife who wished to arrange an impromptu snack without "troubling the kitchen," thus giving her a "thorough grip and control of the chief domestic duties of her home" (Lancaster, 1914:32).

It is intriguing to observe the apparent disparity between marketing these products to individuals who could afford dining at restaurants to experience new innovations, regardless of the value offered, and the individuals typically responsible for cooking in a household setting: the domestic staff. Nevertheless, the dynamics are clear. While domestic servants were not expected to experiment with these advancements, the decision-makers for both their own households and the expanding number of middle-class families without household help were interested in adopting these changes, either for their staff or because they were becoming more self-sufficient.

An Electric Future

It is hard to ascertain how successful the work of spaces like Tricity House and the B&K, or even the numerous other popularising activities, were in encouraging the use of electricity for cooking or how they influenced public perception regarding the relationship between electricity and health. The time that is covered by these case studies was a time of immense fluctuations within the energy supply industries, but it was the electricity business itself that saw the biggest changes. Electricity was growing in popularity and some of the identified hinderances to its acceptance were systematically being removed.

The transformation with the most far-reaching effects was the change in the way that electricity was regulated and supplied in Britain. The patchwork of suppliers that characterised the early years of the electricity industry continued into the 1920s, with 480 different companies in operation throughout the country and a total of 80 in London alone in 1921. This ineffective and inefficient model hampered the adoption of electricity and made implementation difficult for both the suppliers and the consumers. With a clear mandate and need to change the system, the Electricity (Supply) Act of 1926 created an overarching authority—the Central Electricity Board (CEB)—to govern the different electricity supply companies and eventually establish a National Grid transmission system.

Consequently, electric restaurants moved from being demonstration and marketing spaces to accepted technology, with places like the staff kitchen at the London headquarters of Debenham and Freebody, Romano's Restaurant in the Strand and The Old Ship Hotel (Brighton) being early and enthusiastic adopters (Lancaster, 1914:56). In 1921, the London and North Eastern Railway established electric restaurant cars and, in 1924, the Flying Scotsman's daylight catering services went electric (*The Guardian*, 11 March 1929).

The year in which the Electricity (Supply) Act was implemented, the B&K Restaurant shut down, having served over 700,000 meals during its time of operation. Although the restaurant closed, the demonstration space was still in use, with new showrooms opening in 1926 and a further modernisation of the building in 1932. Now, the space was used for meeting places, lectures, cookery demonstrations and also for the popularisation of another new technology—talking pictures—until 1957 when it was finally closed (LMA 4278/01/474).

Tricity House, on the other hand, continued to operate as a restaurant and advertising space for Tricity appliances until the late 1920s. Although no figures exist for how many people they catered for over this time, we do know that they served 20,000 customers in the first three months and continued in popularity (Lancaster, 1914:184). Its owners later announced that the space's role as "purveyor and propagandist" had been so successful that it had made the premises on Oxford Street "too valuable for retention as a restaurant" (*Westminster Gazette*, 30 March 1927).

Highlighting the commercial success of this venture, the directors of Modern Kitchens Ltd and The British Electric Transformer Co Ltd set up a subsidiary company—Tricity Restaurants—in 1926 to open a new space, which would fulfil some of the same functions as Tricity House (National Archives, BT 31/32781/216904). Electricity as a superior technology still formed a large part of the advertising and marketing behind Tricity, with director, Arthur Berry, making a series of statements in the press on the topic, including some rather questionable health claims which, as previously, rooted electrical technology as both modern and an alternative to the highly polluting flame technology:

> Combustion, with its carbon monoxide product, should not be permitted in kitchens, since it produces poison, and I think I am safe in predicting that in 10 years' time there will be no combustion in any kitchen. Then men and women will be enabled to live to five times the period of their natural growth, as they should, instead of to three times that period, which is all they can do at present
>
> (*Leicester Evening Mail*, 11 January 1927)

The new restaurant and dance space—known simply as Tricity—was opened in the heart of London's theatre district in Wellington House on the corner of the Strand. While the intention of the directors may have been the same as with the earlier restaurant, the ambience and tone of the space were very different. Tricity House had focused on combining old-fashioned respectability in décor with the modern utility of their appliances and innovations. The focus of Tricity, however, was to market electricity as something modern, glamorous and luxurious. This can be seen from the descriptions of the dining room, which was decorated in sumptuous pink and gold colours and similar coloured furnishings (*Westminster Gazette*, 11 January 1927).

The demonstrational and educational aspect of the project was partly replaced with an emphasis on music and dancing with a selection of entertainment. There was also dancing from 10 pm to 2 am, with exhibition dancers and dance hostesses ready to entertain on the stage and take to the dance floor with single male guests (*Nottingham Journal*, 11 May 1927). However, the prominence of technological advancement continued into the new space, with advertisements placed in many major newspapers and magazines that provided details of both the entertainment on offer and the conveniences and innovations available at the restaurant. These included marketing the fact that cooking, lighting, refrigeration, ventilation and heating were all carried out with Tricity electrical appliances.

That Tricity continued to see the importance of a demonstration space for their products is evidenced by the decision to open a showroom on the same site. The "Tricity Ideal Electric Home" opened in October 1927 with the intention of attracting both those "who are interested in modern developments of electricity for home use" and those who were visiting the restaurant downstairs (*The Graphic*, 15 October 1927). Just as people had previously been invited to explore the entirety of Tricity House, they were now invited to explore the new demonstration space, which was a series of different rooms, including a dining room, bedroom, bathroom, drawing room and nursery that were fully kitted out with Tricity appliances, such as toasters, kettles and irons. There was also a change of emphasis away from the importance of electricity for cooking towards a campaign to encourage people to adopt the technology for heating.

Both the restaurant and demonstration space also served as vehicles to market a new product launched by Tricity: their Sun Ray system, which encompassed lamps and radiators. These could be standalone objects or integrated into the fabric of the building. One particularly interesting innovation consisted of a heating element attached to a pole, which was weighted at the bottom and included a small circular table for placing ashtrays, coffees and cocktails. Tricity's new system was said to capture the "health giving sun's rays," which "can do so much by scientific means to add to our meagre supply of natural sunshine in this grey clime." They, thus, allowed consumers "To ENJOY GLORIOUS HEALTH" and to "Switch on the SUNSHINE" (*Evening Standard*, 14 March 1928).

The importance of sunshine for health, well-being and beauty was an important concept in the 1920s. Especially in the United States, many people feared that the general population, increasingly living and working in urban environments, was not getting enough sunshine and its health was suffering as a result. Heliotherapy and consumer devices designed to simulate or capture the health-giving benefits of sunshine were popular (Freund, 2012:2). This technology built on the work of physician Dr Niels Finsen who studied light radiation and established that certain wavelengths of light had medical effects. By the late 1920s, it was suggested that specialist glass installed in public spaces could have a beneficial effect on the health of the population. This was trialled by the Pilkington Brothers of St Helens, who established a system called "Vita" which did not filter out (as ordinary glass did) the powerful ultraviolet rays from the sun and was installed in hotels throughout the country, the monkey house at London Zoo and at the Vita Sun Café in 1926.

Tricity's model of a glamorous restaurant and demonstrational space continued to be a success into the 1930s. It was regularly celebrated as one of the top restaurants in London and praised for its food and its entertainment. However, it suddenly closed in 1934 after the resignation of the driving force, Chairman Arthur Berry (National Archives, BT 31/32781/216904). While it is likely that it was the health of Arthur Berry that caused Tricity to shut, it is also clear that the need for this style of space had also largely passed. The closing of Tricity marked the end of the commercial restaurant as an electricity demonstration space in London.

The 1930s saw the continued trajectory of the growth of electricity in the domestic space. The electrical industry had formulated a remarkably effective marketing plan that connected electricity with progress through association with convenience, thereby facilitating its widespread adoption. This was aided by the establishment of the National Grid in September 1933, campaigns by local authorities to introduce assisted wiring schemes and improvements in appliance technology. By the end of the decade, 60% of all homes in Britain had electricity (Sugg Ryan, 2020:162). Nonetheless, there was competition from gas technology, which had gained popularity, particularly in the kitchen. Gas-powered appliances like refrigerators, dishwashers and washing machines all emerged as challengers to electricity's supremacy in the domestic realm (Stevenson, 2007:30).

Despite the widespread adoption of electricity and gas for lighting and cooking, their adoption for heating was considerably slower, and coal consumption remained high (Brimblecombe, 1987:164). Legislative efforts had proven ineffective in addressing air pollution, which continued to pose a significant problem. In early December 1952, London experienced the Great Smog—a thick pollution haze that paralysed the city and resulted in the premature deaths of an estimated 6,000 to 7,000 individuals. The public outcry following this event prompted the enactment of the first Clean Air Act in 1956, which included the establishment of several "smoke control" zones where coal burning was prohibited.

Financial incentives were subsequently provided to individuals looking to shift from coal to gas or electricity. Smokeless fuel—suitable for conventional grates, even within smokeless zones—was introduced under various brand names, such as Cleanglow and Gloco. Although coal's domestic use significantly diminished, it still held a vital position in industries and coal-fired power stations, contributing to low-cost electricity generation until the 1990s when natural gas started its ascension to become the biggest single contributor to power generation in Britain.

Conclusion

This chapter has aimed to enrich the discourse on the relationship between science and healthy living by exploring the concept of "electric restaurants" and how they served as platforms for educating the public about the emerging technology of electric cooking. By tracing the development of electric restaurants in early twentieth-century Britain through two case studies, it has identified some of the diverse approaches through which electric cooking techniques were shown to mitigate the hazards linked with smoke inhalation, as well as their role in enhancing the preservation of nutrients in cooked foods. The significance of this chapter's findings stretches beyond the realm of electric restaurants, however, resonating with wider societal shifts towards modernisation, convenience and technological progress. The specific role that women were to play in the "electric future"—as made clear in the marketing targeted at them—also starts to come into focus. Thus, the chapter not only sheds light on shifting lifestyles and gender roles but also on evolving concepts of health and well-being within the domestic space from an increased emphasis on cleanliness to the adoption of electricity.

Today, there is an urgent need to diverge our electrical supply from using fossil fuels—whether gas or coal—and move to low-carbon sources of power. In the context of cooking, many studies have indicated that gas emits pollutants, including carbon monoxide, nitrogen oxides, particulate matter and formaldehyde, all of which contribute to a range of chronic health problems. Such is the concern that, in January 2023, Richard Trumka Jr, the US Consumer Product Safety commissioner, indicated that the organisation was well within its rights to impose a ban on gas stoves or, at the very least, the new installation of gas appliances. The backlash against this statement went global and resulted in a watering down of this position by the organisation.

Conscious of the criticisms of gas technology, since 2018, the gas industry has launched campaigns targeted at a new generation of people who are instructed by paid social media and well-being influencers that it is better #cookingwithgas. The electricity industry has not been neglectful of the social media space in terms of promoting their own product through campaigns on various media platforms, as well as the largely organic embracing of electric cooking by influencers and chefs like Jon Kung advocating the technology and evidencing its superiority over flame cooking. These examples show that, over the last 120 years, demonstrations of cooking technology have moved from the exposition to the showroom to the electric restaurant and now to our homes.

While this study represents the first in-depth exploration of electric restaurants, it is hoped that it will inspire further research. There are promising avenues for investigating the integration of other technologies within restaurant settings, as well as exploring topics such as Vita ray glass and Tricity health lamps, which could yield valuable insights for future studies. There is also a potential-rich seam of research in focusing more closely on the parallels that we see in the twenty-first century, with a battle again centred around the familiar refrain of environmental concerns, the health of the general population and sources of power.

Note

1 These incidents, which were caused by coal smoke mixing with fog, were known colloquially as "pea soupers."

Bibliography

"Advert for Tricity Ideal Electric Home." 1928. *Evening Standard* (14 March), 19.

"All-Electric Restaurant Trains." 1929. *The Guardian* (11 March), 13.

Apple, R.D. 1997. "Constructing Mothers: Scientific Motherhood in the Nineteenth and Twentieth Centuries" in *Mothers and Motherhood: Readings in American History*, edited by R.D. Apple and J. Golden (Columbus: Ohio State University), pp. 161–178.

Assael, B. 2018. *The London Restaurant 1840–1914*. Oxford: Oxford University Press.

Bell, A. 2021. *Our Biggest Experiment: A History of the Climate Crisis*. London: Bloomsbury Sigma.

Bradley, J. 2008. *Cadbury's Purple Reign: The Story Behind Chocolate's Best-Loved Brand*. Chichester: John Wiley.

Brimblecombe, P. 1987. *The Big Smoke: A History of Air Pollution in London Since Medieval Times*. London: Methuen.

Brompton and Kensington Electric Restaurant, Earls Court Road. London Electricity Board (LEB), 4278/01/474. London: London Metropolitan Archives.

Buckley, M.D. 2009. *Recipe for Reform: The Food Economy Movement in Britain During the First World War*. Unpublished PhD thesis, University of California, Berkeley.

"Combustionless Kitchen." 1927. *Leicester Evening Mail* (11 January), 5.

"Cooking by Electricity." 1912a. *Globe* (7 December), 8.
"Cooking by Electricity." 1912b. *Wakefield and West Riding Herald* (31 August), 2.
"Cooking Demonstrations and After." 1912. *Electrical Times* (11 April), 377.
"Electric Cooking in Practice." 1911. *Electrical Times* (15 June), 603.
"Electric Heating and Cooking." 1911. *Electrical Times* (5 January), 1.
"Electric Kitchen." 1927. *Westminster Gazette* (11 January), 7.
"Electricity in the Home." 1913. *London Evening Standard* (12 May), 8.
Freund, D. 2012. *American Sunshine: Diseases of Darkness and the Quest for Natural Light*. Chicago: University of Chicago Press.
"International Smoke Abatement Exhibition." 1912. *Electrical Times* (28 March), 322.
"Items of General Interest." 1927. *The Graphic* (15 October), 60.
Lancaster, M.L. 1914. *Electric Cooking, Heating, Cleaning, Etc: Being a Manual of Electricity in the Service of the Home*. London: Constable & Co.
"Like Lightning!" 1912. *Sketch* (25 December), 35.
Loeb, L.A. 1994. *Consuming Angels: Advertising and Victorian Women*. Oxford: Oxford University Press.
McWilliam, R. 2020. *London's West End: Creating the Pleasure District, 1800–1914*. Oxford: Oxford University Press.
Miscellaneous Corner House Tariffs and Menus. J. Lyons and Company Limited, ACC 3527/399. London: London Metropolitan Archives.
"Miss Saxophone." 1927. *Nottingham Journal* (11 May), 12.
O'Hagan, L.A. 2020. Pure in Body, Pure in Mind? A Sociohistorical Perspective on the Marketisation of Pure Foods in Great Britain. *Discourse, Context & Media* 34, https://doi.org/10.1016/j.dcm.2019.100325
O'Hagan, L.A. 2021. Blinded by Science? Constructing Truth and Authority in Early Twentieth Century Virol Advertisements. *History of Retailing and Consumption* 7(2):162–192.
O'Hagan, L.A. and Eriksson, G. 2022. Modern Science, Moral Mothers, and Mythical Nature: A Multimodal Analysis of Cod Liver Oil Marketing in Sweden, 1920–1930. *Food and Foodways* 30(4):231–260.
Santos, L.J. 2020. *Half Lives: The Unlikely History of Radium*. London: Icon Books.
Simon, L. 2004. *Dark Light: Electricity and Anxiety from the Telegraph to the X-Ray*. Orlando: Harcout Inc.
"Smoke Abatement Exhibition." 1912. *Electrical Times* (4 April), 351.
Stevenson, G. 2007. *The 1930s Home*. Oxford: Shire Publications.
Stuart, T. 2006. *The Bloodless Revolution: A Cultural History of Vegetarianism from 1600 to Modern Times*. London: W.W Norton.
Sugg Ryan, D. 2020. *Ideal Homes: Uncovering the History and Design of the Interwar House*. Manchester: Manchester University Press.
"The British Electric Transformer Co Ltd." 1927. *Westminster Gazette* (30 March), 8.
"The Cooking Campaign of the B & K." 1912. *Electrical Times* (18 April), 398.
"The Electric Cooking Room." 1912. *Electrical Times* (18 April), 398.
"The Electric Meal." 1912. *London Evening Standard* (7 December), 12.
"The "Electrical" Home." 1908. *Manchester Guardian* (27 August), 8.
"The Exhibition at Olympia." 1911. *Electrical Times* (16 February), 1.
"The Westminster Electric Showrooms." 1912. *Electrical Times* (1 June), 554.
Tricity Restaurants Ltd. BT 31/32781/216904. London: National Archives.
Walkowitz, J. 2012. *Nights Out – Life in Cosmopolitan London*. New Haven: Yale University Press.
"What Science Has Achieved in Modern Cooking." 1912. *London Daily News* (9 December), 3.
Zweiniger-Bargielowska, I. 2010. *Managing the Body: Beauty, Health, and Fitness in Britain, 1800 to 1939*. Oxford: Oxford University Press.

13 Bridging the Gap from the Petri Dish to Natural, Healthy Meat

An Insight into Marketing Communications for Cultured Meat

Andreja Vezovnik

Introduction

Cultured meat—also known as cell-based meat, clean meat, cultivated meat, *in vitro* meat and artificial meat—is a product of tissue engineering technology that grows animal cells, which then become the basis of meat products for consumption as food (Stephens, 2022). Since its inception, tissue engineering technology has been developed to address human health issues in the medical field. The idea of growing human tissue and organs from stem cells is as old as humanity itself, although the implementation of this process did not fully develop until the second half of the twentieth century (Kaul and Ventikos, 2015). In recent years, the food sector has begun to adopt and develop similar technologies, especially in the field of cellular agriculture involving the production of food and other animal-based products (meat, eggs and dairy) directly from animal cells grown in a nutrient-rich growth medium (Cellular Agriculture Europe, 2023).

The idea of cultivated flesh springs from the realisation that modernity has failed to meet the challenges of delivering healthy, nutritious and environmentally friendly food for the global population. After World War Two, the goal of the food industry was to increase food production in order to produce enough food for the world and to alleviate Malthusian concerns over food security and neo-Malthusian concerns over environmental problems. Strongly supported by the Green Revolution of the twentieth century, this project led to significant increases in crop yields and agriculture in industrialised countries. However, more recently, investments in technologies such as chemical fertilisers, pesticides, controlled irrigation and genetically modified organisms have been perceived as dystopian, inefficient and harmful to human health and the environment. Therefore, with the consolidation of biotechnology, new solutions have emerged over the past 20 years. Besides cultured meat, these solutions involve other types of alternative proteins such as plant-based meat, insects, algae and fermentation.

Unlike the conventional meat industry, which is criticised for being unsustainable, the cultured meat industry claims that cultured meat products are animal-friendly, use less water and energy, emit fewer pollutants and fewer

DOI: 10.4324/9781003450276-19

greenhouse gases and are healthier overall because they do not cause food-borne and zoonotic diseases. In addition, the cultured meat industry claims that its products will successfully contribute to solving the problem of global protein security and safety, especially if produced with plant-based growth serum (Volden and Wethal, 2021:187).

The focus of this chapter is to examine the promotional discourses for cultured meat as presented in marketing communications. These promotional discourses will be approached from a transhistorical perspective in order to provide an important "genealogy" of how the scientific and technological discourses used in the promotion of cultured meat became embedded in notions of naturalness, health and cleanliness. To this end, the method of multimodal critical discourse analysis (MCDA) is applied (Machin and Mayr, 2012), which is a form of critical linguistic analysis that also includes visual representations and design. In MCDA, texts are analysed in terms of lexical, grammatical and semiotic choices to reveal the underlying discourses and the power relations that sustain them (Ledin and Machin, 2015). The following analysis focuses on the visual and linguistic features of three websites of three major cultured meat producers—namely Eat Just, Mosa Meat and Upside Foods—with the aim of deciphering the nature of the discourses, that is the broader ideas and values conveyed through texts and used in the marketing of cultured meat. Before the actual analysis, however, I present the history of how the idea of cultured meat was developed and marketed.

Ways to Cultivated Meat

In recent decades, policymakers, industry and academia have worked together to find a solution to the unsustainable food system, where meat production is seen as particularly problematic due to its impact on the environment, global warming, animal welfare and food safety. In addition to technological innovations and changes in animal production, which include changes in soils and feed, genetic manipulation and changes in animal species and/or breeds (Zhang et al., 2017), alternative proteins are expected to play an important role in the new food system. The alternative protein industry—particularly plant-based meat analogues is now developed, especially in the United States, and has launched products such as plant-based burgers, chicken nuggets and sausages. These products are not only sensory similar to real meat but also aim to provide essential macronutrients found in real meat, particularly protein.

Plant-based protein sources such as tofu, tempeh and seitan have been around since ancient times and were mainly consumed in Asia (He et al., 2020; Bakhsh et al., 2021). In Western markets, plant-based meat substitutes emerged in the late nineteenth century when pioneers such as John Harvey Kellogg developed nut- and grain-based products and sold them under the names Nuttose and Protose to promote health. After World War Two, noticeable advances were made in food packaging manufacturing, which accelerated the development of plant-based protein concentrates, isolates and texturised proteins. Soy-based meat alternatives proliferated, targeting the vegetarian niche, while products such as Tofurky were launched in the United States in the 1990s (He et al., 2020; Bakhsh et al., 2021) and were primarily used to replace meat.

In recent years, companies such as Impossible Foods and Beyond Meat have developed a new generation of plant-based meat substitutes to satisfy meat eaters. The latest versions of plant-based analogues have similar textures, comparable smells and even a bloody appearance to mimic animal meat. These analogues include hamburger patties, hot dogs, bacon, lunch meat and ground beef. While these products are well received by vegetarians who do not want the taste of real meat, meat consumers are often not satisfied with their appearance, taste and flavour when they consider them as meat alternatives (He et al., 2020).

Meat-eating consumers' dissatisfaction with the sensorial features of plant-based analogues hastened the development of cultured meat. In the process of making cultured meat, stem cells are grown until they develop into muscle, fat or other tissues, which become animal products such as meat, fish, milk or eggs (Cellular Agriculture Europe, 2023). The process takes place outside the animal's body in the laboratory; the only stage involving animals is the biopsy for suitable cells. There are two ways to produce cultured meat: (1) to cultivate cells and (2) to ferment bacteria. So far, the main focus has been on cell cultivation. Cells are grown and propagated in a plant-based serum consisting of amino acids and glucose and are cultured in bioreactors (Volden and Wethal, 2021:186). After about three weeks, the finished product can take different forms: a meat patty, a chicken nugget, a steak or a meatball.

Although the history of cultured meat production now spans more than two decades, the idea is much older. The first mentions of cultured meat occurred in the context of science fiction literature and chemistry and came from German writer and scientist Kurd Lasswitz, who mentioned cultured meat in his 1897 novel *Two Planets* (Jönsson, 2016). A few years before him, in 1894, a famed French chemistry professor Pierre-Eugène-Marcellin Berthelot claimed that, by the year 2000, humans would dine on meat grown in a lab rather than from slaughtered animals (Shapiro, 2018). The first political figure to dream of producing meat without animals was British politician Winston Churchill. In 1932, he stated that "we shall escape the absurdity of growing a whole chicken in order to eat the breast or wing, by growing these parts separately under a suitable medium. Synthetic food will, of course, also be used in the future" (Ford, 2013).

Churchill's words became reality in 1999 when the first patent for *in vitro* meat was granted in the Netherlands, filed by three Dutchmen: Willem van Eelen, Willem van Kooten and Wiete Westerhof (Jönsson, 2020). Van Eelen was a medical doctor who had been interested in finding ways to produce meat *in vitro* for five decades. While imprisoned and starving during World War Two, he developed the idea of growing meat in a laboratory and outside the animal's body to avoid inflicting pain on the animals (Wurgaft, 2015; Jönsson, 2016).

The patent consisted of placing the muscle cells in a collagen matrix, holding them in a nutrient solution and causing them to divide (Chodkowska et al., 2022). Almost at the same time, in 2000, the National Aeronautics and Space Agency (NASA) was growing goldfish meat (and later turkey meat) as part of food production research that could be successfully used as food in spaceflight (Chodkowska et al., 2022). The project was initiated much earlier, in 1995, when the Food and Drug Administration (FDA) approved NASA's *in vitro* meat production techniques, and it was intended to comfort astronauts on their mission to Mars (Jönsson, 2016:730).

The concept of cultured meat was introduced to a wider audience in the early 2000s by Jason Matheny. He co-authored an article on cell-cultured meat and was the founder of the NGO New Harvest—an *in vitro* meat research organisation founded in 2004 (Chodkowska et al., 2022). Matheny became interested in cultured meat when conducting research on infectious diseases in India. After visiting a poultry farm outside Delhi, he recognised the need for a new way to meet global demand for meat. In 2004, New Harvest was invited to present on cultured meat at the PROtein Foods, Environment, Technology and Society (PROFETAS) conference in Wageningen (Netherlands). Matheny subsequently met with the Dutch Minister of Agriculture to advise him on funding for cultured meat research. In 2005, the Dutch cultured meat project began. Although this project was the first government-funded project, with the Dutch government providing €2 million to a consortium of three universities and an industrial partner, meat producer Meester Stegeman, no edible products were produced from this project (Jönsson, 2020). However, in 2011, the first commercial meat cultivation project, Modern Meadow, was founded in the United States. Meanwhile, Dutch physiology professor Mark Post, who was previously involved in the Dutch project, secured funding from Google co-founder Sergey Brin to produce the first cultured beef burger (Jönsson, 2020).

The first piece of cultured meat served to an audience, however, was not Mark Post's burger but a chop made from frog cells, served in 2003 in Nantes (France) as part of Disembodied Cuisine—an artwork created and performed by bioartists Oron Catts and Ionat Zurr. The cutlet was a tissue of frog cells marinated in Calvados and fried in honey and garlic (Wurgaft, 2020:16). It was not until ten years later, in 2013, that Mark Post—who received a substantial grant from the government thanks to the persistence of van Eelen—presented to the public the first cultured meat burger, which was made from cow cells. The patty reportedly cost €250,000 to produce (Jönsson, 2016:730). Experts who tasted the burger felt that it lacked fat and was, therefore, rather dry and tasteless (Spector, 2013), but this did not stop scientists and entrepreneurs from developing the product further.

The sector has grown significantly since Post's public tasting, largely due to the rise of startups. Given very limited public funding, many cultured meat developers were founded by wealthy philanthropic individuals and the investment streams associated with high-tech companies. The expansion of the field was accompanied by the creation of research teams that used tissue engineering technologies to produce meat by companies that used genetic modification to produce other animal products, such as yeast to produce milk and protein, casein for whey and ice cream, gelatine and collagen. These startups grew out of a San Francisco-based biotechnology accelerator for the cellular agriculture field. However, the field has also expanded by turning to venture capital. In just a few years, from 2016 to 2020, the number of companies involved in cultured meat has grown from four to more than 40, including companies focused on pet food, technology platforms and non-edible products. A handful of other companies are engaged in cellular agriculture based on genetic modification (Jönsson, 2020).

A striking concentration of these cultured meat startups occurred in Silicon Valley, reflecting growing institutional interest and investment in food technology in the region over the past decade aimed at improving global food security. Outside of Silicon Valley, namely in the Netherlands, the United Kingdom and Israel, other cultured meat companies tend to have their origins in academia, with a number of college-based projects without links to corporations. In other parts of the world, such as Japan, China and Singapore, government-funded agencies have been involved in funding cellular agriculture projects.

Until 2023, Singapore was the only state where cultured meat was approved for human consumption. In 2023, the Dutch Mosa Meat received parliamentary approval to use cultured meat for tasting purposes in the Netherlands, while Silicon Valley-based companies Upside Foods, Eat Just and Good Meat received the green light from the FDA and USDA (United States Department of Agriculture) for their cultured chicken products. In 2024, the Israeli Cultured Meat Consortium received regulatory approval as well. This means that, in the next decades, cultured meat products will probably enter Western markets.

Marketing Cultured Meat to Consumers

Although cultured meat companies have mainly focused on developing, perfecting and testing their products, they have recently begun to develop marketing communications aimed at consumers. Marketing communication is an activity that includes all messages and media disseminated by companies to communicate with the market. It comprises advertising, direct marketing, branding, packaging, online presence, printed materials, public relations activities, sales presentations, sponsorships and trade show appearances, with the goal of creating and maintaining demand and preference for a product (Smith and Taylor, 2004:8). The marketing communications of cultured meat companies have mainly consisted of informing the target audience about the company's activities. This has taken the form of blogs and press releases focused on major company milestones such as sales approvals, technical advances (i.e., the introduction of the animal-free growth serum), major funding from venture capitalists and promotion of their products through social media and informative advertisements. The companies conduct their marketing communications predominantly through two mediums: corporate websites and social media, which include YouTube commercials and other types of videos, as well as Twitter, Facebook, Instagram and TikTok posts. Recently, some print media activity has also been noted; in 2023, Upside Foods, for example, published an advertisement in the *New York Times* to celebrate the FDA's approval of their chicken nuggets.

More and more market research indicates that cultured meat will become a permanent fixture on store shelves and restaurant menus. The cultured meat market is estimated at $214 million in 2025 and $593 million by 2032. The product with the largest market will most likely be burgers, followed by nuggets and meatballs (Chodkowska et al., 2022). There are many studies looking at consumer acceptance of and willingness for cultured meat, but they all show consumer hesitation, with food neophobia—the reluctance to try new foods—emerging as a key barrier. However, consumers' perceived benefits of cultured meat are still many. Primarily, consumers associate cultured meat with less animal suffering, protection of the environment, especially reduction of greenhouse gas emissions, and personal health benefits such as fat reduction and increased food safety. On the other hand, safety concerns, unnaturalness, nutritional concerns, disgust, neophobia, economic fears and ethical concerns have also been identified as barriers to the acceptance of cultured meat (Bryant and Barnett, 2020).

Health, Nature and Science in Food Marketing

Therefore, the marketing of cultured meat is primarily concerned with concepts such as cleanliness, genuineness, naturalness and scientificity. Marketing attempts to describe food as natural, healthy, clean, pure and scientific have been around since the late nineteenth century (see Domosh, 2003; O'Hagan, 2020; Eriksson and O'Hagan, 2021). As demonstrated by Domosh's (2003) analysis of Heinz mayonnaise, the use of these concepts in food marketing can be traced back to Victorian notions of purity, whiteness and civilisation, as well as to ideas of the Physical Culture Movement in Europe and in the United States that emerged right after and promoted a healthy diet and regular physical activity for building a healthy (male) body and nation (O'Hagan, 2022b). Furthermore, the promotion of healthy food at that time was closely linked to the idea of naturalness, which was accompanied by food advertisements showing images of national natural landscapes which, used together with national symbols in milk marketing, functioned as manifestations of banal nationalism (Billig, 1995) constitutive for the formation of national identities (Andersson, 2019, 2020).

The purity and naturalness of promoted food products symbolically reflected national ideologies of the racial purity of the white race, which gained prominence over the "dirty other" who needed to be civilised and purified, which was ultimately the goal of British and American colonisation projects (Domosh, 2003). The purification of colonial India and the Philippines, for example, was most evident in the introduction of Western standards of hygiene in the process of food preparation to the colonised people (Samiparna, 2021; Orquiza, 2021). However, the notion of natural and pure food also arose from the fear of food adulteration, which was regulated in England in 1875 with the Food and Drugs Act (O'Hagan, 2020) and in the USA with the Pure Food and Drug Act (Domosh, 2003). Both acts aimed to protect public health by regulating the composition of food.

The "purity" of food, therefore, has two meanings. It refers to terms such as natural, untainted, unadulterated, simple, earthy and unprocessed by humans, but it also relates to safety in the sense of biologically purified, scientifically aseptic, hygienic and germ-free food (Mintz, 1996). This dual meaning of purity is ubiquitous in modern and postmodern food marketing. In the postmodern era, where technological advances, such as genetically modified crops or highly processed foods on which the modern food industry relied, have been called into question—especially in the context of human health and zoonotic disease outbreaks—the concept of clean and safe food remains at the forefront. However, this does not mean that the concept of naturalness has disappeared. On the contrary, Hansen (2002:502) notes that a number of studies in the late 1980s and early 1990s observed an upsurge in so-called "green advertising" and "green marketing" in which naturalness and pastoralism are evoked, reminiscent of an idyllic rural scene showing cows on green grass fields in advertisements for animal products such as meat and dairy (Borkfelt et al., 2015; Andersson, 2019, 2020). Indeed, in green marketing, nature becomes synonymous with human health and well-being (Andersson, 2019).

If modern references to the health and purity of food are based on the Victorian notion of purity, nature and health of body and nation, the postmodern appeals of food marketing "back to nature" should rather be interpreted as a reaction to modernity's project to produce convenience in the form of ultra-processed foods that have not fully convinced consumers of being truly healthy, pure and natural. Modern food has tended to be perceived as disconnected from nature because it is highly processed and, as such, unnatural and unhealthy. It is, therefore, unsurprising that the commercialisation of food has recently provided an opportunity to consume nature in its purest form, which typically means consuming images, representations, experiences and simulations of the non-human environment in all its forms, but with the scope to question the transgressions of modernity (Vezovnik, 2023).

In the past decades, consumer studies have shown that perceived naturalness is a particularly important variable in the acceptance of food and food technologies. The greatest decrease in perceived naturalness is observed when an item is the product of genetic modification. However, what consumers perceive as unnatural foods also include foods with additives, artificial colours and flavours, chemicals, hormones and pesticides, preservatives and artificial ingredients (Rozin, 2005; Román et al., 2017). One possible explanation for consumer preference for natural products is that these products are perceived as healthier. This suggests that naturalness per se is perceived as a desirable product attribute (Rozin, 2005; Román et al., 2017). Moreover, psychological factors such as idealism, traditionalism and universalism were found to be positively related to preference for naturalness in food, along with an interest in health. The importance of naturalness in food also influenced the intention to eat foods perceived as more environmentally friendly, more natural, local, traditional and lower in calories (Rozin, 2005; Román et al., 2017).

In promoting cultured meat, references to naturalness and health are backed up with references to safety assured by science and technology. Studies focused on the use of scientific language and references to science in food marketing have examined how scientific evidence is cited to promote claims about specific foods with specific health benefits (e.g. Koteyko, 2009; Ledin and Machin, 2020a; Eriksson and O'Hagan, 2021; Chen and Eriksson, 2022). Referencing science allows marketers to take advantage of the social impact of science to emphasise the positive effects of products and offer hope and promise to consumers, and is most often used to give products health value (Koteyko, 2009; Ledin and Machin, 2020a; Eriksson and O'Hagan, 2021; Chen and Eriksson, 2022).

The marketing of cultured meat is, thus, a curious mixture of codifications with scientific and technological signifiers, on the one hand, and signifiers of "nature" and health on the other. In this sense, the promotion of cultured meat as natural and healthy and simultaneously scientific and technological seems counterintuitive, although it is already found in historical examples of food marketing (cf. Eriksson and O'Hagan, 2021; O'Hagan, 2022a). As Mintz (1996:92–93) points out, this is because the contrast in meaning is based on two quite different understandings of nature which many of us seem to hold simultaneously. Nature, precisely because it is natural, is not chemically clean. But scientific purity, precisely because it is chemically clean, is not natural. This conundrum embodies a clear and irresolvable conceptual polarity in our thinking that is exploited by the cultured meat industry in the marketing of cultured meat products.

Because cultured meat is artificially produced and contains very little of what people perceive as "natural" ingredients, references to nature are key to appealing to consumers who want to associate their food with nature. Due to its artificiality, cultured meat is not usually perceived as a healthy product in the eyes of consumers (Bryant and Barnett, 2020). Furthermore, the majority of cultured meat advertisements consist of images and references to fast food products such as chicken nuggets and burgers, which are generally considered unhealthy. At the same time, however, cultured meat advertisements emphasise the characteristics of naturalness and health, especially because it is declared GMO-free and ecologically sustainable.

With this duality in mind, I now turn to an analysis of three websites of three leading cultured meat companies, namely Silicon Valley-based Upside Foods and Eat Just, and Dutch company Mosa Meat.[1] I will focus on how the promotion of cultured meat is codified through scientific and technological discourses to decode its construction as a transparent, real, natural and healthy food.

"It's science (but not rocket science)"

In order to familiarise the consumer with the technological processes of meat production, all three websites provide a step-by-step presentation of their meat production technology. At Upside Foods, the first thing we see at the top of their webpage is a short 3D video clip of a fully grown chicken against a bright red background. The image of the chicken is very realistic. It is not altered or modified. We see the chicken in motion. The way it moves its body reinforces the viewer's feeling of looking at a real animal. Next to the video clip, there is a caption that reads: "Cultivated meat. It's science (but not rocket science)." The text implies that producing cultured meat is a scientific process, but the use of the metaphor—*it's not rocket science*—negates the suggestion that making cultured meat is a complicated procedure. The metaphor is, therefore, used to demystify the supposedly mysterious nature of the science behind cultured meat production and reassure viewers that the process of meat production is not difficult to understand (Machin and Mayr, 2012:13). The image of the chicken suggests that cultured meat is paradigmatically associated (cf. Barthes, 1967:48) with a real chicken used to produce conventional meat. In this sense, the associative link between chicken and meat is established and serves to allay consumer scepticism about artificially produced meat.

In the second step of the meat production presentation, visitors to the Upside website can see chicken cells in a realistic 3D video animation. In this visualisation of the science behind cultured meat, the cells are depicted as a dark, red, uneven and internally rounded mass that likely represents a cell nucleus encased in a bright red, transparent membrane. The short 3D video clip of the cells shows a zoom-in on the cells to simulate the gaze of the scientist selecting them through a microscope. The view from the microscope, associated with the ability to reveal what was previously hidden, to give access to what is otherwise inaccessible, signifies transparency. Looking at the cells informs the consumer about the biological matter used in cultured meat that is invisible to the naked eye and, therefore, difficult for the layperson to imagine. This highly digitised and realistic image of the cell also connotes advanced technology (Chen and Eriksson, 2022:15) and relates to medical representations of red blood cells, which can make this image comprehensible to consumers. The cell is presented as a matter between chicken and meat, and its importance is still mainly in the scientific and biological framework, not in the culinary one.

However, in the next step, the 3D image shows how cells divide and grow. Starting from one cell, viewers can see how the cells start to multiply until they are zoomed out and look smaller and smaller but more and more numerous. The last thing we see is a Petri dish-shaped pile of small red cells that already resemble a raw burger patty. This is the point at which biological matter takes on the form of food. The aesthetic appeal of the images of cells described above is an important means of presenting scientific content to a wider audience (Ruivenkamp and Rip, 2014:183). The iconography of science has a greater impact on the public than words, which may be incomprehensible to them (Myers, 1990:231). However, to persuade viewers, written messages must appear alongside the images. In one of the captions, Upside Foods explains:

> We kick off the cultivation process by placing cells from a selected cell line into a cultivator and feeding them with a blend of nutrients, which includes water, sugars, amino acids, vitamins, minerals and salt. As these small batches of cells, called seed trains, multiply, we increase the size (and/or number) of the cultivators to give them more space to grow.

The text begins with the idiomatic verb "kick off," borrowed from the popular sport of football to indicate the start of an activity and used to explain how the intervention of "us" (i.e., Upside and our scientists) will turn cells into meat. In the example, the use of the pronoun "we" represents collective scientific action and camaraderie among scientists. The pronoun "we" combined with verbs that imply action (kick off, feed, increase, give) reinforces the idea that the scientists are actively involved in finding a solution. A mix of lay and scientific language is used to demystify the scientific process while making it clear to consumers that it exists. The use of scientific language informs potential consumers of technical terms such as "seed trains," "cell line" or "cultivator" to familiarise them with the otherwise hidden processes that are characteristic of the conventional meat industry, without losing the scientific language level.

In the last step, the image changes. Instead of cells, a pink tablecloth appears in the background and a colourful chicken salad in a yellow bowl is moved to the foreground, making it stand out and emphasising its importance (Machin and Mayr, 2012:223). In food advertising, the colour yellow is associated with sunshine, happiness and warmth (O'Hagan, 2022c) and generally stands for brightness and optimism (Ledin and Machin, 2020b:31). This is the point at which abstract biological matter becomes a pleasant consumer good. The image is complemented by the statement: "Now all that's left is to cook, eat and enjoy!"

This step-by-step approach to the presentation of cultured meat ensures transparency but is also similar to the manuals and instructions consumers receive when buying technical goods, which communicate without possible ambiguity. The main goal is to teach consumers how to use a purchased technology. Providing insight into the technical features of devices and equipment serves to demystify the technology, which may seem unfamiliar and sometimes even frightening to consumers. Further evidence of this can be seen in the efforts of cultured meat producers to provide potential consumers with all sorts of information about their product: "We can tell you everything that goes into it."

Convincing viewers of the transparent process of producing cultured meat also happens by arousing consumer curiosity about technological processes to inform them. Upside Foods and Mosa Meat use rhetorical questions that viewers encounter as they scroll through their websites. "Still curious?" and "Want to see more?" are questions that invite potential consumers to engage with cultured meat with scientific curiosity. Consumers are offered the opportunity to learn more about the details of cultured meat technology. Upside Foods encourages them to familiarise themselves with the "Cultivation Glossary," while Mosa Meat offers sections titled "Lab Notes" where potential consumers can familiarise themselves with the scientific vocabulary that will enable them to "speak like a scientist." The "Cultivation Glossary" provides basic definitions of various terms such as "cell bank," "cell feed," "cell line" and "cell sample" with brief explanations in layman's terms, while Mosa Meat's "Lab Notes" uses words such as "myotubes," "myosatellite cells," "fibers" and "tissue strands" that suggest expertise and scientificity. The "Cultivation Glossary" describes cell feed as "media," "food for cells" and "a liquid diet" for cells. The metaphorical language used by Upside, such as "food for cells" and "liquid diet," facilitates the understanding of the abstract biological procedures associated with the process of cell cultivation (Machin and Mayr, 2012:13). In this way, companies attempt to present complicated scientific processes and technologies in a demystified way, making them accessible and understandable to consumers. The more familiar the consumer is with the product, the less scepticism and reluctance can be expected (Raudenbush and Frank, 1999). With newly acquired knowledge on the internet, the site visitor is no longer a simple consumer but is upgraded to a "subject of knowledge," which symbolically places him or her alongside visionary cultured meat scientists.

"How do we do it? With science, naturally"

The cultured meat industry's emphasis on naturalness, health and cleanliness must be understood as a set of values that contrast with the polluting, unhealthy and dirty methods of conventional meat production. According to the cultured meat industry, these problems, which are characteristic of food production in the modern era, require a technological solution offered by biotechnology start-ups, which aim to solve the problem by inventing a clean, healthy and environmentally friendly way of producing meat. Unlike industrialised forms of food production, the appeal to nature is key for cultured meat companies. The naturalness of cultured meat is asserted in many ways, from simple images of idyllic natural landscapes to more complex connections between nature and science and nature and health. I first review examples of nature imagery used on websites and then turn to an examination of the connection between nature, science and health.

Upside Foods places images of nature under the heading of "Progress." At the top of the section is a photo of a human hand holding a burger. The angle from which the image was taken is slightly upwards so that the viewer is looking up at the burger, suggesting the importance and magnificence of this new food (Machin and Mayr, 2012:100). Behind the burger is a blue background reminiscent of a cloudless sky. The caption, which is partially above the image, reads, "Progress for people, animals, and the planet." If you scroll to the bottom of the web page, several short 3D video clips appear: a video of a calf running free in the meadow, a clip of a clear, light blue water surface with calm waves, a clip of green trees swaying in the wind and a blue sky with white clouds drifting across the screen. These images of nature are accompanied by slogans such as the following: "Mindful Methods," referring to the use of meat production methods that respect animal welfare; "Clean Currents," referring to water conservation; "Room to Grow," referring to land use and forest conservation; and "Great Atmosphere," referring to climate change and air quality. The burger in the first image is paradigmatically positioned alongside other images of nature to suggest a connection between eating cultured burgers and protecting nature. The burger, thus, functions as a signifier (Barthes, 1987) of progress in the meat industry that allows nature to be preserved rather than destroyed by pollution from the conventional meat industry.

So, cultured meat companies claim that the preservation of nature depends on the high-tech solutions they offer. On Mosa Meat's website, we find the following question and answer: "How do we do it? With science, naturally." The sentence takes advantage of the double meaning of the word "natural." In the second sentence, "natural" has two meanings: the first meaning is "natural, as to be expected" and the second meaning is that something happens without intervention and is done by nature. The assertion that "made by nature" is "made with science" introduces an interesting paradox that encodes conflicting expectations, countering the traditional belief that meat comes from animals, creatures that are part of nature (Ledin and Machin, 2020b). If something happens naturally, it cannot also happen artificially at the same time because nature and artificiality are usually at odds with each other (Segal, 1994:13). However, the intervention of science and technology apparently resolves this paradox. As Mosa Meat explains, they grow their:

> beef by harnessing the same natural process responsible for muscle growth in a cow. We start by taking a sesame-seed sized sample of cells, and nurturing them to naturally grow into beef [...] And just like a farmer cares for their herd, we give the same care and attention to every cell.

To reinforce the impression that the cells have grown naturally, Mosa Meat presents the viewer with a 3D image reminiscent of the aesthetics of renders. The image suggests realism because it is highly iconic (Chandler, 1994) and resembles the material object it represents. The image consists of a cow standing on a square, minimalist sketch of a grassy area drawn in purple paint. An arrow points to the cow's back and a circle, in the centre of which a small, dark, rectangular mass appears in 3D. This circle resembles the shape of a microscope, and the mass is the matter we can see through it. The arrow indicates the cow's back so that the viewer can see where on the cow's body the cells come from and what they look like. Next to the mass in the circle is a line segment and below it is written "3 mm," indicating the size of the mass and pointing to an objective scientific measurement (Chen and Eriksson, 2022). From the text on the right side of the image, we learn that this mass is myosatellite cells taken from the cow to initiate the process of burger production. The realistic image of the cow represents the real animal as it exists in nature as a source of cultured meat, while the scientific explanations and visualisations explain the technological intervention in the animal's body. Furthermore, Mosa Meat explains that the cells are "grown naturally" and refers to the cow's body as an analogue of the bioreactor in which the cultured meat cells are grown. They explain, "The finest livestock start their journey on a free-range farm. Natural food and a natural environment help them grow strong." In the "Lab notes," they explain that the entire process of growing cells in bioreactors is a "replication of the natural environment." On their website, we learn, "By allowing nature to take its course, the cells we started with grow to become fully fledged muscle and fat—just like they would inside a cow." The appeal to go "back to nature" here differs from the above-described pastoral and romantic ideas of discarding technology and returning to pre-modern methods of animal breeding (Vezovnik, 2023); rather, the message is to use technological advances to circumvent the harmful exploitation of natural resources and, as suggested by Eat Just, to consider the connection between human, animal and planetary health.

"Safe, high-quality meat"

For the first time, meat marketing expands the concept of health beyond human (and nation's) health, envisioning that cultured meat will positively impact the health of the entire planet Earth. In the analysed material, images of wild nature and rainforests appear along with messages such as "Our health and our planet's health are deeply connected" (Eat Just), suggesting that concern for the health of the planet also means concern for human health. Health also refers to the way cultured meat is produced, free from dystopian modern processes and technologies such as slaughter, GMOs, growth hormones and the use of preventative antibiotic cures for farm animals. Eat Just states that the company is "mirroring how an animal grows" when producing cultured meat, avoiding "slaughter, antibiotics or hormones" and also using "no GMOs." The promise of a "cleaner way of producing beef" (Mosa Meat) is directed against all dirty and polluting practices of modern conventional meat production and refers specifically to the cultural perception of slaughterhouses as dirty and polluting, with many contamination problems (Samiparna, 2021). The healthiness and safety of cultured meat is strongly connected to cleanliness. Cultured meat is claimed to be clean for the same reasons: free of viruses and bacteria, hormones and GMOs, and free of slaughter. Along these lines, Eat Just claims, "We produce GOOD Meat in a sterile, controlled environment from a single cell, removing slaughter from the process and nearly eliminating the risk of food-borne illness."

However, in cultured meat promotion, health is also related to the quality of the meat. In selecting cells, Eat Just says that they "examine the cells and choose the ones most likely to produce the healthiest meat," while Upside points out, "Our team selects the best cells—based on their ability to consistently and efficiently produce safe, high-quality meat."[2] This results in a high nutritional profile for the cultured meat products. With this in mind, Eat Just explains its cultured meat: "It's real, delicious meat with an identical nutritional profile to conventionally raised meat, but with less impact on our planet and less risk of contamination." Similarly, Upside Foods promotes its chicken meat by saying, "We created our first product, chicken, from a fertilized heritage-breed chicken egg." Heritage-breed chickens were consumed by Americans before the rapid mass breeding of hybrid chickens in the 1960s, so they are a guarantee of high quality. They are not genetically modified and are considered more sustainable, unlike the meat chickens used in the conventional meat industry. The selection of cells from "heritage-breed chicken" inspires confidence in the scientists who select only the best for the consumer's diet.

The trustworthiness of scientists and the products that they create is further underscored by the use of images of high-tech equipment and technology used in meat factories. Scientists are portrayed as controllers and conductors of this complicated system of meat production. Demystifying the scientific workspace occurs with the "virtual tour" of Upside's production facility named EPIC. Virtual visitors can explore the sights, such as the "cultivation room" where scientists in full laboratory gear with white hats, protective gloves, masks and white uniforms manage a tangle of stainless pipes and tanks, which the text reveals to be production vessels, cultivators. The whole image suggests the cleanliness and sterility of the process and, therefore, of the product, high technology and scientificity. The "control room" is described as "the brain" of the plant, supposedly used to "constantly monitor safety and quality," but also to "detect problems early." There is a picture of scientists portrayed from behind, looking at their computer screens that show graphs and charts, and looking at the large glass window through which the grow room is monitored. This portrayal of scientists as attentive controllers and the view of the sterile environment in which the meat is produced reinforces confidence in the quality and safety of the product.[3]

Conclusion

The marketing of cultured meat companies is undoubtedly in line with the general increase in public concern, awareness and media coverage of public health and environmental issues. With the goal of fixing the conventional meat industry, cultured meat marketing focuses on promoting values related to environmental preservation, using scientific authority and technical arguments to reinforce cultured meat beliefs. Scientism, that is the unconditional belief in scientific arguments, is the main source of promotion of cultured meat. By referring to science, cultured meat is constructed as a trustworthy, new food product, the production process of which is sold to consumers as completely transparent. Apart from being scientific, clean and, therefore, environmentally friendly, cultured meat is also marketed as real, natural and healthy.

As I have shown, the terms health, purity, naturalness and cleanliness have been used in food marketing since the late nineteenth century and were then associated with ideas of modernisation, according to which a white Western nation would emerge from strong and healthy (male) bodies powered by food with ingredients derived from nature and then transformed by scientists into powerful food products. The use of the imaginary of nature in late nineteenth- and early twentieth-century food marketing aimed to consolidate natural landscapes as national and played an important role in national identity formation. In the marketing of cultured meat, however, references to naturalness and health have nothing to do with modern nationalist narratives, but rather aim to respond to the failures of modern Western food production. The idea of nature no longer involves national and local natural landscapes but appears primarily global and shared by the whole humanity. For this reason, the concept of preserving nature relates to solving global environmental problems. Therefore, in the marketing of cultured meat, the health of the body is extended to the health of the environment and the planet, while the concept of naturalness refers to the preservation of pristine natural landscapes and resistance to the modern project of exploiting and subjugating nature (and animals as part of it) to satisfy human needs.

Cultured meat is primarily a symbol of scientific advances, especially in the field of food technology. This is because the idea of cultured meat is based on the logic of solutionism, in which technology is seen as the ultimate solution to the environmental and health problems caused by modern technology. Solutionism aims to improve, enhance and change things to make them better (Morozov, 2013). However, the technologies that emerge from this logic mainly enable opportunities for economic growth. Not coincidentally, they emerged in response to the economic crisis in the United States in the 1970s (Cooper, 2008:16; Vezovnik and Kamin, 2020:6) and spread to the venture capital–driven space that is Silicon Valley. Although we now appreciate the glory of solutions for animals, humans and nature, biotechnology and microbiology are among the most competitive, profitable and prestigious scientific activities of the late twentieth century (Fiddes, 1991). The notion that food companies and corporations are no longer the enemy of the environment, but rather its promoters, is based on scientific discourses that contribute to the idea that solving environmental problems is not only the responsibility of industry but also of the consumer. The variety of choices amongst different food products offered to consumers, along with the increased environmental and ethical concerns in late modernity, resulted in the idea that consumers can be most effective in mitigating environmental and health problems through their purchasing decisions. The exhortation to not consume is being pushed aside in favour of an exhortation to simply consume better. The cultured meat industry is divorced from any sustained critique of the broader structural forces that also cause environmental problems, offering instead a simpler and necessarily limited engagement with why environmental problems arise and how they can be addressed (Rutherford, 2011:187).

Notes

1 The websites can be found at the following addresses: https://upsidefoods.com/ (Upside Foods), https://www.ju.st/ (Eat Just) and https://mosameat.com/ (Mosa Meat).
2 Similar arguments were at work in early twentieth-century advertisements for radium in which products were said to be carefully monitored by teams of scientists to ensure the best quality (see Eriksson and O'Hagan, 2021).
3 Similarly, in the early twentieth century, the Postum Cereal Company invited the public to tour the factory to promote cleanliness, purity and transparency and to reassure consumers that there was no fear of food adulteration (O'Hagan, 2023).

References

Andersson, H. 2019. Recontextualizing Swedish Nationalism for Commercial Purposes: A Multimodal Analysis of a Milk Marketing Event. *Critical Discourse Studies* 16(5):583–603.

Andersson, H. 2020. Nature, Nationalism and Neoliberalism on Food Packaging: The Case of Sweden. *Discourse, Context & Media* 34, https://doi.org/10.1016/j.dcm.2019.100329

Bakhsh, A., Lee, S.J., Lee, E.Y., Hwang, Y.H. and Joo, S.T. 2021. Traditional Plant-Based Meat Alternatives, Current, and Future Perspective: A Review. *Journal of Agriculture & Life Science* 55(1):1–10.

Barthes, R. 1967. *Writing Degree Zero*. London: Cape.

Barthes, R. 1987. *Mythologies*. New York: Hill and Wang.

Billig, M. 1995. *Banal Nationalism*. London: SAGE.

Borkfelt, S., Kondrup, S., Röcklinsberg, H., Bjørkdahl, K. and Gjerris, M. 2015. Closer to Nature? A Critical Discussion of the Marketing of "Ethical" Animal Products. *Journal of Agricultural and Environmental Ethics* 28:1053–1073.

Bryant, C. and Barnett, J. 2020. Consumer Acceptance of Cultured Meat: An Updated Review (2018–2020). *Applied Sciences* 10(15), https://doi.org/10.3390/app10155201

Cellular Agriculture Europe. 2023. About Us. Available at www.cellularagriculture.eu (Accessed: 7 November 2023).

Chandler, D. 1994. Semiotics for Beginners. Available at https://www.academia.edu/download/34512504/Semiotics_for_Beginners.pdf (Accessed: 3 October 2023).

Chen, A. and Eriksson, G. 2022. Connoting a Neoliberal and Entrepreneurial Discourse of Science Through Infographics and Integrated Design: The Case of "Functional" Healthy Drinks. *Critical Discourse Studies* 19(3):290–308.

Chodkowska, K.A., Wódz, K. and Wojciechowski, J. 2022. Sustainable Future Protein Foods: The Challenges and the Future of Cultivated Meat. *Foods* 11(24), https://doi.org/10.3390/foods11244008

Cooper, M. 2008. *Life as Surplus: Biotechnology and Capitalism in the Neoliberal Era*. Washington: University of Washington Press.

Domosh, M. 2003. Pickles and Purity: Discourses of Food, Empire, and Work in Turn-of-Century USA. *Social and Cultural Geography* 4(1):7–26.

Eriksson, G. and O'Hagan, L.A. 2021. Selling "Healthy" Radium Products with Science: A Multimodal Analysis of Marketing in Sweden, 1910–1940. *Science Communication* 43(6):740–767.

Fiddes, N. 1991. *Meat: A Natural Symbol*. London: Routledge.

Ford, B.J. 2013. Impact of Cultured Meat on Global Agriculture. *World Agriculture* 2(2):43–46.

Hansen, A. 2002. Discourses of Nature in Advertising. *Communications* 27:499–511.

He, J., Evans, N.M., Liu, H. and Shao, S. 2020. A Review of Research on Plant-Based Meat Alternatives: Driving Forces, History, Manufacturing, and Consumer Attitudes. *Comprehensive Reviews in Food Science and Food Safety* 19(5):2639–2656.

Jönsson, E. 2016. Benevolent Technotopias and Hitherto Unimaginable Meats: Tracing the Promises of In Vitro Meat. *Social Studies of Science* 46(5):725–748.
Jönsson, E. 2020. On Breweries and Bioreactors: Probing the "Present Futures" of Cellular Agriculture. *Transactions of the Institute of British Geographers* 45(4):921–936.
Kaul, H. and Ventikos, Y. 2015. On the Genealogy of Tissue Engineering and Regenerative Medicine. *Tissue Engineering* 21(2):203–217.
Koteyko, N. 2009. "I am a very happy, lucky lady, and I am full of vitality!" Analysis of Promotional Strategies on the Websites of Probiotic Yoghurt Producers. *Critical Discourse Studies* 6(2):111–125.
Ledin, P. and Machin, D. 2015. The Semiotics of Modernist Space in the Branding of Corporations: A Multimodal Critical Discourse Analytic Approach. *International Journal of Marketing Semiotics* 3:19–38.
Ledin, P. and Machin, D. 2020a. Replacing Actual Political Activism with Ethical Shopping: The case of Oatly. *Discourse, Context and Media* 34, https://doi.org/10.1016/j.dcm.2019.100344
Ledin, P. and Machin, D. 2020b. *Introduction to Multimodal Analysis*. London: Bloomsbury.
Machin, D. and Mayr, A. 2012. *How to Do Critical Discourse Analysis*. London: Sage.
Mintz, S. 1996. *Tasting Food, Tasting Freedom: Excursions into Eating, Culture, and the Past*. Boston: Beacon Press.
Morozov, E. 2013. *To Save Everything, Click: The Folly of Technological Solutionism*. New York: Public Affairs.
Myers, G. 1990. "Every Picture Tells a Story: Illustrations in E.O. Wilson's Sociobiology" in *Representation in Scientific Practice*, edited by M. Lynch and S. Woolgar (Massachusetts: MIT Press), pp. 231–266.
O'Hagan, L.A. 2020. Pure in Body, Pure in Mind? A Sociohistorical Perspective on the Marketisation of Pure Foods in Great Britain. *Discourse, Context and Media* 34, https://doi.org/10.1016/j.dcm.2019.100325
O'Hagan, L.A. 2022a. All that Glistens is Not (Green) Gold: Historicising the Contemporary Chlorophyll Fad Through a Multimodal Analysis of Swedish Marketing, 1950–1953. *Journal of Historical Research in Marketing* 14(3):374–398.
O'Hagan, L.A. 2022b. Flesh-Formers or Fads? Historicizing the Contemporary Protein-Enhanced Food Trend. *Food, Culture & Society* 25(5):875–898.
O'Hagan, L.A. 2022c. Selling Swedish Summer: The Marketing of Pommac, 1920–1960. *History of Retailing and Consumption* 8(2):171–199.
O'Hagan, L.A. 2023. "Welcome to Pure Food City": Tracing Discourses of Health in the Promotional Publications of the Postum Cereal Company, 1920–1925. *Journal of Historical Research in Marketing* 15(3):171–200.
Orquiza, R.A.D. 2021. "Old is Bad, New Is American: Philippine Food Consumption and Production During the American Empire in the Early 1900s" in *Acquired Tastes: Stories about the Origins of Modern Food*, edited by M. Kideckel, B.R. Cohen and A. Zeide (Cambridge: MIT Press), pp. 51–65.
Raudenbush, B. and Frank, R.A. 1999. Assessing Food Neophobia: The Role of Stimulus Familiarity. *Appetite* 32(2):261–271.
Román, S., Sánchez-Siles, L.M. and Siegrist, M. 2017. The Importance of Food Naturalness for Consumers: Results of a Systematic Review. *Trends in Food Science and Technology* 67:44–57.
Rozin, P. 2005. The Meaning of "Natural" Process More Important Than Content. *Psychological Science* 16(8):652–658.
Ruivenkamp, M. and Rip, A. 2014. "Nanoimages as Hybrid Monsters" in *Representation in Scientific Practice Revisited*, edited by C. Coopmans, J. Vertesi, M. Lynch and S. Woolgar (Cambridge: MIT Press), pp. 177–200.

Rutherford, S. 2011. *Governing the Wild: Ecotours of Power*. Minneapolis: University of Minnesota Press.
Samiparna, S. 2021. *Meat, Mercy, Morality: Animals and Humanitarianism in Colonial Bengal, 1850–1920*. Oxford: Oxford Academic.
Segal, H.P. 1994. "The Cultural Contradictions of High Tech: Or the Many Ironies of Contemporary Technological Optimism" in *Technology, Pessimism, and Postmodernism*, edited by Y. Ezrahi, H.P. Mendelsohn and H. Segal (Berlin: Springer Science & Business Media), pp. 175–216.
Shapiro, P. 2018. *Clean Meat: How Growing Meat Without Animals Will Revolutionize Dinner and the World*. New York: Gallery Books.
Smith, P.R. and Taylor, J. 2004. *Marketing Communications: An Integrated Approach*. London: Kogan Page Publishers.
Spector, D. 2013. The World's First Test-Tube Burger Was Just Cooked and Eaten. *Business Insider* (5 August). Available at https://www.businessinsider.com/first-ever-public-tasting-of-cultured-beef-burger-in-london-2013-8 (Accessed: 22 January 2024).
Stephens, N. 2022. Join Our Team, Change the World: Edibility, Producibility and Food Futures in Cultured Meat Company Recruitment Videos. *Food, Culture and Society* 25(1):32–48.
Vezovnik, A. and Kamin, T. 2020. Good Food for the Future: An Exploration of Biocapitalist Transformation of Meat Systems. *Discourse, Context and Media* 33, https://doi.org/10.1016/j.dcm.2019.100354
Vezovnik, A. 2023. Romantic Narratives on Nature and Environment in Meat-Focused Food Documentaries. *Food, Culture & Society*. https://doi.org/10.1080/15528014.2023.2260974
Volden, J. and Wethal, U. 2021. "What Happens When Cultured Meat Meets Meat Culture? (Un)naturalness and (Un)familiarity in the Meat of Today and Tomorrow" in *Changing Meat Cultures: Food Practices, Global Capitalism and the Consumption of Animals*, edited by A. Hansen and K. Lykke Syse (Lanham: Rowman and Littlefield), pp. 185–206.
Wurgaft, B.A. 2015. Godfather of Cultured Meat: Willem Van Eelen Passes Away at 91. *New Harvest* (8 April). Available at https://new-harvest.org/willem-van-eelen-passes-away/ (Accessed: 22 January 2024).
Wurgaft, B.A. 2020. *Meat Planet: Artificial Flesh and the Future of Food*. Berkeley: University of California Press.
Zhang, Y.W., McCarl, B.A. and Jones, J.P.H. 2017. An Overview of Mitigation and Adaptation Needs and Strategies for the Livestock Sector. *Climate* 5(4), https://doi.org/10.3390/cli5040095

Afterword

A Transhistorical Semiotics of Food Marketing

Caroline Tagg

This fascinating edited volume sets out the groundwork for a transhistorical semiotics of food marketing. In doing so, O'Hagan and Eriksson draw on the transhistorical approach laid out in my and Mel Evans' earlier work, *Message and Medium* (Tagg and Evans, 2020), which focused on exploring how "elements of human communication endure across time despite the different technologies that shape how a message is conveyed" (1). Our transhistorical approach started from the premise that new media do not immediately disrupt what came before them. Instead, they *remediate* (Bolter and Grusin, 2020) existing forms of communication in familiar ways, and the message—the content of the communication—shapes the way technologies are used as much as the medium shapes the message. Whilst drawing closely on the principles that underlie our approach, the transhistorical semiotics of food marketing builds on that initial work in at least three important ways—one methodological, one empirical and one conceptual.

The first contribution of this well-researched volume is to lay out and illustrate a clear methodological approach for carrying out transhistorical semiotic work. Central to O'Hagan and Eriksson's transhistorical semiotic approach is the case study, usually focused on a product or brand (be it muesli or Allinson wholemeal bread, baby milk or anti-ageing milk, blackcurrant drink or coffee substitute, ghee or chia). It is not inevitable that food marketing case studies would be organised in this way; they could alternatively track a particular marketing trope, such as the use of sunshine to convey health or happiness, over time and across brands. However, their focus on a product provides a constant against which social and ideological shifts can be discerned. The case studies are interrogated using either a comparative approach which compares two moments in time, such as the contrastive analysis of Alpen and Troo muesli (Chapter 4), or a diachronic study of the evolution of a product's marketing through core periods, many of which stretch up to the present day, as with the discussion of dairy products and plant-based alternatives in Denmark (Chapter 2), the story of ultra-processed food in Mexico (Chapter 3) or the changing portrayal of Ribena blackcurrant drink in the UK since the 1930s (Chapter 6). Other diachronic studies track developments over a historical period, as with

DOI: 10.4324/9781003450276-20

the promotion and use of cow's milk for feeding infants in early twentieth-century China (Chapter 5) or of coffee substitutes in Sweden between 1870 and 1914 (Chapter 7). In each chapter, the case study involves detailed, multimodal analysis of diverse marketing materials, from posters, print advertisements and packaging to television commercials and websites, utilising a range of analytical frameworks drawn largely from (multimodal) critical discourse analytical approaches. Crucially for transhistorical semiotics, each case study is interpreted against the wider backdrop of relevant historical trends, as outlined by the editors in their chapter, "From Foods to Nutrients: 150 Years of Modern Nutrition Science", and also contextualised by a historical account of the particular shifting sociohistorical, economic and ideological contexts in which the product or brand is embedded. The approach to the transhistorical semiotics of food marketing developed and amply illustrated in this volume provides a blueprint for future investigations of other marketing and communicative practices.

The second contribution lies in the rich and detailed case studies that make up the volume, each of which shows how food marketing not only reflects but also exploits existing sociocultural values and ideologies, immediate problems and concerns, and popular and scientific ideas about health and nutrition in particular times and places. For example, the marketing of baby milk (Chapter 5) and anti-ageing milk (Chapter 8) in China and Hong Kong, respectively, must be understood against the history of the Chinese diet, which did not customarily feature cow's milk until its introduction by Western traders and missionaries in the early 1800s. Advertisers of baby powder milk in early twentieth-century China, thus, had to adapt their advertising for an audience unfamiliar with the bottle-feeding of cow's milk, resulting in text-heavy advertisements, as well as the blending of Western scientific ideas with traditional Chinese medical concepts. The subsequent marketing of milk as an anti-ageing product for adults in Hong Kong built on the success of the baby milk campaigns, spurred by concerns around a rapidly ageing population and growing awareness of illnesses such as osteoporosis and shaped less by notions of individual responsibility for self-care (as in the West) but by Confucian familial values which encouraged older Chinese women to stay healthy for others.

To take a second example of the situated nature of food marketing, the emergence of electric restaurants in twentieth-century London (Chapter 12) was very much a product of the contemporary craze for electricity, as companies tried to convince reluctant or anxious customers of its benefits for cooking in comparison to coal, which was smoky and dirty. This new marketing strategy also reflected the new-found popularity of dining out, due in part to a growing urban population. Electric restaurants remediated the practice of "showcasing" first realised in nineteenth-century expositions which, among other things, put kitchens on display to an audience. Restaurants, however, allowed electricity companies to demonstrate their appliances in quieter, more intimate spaces, creating an association between electric innovations and the reassuring familiarity of country inns with "oak beamed ceilings, antique candelabra and red tile floors" (p. X). A century later, international attempts to convince customers of the benefits of cultured meat (Chapter 13) reveal parallels with the electricity campaigns of Edwardian Britain: like electricity, cultured meat is now being harnessed thanks to developments in technology to tackle the problem of the day: not coal this time, but the pressing need for environmental sustainability and the failures of modern food production processes. As with electricity, advertisers must overcome consumers' reluctance, anxiety and disgust, which they do by associating the product with cleanliness and naturalness, as well as scientific innovation, at a time when technology is often positioned as the solution to environmental problems. Across the book, we see, time and again, how a product emerges in response to immediate socioeconomic and public health issues: the physical culture movement emerging amidst concerns about the British physique following the country's performance in the Anglo-Boer War (Chapter 1); Ribena marketed on the back of concerns around vitamin deficiency during World War II (Chapter 6); and the promotion of vegetable ghee in India in the face of concerns around adulterated traditional ghee (Chapter 9).

The food marketing case studies in this book also demonstrate *par excellence* the key role that modes other than language play in putting across a message, a point that is foregrounded by a transhistorical semiotics approach which points to the ways in which messages are legitimised and brands familiarised through carefully designed modal choices that recur over time—the swirl of a signature (such as Allinson's on his wholemeal bread), the image of a mascot (from the Bimbo bear to the Kellogg's tiger) or a particular colour.

The third contribution made by a transhistorical semiotics of food marketing is to foreground how certain messages persist across time, not because of something inherently human but because they are delivered by people and corporations who own the technologies of production and communication and who have a vested interest in remediating the same message through the media they control. The most striking aspect of food marketing as a transhistorical phenomenon, as revealed in this volume, is its seeming timelessness. The continuities in both its messaging and media are experienced by consumers in many societies today as so mundane and prevalent that they come into focus only through a transhistorical lens. One huge strength of the volume is that it is not only transhistorical but translocal, with studies rooted in Australia, China, Denmark, Hong Kong, India, Mexico, Sweden and the UK, revealing and detailing similar ideologies, tropes and strategies across time *and* space. As already anticipated in the introduction to this volume, the food marketing analysed across the chapters—and across time and space—draws consistently on notions of purity, naturalness, individual responsibility, health and science. These seemingly contradictory neoliberal discourses come together to manipulate consumers into making purchases. On the one hand, it is the individual who is held up as responsible for the health of the nation (in the late 1800s and early 1900s), their own individual health (in the twentieth century) and, most recently, the health of the planet; on the other, the individual is simultaneously positioned as agentless and reliant on the scientific understanding of health and nutrition in their own decision-making. The solution put forward by the advertiser is a product that is at once natural and traditional, and packed with scientifically endorsed nutrients. As this shows, these apparently timeless and universal themes do not, in fact, represent unchanging continuities, but are rather constantly refashioned or remade for the immediate sociohistorical, economic and ideological contexts in which a food and its marketing are embedded.

Alongside these recurring discourses are many marketing tropes that may seem at first to be new: the involvement in selling both products and lifestyles of what we might now call wellness influencers—from the physical culture movement hero, Eugen Sandow, and breadmaker Thomas Allinson in the early twentieth century to Gwyneth Paltrow in the twenty-first; the role of superfoods, from Plasmon in Edwardian Britain and Horlicks in mid-twentieth-century Hong Kong to chia seeds today; and calls to the past, whether to traditional village life in India, ancient Aztec culture in Mexico or the Second World War in the UK. And, across the years, despite an increase in the multimodal resources available to marketers over time, we see the same semiotic resources being deployed in similar ways: image, gaze and gesture, visual arrangement, slogans, synthetic personalisation and, more recently, colour. The reason these marketing themes and tropes persist is not due to any human need to communicate, as assumed by Tagg and Evans (2020) in discussion of personal and literary texts but because they help corporations sell products. As discussed in the introduction to this volume, the asymmetry of mass advertising reflects unequal power relations between corporations, their advertisers and people positioned as consumers, and it is in the former's interests to exploit emerging technologies to keep their audience anxious, confused, overwhelmed, vulnerable and buying.

This observation raises questions as to the role that new media play in twenty-first-century marketing. There are insights throughout the book regarding the role of earlier new media in food marketing. It is interesting to learn of the role played in Europe by touring and speeches (Chapter 1), exhibitions and world fairs (Chapter 13) in educating the public and marketing products at a time before mass literacy and the ways in which the Chinese public addressed low literacy rates in the early 1900s by reading newspapers aloud in teahouses, as well as displaying them on walls (Chapter 5). As the editors point out in the introduction to this volume, it was the expansion of mass communication from the nineteenth century that made possible the food marketing industry we know today. We also learn of a mail-order health service (Chapter 1) and baking competitions and agony aunt columns (Chapter 4) as intriguing exploitations of available media. The volume does not engage in any significant way with social media but occupies itself with more traditional media—the poster, the printed advertisement, the televised campaign and the corporate website. The remediation of a familiar marketing message through each of these new technologies—printed advertisements in the 1800s, radio in the 1920s, television in the 1950s and the World Wide Web from the 1990s—draws closely on existing advertising practices and is governed by established power relations and commercial imperatives. As a result, any change is slow and incremental and the medium recedes into the background. In Bolter and Grusin's (2020) words, the medium is *im-mediate*, in the sense that it is highly transparent; attention is not drawn to the medium through which marketing takes place, giving consumers the impression of direct contact with the product. This is no doubt due to familiarity with the now well-established marketing media covered in this book, as well as with the marketing genre and its recurring tropes. We do not easily discern the ways in which the medium makes available particular resources and nuanced changes in affordances which might subtly shape how a message is conveyed.

Social media and contemporary digital technologies appear, on the surface, to have transformed food and lifestyle marketing, as a platform for lay participation in food matters (Gerhardt, 2020; Rüdiger, 2022) and through, for example, social media influencers (Zhao and Bouvier, 2021), heightened opportunities for interaction between corporations and publics (Catenaccio, 2021) and restaurant review sites (Vásquez and Chik, 2015), not to mention the looming promise of artificial intelligence, evident in, for example, AI-generated online reviews (Vásquez, 2023). These developments are not necessarily unprecedented; as already mentioned, this volume points to the role of influencers in early food marketing, as well as to historical opportunities for "interactive experiences" through user endorsements and testimonials, and at speeches, expositions and electric restaurants where visitors were encouraged to inspect and try out appliances during their meal. Future transhistorical work is needed to unpack today's social media marketing and place it in the contexts of both its immediate sociocultural setting and the wider historical backdrop in order to fully understand the impact of these newest new media. For the moment, the transhistorical semiotic lens established in this volume urges us not to assume that the seeming innovation and promise of new technologies will do much to change the long-standing message of food marketing.

References

Bolter, J.D. and Grusin, R. 2020. *Remediation: Understanding New Media*. Cambridge: MIT Press.

Catenaccio, P. 2021. Discursive Strategies of Legitimation on the Web: Stakeholder Dialogue in the Agri-Biotech Industry. *Discourse, Context & Media* 43, https://doi.org/10.1016/j.dcm.2021.100535

Gerhardt, C. 2020. "How Less Means More in the Comments Section of Vegan Food Blogs: Exgredients Such as Gluten-Free and Extreme Case Formulations" in *Talking about Food: The Social and the Global in Eating Communities*, edited by S. Rüdiger and S. Mühleisen (Amsterdam: John Benjamins), pp. 15–34.

Rüdiger, S. 2022. Intimate Consumptions: YouTube Eating Shows and the Performance of Informality. *Internet Pragmatics* 5(1):115–142.

Tagg, C. and Evans, M. eds. 2020. *Message and Medium: English Language Practices Across Old and New Media*. Berlin: de Gruyter.

Vásquez, C. 2023. The Evolution of Online Reviews: From Grassroots Practice to Commodified Product. Plenary Talk Given at Approaches to Digital Discourse Analysis (ADDA4), Universität Klagenfurt, 12–14 October.
Vásquez, C. and Chik, A. 2015. "I am not a foodie…": Culinary Capital in Online Reviews of Michelin Restaurants. *Food & Foodways* 23(4):231–250.
Zhao, W. and Bouvier, G. 2021. Where Neoliberalism Shapes Confucian Notions of Child Rearing: Influencers, Experts and Discourses of Intensive Parenting on Chinese Weibo. *Discourse, Context & Media* 45, https://doi.org/10.1016/j.dcm.2021.100561

Index

Pages in *italics* refer to figures and pages in **bold** refer to tables.

For Product Safety Concerns and Information please contact our EU representative GPSR@taylorandfrancis.com
Taylor & Francis Verlag GmbH, Kaufingerstraße 24, 80331 München, Germany

www.ingramcontent.com/pod-product-compliance
Ingram Content Group UK Ltd.
Pitfield, Milton Keynes, MK11 3LW, UK
UKHW020153200926
475702UK00016B/2689

9781032584812